D1229769

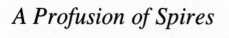

A Profusion of Spires

THE ONTARIO HISTORICAL STUDIES SERIES

The Ontario Historical Studies Series is a comprehensive history of Ontario from 1791 to the present, which will include several biographies of former premiers, numerous volumes on the economic, social, political, and cultural development of the province, and a general history incorporating the insights and conclusions of the other works in the series. The purpose of the series is to enable general readers and scholars to understand better the distinctive features of Ontario as one of the principal regions within Canada.

J.M.S. Careless, ed., *The Pre-Confederation Premiers: Ontario Government Leaders, 1841–1867* (1980)

Charles W. Humphries, *'Honest Enough to Be Bold' : The Life and Times of Sir James Pliny Whitney* (1985)

Charles M. Johnston, *E.C. Drury: Agrarian Idealist* (1986)

Peter Oliver, *G. Howard Ferguson: Ontario Tory* (1977)

A.K. McDougall, *John P. Robarts: His Life and Government* (1976)

Christopher Armstrong, *The Politics of Federalism: Ontario's Relations with the Federal Government, 1867–1942* (1981)

David Gagan, *Hopeful Travellers: Families, Land and Social Change in Mid-Victorian Peel County, Canada West* (1981)

Robert M. Stamp, *The Schools of Ontario, 1876–1976* (1982)

John Webster Grant, *A Profusion of Spires: Religion in Nineteenth-Century Ontario* (1988)

Ian M. Drummond, *Progress without Planning: The Economic History of Ontario from Confederation to the Second World War* (1987)

K.J. Rea, *The Prosperous Years: The Economic History of Ontario 1939–1975* (1985)

Olga B. Bishop, Barbara I. Irwin, Clara G. Miller, eds., *Bibliography of Ontario History 1867–1976: Cultural, Economic, Political, Social* 2 volumes (1980)

R. Louis Gentilcore and C. Grant Head, *Ontario's History in Maps* (1984)

Joseph Schull, *Ontario since 1867* (McClelland and Stewart 1978)

JOHN WEBSTER GRANT

A Profusion of Spires:
Religion in
Nineteenth-Century Ontario

A project of the
Ontario Historical Studies Series
for the Government of Ontario
Published by University of Toronto Press
Toronto   Buffalo   London

ISBN 0-8020-5798-5

Printed on acid-free paper

Canadian Cataloguing in Publication Data
Grant, John Webster, 1919–
    A profusion of spires

(Ontario historical studies series, ISSN 0380-9188)
Includes bibliographical references and index.
ISBN 0-8020-5798-5

1. Ontario – Religion – 19th century. 2. Ontario –
Church history – 19th century. 3. Religious
thought – Ontario – 19th century. I. Title.
II. Series.

BR575.05G73 1988   209'.713   C88-093905-2

This book has been published with the assistance of funds provided by the Government
of Ontario through the Ministry of Culture and Communications.

Contents

The Ontario Historical Studies Series

For many years the principal theme in English-Canadian historical writing has been the emergence and the consolidation of the Canadian nation. This theme has been developed in uneasy awareness of the persistence and importance of regional interests and identities, but because of the central role of Ontario in the growth of Canada, Ontario has not been seen as a region. Almost unconsciously, historians have equated the history of the province with that of the nation and have depicted the interests of other regions as obstacles to the unity and welfare of Canada.

The creation of the province of Ontario in 1867 was the visible embodiment of a formidable reality, the existence at the core of the new nation of a powerful if disjointed society whose traditions and characteristics differed in many respects from those of the other British North American colonies. The intervening century has not witnessed the assimilation of Ontario to the other regions in Canada; on the contrary it has become a more clearly articulated entity. Within the formal geographical and institutional framework defined so assiduously by Ontario's political leaders, an increasingly intricate web of economic and social interests has been woven and shaped by the dynamic interplay between Toronto and its hinterland. The character of this regional community has been formed in the tension between a rapid adaptation to the processes of modernization and industrialization in modern Western society and a reluctance to modify or discard traditional attitudes and values. Not surprisingly, the Ontario outlook is a compound of aggressiveness, conservatism, and the conviction that its values should be the model for the rest of Canada.

From the outset the objective of the Board of Trustees of the series has been to describe and analyse the historical development of Ontario as a distinct region within Canada. The series as planned will include thirty-two volumes covering many aspects of the life and work of the province from its original establishment in 1791 as Upper Canada to our own time.

Among these will be biographies of several premiers, numerous works on the growth of the provincial economy, educational institutions, minority groups, and the arts, and a synthesis of the history of Ontario, based upon the contributions of the biographies and thematic studies.

In planning this project, the editors and the board have endeavoured to maintain a reasonable balance between different kinds and areas of historical research, and to appoint authors ready to ask new questions about the past and to answer them in accordance with the canons of contemporary scholarship. *A Profusion of Spires: Religion in Nineteenth-Century Ontario* is the sixth theme study to be published. It is a comprehensive account of the development of the religious traditions and institutions of this province, which begins with a description of the Indians' religion and ends in 1900 when the Christian churches had achieved a dominant position in the Ontario community.

John Webster Grant has given us a very perceptive and well-balanced analysis of the ways in which religion, principally in its Christian forms, came to permeate the consciousness of the peoples of Ontario, and a judicious assessment of the impact of religion on provincial society. We hope that it will encourage others to look closely at this vital element of our cultural inheritance.

The editors and the Board of Trustees are grateful to Professor Grant for undertaking this task.

GOLDWIN FRENCH
PETER OLIVER
JEANNE BECK
MAURICE CARELESS, Chairman of the Board of Trustees

Toronto
25 May 1988

Preface

Much of the religious history of Ontario has perished with those who made it. The religious practices of earlier generations are fairly well known, though there are surprising gaps in our knowledge even of them. The motives underlying these practices are not so easily ascertained, for most Ontarians did not put their inmost thoughts on paper and the inquisitive employees of the Gallup Poll were not on hand. Inevitably we attach undue weight to the writings that have come down to us, which represent in the main the opinions of clerics and heretics, or we draw such inferences as we can from the public activities of Ontarians. Perhaps some day a massive exploration of private diaries will make possible a more thorough exposé of the religious mind – or minds – of the province. What is offered here may serve in the meantime to trace the formation and transformation of distinctive patterns of religious life.

One word that may cause the reader some puzzlement is 'evangelical.' To speak of evangelicals today is to conjure up a picture of embattled Protestants who deplore the liberal attitudes to doctrine and morality which they attribute to the leaders of the churches that dominated the scene in the nineteenth century. That most evangelicals of that era resembled their conservative successors in their moral precepts and in their views of biblical authority can scarcely be doubted. In those days, however, the term 'evangelical' denoted a belief in the transforming power of faith in Christ to which the great majority of Protestants would have laid claim. Liberal views of biblical inspiration and social responsibility made their way at least as readily in denominations that considered themselves evangelical as in others, and the designation 'liberal evangelical' seemed in no way paradoxical. With this explanation, it is hoped, readers will be able to follow without confusion the use of an inescapable word.

In writing this book I have been able to stand on many shoulders. Archivists, too numerous to mention by name, have been uniformly helpful both in making information available and in suggesting sources of which I should not otherwise have been aware. I am also indebted to them, along with Elwood Jones, for the illustrations that accompany the text. William Magney and Robert Black carried out helpful statistical research. Glenn Lucas, the former archivist-historian of the United Church of Canada, read the manuscript at my request and offered candid comments that saved me from some serious blunders. I must content myself with a general word of thanks to the anonymous outside readers for their perspicacious advice. Nor should I forget a graduate class at the University of Toronto's Centre of Religious Studies on whom I tried out many of the ideas contained here, as well as some other notions which their criticisms have dissuaded me from including. All of these helped me to write this book, but none can be held responsible for its contents.

I owe a special debt of gratitude to Goldwin French, Peter Oliver, and Jeanne Beck of the Ontario Historical Studies Series for their constant encouragement and forbearance. It has been a pleasure and privilege to work, once again, with Gerald Hallowell of the University of Toronto Press. The final product, however imperfect, is distinctly less so after the careful copy-editing of Kathleen Johnson.

Not least, I am mindful of the caring patience of my wife, Gwen, over a period of gestation that must have seemed interminable.

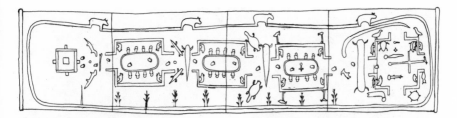

Like others of its kind, this elaborate *midewiwin* scroll represents both the path of a ceremonial procession through the medicine lodge and the road that an initiate was expected to take through life.

The visions of Ganiodaio, or Handsome Lake, led him in 1799 to recall the Iroquois to a purified version of their traditions. This imaginative reconstruction, painted by the Seneca artist Jesse J. Cornplanter in 1905, shows Ganiodaio presenting his Good Message with the aid of a wampum belt.

Alexander Macdonell (Alasdair Mor) helped Roman Catholic Scottish Highlanders to emigrate to Glengarry; he followed them in 1804, and became in 1826 the first bishop of Kingston.

Suggestions in a sermon in 1825 by Archdeacon John Strachan of Toronto (right) that Methodist preachers were both ignorant and disloyal called forth a vigorous rebuttal from Egerton Ryerson (left), then a Methodist probationer stationed at York.

Dettweiler Mennonite Meetinghouse, built in 1855 near Roseville, was in continuous use until the congregation disbanded in 1965.

John Roaf, minister of the 'radical' Zion Congregational Church in Toronto, claimed to be non-political but urged exiled leaders of the 1837 rebellion not to give up their cause.

The centrepiece of the Sharon Temple of the Children of Peace, constructed in the late 1820s for use on festive occasions, was this ark of the covenant.

One could be admitted to an early Presbyterian communion only on the presentation of a metal token. Tokens were given out by the local session of elders on a careful scrutiny of a member's faith and character, but such was the desire to participate that they were sometimes counterfeited.

This drawing of a Methodist camp meeting in 1859 is the earliest extant contemporary record of such a gathering in the province. Already a well-established institution, the camp meeting was then taking on a new lease on life under the influence of American holiness movements.

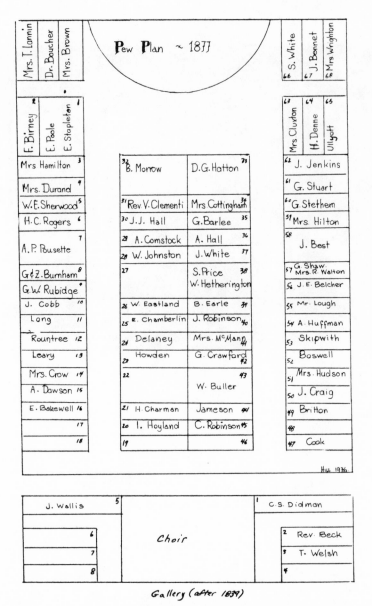

Until almost the end of the nineteenth century, churches of most denominations counted on paying for buildings by selling or renting pews in them. Affluent families often added their own upholstery, sometimes in jarring colours that gave a motley appearance to the church interior. The system was still in operation at St John's Church of England in Peterborough in 1877.

Torah scrolls are an essential adjunct of Jewish worship. This scroll was donated to the Toronto Hebrew Congregation (now Holy Blossom Temple) in 1857. (Photograph courtesy of the Toronto Jewish Congress Archives)

The great ambition of Senator William A. McMaster was to bring Canadian Baptists together in a single organization that would operate effectively from sea to sea. His dream has never been fulfilled, but McMaster University in Hamilton and Jarvis Street Baptist Church in Toronto represent but two of his many benefactions.

Under the leadership of Letitia Youmans, first president for Ontario in 1877 and for Canada in 1883, the Women's Christian Temperance Union became a force to be reckoned with. Dedicated primarily to the enactment of prohibition, it also pressed for woman suffrage and other reforms.

Voluntary organizations, such as this auxiliary to the Methodists' downtown Fred Victor Mission, drew much of their support from the wives of prominent businessmen. Some well-known Toronto names may well be represented in this camera-shy 'ladies' group.'

A few members of this Student Volunteer band at Queen's University, such as Omar L. Kilborn of West China (centre front, above small picture), went on to become noted foreign missionaries. Significantly, three of the four women in the group achieved medical degrees.

Francis McSpiritt, shown with a typically Irish stove-pipe hat, is still remembered in Peel County for his sanctity and miraculous cures. In return for healing he exacted stiff penance and the promise of reformed behaviour.

Hugh T. Crossley (left) and John E. Hunter (right), who began their career as a team of travelling Methodist evangelists in 1884, drew crowds and made converts wherever they went. In line with the conventions of the time, the photographer has posed them carefully against an artificial backdrop.

Best known for its service work, the Salvation Army had its greatest success in residential areas such as this quiet Toronto street.

The evangelist Ralph Horner (holding book), shown here with several associates, claimed to draw on 'cyclones of power' that would melt the heart of the most hardened sinner. After being deposed from the Methodist ministry in 1894 for insubordination, he then founded the Holiness Movement Church of Canada.

The funeral procession of Bishop John Strachan on Yonge Street in Toronto on 5 November 1867 not only marked a notable point of transition but was, in its arrangements, a model of hierarchical organization.

An Orange parade, snapped from the same vantage-point during the same period, has the straggling appearance more characteristic of Ontario folk religion.

Looking north along Bond Street, Toronto, in the 1890s, the eye is caught by a profusion of spires from Metropolitan Methodist past St Michael's Cathedral to Bond
Street Congregational. In the distance can be seen the only relatively more secular tower
of the Toronto Normal School.

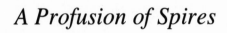

A Profusion of Spires

1 Spirits of the Land

To think of Ontario as it was when it became a Canadian province more than a century ago is to conjure up a picture of church-centred communities whose inhabitants wholeheartedly professed the traditional doctrines of Christianity, regularly said their prayers, and participated in a variety of communal religious activities with a fervour seldom approached today. This inherited memory of 'old-time religion' is substantially accurate, but the situation thus described had come about as the result of a long process of religious acculturation and was always subject to significant exceptions. In the long run it also proved to be unstable, for time refused to stand still.

The usual difficulties of transplanting religious institutions and attitudes to new soil were in some respects compounded in Ontario. Few immigrants chose the province for religious reasons, and a fair number came from areas where indifference and even hostility to religion were common. Staving off further erosion of faith in the new setting called for the immediate provision of pastoral leadership, which was not easily attracted to a province widely regarded as a cold and insignificant backwater. A diversity of religious expectations introduced further complications. While the overwhelming majority of the population was of British or American origin, differences of ethnic background, ecclesiastical affiliation, and length of residence ensured that no single approach would suit everyone. The inevitable result was not only competition but conflict, which was considerably exacerbated by the coincidence of the formative period of Ontarian religion with a general transition in Western societies from aristocratic (or oligarchic) to bourgeois social patterns.

The triumph of secular democracy, which eventually made possible the emergence of a practical religious consensus, also brought into play new forces that immediately threatened it. In the long run, as we know now, these resulted in a substantial weakening of the hold of traditional religious beliefs and values. The immediate response was to seek to shore up the defences of various citadels of faith by reasserting neglected elements of tradition, though not without introducing elements of novelty in the process. Within a few decades serious challenges to received beliefs, along with social problems to which they seemed to offer no adequate solutions, were leading many Ontarians to attempt new religious formulations. Thus, the career of religion in nineteenth-century Ontario was marked less by uniformity or stability than by variety and change.

To an important segment of the Ontario population 'old-time religion' represented a complex of beliefs and practices with local roots that long antedated the appearance of the first European settlers. Despite the lapse of several millennia since the last important migrations, ethnologists have been able to identify common elements linking many religious traditions of the Indians of Ontario with prototypes in northern Asia. Some of these parallels, such as the identification of certain lakes or mountains as sacred, the clothing of spiritual forces in animal forms, and the linking of origin myths with natural phenomena, are so general as to admit the possibility that independent invention was inspired by similar living conditions. Others are striking in their specificity. Particular honour has been paid to the bear by people living in a band of northern forest that stretches without a break from Europe through Asia to North America. The sweat lodge, used almost universally by the Indians for spiritual purification, has affinities with the Finnish sauna so familiar to modern apartment-dwellers. Most significant of all as evidence of a common heritage is the prominence on both sides of the Bering Strait of the shaman, or medicine-man or -woman, a mediator with the unseen whose power depends on personal experience rather than official appointment. A shamanic performance that particularly impressed early visitors to North America was the summoning of spirits who made tents move without any apparent human intervention. That phenomenon too was shared with Asia, and speaking in tongues has been associated with shamanism on both continents.[1]

Research is steadily pushing back the time-line of human occupation in America, and newspapers periodically report discoveries that promise to revolutionize our view of native origins. Dates as early as 20,000 BC are generally accepted, and only the supposed appearance of *Homo sapiens* around 50,000 BC sets an apparent upper limit to what may yet be discovered.[2] Scholars agree, however, that the present Indians of Ontario are descended from wanderers from northern Asia who began to leave traces of their presence in many parts of America around 10,000 BC. The original colonizers were probably not intentional migrants but nomads who during the last ice-age followed the tracks of mammoths across a vanished land-bridge into what later became a separate continent. As early as 25,000 BC some of them may have been living at Old Crow in the Yukon, a locality that escaped the glaciation that engulfed most of northern North America. Some millennia later, as the ice melted, corridors opening to the south made larger migrations possible. The first concentration of population seems to have been on the plains of the western United States, where mammoths, giant sloths, and larger-than-life bison provided abundant game for hunters who had already acquired the necessary skills for exploiting it. Within another millennium or two there were Indians in every accessible part of America. Ontario, just emerging from its burden of ice, was reached not from the northwest but from the south and west.

When the original settlers of America left Siberia, neither the civilizations nor the major religions of the Old World had yet taken shape. Indians established their own precedents, drawing to some extent on an archaic common stock of tradition but innovating when necessary with little or no reference to Eurasian developments. The lapse of time between first settlement and European contact was sufficient to permit both the emergence of autonomous civilizations and a differentiation of language and culture at least as great as in the eastern hemisphere. This diversity extended to religious beliefs and practices, which ranged from the brutally efficient mania of the Aztecs for human sacrifice to the mysticism of solitary seers. Generalizations about native American religion are apt to be as misleading as generalizations about the religion of Eurasia would be.

Archaeology and analogy provide our best clues to the specific religious beliefs and practices of the Indians who inhabited Ontario over ten millennia. Many of those described by the first European explorers had probably been in place for a long time, but it is not always easy to know which ones. Change was as incessant in America as elsewhere, despite the propensity of Europeans to think of other cultures as fossilized and the tendency of native folk tradition to read current manifestations back into the distant past. Prophetic movements within historic times have demonstrated the capacity of native Americans for religious innovation, and there is reason to think that in some areas European trade had inspired religious change even before the establishment of direct personal contact.

Archaeology can tell us more, though in intangible matters its signals are not always easily read. Early evidence of care in funerary practices, whether through cremation or the preparation of bodies for burial in communal cemeteries, testifies to a belief in some sort of survival after death. The discovery of masks and other ceremonial paraphernalia points to the existence of shamans or other religious practitioners. The picture becomes clearer about 1000 BC when elaborate cultic practices began to move north from Mexico along with a knowledge of agriculture. Among Indians of the Hopewell culture, which flourished around the time of Christ, a religion that included an elaborate cult of the dead and in some places human sacrifice achieved such prominence that priests were able to command the services of artisans to produce elaborate grave-goods and of labourers to erect burial mounds of startling size. Their range, which extends into southern Ontario, attests to the local influence of the Hopewell cult.[3]

Until about the beginning of the Christian era, and in many parts of the province until the present, Indian economies in Ontario have been based on the search for game, fish, and other products of nature. Archaeology has shed less light on the religion of migratory than of settled Indians, although it has been able to demonstrate in both types of society the existence of ceremonial practices implying religious belief. Since even into historical times the religion of Indians relying on the primary resources of the land has exhibited considerable homogeneity, however, we can safely assume that the early Indians of Ontario conformed in the main to this widely distributed pattern. Hunter-gatherers lived literally from hand to mouth, depending for survival not merely on their own efforts or skills but on the timely bounty of an apparently capricious nature. They found it natural, therefore, to think of the cosmos not as a self-regulating machine but as an arena for the interplay of vital forces which they associated with whatever promoted or threatened human life: celestial bodies, elemental forces, and above all animals, or rather the 'bosses' or 'masters' who were supposed to control them.[4] Traffic with these spiritual powers, like contact with electricity, was dangerous but nevertheless essential to success. Religious practice, therefore, had to do mainly with gaining the favour of the spirits, avoiding offence to them, and showing due appreciation for the benefits they bestowed. In the context of the hunt this implied such well-known practices as apologizing to animals for killing them and paying scrupulous respect to their remains.

Ability to make contact with the spirit world depended not on official ordination or on the correct performance of rituals, as in more settled societies, but rather on the special insight that came in part through instruction in occult practice but primarily through a personal vision of ultimate reality. These qualifications were the special property of the shaman, who in an illness or other 'boundary experience' had been transported into the world of spirits only to emerge with a wisdom unattainable by purely natural means. In the northern forests of America, however, to a greater extent than in most other parts of the world, each person was expected to have some of the properties of the shaman. Dreams were a readily available window to the realm beyond, a means of foretelling the future or expressing needs otherwise unknown to the dreamer. Communal rituals stimulated the search for ecstasy, employing for this purpose drums, dancing, and sometimes mild hallucinogenic drugs. A decisive turning-point in the life of each Indian was the personal vision quest, which commonly took place in late childhood. After careful instruction the young person undertook a fasting vigil in a lonely spot, emerging if successful with a message from a spirit, usually that of an animal, that would act as a guardian and provide a direction for life. A tangible token of this visitation, such as an eagle feather, would become the most valued ingredient of a medicine bundle that represented the individual's draft on the spirituality inherent in nature.[5]

The traditions of a tribe were embodied in myths and legends that were incorporated into rituals and dances, taught to grandchildren, and often recounted in detail during a long winter evening. There were also didactic tales, perhaps the result of borrowings from Europeans, that explained why a certain thing was so or drew an obvious moral. These stories belong to the same genre as Aesop's fables, and one does not have to be an Indian to appreciate them. The myths and legends, however, are much less accessible to a reader of European background. Designed mainly to account for the origins of the tribe and to reinforce its view of the world, they abound in dealings among animal spirits with complicated family trees and occasionally bring in the sun, moon, and other celestial bodies as actors in the drama. Prominent in many of the legends is a figure commonly known as the Trickster-Transformer, who combines human, animal, and supernatural properties and engages in activities that range from the cosmic to the amorous and sometimes the scatological. The status of the Trickster-Transformer varies remarkably from one culture to another. In some he appears as a hare, in others as a coyote. In some he has considerable dignity, in others he takes pratfalls. He has some of the features of a creator, but he is far from omnipotent or even all-wise.[6]

This approach to religion is commonly called animism, and it is not easily appreciated by those who are accustomed to European patterns of thought. To the sceptic it appears superstitious, to the fundamentalist idolatrous, and to the desacralized occidental merely untidy and confusing. If we can rid our minds of the expectation of linear consistency, however, we may discern an approach to reality that is in some respects highly sophisticated. To the animist the cosmos is a complex organism that is held in equipoise by the interplay of spiritual forces. The universe as the Indian sees it has been described as a 'sacred hoop,' symbolized by the campfire circle, in which humanity can survive and prosper only by being in harmony with the plants, animals, and heavenly bodies that constitute the rest of nature.[7] Taboos were intended to preserve this harmony, rituals of propitiation to restore it. Even the Trickster-Transformer can be regarded as an embodiment of the essential ambiguity of nature, which depends for its health not on the triumph of any single organizing principle but on the interplay of varied and sometimes apparently contradictory elements.

The first Europeans who ventured into what is now Ontario encountered both hunting-gathering (and, to an even greater extent, fishing) peoples and ones who lived mainly by agriculture. The Canadian shield from Sault Ste Marie to the Quebec border was occupied by tribes fitting into the former category who spoke closely related dialects of what was essentially a single central Algonquian language. Along the Ottawa River were the Algonquins. The Ottawas lived not on that river, to which their name was given merely because the river allowed the French access to their country, but mainly along the eastern shore of Lake Huron. In between these and to the north of the lakes were a number of groups that today constitute the Ojibwas but were known to the French under a variety of designations: Nipissings on the lake of that name, Mississaugas on the north shore of Lake Huron, Saulteaux around the Sault, and many others. Farther north, beyond the height of land, were Crees, who represented a separate linguistic and cultural subgroup of the Algonquian family. Other Crees, mingled with Assiniboines of Siouan language, occupied the northwestern corner of the province. (These last no longer inhabit the province, having left it for the prairies during the eighteenth century.) Southern Ontario, then as now, was hospitable to agriculture. Peoples of Iroquoian speech – Hurons in Simcoe County, Khionontateronons or Petuns immediately to the west of them, and Neutrals around what is now the Golden Horseshoe – subsisted mainly on corn but also grew squash, beans, sunflowers, and some tobacco. In practice the distinction between primary-resource and agricultural peoples was not clear-cut. The Ottawas grew a fair amount of corn, the Ojibwas cultivated 'wild' rice, and Iroquoians depended on the hunt both for fur clothing and for variety in their diet. Nevertheless, the difference had far-reaching effects on patterns of spirituality.

Contrary to earlier opinion, it is now generally agreed that most of the Ontario Indians had occupied for some centuries the territories in which Europeans first found them. As usual, there were exceptions. The Huron confederacy included several tribes that had joined the main body along Georgian Bay fairly recently, and there is some reason to think that the Algonquins had been displaced from a more easterly location. Even these movements have been attributed to the dislocation occasioned by early French trading activity, however, so that we can asume that in most cases long stability of residence had encouraged a corresponding stability in religious practice. Movements of population since contact have also brought into the province several groups of Indians whose traditional homes were elsewhere. A large segment of the Six Nations Iroquois entered Ontario from western New York after the American war of independence. With them came a number of Delawares from Pennsylvania, who spoke an Algonquian tongue but practised agriculture; others of this tribe followed in 1792. During the nineteenth century the province became a refuge for many Potawatomis, close associates of the Ojibwas and Ottawas and near kin to them in language and culture.[8] To understand ⁄ the religious backgrounds of aboriginal residents and newcomers alike, we need to know something of the beliefs characteristic of the Algonquian and Iroquoian families.

Apart from a few practices of agricultural origin such as the ceremonial sacrifice of a white dog, which can be traced to Mexico, the religion of Ontario Algonquians fitted with almost classic precision into the pattern posited for societies dependent on primary resources. The north was a stronghold of shamanism, and the weakness of other bonds of social cohesion made shamans the most powerful members of many communities. Three general types have been distinguished. The *wakano*, or 'fire-handler,' operated at night, drawing on the powers of dangerous spirits to prescribe potions for hunting, healing, and seduction. The *jessakid* specialized in divination by means of the spectacular spirit lodge or 'shaking tent' ceremony. The third type has been identified variously as 'seer,' 'sucking-doctor,' or 'herbalist.'[9] Despite the importance of the shaman, or perhaps in line with it, the religious practice of central Algonquians was highly individualistic. Everyone sought religious power, usually for his or her own benefit. The vision quest was universally pursued; dreams were assiduously cultivated; and each individual prized a bundle of sacred objects. Success in hunting and war was sought in appropriate rituals, and travellers made offerings of tobacco at every dangerous passage.

Religious ideas adhered to the same general pattern. Behind every significant manifestation of nature, whether animate or cosmic, was seen the operation of a *manito* or spirit. Behind these in turn might be discerned the power of one who was the master of spirits, as each spirit was the master of its own kind. Here, however, we are on uncertain ground. A contrast between the good *Kitchi-manito* and the evil *Medji-manito* that is regularly made today appears to have been of late origin, the result of Christian influence or perhaps of intimate contact with such agricultural peoples as the Hurons. Even the currency of the term *Kitchi-manito*, or 'great spirit,' prior to contact is widely doubted. Neither monism nor dualism suited the Algonquian mentality, which conceived reality in terms of a multiplicity of beings with personal souls and attributes. Spirits might be helpful or harmful, friendly or hostile to humanity, but the essential fact was that they existed and had somehow to be lived with. In practice the recognition of *Kitchi-manito* was limited to special occasions; he was seldom mentioned even in connection with the paradise in the west or at the end of the Milky Way to which the Indian hoped to attain after death. More prominent in Algonquian spirituality was the cosmic vision of a great mountain or tree, symbolizing the centre of the earth, that might be created ritually by the erection of a sacred tent or lodge.[10]

Religious belief and practice varied from tribe to tribe, band to band, and even individual to individual. Ottawas and Potawatomis are said to have attached particular importance to medicine bags and bundles. Among the Crees, who had even fewer opportunities than their neighbours to the south for contact with others of their kind, individual and family rituals took on enhanced importance, and in the long winters the starvation-spirit *windigo* continually threatened to infect others with his cannibal appetite. The Ojibwas have been credited with an unusual wealth of religious concepts. Among them, for example, alone among North American tribes, does one encounter a parallel to the Greek myth of Orpheus. More conspicuous to early travellers, however, was the popularity of stories about the beneficent though capricious culture hero Nanabozho, the Great Hare, and the fear inspired by a surprisingly feline marine monster. Delawares shared many of the traditions of their more northerly relatives, but with substantial modifications introduced by a more sedentary and affluent way of life. In their annual 'big house' ceremonial, which lasted for twelve days, members of the community reconstituted the 'centre of the world' by re-enacting visions and dreams from their own experience.[11] It is difficult, however, to identify features unique to any one group or even to be certain that apparent differences in emphasis represent anything more than uneven reporting.

Since the spirit world stood in a somewhat ambivalent relation to human desires, religious practice inevitably contained a similar element of ambivalence. Spiritual power was meant to be used for good ends, but there was nothing to prevent one's drawing on it to cause harm. The temptation to misuse it was strong, and always it was there to be used rather than served. Shamans were regularly suspected of sorcery, and the greater the access to spiritual power the stronger the suspicion. Tales of harmful or even fatal spells circulated constantly, though more often at second hand than out of personal experience.[12] This moral ambiguity was intrinsic to the religion of hunters, who needed to be aggressive in order to survive. At its best, however, central Algonquian religiosity was unusually impressive. Spirituality was not relegated to the edges of daily life; it permeated every action. Spiritual power was the most significant of all powers, even ultimately the only power, and the vision that made it possible was universally regarded as the pearl of great price. Only when Christian teaching brought shamans into disrepute and traditional folkways began to break down did its sinister applications come to the fore.

To pass from Algonquian to Iroquoian religion is to recognize much that is familiar and to become aware of some features that are strikingly different. Few of the elements that have been noted in Algonquian religion were absent from that of Iroquoians. Young people undertook vision fasts, hunters and warriors sought to propitiate the spirits, and shamans performed their accustomed roles. Dreams received even greater attention, if that was possible, than they did among hunting peoples. They were believed to reveal hidden desires or to foretell calamities, and their messages had to be acted out if the desires were to be fulfilled or the calamities averted. The persistence of these common elements recalled an earlier period when Iroquoians too had depended solely on primary resources. Although hunting had lost much of its economic significance, its importance as a means by which a young man might attain prestige kept alive the religious practices associated with it. Indeed, the existence of sizeable village communities made possible corporate participation in them on a scale that would have been inconceivable farther north.[13]

What was different in Iroquoian religion sprang, as we might expect, from the centrality of agriculture and from openness to influences from the south where agriculture had been practised for an even longer time. Whereas hunter-gatherers usually staged feasts and other rituals in response to local emergencies or under the inspiration of dreams or visions, Iroquoians added to these a sequence that followed the round of the agricultural calendar from midwinter to harvest, with special ceremonies dedicated to various fruits of the earth.[14] The ritual torture of captives taken in battle, which excited first horror and then imitation among the French, was not an expression of innate cruelty but rather a vestige of the human sacrifice commonly associated with agricultural societies. It had originally formed part of a cult of the sun that was solidly established among more southerly tribes and exerted some influence over almost all Indian societies. No matter how extreme the tortures, it was essential that the victims should be kept alive until dawn so that the virtue of their sacrifice might be visible to the sun and thus contribute to the fertility of the soil.[15]

In no respect was the influence of agriculture more conspicuous than in the prevalence of a dualistic conception of reality. This polarity was represented in myth by the primordial twins Oterongtognia ('maple sapling') and Tawiskaron ('flint'), of whom the former was the constant benefactor of humanity and the latter an implacable enemy. It was mirrored in ritual by the division of roles in ceremonies between two halves of the total group – men and women in most tribes, but members of clans composing contrasting moieties among the Cayugas. The calendar itself was divided into two halves, the winter being given over to thanksgiving rites performed by men and the summer to prayers for a favourable harvest by the women. The entire cycle, even after post-contact adaptations, betrays an original division into rituals offered to Oterongtognia and to Tawiskaron. Although this polarization is obervable throughout Iroquoian religion, we should be wary of identifying Oterongtognia with good and Tawiskaron with evil or of supposing that the purpose of the ritual was to ensure the triumph of good over evil. The twins represented not so much good and evil as light and dark aspects of nature; Iroquoians, like Hindu Shaivites, considered darkness and light equally essential to the continuance of the world. Indeed, the practices of Iroquois curing societies retain traces of an original dedication to Tawiskaron.[16]

Among central Algonquians social organization was rudimentary, and depended largely on real or assumed family ties; Iroquoians, in contrast, grouped themselves in villages, tribes, and in the case of Hurons and Iroquois, even confederacies. And whereas authority among the former depended on the possession of personal qualities that were conferred by the spirits and merely recognized by band elders, Iroquoian sachems were *chosen* by the women of the tribe. The distinction was not absolute, for leaders were selected for their spiritual as well as political qualifications, but it is significant that the names of original office-holders passed to their successors and thus in effect became titles. Iroquoian religion bore the marks of this politicization of culture. The 'Book of Rites,' probably the Iroquois's most prestigious ceremonial document, consisted essentially of directions for giving religious sanction to the orderly transmission of offices.[17] The communal element in Iroquoian religion was also evident in the Huron custom of disinterring the bones of the deceased after temporary burial, carefully cleaning them, and reinterring them along with elaborate funerary offerings in a common grave. It also found expression in the popularity of voluntary religious societies, which recruited their members across clan lines and thus provided a counterweight to exclusive family loyalties.

These long-established religious traditions were challenged early in the seventeenth century by Christian missionaries from France. Their first efforts in Ontario were among the Hurons, who were trading partners of the French and attractive to the missionaries because of the favourable opportunities for regular teaching promised by their sedentary manner of life. Joseph Le Caron, a member of the Récollet branch of the Franciscan order, surveyed the area soon after his arrival at Quebec in 1615, and again in 1623 when he was accompanied by another priest and a lay brother.[18] An attempt to set up a permanent mission, inaugurated in 1626 when the Récollets had been joined by several members of the Society of Jesus, was aborted in 1629 by the capture of Quebec by English raiders and the enforced return of the missionaries to France. In 1634, however, the

Jesuits, who had now been granted a monopoly of the Canadian missions, were able to carry out their long-contemplated design.[19] With the advantage of a ready supply of personnel they were able to increase their complement of priests in Huronia to thirteen by 1639 and to nineteen by 1647. Most of the priests had served long enough to become familiar both with the language and with local customs. The Jesuits were also able to attract a number of *donnés*, laymen who served the mission without salary in return for the promise of lifetime subsistence.

Christianity as expounded by the Jesuits presented to the Hurons both attractions and difficulties. Since even among Iroquoians political alliance was inconceivable apart from mutual adoption as kin, association with the French implied some measure of recognition of the spirits who presided over their destiny. The exclusiveness of Christian claims to truth was beyond their comprehension, however, and even seemed to violate the essential requirements of courtesy. At first the Hurons were prepared to recognize the Jesuits as possessing some shamanic qualities, though they showed not the slightest desire to adopt their religion. In succeeding years, as a series of devastating epidemics swept the country, the qualities that had secured for the Jesuits some grudging respect as shamans aroused suspicions that they might instead be sorcerers. Death would have been their reward if French trade goods had not by this time become practically indispensable to the Hurons. Among the missionaries none commanded more admiration or aroused more suspicion than Jean de Brébeuf, who was the Jesuits' most accomplished linguist and most effective debater. In time, despite setbacks, the Jesuits secured a nucleus of followers, especially in the village of Ossernenon, where they had been longest established. During the 1640s, as Iroquois attacks began to threaten the existence of the confederacy, an increasing number of Hurons turned to the Jesuits for leadership. According to the *Jesuit Relation* of 1648–9, more than 2,700 had been baptized in the previous thirteen months. Most of these baptisms appear to have been indiscriminate, although in earlier years the Jesuits had scrutinized adult candidates with meticulous care.

While concentrating their energies upon the Hurons, the Jesuits reached out as their resources allowed to other groups. A visit to the Neutrals of the Niagara Peninsula in 1640 proved unproductive, but a mission opened among the Petuns in the previous year managed to maintain a precarious existence. Isaac Jogues, who was captured by the Iroquois in 1642 and released after torture according to custom when a Mohawk woman adopted him as her son, returned to the Iroquois country during a truce in 1646 in the hope of securing converts. Unfortunately, a poor harvest during the year of his previous visit had been blamed on contagion from a small chest he had left behind, and he was quickly struck down as a sorcerer. Contacts with

Algonquian peoples were limited to the summer season when there was some chance of securing a sizeable audience. Visits were paid in 1642 to the Nipissings, who customarily wintered among the Hurons, and on invitation to the Saulteaux or Ojibwas of Sault Ste Marie.

Iroquois attacks, inspired by an ancient grudge and by a desire to share in the profits of the fur trade, soon wiped out the earliest Christianity of Ontario. After several Huron defeats the Jesuits suffered their first loss of life in 1648 when Antoine Daniel was killed by a volley of arrows in his church in the outlying village of Saint Joseph. In the following year Brébeuf and the young Gabriel Lalemant were put to death at Saint Louis with the tortures customarily inflicted on distinguished prisoners.[20] By 1650 Huronia no longer existed, and its former inhabitants were starving refugees on nearby Christian Island. Within a short time the Petuns and Neutrals suffered similar fates, and the Algonquins fared little better. Apart from a small group of Hurons who followed the missionaries to Quebec, the remnants of these peoples either joined the Iroquois or fled from their ancestral homes. As Iroquois aggression continued, most of the northern tribes withdrew temporarily to what is now Michigan and Wisconsin. For some years the southern part of the province was left virtually empty.

At the time, many Indians attributed the downfall of the Hurons to the presence of the Jesuits, and not a few scholars since have agreed with them. That judgment cannot be accepted without qualification. All-out warfare such as the Iroquois waged in the 1640s was unprecedented, and neighbouring tribes proved as vulnerable to it as the 'missionized' Hurons. The diseases that decimated the Hurons cut a wide swath across eastern North America, and proved equally destructive to the Iroquois. Nor need we take seriously suggestions that the Christian ethic of love weakened the fighting spirit of converts, for Christian Europe set no example of pacifism and the Jesuits could claim with some plausibility that Christian warriors maintained stricter discipline than others. Huron resistance was certainly weakened, however, by the existence of divisions so deep that many traditionalists preferred absorption by the Iroquois to acquiescence in Jesuit designs.[21]

Despite the magnitude of the catastrophe, the Jesuits had no thought of quitting. Missionaries soon appeared at Saint Esprit on the south shore of Lake Superior, at Green Bay off Lake Michigan, and at Sault Ste Marie. Claude Allouez, who arrived in the region in 1665, devoted much of his time to the Indians who remained in northwestern Ontario or had taken refuge there. Until the end of the French regime the Jesuits retained precarious footholds on the upper lakes. Farther north, Antoine Silvy spent the years from 1687 to 1693 among the Crees around Fort Sainte Anne other.

The modern mind overleaps the strict dualism of a divine sphere in heaven and a human sphere on earth which developed in the later ancient world. The divine sphere is not some place alongside of the world or above the world, but is present in everything human and natural. In some respects one can say that modern naturalism was born out of the mystical idea of the coincidence of opposites. This was not simply a methodological approach to reality, rationalistic or empiricistic. Behind it [10] was an experience that nature is not outside of creative reality, but is potentially before the creation in God — of course this is not meant temporally but logically — and then after the creation the divine is within it. This means that the finite is not only the finite, but in some dimension it is also infinite and has the divine as its center and ground.

This principle of the relation between the finite and the infinite is the first principle of Romanticism on which everything else is dependent. Without it Romanticism and a theologian like Schleiermacher become completely unintelligible.

II – 1. Colonial Period

II – 2. N.A. History – 19th Cen.

II – 2 – 1. Canada

II – 2 – 2. United State

Survey & General History

Intellectual History =

= Pragmatism

12,000
350,000
300,000
35,000

(later Fort Albany). Other Jesuits, taking advantage of lulls in warfare between the French and the Iroquois, opened missions among all of the five nations that then constituted the Iroquois confederacy. They were welcomed at first chiefly by Huron captives who were grateful not to have been altogether abandoned, though others greeted them with undisguised hostility. The last of these missions came to an end only in 1709, when British influence had become paramount among the Iroquois. From 1668 to 1680 the Sulpicians of Montreal maintained a mission among some Cayugas who had sought a temporary retreat on the north shore of Lake Ontario from attacks by the Susquehannock tribe to the south. The Quinte mission was never conspicuously successful, but is of interest because it provided the first Christian services within the limits of metropolitan Toronto.[22] When Fort Frontenac was founded in 1673, its complement included a Franciscan chaplain who likewise paid some attention to Iroquois in the neighbourhood. The western missions left few permanent results apart from the retention of the Wyandots of the Windsor area, a remnant group consisting of Petuns with some Huron intermixture. Missions among the Iroquois, however, were more successful than they have sometimes been reckoned. Although they left no residue of Roman Catholics in the Iroquois homeland, they attracted a significant proportion of the population to mission settlements in the St Lawrence valley. The Catholic Indians who reside in the portion of the Aquasasne, or St Regis, reserve that lies within Ontario constitute their legacy to the province.

Although they were excluded from areas under French control, Protestant missionaries engaged in activities elsewhere that would have a later impact on the province. The Dutch of the Hudson Valley, with a base at Fort Orange where Albany now stands, were in a more strategic position than the French to influence the Mohawks. Johannes Megalopensis, who became a Dutch Reformed pastor there in 1642, may well have made the first Christian converts among them, and the church he served had sixty Mohawks on its communion roll before the end of the seventeenth century. In 1704, when the English were cultivating the friendship of the Mohawks, the Society for the Propagation of the Gospel (SPG) established a mission among them. At first its success was limited, but after the appointment as chaplain in 1735 of Henry Barclay, the son of a former missionary who had the advantage of familiarity with Indian ways from childhood, the Mohawks of the upper country gradually became Anglican.[23] A significant indicator of success was the ability of the society to enlist such native translators as Joseph Brant, who later became an acknowledged leader of his tribe. In 1767 Samuel Kirkland, a Presbyterian of revivalist tendencies, was able to organize among the Oneidas a church that attracted many of the warrior class. Farther south, in Pennsylvania, Moravians of German background established missions among the Delawares. They were even able to convert many of them to the traditional Moravian pacifism, which created difficulties in dealing with other tribes and even greater ones in coping with rapacious settlers.

Although these last efforts may seem remote from Ontario, they were influential in determining the later affiliations of significant segments of its Indian population. John Stuart, the SPG chaplain at Fort Hunter, New York, from 1760, came to Canada during the American Revolution with his Mohawk parishioners and continued for many years to minister from his home at Kingston to the Thayendanegea reserve near Deseronto. Churches both at Thayendanegea and Brantford still count among their treasures silver vessels presented by Queen Anne to the chapel at Fort Hunter in 1710. Meanwhile, David Zeisberger, a particularly appealing Moravian missionary, was leading a group of Delawares on an enforced migration in search of peace that took them to the Wyoming Valley of northern Pennsylvania, then to various locations in Ohio, and finally in 1792 to Fairfield on the Thames. Nor do such obvious connections exhaust indications of continuity. Members of the Chapel of the Delawares on the Grand River reserve, which is now affiliated with the United Church of Canada, trace their origin to an earlier Moravian church of the same name in Pennsylvania that had been burned in the course of a murderous attack by settlers.[24] And though Kirkland's republicanism led most of his followers to opt for continued residence in the United States, descendants of Tuscaroras whom he had influenced would form the nucleus of a later Baptist community on the Grand River.

The introduction of Christianity was not the only religious change to affect the native peoples of Ontario within historic times. Among North American Indians, as among aboriginal peoples in various parts of the world, so-called nativistic movements were a common response to the dislocation caused by European activities. Most of these combined selected elements of native tradition with borrowings from Christianity or, in some instances, from the framework of structures and attitudes within which Christianity was presented. This latter type of borrowing is often extremely difficult for people of European background to recognize, simply because they take this framework so much for granted that they assume it to be the common property of all religions. A complex of religious ideas and practices that seems to white observers to have been manufactured entirely out of traditional cloth may, however, strike an Indian as distinctly novel. The Indians of Ontario were by no means immune to the attraction of such movements. The so-called Delaware prophet of 1762 who helped to inspire Pontiac's rebellion against newly imposed British rule attracted a large following among the Ojibwas and their Ottawa and

Potawatomi associates, and so did the visions of Tenshwatsiwa, or Open Door, in 1805 that spurred Tecumseh to resist American inroads into Indian hunting territories. So little documentation exists with regard to their long-term influence in Ontario, however, that it seems advisable to restrict attention to two developments that have borne conspicuous and continuing fruit.

Around the turn of the eighteenth century some Ojibwas living along the southern shore of Lake Superior instituted the *midewiwin*, a lodge dedicated to the shamanic curing of initiates. Membership was open to those who required healing or were led to the society by a dream or vision, and who were prepared to pay a stiff initiation fee. Admission was by a ceremony of which the central feature was the ritual shooting of a mystical *megis*, or conch shell, into the candidate's body. From this stage the candidate could proceed, rather as in the Masonic order, through a series of three further degrees. Rituals for the various degrees were almost identical, but the steep escalation of fees as well as the fear of coping with the spiritual forces associated with the higher degrees kept most members within the first two. For the rich and venturesome, however, there were even four 'sky' degrees beyond the standard four. The ceremonies drew their significance from a mythology that explained the origins of the world and humanity, of the Ojibwas, and of the *midewiwin* itself. This mythology, recorded for easier recall on pictographic charts of birch-bark, described an earlier migration of the tribe from the east coast, although there is reason to suspect that it was originally the *mide* message that had been brought from there by the visionary Cutfoot. Along with traditional material it incorporated elements of biblical cosmology drawn from the book of Genesis.[25]

This reconstruction of events is still somewhat controversial, for until recently anthropologists did not doubt that the institution had existed among the Ojibwas from time immemorial. In 1962, however, Harold Hickerson argued that missionary records prior to 1700, though eloquent on other religious practices of the Ojibwas, contained no references to the *midewiwin*. Since *mide* rites are performed in public and figure prominently in later descriptions, this argument seems fairly conclusive. More recently, Selwyn Dewdney, in investigating scrolls embodying *mide* tradition, came unequivocally to the same conclusion. He argued further that the cosmology embodied in the charts had undergone considerable development over the years and identified Cutfoot as a historical figure whose vision could be dated to some time after 1780.[26] There can be no doubt, of course, that the shamanic features incorporated into the *midewiwin* were of long standing, and it is possible that the concept of a medicine lodge antedated contact.

If this interpretation is correct, many features of the *midewiwin* make sense in terms of the social context in which it originated. Medicine societies, as has been noted in the case of the Iroquois, were commonly associated with settled communities. During the late seventeenth century, under Iroquois pressure, many Ojibwas began to come together for the first time in permanent villages. The authority of clan elders and clan societies no longer sufficed, and a need was felt for an institution that would bind the whole tribe together. Indicative of this integrative function were the identification of Nanabozho as the founder of the *midewiwin* and an attention to *Kitchi-manito* that had not been customary in the operations of individual shamans. Although specifically Christian elements were few, the public nature of the society suggests a Christian influence; the Roman Catholic Church was, after all, the most obvious example available to the Ojibwas of an institutionalized religion with regularly instituted officers. The *midewiwin* has won little acceptance among Canadian Ojibwas, who in line with the relatively recent origin suggested here resist it as an innovation. In Ontario it reached as far south as Parry Island, at the entrance to Parry Sound, but was brought there by Potawatomis and was not well regarded locally.[27] It has been of considerable importance, however, in parts of northwestern Ontario, where regular contacts are maintained with Minnesota.

Another religious development, somewhat outside the period dealt with in this chapter, seems to fit naturally here as an illustration of the diversity of Indian responses to the white presence. Ganiodaio, or Handsome Lake, a Seneca of the Allegany band in western New York, shared in the general demoralization of the Iroquois of his area that followed the American Revolution and the loss of most of their lands. Laid low in 1799 by an illness generally attributed to alcoholism, he fell into a deep trance from which he awakened with a program for the renewal of his people that was subsequently expanded as the result of further visions. On the one hand, the Iroquois should accommodate themselves to the new circumstances imposed by the hegemony of the white man. They should take up the plough, renounce alcohol, and eliminate religious practices such as sorcery that would discredit and handicap them in American society. On the other hand, they should hold fast to elements of tradition, notably the strawberry feast and other calendrical rituals, which he recognized as good. Those who wished to embrace Christianity were free to do so, but those who accepted 'the Good Message' were to hold to the ancient ways. Although it was conceived in the United States, this 'Longhouse' religion quickly penetrated the Grand River, where it appealed most strongly to the Senecas and Cayugas in the lower part of the reservation.

Handsome Lake's experience is inexplicable apart from the arrival at his village in 1798 of three Quaker missionaries who eschewed proselytizing in favour of helping the Iroquois to find their own way; his moral ideas undoubtedly owed a good deal to their influence. That significant Christian elements were present in his religious teachings is denied by Anthony F.C. Wallace, who has made a detailed study of the movement.[28] This is the view of an outsider, however, and a more authentically Iroquois perception may have been expressed by a young Mohawk traditionalist who attended a symposium on native spirituality at Edmonton in 1977. To him the annual recitation of Handsome Lake's code, followed by four days of public repentance in order to avoid hell-fire, was 'very much like the Baptist talk,' and he added the significant complaint that what had been a way of life was now transformed into a religion.[29] What Handsome Lake did, in effect, was to resolve a duality that the Iroquois traditionally had seen no need to resolve. Feasts and dances hitherto offered to Tawiskaron were either suppressed or transformed into purely social occasions. Instead, all offerings were to be made to Haweniyo, a deity in whom there was no shadow of darkness. Some dualism remained, for Haninseono represented an opposing power, but the contrast was no longer one of yang and yin but rather of God and devil.

With Ganiodaio's movement, however, we have leapt forward to a period when the Indians were already vastly outnumbered by white settlers. At the time of the British conquest, the land that would become Upper Canada was peopled largely by Ojibwas, who had gradually become more than a match for the hitherto invincible Iroquois. About 1700 they were able to wrest from them the right to occupy the north shore of Lake Ontario and thus to gain a share of the lucrative Albany trade, and by 1720 they were firmly established throughout southern Ontario.[30] Although they retained vague memories of Roman Catholic teaching, they adhered tenaciously to traditional practices and beliefs. The same was true of the Crees of the remote north, who had been reached even more intermittently by Jesuit missionaries. Only along the Detroit River, where from 1746 until his death in 1781 the scholar-priest Pierre-Philippe Potier served a Jesuit mission to the Wyandots, did there remain a significant pocket of Christian influence. No immediate change in this situation was in prospect, for the British government regarded the area around the Great Lakes as Indian territory and placed severe limitations on white settlement.

2 *Uprooted Traditions*

Events soon dispelled any expectation that the ancestral spirits might retain undisputed possession of the land. Even at the time of the British conquest European Christianity had a foothold in what was to become Ontario, for in 1749 French settlers had begun to establish themselves on the south – later the Canadian – bank of the Detroit River. Assumption parish in Windsor, founded in 1767 for those settlers and their Wyandot neighbours, maintains to the present the longest continuous Christian witness in the province. With the outbreak of the American revolutionary war, Montreal and Niagara became bases from which colonists loyal to the Crown carried out guerrilla warfare on the frontiers of New York, Pennsylvania, and New Jersey. During the war some of them moved their families across the Niagara River, while many of their wives and children were crowded into camps at Sorel and at Yamachiche near Trois-Rivières. The unsuccessful end of the struggle made their resettlement necessary, and the fertile lands above Montreal became their obvious destination. By 1783 a village had sprung up at Kingston, and in 1784 and 1785 the main body of loyalists moved into lands set aside for them between the present Quebec border and the Bay of Quinte. Others established homes on the Niagara and Detroit frontiers.

Many of those who opposed separation from Britain lived on the eastern seaboard, ranked somewhat above the average in wealth and social position, held a government post or engaged in overseas trade, and adhered to the Church of England.[1] Insight into factors shaping the American Tory mind is of no help, however, in identifying the origins of those who came to be known in Upper Canada as United Empire Loyalists. Prominent Tories found a refuge in the maritime provinces or, more often, in England. Well over half of the roughly seventy-five hundred loyalists who settled in what is now Ontario came from the three least developed counties of New York, which were also those closest to Canada.[2] A remarkable proportion had been dependants of Sir William Johnson, who ruled the Mohawk Valley as a benevolent feudal lord until his death in 1774. The largest other single group consisted of two boatloads of refugees from New York City, mostly civilians, who chose to sail to Quebec rather than Halifax;[3] even some of these, including their leader Captain Michael Grass, were from the Johnson country.[4] Fully 90 per cent of these loyalists were farmers, for the most part on a small scale, while those of any social standing could be counted on one's fingers. Ethnically they were a mixed group: Germans, Highland Scots, Dutch of the old Yorker stock, and some whose Old Testament names suggested a New England background. Considering themselves independent nations, and therefore not necessarily wishing to be called loyalists, were more than two thousand Indians who went into exile with their British allies. Captain Deserontyon's band of Mohawks settled on the Bay of Quinte, while a more numerous group of Six Nations and allied tribes preferred to accompany Joseph Brant to the Grand River.

The presence of a sizeable body of white settlers attracted others. Some disillusioned loyalists moved up from New Brunswick, while others discovered belatedly the disadvantages of living under a republican government. Britain supplied a few officials and military officers, while common soldiers were brought from all parts of the United Kingdom. Groups of Highland Scots joined their loyalist compatriots in Glengarry County from time to time, and a few Lowland merchants sought their fortunes in Niagara and other centres of trade. Prior to 1812, however, the great majority of immigrants were Americans whose motives had little to do with politics. At first they came mainly from the hill country of western and northern New England. The Duc de La Rochefoucauld-Liancourt, a French émigré who toured the province in 1795, cited Connecticut, Vermont, and New Hampshire as the chief sources. During the early years of the nineteenth century the western part of the province, then opening up, attracted many from the middle states. In his *Statistical Report of Upper Canada*, published in 1820, Robert Gourlay identified New York, New Jersey, and Pennsylvania as the sources of much of the population of the Niagara and London regions. Lieutenant-Colonel John Graves Simcoe, the first lieutenant-governor of Upper Canada after its separation in 1791, sought to establish a credible British presence in the interior of North America by attracting 'loyal' residents of the United States into the province. Most of those who took up his offer of generous land grants, it may be presumed, were simply part of a general westward movement across the continent that paid little heed to political boundaries.[5] By 1812 Upper Canada had roughly seventy-five thousand inhabitants.[6] Of these, a visiting Baptist minister estimated, eight of every ten were of American origin, but only two were of loyalist stock.[7]

Along with their household effects and the few heirlooms they were able to take into the wilderness, these early inhabitants brought with them a considerable body of religious beliefs, practices, and prejudices. In time their descendants would be vastly outnumbered by later immigrants and their contributions to the religious life of the province substantially modified by the efforts of preachers, journalists, Sunday school teachers, and distributors of tracts. But just as they bequeathed to the province a mid-American accent that would persist through many demographic changes, so they established a religious pattern that has never been totally obliterated. Reflecting the religious diversity of the middle states, from which much of Upper Canada's early population was derived, this pattern embraced a considerable spectrum of conviction and custom.

Easily overlooked were the venerable traditions of the native peoples. To most whites the Indians were a dying race, their religious customs of interest only to antiquarians. Yet even after the entry of the loyalists they constituted approximately half of the population, and no early traveller's reminiscences were complete without an account of these 'picturesque' people who formed a conspicuous presence even in the towns. The Mississaugas along Lake Ontario, who most keenly felt the loss of traditional hunting-grounds, were already beginning to wonder about the efficacy of their rituals.[8] Elsewhere, Ojibwas held tenaciously to their ancestral ways, as did several of the Iroquois nations.

Roman Catholics, in sum fairly numerous, were of several ethnic backgrounds. The French and Wyandots of the old Essex settlements represented a tradition that already seemed indigenous to the province, though the Wyandots were somewhat unsettled in their Catholicism. In Glengarry County, at the other end of the province, was a colony of Scots that reproduced in the new world the customs and manners of the old Glen Garry above Loch Ness. After fighting on the losing side in four Jacobite campaigns, some of these Catholic Highlanders had taken up lands in the Mohawk Valley in 1773 on the invitation of Sir William Johnson, who despite his Irish birth and Anglican religion was of Macdonell descent.[9] So little time intervened before the outbreak of the revolution that they would have carried to Canada as loyalists much more vivid memories of Scotland than of New York. Those who followed them to Glengarry directly from the home glen were equally retentive of their clan attachments and their distinctive language and dress. In the garrison towns, after enlistment in the army was opened to them in 1793, there were also a considerable number of Irish soldiers of the Roman Catholic faith. As yet relatively inconspicuous, they were the forerunners of a larger migration.

Belief in the transubstantiation of the elements in the mass, the veneration accorded to the Virgin and the saints, and recognition of the pope as the vicar of Christ on earth gave Roman Catholicism a distinctiveness that does not need to be elaborated in detail. At this time, however, the church was less centralized in government and less uniform in practice than it would later become. Prelates customarily deferred to secular authorities in matters that did not concern the faith, and many national and regional usages persisted. Bishop Joseph-Octave Plessis, who toured the province in 1816, left a generally unfavourable report of his impressions. The Irish of Kingston, he complained, were more concerned to make money than to work for their salvation, and days of abstinence, fasts, and feasts of obligation seemed foreign to them. Of the French Canadians of Malden he wrote, 'Everything is here in miniature except irreligion and libertinage.' To a considerable extent these negative judgments reflected expectations shaped in Quebec. In general, the Irish were fervently attached to their church but unaccustomed to a strict application of its rules. The French of the Detroit area knew the rules, but long association with the fur trade had made them impatient of restraint. While Plessis recorded no comparable observations on the Glengarry Scots, we may surmise that their behaviour and attitudes were similar to those he encountered on pastoral tours through eastern Nova Scotia in 1812 and 1815. On these visitations he was distressed by the clumsiness of Highland priests on ceremonial occasions and disturbed by the attendance at mass of barking dogs and women with uncovered throats; he was also greatly moved by the spontaneous fervour of people who had long suffered persecution for the faith. Unlike Cape Breton, however, Glengarry maintained many features of the old clan system under leaders, mainly military Macdonells of courtly bearing, who would have had a greater feeling for propriety in worship.[10]

At the other end of the theological spectrum were representatives of several movements that sought in varied ways to move beyond the positions of conventional Protestantism. Some Mennonites settled in the Niagara Peninsula in 1786;[11] others began to locate around Waterloo in 1800 and in Markham Township in 1803. They were spiritual, and mainly lineal, descendants of the Anabaptists who in the sixteenth century had set out to reproduce literally the church life described in the New Testament. Insisting that members should be fully committed Christians, these Anabaptists had denied the validity of infant baptism. Insisting also that they should hold themselves aloof from a sinful world, they embraced pacifism and advocated the strict separation of church and state. These radical positions, often urged with deliberate aggressiveness, had called forth severe persecution by both Protestant and Roman Catholic governments. When the movement seemed doomed, Menno Simons rallied some Dutch followers and persuaded them to withdraw from public agitation in order to live out their convictions within their own communities. When these Mennonites were subjected to intolerable pressure to conform, their habitual response was to seek new homes where their convictions would be respected. In 1683 some of them began to settle in Pennsylvania in response to a general invitation issued by a fellow pacifist, the Quaker William Penn. It was from these 'Pennsylvania Dutch' that the early Mennonites of Upper Canada originated. Economic opportunity was an important motive in their choice of the province, but doubtless the instability of the post-revolutionary United States and its suspicion of all who refused to fight for independence also brought into play the Mennonite instinct for migration in time of danger.[12]

Closely associated with the Mennonites were the Tunkers,[13] who resembled them in many respects but traced their origin to a different source. In 1719 some Germans who had left the Reformed Church in protest against its baptism of infants began to move to America in hope of greater freedom. About 1780 their movement took more definite shape under the name of 'River Brethren.' Seeking to adhere ever more strictly to New Testament precedent, the Tunkers practised triple immersion and held periodic love-feasts with mutual foot-washing and the exchange of the kiss of peace. Among the more tradition-bound Mennonites they operated as a revivalist leaven, insisting on a personal conversion that had become largely a formality in the older group.[14]

Some members of the Religious Society of Friends, or Quakers, followed so quickly on the heels of the first loyalists that they are often accounted part of their migration. Probably the chief factor in their decision to leave the United States was resistance to pressure for military involvement in the revolution. Others followed as part of the general westward movement of the time, spurred on by a conviction that their societies had a special mission on the frontier. Quakerism, which had originally taken shape on the left wing of the Puritan movement in seventeenth-century England, was based on the teaching of George Fox that the ultimate criterion of truth is not a book but an 'inner light' through which Christ reveals himself to the heart. In the early years its adherents had been noisy and disruptive, scattering through western Europe and America in an effort to summon the rulers of the nations to join in the 'Lamb's War' for the renovation of society.[15] Later they moved to a more liberal theology and to a commitment to advanced social causes, while clinging to the antique customs that symbolized their separateness. With their distinctive forms of dress and address, their puzzlingly quiet worship, and their abnormally tender consciences on the making of war and the taking of oaths, they were a conspicuous presence during the early nineteenth century. They were also a considerable presence, absolutely more numerous than today and proportionately much more so. In Prince Edward

County they were for a time the largest denomination, and provided the pioneer schooling on the peninsula. They also dominated a portion of Yonge Street around Newmarket and were strong in the Long Point area.

A body of unusual origin that touched the life of Upper Canada was the Unitas Fratrum, or Unity of Brethren, commonly known as the Moravian Church. From the late fourteenth century some followers of the Czech reformer Jan Hus had maintained a precarious separate existence in the mountains of their homeland. Their typically medieval style of life was based on a tight communal discipline, with stress placed on singing in choirs segregated by age and sex. Forced out of the Hapsburg dominions by unrelenting persecution, some of them found a refuge in 1722 on the Saxon estate of Count Nicolas von Zinzendorf. Zinzendorf had already collected around him a number of Lutherans who sympathized with his emphasis on the religion of the heart. The two groups merged in 1727 and immediately launched the most ambitious Protestant foreign missionary enterprise of the eighteenth century, an enterprise based on the unusual technique of sending in an economically self-sufficient community of believers who might attract others to their way of life. It was a Moravian, Peter Böhler, who guided John Wesley to his evangelical conversion, although Wesley later became dissatisfied with the depth of Moravian spirituality. At the outset of the American revolution there were as many Moravians as Methodists in New York City, and some of them showed up along the Bay of Quinte as loyalists. The most significant body of Moravians in the province, however, consisted of the colony of Delaware Indians who moved with David Zeisberger to Fairfield in 1792.[16]

Religious variety in the infant colony was thus considerable, but its range was still relatively narrow. The denominations already discussed constituted no more than spice in the cake; Christians of eastern traditions were unrepresented, and the religions of the Orient were known only by vague rumour. The great bulk of early settlers would have identified themselves without hesitation as belonging to the mainstream of Protestantism. Even those who did not attend church had been formed, more than they knew, by its precepts and presuppositions. Their very doubts and objections were Protestant.

Persons who had been raised in the original Protestantism of Martin Luther made up a substantial proportion of the population, probably a greater proportion than at any time since. In 1708 a number of 'Palatine' Germans left the Rhine valley for America to escape economic hardship and religious persecution, and many of them ultimately settled on a fifty-mile stretch along the Mohawk known as the German Flats. When lands were allotted to the loyalists, Dundas County was assigned to members of this group. They included Lutherans and Reformed, but

Lutherans were the larger group. Disbanded Hessian soldiers formed another concentration of Lutherans around the Bay of Quinte and in Prince Edward County. In 1794 William Berczy sponsored a further Palatine settlement in Markham Township, and a succession of convoys of Conestoga wagons brought many Lutherans from Pennsylvania to neighbouring Vaughan both before and after 1800.[17]

Lutherans insisted, against much medieval understanding, that salvation is through the unmerited grace of God appropriated by faith alone. In worship Luther discarded only what he regarded as theologically objectionable, while his followers tended to have a more relaxed attitude to common amusements than some other Protestants. Those who settled in America were pulled in two directions. On the one hand, they treasured Luther's German Bible and hymns and sought to uphold his doctrines with integrity. On the other hand, many of them were attracted by the informality and emotionalism of eighteenth-century pietism and affected by the revivalism and strict moralism of their American neighbours. The architecture of their churches, which tended to be bare meeting-halls, suggests that the process of acculturation had gone quite far. While they were eager to hold on to their traditions, many Lutherans of the period would have been hard put to say precisely what those traditions were.

The Reformed or Presbyterian tradition traced its origin to John Calvin, a native of France who became the leading Protestant reformer of Geneva. Although he regarded himself as essentially a follower of Luther, Calvin imposed a stricter discipline on his followers and made a much more thorough effort to rid worship of medieval accretions and base it on biblical precepts. The presence of Christ in the elements of the Lord's Supper he described as 'spiritual,' to the scandal of Lutherans who saw in his terminology a denial of reality of that presence. The cornerstone of Calvin's theology was the sovereignty of God, who became the chief and in a sense the only significant actor in history. A corollary of this belief was the predestination of each individual even before birth to eternal salvation or damnation, a doctrine that Calvin accepted, in common with most Western theologians, while relegating it to a few chapters in the latter part of his massive *Institutes of the Christian Religion*. Later generations made predestination the centrepiece of a Calvinistic system while adopting a strict sabbatarianism that would have astonished Calvin.[18]

Calvin's influence extended to a number of European countries, inspiring the formation of national churches that differed in emphasis and ethos but agreed on the essentials of belief. Several of these were represented among the settlers of Upper Canada. Those of continental origin were destined not to remain distinct entities in the province beyond the pioneer period, but they call at least for brief notice. Loyalists of

German Reformed background constituted a significant bloc in Dundas County. Other loyalists, who sailed from New York under the leadership of Peter Van Alstyne and settled along the Bay of Quinte, represented the venerable Dutch Reformed tradition of New Amsterdam. Here and there also might be found descendants of the Huguenots who represented the Calvinist tradition in France. Continental Reformed churches tended to be austerely formal, although doctrinally less rigid than Lutheran churches. Their esteem for the preaching of the Word, which they shared with other Calvinistic churches, made the minister a figure of great prominence, dignity, and authority. By the end of the eighteenth century, however, both Dutch and German Reformed churches had undergone considerable Americanization. Although some of their members held strictly to national traditions, others could not readily be distinguished from the general run of American Protestants. The Huguenots never set up a separate organization in America, and those who came to Upper Canada were already scattered among several denominations.

Scottish Presbyterians, who may have been outnumbered at first by their fellow Calvinists from continental Europe, were to have a greater impact on the religion of the province. Their early stronghold was Glengarry, where demobilized Highlanders of the 84th Regiment shared the Gaelic language of their Roman Catholic neighbours. The established Church of Scotland – the 'Auld Kirk' in Presbyterian shorthand – had imbibed a strong dose of Calvinism in the sixteenth century under the leadership successively of John Knox and Andrew Melville. The 'moderates' who controlled the church in the eighteenth century were more interested in raising the standards of literature and learning in what had been a semi-barbarous country, a project in which they were notably successful. Neither development had major repercussions in the Highlands, where beyond a drastic simplification of worship the Reformation had had little effect on the mentality of the people and where differences between Protestants and Roman Catholics owed more to political allegiance and clan loyalty than to theological conviction. During the eighteenth century, however, the Edinburgh-based Society for Propagating Christian Knowledge (not to be confused with the Anglican Society for Promoting Christian Knowledge) established schools that gradually introduced literacy and evangelical piety to the Highlands. That their efforts had made relatively little impression on the first Protestant settlers of Glengarry, most of whom had spent some years in army barracks, is suggested by occasional reports of conversions to Roman Catholicism. Later arrivals, including an important contingent of pious MacMillans, helped to solidify their Presbyterianism and to naturalize the *Shorter Catechism,* the Scottish metrical psalter, and the authority of the Kirk session.[19]

The appointment of Kirk ministers in Scotland was in the hands of patrons, often local lairds, who preferred cultured moderates to the more fervent preachers whom the people would have chosen. In 1733 the brothers Ebenezer and Ralph Erskine led a secession in protest. Their followers ultimately split into four irreconcilable fragments that spawned counterparts and variants in Ireland and America. None of these, nor other splinter groups that followed them, had more than a handful of adherents in Upper Canada before 1812. Nevertheless, since they appealed to a class of merchants and artisans that was beginning to appear in the province and would attain considerable importance, they deserve a brief introduction. The Seceders were democratic in temper, often radical in politics, and strong on personal piety. They were noted for the strictness of their Calvinism, and their dedication to principle manifested itself in their division into Burgher and Antiburgher segments over the acceptability of an oath requiring civic officials to acknowledge 'the true religion presently professed in this realm.' Although Burghers condemned Antiburghers as narrow, they themselves seemed broad only to other Seceders. By the end of the eighteenth century, however, 'New Lichts' in both camps were diverting some of their attention from the defence of orthodoxy to the organization of prayer meetings and missionary societies.

To a considerable extent the Church of England also had been shaped by Calvinism, though always in conjunction with other impulses such as the renaissance of classical letters, the high churchmanship of Archbishop Laud, the tolerant latitudinarianism inspired by the Cambridge Platonists, and the varied evangelical movements of the eighteenth century. Traces of all of these influences could be detected among the church's adherents in early Upper Canada. For most of them, however, the essential fact about their church was simply that it was the Church of England and thus the embodiment of all the values that were held to qualify England to an unusual degree as a Christian nation. The factors that entered into this evaluation were remarkably diverse: the link with the universal church represented by episcopal succession but also independence of any foreign authority, the institution of a limited monarchy along with freedom from the mob rule commonly associated with republican government, and perhaps most of all the profession of a 'rational religion' with doctrines 'as far removed from Enthusiasm on the one side as they are from Superstition on the other.'[20]

In the minds of its zealous adherents those who declined to belong to it, apart from respectable members of the Church of Scotland and incorrigible followers of Rome, were dissenters whose obstinacy could be traced only to ulterior and probably political motives. The term 'Anglican' not yet being in general currency, members commonly referred simply to 'the

Church'; outsiders who balked at admitting that status spoke of 'Episcopalians.'

What proportion of pre-1812 settlers may have been of 'Church' or 'Episcopalian' background has long been a matter for dispute. Chancellor Nathanael Burwash of Victoria University was among those who accepted a traditional view that they held the first rank among the loyalists. At the other extreme Richard Cartwright, himself a member of the Church of England, estimated in 1792 that not more than one hundred families in the province adhered to it. Cartwright was a foe of religious establishment, and this bias may have skewed his figuring. But apart from the Mohawks, who constituted the largest single body of Anglicans, it is difficult to identify a much greater number of practising members during this period. John Stuart, the first rector of Kingston, conceded that his church was in a minority both there and at Niagara. Despite suggestions of significant concentrations in Grenville County and along the Bay of Quinte, Episcopalians were even less visible in rural districts. Nor is it easy to see where many would have come from, for they were scarce in New York beyond the vicinity of the city. To loyalists from the Mohawk Valley, however, the services of the Church of England would have been familiar. Stuart, who for many years had been a missionary to the Mohawks of Fort Hunter in that region, had also provided pastoral oversight to white settlers of various denominations and served many others during the war as a chaplain. In an invitation to him in 1788 to become their missionary, the people of Niagara specifically recalled favourable associations from the past.[21] Later years brought to the province a number of officials and military men who would most naturally associate themselves with the Church of England, and among American immigrants there were undoubtedly some who retained a lingering affection for their ancestral church. On any reckoning, however, Episcopalians constituted at most one among a number of minority groups.

Methodism, an offshoot of the Church of England, was introduced to Upper Canada by some of the original loyalists. John Wesley, an Oxford don and a priest of the established church, experienced in 1738 a conversion that brought him an assurance of salvation which strict keeping of the rules of the church had failed to deliver. From the following year until his death in 1791 he engaged in an itinerant ministry that was intended not merely to induce similar conversions but, in his words, 'to spread scriptural holiness over the land.'[22] Implicit in this purpose was the conviction that actual sinlessness is possible in this life, though Wesley never claimed to have attained it. His view of salvation, associated with the Dutch theologian Arminius and therefore known as Arminianism, stressed as strongly as Calvinism our inherent incapacity to choose the way of salvation but insisted that each person had been granted sufficient 'prevenient' grace to be able to accept God's offer of it. The possibility of both redemption and perfection could therefore be held out to all. Wesley gathered his followers into societies, not intending thereby to detach them from their allegiance to the Church of England or any other to which they might belong. When the national clergy proved unwilling to co-operate, however, he called laymen to assist him as both local and itinerant preachers.

Among those who entered Upper Canada as loyalists were a cluster of Methodist families who established themselves on the Bay of Quinte and in Augusta Township of Dundas County. Descendants of Palatine Germans who had taken refuge in Ireland in 1709, they had come under Wesley's influence there and in 1760 moved on to New York City. They constituted a very important group, for in 1766 Philip Embury and Barbara Heck were chiefly responsible for the organization there of what was probably the second Methodist society in America. In 1770 most of these families settled in the Camden Valley on what is now the New York-Vermont border, a location from which it was possible for several men in the party to escape to Canada and enlist in the British forces during the revolution. The religious tradition they carried to Upper Canada was thus one of unusual vitality. Since the total membership of their society in New York in 1776 was only 180, however, it is unlikely that loyalists who entered the province as Methodists can have been very numerous. Among later immigrants the proportion would have been considerably higher, for Methodism expanded with unprecedented rapidity during and after the revolution.[23] Many others, especially from the New York area, would have heard and responded favourably to Methodist preaching.

Those who came to Upper Canada as loyalists had known Methodism not as a religious denomination but merely as a voluntary association for the cultivation of holiness. For a time the Emburys and Hecks were members of a Lutheran congregation in New York, and after their removal to Upper Canada the Hecks did not scruple to attach themselves to the Anglican Blue Church at Maitland. After the revolution, however, when the Church of England was practically derelict in the United States, Wesley commissioned two superintendents to ensure that his followers would have access to the sacraments.[24] One of them, Francis Asbury, became in 1784 the first bishop of the newly formed Methodist Episcopal Church. Thus, later Methodist immigrants reflected the outlook of a full-fledged ecclesiastical body, furnished with a threefold ministry of bishops, elders, and deacons, and disinclined to defer to the Church of England.

Left to the last in this discussion has been a category that almost certainly accounted for a larger proportion of pre-1812 settlers than any other. This was the Puritan tradition that had been carried to New England in various forms by waves of colonists beginning with the Pilgrim Fathers in 1620. Originally, Puritanism had signified simply uncompromising Calvinism as professed in England, but it was soon characterized also by a heightened emphasis on personal spirituality and a tendency to take constant stock of spiritual progress. This insistence on internalizing religion left many New Englanders open to outbursts of emotional revivalism, which began around 1690 under Solomon Stoddard at Northampton, Massachusetts, recurred there in the 1730s under the ministry of his grandson Jonathan Edwards, and became regular occurrences largely as the result of successive American tours by Wesley's one-time associate George Whitefield. 'New light' preaching stressed the importance of personal conversion, which was expected to be sudden and dramatic, and belittled the starchily theological sermons that had become standard fare. New Englanders continued to defend Calvinism with a vigour that led the Methodist itinerant Freeborn Garrettson to complain that planting Arminianism on their borders called for 'the wisdom of the serpent and the harmlessness of a dove.' In fact, however, predestination counted for little when conversion was being pressed on all, and New England theology was moving ever closer to Arminianism. Universalists, occasionally encountered in Upper Canada, even argued that everyone would ultimately be saved.[25] Meanwhile, in reaction against the emotionalism associated with revivals, much of urban New England was moving towards Unitarianism.

Most readily distinguished among the orthodox heirs of the Puritan tradition were the Baptists. For the most part their churches were secondary products of 'new light' revival, formed by groups of converts who studied the New Testament closely and tried to model their congregational life on the procedures they found there. To Baptists these implied the baptism by immersion of believers only and the independence of each congregation from any form of centralized control, and they held to these principles with great tenacity. Despite their revivalist origin, most of them resisted any tendency to water down their inherited Calvinism. Yet there were also Free Baptists, especially strong in Maine, who professed an Arminian theology and communed more readily with churches practising infant baptism. We hear of no Baptists in the loyalist migration to Upper Canada, for they were virtually unknown in the areas from which it drew. Small groups began to appear in eastern Upper Canada before the turn of the century; most of these soon disintegrated. The largest concentration later developed in the area north of Lake Erie, which was on a path of westward migration from upstate New York.

Congregationalists, seeking to apply Jesus' statement, 'Where two or three are gathered together in my name, there am I in the midst of them,' believed like Baptists that ultimate authority resided in a local worshipping community whose members were bound to God and one another by a covenant of belief. Their most characteristic institution was a monthly meeting at which, they believed, the Holy Spirit guided the church to a consensus in the transaction of its business. From the outset theirs was the favoured polity of New England. As Congregationalism became the' official religion there, the church meeting and the town meeting tended'' more and more to coalesce. When New Englanders moved to areas where Congregationalism was not so privileged, therefore, they had great difficulty in carrying their institutions with them. Late in the seventeenth century the Congregationalists and Presbyterians of England had arranged to unite. Although their union was short-lived, the Heads of Agreement of 1691 that had served as a constitution provided a precedent for Puritans in the middle colonies. In 1706 the presbytery of Philadelphia was formed, and before long, especially on Long Island and in New Jersey, most erstwhile Congregationalists had adopted the Presbyterian name along with the Presbyterian system of government by representative church bodies.[26] Inevitably, the Presbyterianism of these colonies acquired some'' Congregational characteristics, and members passed from one designation to the other without noticing much difference. In 1801 the two denominations moved even closer together by adopting a Plan of Union that made the Presbyterians responsible for organizing new congregations outside New England.

There were probably a few New Englanders among the loyalist settlers,'' and there were many among those who reached the province in the later years of the eighteenth century. Most came as farmers, but a fair number'' were entrepreneurs who set up local industries and often hired some of their former neighbours to work for them. A large proportion came from parts of New England where revivalism was endemic. During the early years of the nineteenth century, when the central states began to provide the bulk of immigrants, Presbyterians predominated but represented essentially the same tradition. In Upper Canada, especially after the Plan of Union, the designation 'Presbyterian' was almost always used by American settlers. Thus concealed, the attitudes and beliefs of Congregational New England would continue to colour the provincial mentality.

Climbers of family trees, who are often surprisingly successful in tracing New World ancestors, find their chief resources to be church records and churchyard inscriptions. The founders, it seems, maintained contact with some religious denomination or other at least in the crises of birth, marriage, and death. Such details tell us little, however, about the quality of their commitment. Did they attend services regularly? Did they obey the rules of their churches and fulfil the duties expected of them? Were they generous in support of religious institutions? Did they say their prayers? To what extent did religious faith shape their behaviour?

If the first clearers of the land had confided more of their inmost thoughts to paper, we should be in a better position to answer such questions. Early missionaries tended, on the whole, to a rather negative appraisal. Asahel Morse, a Baptist missionary who toured the province in 1807, described it as a 'dismal region of moral darkness and the shadow of death.' Nathan Bangs, a Methodist itinerant, recalled York as in 1801 a 'new little village, the settlers of which were as thoughtless and wicked as the Canaanites of old.' William Smart, the first Presbyterian minister of Brockville, was more specific in his complaints: he cited intemperance, gambling, card-playing, and the lack of sabbath observance, and added piously that people would be better occupied in reading books. Even John Stuart, who as an Episcopalian was more tolerant of human foibles, characterized the New York loyal refugees who constituted the bulk of his congregation as 'a Description of men not remarkable for either Religion, Industry or Honesty.' Everyone seemed happy with him until a subscription list was passed around, he added, when he discovered that the proportion of church to dissenters was very small. While lamenting the scarcity of communicants, he could identify 'but few of good character & morals, professing themselves members of our Church, who [were] not already Communicants.'[27]

Even when due allowance is made for the propensity of the clergy to magnify the difficulties confronting them, what we know of the state of religion in this period lends credence to their assessment. It is generally conceded that the commercial spirit had eroded the early zeal of Puritan New England to the point where only the direct approach of high-pressure revivalists could stem the tide. New York, from which Upper Canada drew much of its early population, had the reputation of being one of the least religious colonies; in 1687 Governor Thomas Dongan wrote of its inhabitants, 'Of all sorts of opinions there are some, the most part none at all.' The outbreak of the revolution induced in some quarters a seriousness favourable to religious commitment, but also popularized the anti-Christian polemic of Thomas Paine. By 1790, it has been estimated, not more than 10 per cent of the American people were church members; 'the majority had no significant connection with any religious organization.'[28] In the early years of the nineteenth century a great religious awakening swept the United States, but only a small proportion of those who emigrated to Upper Canada before 1812 would have been affected by it.

The circumstances of settlement were no more conducive to religious interest. Most loyalist men had spent the war years in military service, usually in situations where daring and ruthlessness were more valued than self-discipline, while their families had suffered the irritations and boredom of life in a refugee camp. Small wonder that a military officer commented, after a tour of the Kingston area, 'Strange is the Collection of people here.' Even when the circumstances of arrival were less unsettling, the task of rendering operative a farm or business called for an expenditure of time and energy that left little surplus for prayer and religious instruction and little incentive for distinguishing the days of the week. Compounding these preoccupations was a falling away of familiar sanctions to which John Strachan gave eloquent, if possibly exaggerated, testimony:

Persons going into a wilderness, though far better prepared than the generality of Loyalists, are found greatly to relax in their religious observance, and to fall into a sort of moral bondage – they are not restrained by public opinion, or kept under any regularity of deportment by the rules of decorum – the eye of those whom they fear is not present to put them on their guard, nor are they often beheld by those whom they love and whom they are unwilling to offend. Experiencing no moral restraint from the example and opinion of others, they feel at length little from themselves; whatever vigour and resolution they bring with them gradually diminish, their passions and appetites assume the reins; so that while many of their most pressing difficulties are removed, they have little or no disposition to support religion or to attend to its institutions.[29]

There were also countervailing forces. Especially among farm women, loneliness could induce a desire for community that might not be satisfied by the usual round of parties and frolics. Immersion in a round of household chores could create an appetite for activities more satisfying to the intellect or the emotions. Not least among factors favouring religious awareness was a nostalgia that led the pioneer to wish to recreate some of the familiar atmosphere of home. Students of the immigrant experience have often noted that even many of those who had not displayed great piety in their homelands turned to familiar churches in their countries of adoption as means of solidifying or refurbishing a threatened sense of personal identity. What back there had been merely religion now came to be seen as one's *own* religion, and the appearance of a preacher who could evoke memories of past associations might set in motion a train of powerful feelings. Among settlers such as the loyalists, who had come to the province not in search of Utopia but in the hope of reconstructing blasted careers, such feelings must have been especially strong.

Despite the generally pessimistic tone of contemporary accounts, we know of a fair number of settlers who sought to keep the torch of religion alight in their communities. Colonel John Clark, reminiscing about early times in Lennox and Addington County, recalled an era of bucolic innocence: 'There were no squabbles about churchwardens or decorations – formalities, divisions of sects, fasts, holidays or particular days. Those residing within a short distance of each other would meet once a week to hold social converse, read the scriptures and instill into the minds of the children the principle of dependence upon God.' Although this picture appears somewhat idealized, a number of firsthand references testify to such practices. In the Thames Valley, a region not noted for its early piety, a Yankee immigrant named Francis Cornwall read to his neighbours on Sundays when no preachers were available. At Long Point, Amelia Harris later recalled, her father had initiated the practice of reading the church service every Sunday to his household and any hired men who could be persuaded to attend. Methodists at Augusta and Niagara organized unofficial classes without waiting for preachers, and during a vacancy at York the schoolmaster William Cooper read the church prayers and book sermons not only to the townspeople but to the inmates of the local jail.[30]

The Methodist itinerant John Carroll noted among the early settlers 'a marked line of distinction between the righteous and the wicked,' and so it often appeared. In assessing their religious state, however, we should do well to bear in mind the familiarity of most of those of American origin with the revivalist tradition that had taken deep root in the colonial mentality long before the revolution. In this tradition it was generally believed that only those who had gone through the crisis of conversion qualified as Christians. Even the converted might back-slide, always with the possibility of recovering their Christian status at the next revival. Those who had not experienced conversion or had forfeited the benefits of an earlier awakening allowed themselves in practice a fair measure of spiritual and moral latitude, but to reckon them, without qualification, among the irreligious would be in some respects unrealistic. Many of them were, in effect, merely not yet converted or enjoying a temporary holiday from grace. Such people might give the impression of utter carelessness in religious matters, but they were not necessarily closed to the possibility of quickened zeal if some impulse should fan the embers.[31]

3 Foundations

The memories, convictions, devotional habits, and aspirations that the first generation of immigrants brought with them to Upper Canada constituted some of the raw material out of which an Ontario religious tradition would begin to take shape. As yet this religiosity lacked cohesion, being merely the sum of the religious baggage of individual settlers. Much of it was latent, and all of it was fragile. Whether it would be strengthened or further dissipated would depend to a great extent on the effectiveness of the religious leadership that could be made available to the province. The task would not be easy. Reinforcing the faith of those who had entered the province with solid convictions would be a challenge in itself, and winning over the majority who lacked firm church connections would require even more heroic effort. Yet prompt action promised rich returns, for one could apply to many Upper Canadian communities Sir William Johnson's analysis of the situation in the Mohawk Valley in 1774: 'The first Church which goes in successfully & without interruption must attach them all.'[1] In practical terms these tasks called for buildings, budgets, organization, and, above all, ministerial leadership. Efforts to provide these necessities would constitute a dominant theme in the religious history of the province through a large part of the nineteenth century. By 1812 a significant beginning had been made and some elements of a denominational pattern put in place.

The formation of religious institutions in a newly settled area calls for initiative on someone's part. Action may originate internally when local inhabitants take steps to secure religious services for themselves. They may organize congregations, erect church buildings, or petition governments or religious agencies for aid. In the absence of outside leadership, they may, as we have already seen them do, continue the practice of family worship, gather for informal services in homes or schoolhouses, or ask one of their company to read prayers or conduct a Sunday school. They may even devise new forms of religious expression and raise up their own locally authorized leadership. Alternatively, initiative may be taken from without by governments, churches, or missionary agencies, or by concerned or merely unemployed preachers or priests. Their help can take a variety of forms – the direct provision of personnel or money, the conferral of religious privileges, or merely the offer of encouragement and advice by correspondence or personal visitation. Typically, there will need to be some action at each end. Pleas for help will be of little avail unless external agencies show interest. Missionary outreach will depend for its effectiveness on the willingness or ability of colonists to take increasing responsibility for their own religious needs. We shall see all of these processes at work in Upper Canada.

Lines of authority differ from one religious denomination to another, and these differences can greatly affect the manner in which organizations are created and leaders secured. In denominations such as the Congregationalist and Baptist, where ultimate authority rests with the local church, each congregation is responsible for its own arrangements for ministerial supply. Churches of the Presbyterian or Reformed family have a graduated system of legislative bodies or 'courts' that oversee and presumably assist local congregations. Ministers can be settled only when congregations call them, however, and congregations must co-operate in order to bring the higher courts into existence. Outside assistance must therefore await the organization of regular congregations and, in theory at least, of presbyteries to 'moderate' calls. An episcopal system, such as prevails among Roman Catholics, Anglicans, and American Methodists, allows for much greater initiative from the centre. Bishops normally make appointments, and parishes or circuits are expected to accept the priests or ministers they are sent.

Such, at any rate, are the classical expressions of these various ecclesiastical polities. In practice, as will become evident, their operation in Upper Canada was greatly affected by custom and circumstance and by the existence of power structures that escaped the neat definitions of ecclesiastical theory. Churches adhering rigidly to congregational independence might prove more adept at concerted action than denominations of more centralized polity. Missionary societies and religious orders might, by virtue of the money and personnel at their disposal, sometimes have more actual influence in the province than bishops or presbyteries. Until 1815 the state paid the stipends of Church of England missionaries, and governors were not slow to claim the voice in appointments to which this subsidy entitled them. Removed as they often were from effective supervision, moreover, ministers and congregations did not always adhere to the principles of church government to which in theory they were committed; in 1807, for example, the Roman Catholics of York elected officials whom they designated, in Presbyterian fashion, 'elders.'[2]

As one might expect, the relative importance of internal and external initiative varied from one denomination to another. Among groups fortunate enough to be able to carry their institutions with them, the two virtually coalesced. This was notably the case with the Mennonites, who moved from Pennsylvania to Upper Canada as extended family groups and sometimes as sizeable portions of established communities. Their ministry of bishops and elders, which they retained from earlier days, was chosen from among the most trusted members of the community by a system of lots that depended in practice on the attainment of consensus. Even when authorized ministers did not take part in a local migration, the Mennonites were able to institute their accustomed order without delay or upheaval. Since new colonies required time for adjustment, however, the communities in Pennsylvania from which they had come made themselves available for advice and for the adjudication of disputes. The fruits of this continuity were most strikingly evident in the emergence of such leaders as Benjamin Eby, who served the Mennonites of the Waterloo area not only as bishop but as the founder of industries that gave the city of Kitchener its start. Even so, failure to secure the solid blocks of land to which they had been accustomed resulted in the falling away of some members.[3]

Moravians and Quakers were similarly situated. Moravian Fairfield was essentially the product of a series of moves that had taken its Delaware inhabitants from Pennsylvania to Ohio to Upper Canada and would take most of them on to Kansas in 1837. Its German-speaking leaders were already well known to their people, and its hierarchically arranged streets replicated the pattern of previous settlements. Although the Friends spoke English and were therefore more open to outside influences, their distinctive dress and vocabulary served as badges of identity and aids to cohesion. Like the Mennonites, too, they tended to settle in close proximity to one another. They had the further advantage of being able to apply a Presbyterian polity more effectively than the Presbyterians. Quaker organization consisted of a graduated series of 'meetings,' from weekly local gatherings to an all-embracing yearly assembly. From 1797 superior meetings in the United States sent delegates to examine and authenticate Canadian branches, and exchanges of authorized messengers of either sex bearing particular 'concerns' were a regular feature of Quaker life.[4]

In almost every denomination, indeed, there were cases where ministers and people virtually moved into the province together. With one brief exception the early priests of Glengarry were not merely Highlanders but Macdonells of the Scottish Glen Garry who possessed a native understanding of the mentality of their flocks. Eminent among them was Alexander

Macdonell – Alasdair Mor, or Big Alex – who sponsored the emigration of some of his people from Scotland and followed them to Upper Canada in 1804. More than three hundred pounds of formidable presence, he was soon fulfilling many of the functions of a clan chief and in 1826 would become the first bishop of Kingston. John Bethune and John Stuart had been known to many of their parishioners as military chaplains, and Stuart was able to maintain close contact with the Quinte Mohawks to whom he had been a missionary in New York. Asa Turner, the first ordained Baptist minister in Upper Canada, regularly preached to a group of settlers whom he had led to the Moira River in 1789. Abel Stevens, an entrepreneur who attempted to set up an ironworks on the Gananoque River, was another Baptist who served as both colonizer and minister.[5] Such connections greatly eased the shock of transplanting religion into a new soil. They offered no pattern for the future, however, and unless some other provision was made for continuance, causes founded on individual initiative tended to die with their founders.

In any case such ready-made connections were exceptional. Typically, a minister had to be found somewhere, and in denominations where the call system applied the search process could be cumbersome. First, a local group had to be assembled and persuaded to make a financial commitment; next, contacts had to be made in the United States or Britain that would discover a suitable candidate; finally, all parties had to be brought to agreement. The Lutheran experience in Upper Canada illustrated both the possibilities and the difficulties of this procedure. Lutherans demonstrated their determination to preserve their faith by instituting services and erecting church buildings without waiting until ministers became available. They were fortunate enough to receive a sympathetic hearing from the New York Ministerium, which adopted Upper Canada as a special mission field and provided several ministers. In 1790 the Lutherans of Williamsburg in Dundas called Samuel Schwerdfeger, who had been imprisoned during the war for his loyalist views. Other early congregations had pastors by the end of the century, but keeping them was another matter. Mainly because of a lack of money, but perhaps also because in Germany the clergy had been paid by the state, Lutherans failed to pay their pastors a living wage. In desperation, two ministers took orders in the Church of England, and the supply of replacements gradually dried up. Among these early congregations only Williamsburg would retain its Lutheran affiliation; several others eventually defected to the Methodists.[6]

Presbyterians were, on the whole, slower than Lutherans to organize congregations and procure ministers. As in the case of Bethune's Glengarry, they fared best when a significant number of people from a single ethnic background settled together. In 1795 the German Reformed people of Dundas were able to secure the services of John Ludwig Broeffle, who, despite what James Croil described as 'the extreme niggardliness of their contributions to his support,' served them faithfully until his death in 1815. Peter Van Alstyne, the leader of the loyalists from New York City who had settled on the Bay of Quinte, is said to have been instrumental in persuading the Dutch Reformed Classis of Albany to send a young man named Robert McDowall on a mission to his area in 1790. After college training and ordination, McDowall returned in 1798 and within two years succeeded in organizing a regular congregation. The other important centre of Presbyterian activity was the Niagara Peninsula, where a handful of Scots leavened a largely American population. The first minister to arrive in this general area was Jabez Collver, who in response to Simcoe's invitation to American settlers took up a land grant in Norfolk County and removed there in 1794 at the age of sixty-four with eight of his thirteen children. Once on the scene, he organized a preaching circuit of neighbouring communities. In the same year the Presbyterians of Stamford were sufficiently well organized to call the first of a succession of ministers of Scottish background, and in 1808 Lewis Williams from Wales arrived at St Catharines to serve a mixed congregation of Presbyterians and Episcopalians. The best-remembered pioneer of the Niagara region, however, was Daniel W. Eastman from western New York, who from 1801 almost until his death in 1865 itinerated through the back country. Despite the presence of ministers from Scotland and Wales, the Presbyterianism of the region had more in common with the Congregationalism of New England than with the more traditional strains represented by Bethune and McDowall. Eastman was ordained by a Congregational association shortly after his arrival in the province, while Collver had worked for some time as an organizer of Congregational churches for the Connecticut Missionary Society. The only church bearing the Congregational name in Upper Canada before 1812, however, was erected in 1804 at Martintown, in Glengarry County, by Scottish settlers who had been affected by revivals in the homeland led by the brothers Robert and James Haldane.[7]

Measured against the likelihood that heirs of the Congregational-Presbyterian-Reformed tradition constituted the largest body of Christians in the province, the presence of six ministers by 1806 did not represent an impressive achievement. McDowall, whose energetic itinerating had convinced him that the field was ripe for harvesting, appealed in that year to the synod of the Dutch Reformed Church for assistance. The outlook seemed promising, for the synod had an expanding supply of ministers. It had already sent a number of missionaries on exploratory sallies, and would continue to do so in succeeding years. McDowall co-operated by organizing congregations, of which at one time he was able to report fourteen. By 1806 one of these, at Brockville, had already made two unsuccessful attempts to secure a minister from Scotland or the United States. It was eventually rewarded in 1811 when the London Missionary Society sent out William Smart, even though the society was primarily interested in foreign missions and had intended its appointees to Upper Canada to evangelize Indians. Apart from McDowall, however, no Dutch Reformed minister settled in the province.[8] Ethnic prejudice may have been a factor, but the lack of credible assurances of financial support was probably at this stage a greater one. The failure of this energetic promotion, even more than the apathy evident in some quarters, demonstrated the difficulties of using the call system in a pioneer province.

The breakdown of familiar social patterns has sometimes inspired the rise of indigenous movements of religious renewal, usually stimulated by the emergence of a charismatic leader. A notable example occurred in the maritime provinces, where the conversion of Henry Alline in 1775 and his subsequent conviction that God had called him to preach despite his lack of education and ordination radically altered the religious complexion of the region. Two movements of this kind affected Upper Canada in its early years. Rather remarkably, both reflected at least indirectly the influence of the Quakers, whose role as pioneer missionaries of the frontier has generally been underestimated. One of them, the Good Message of Ganiodaio, has been discussed in chapter 1. Although it fitted within a specifically Indian tradition of revitalization movements, the circumstances under which it arose were not altogether unlike those of white settlers coping with the disappearance or disarray of familiar institutions. The other movement of this type issued from a schism among the sober Friends of Yonge Street.

David Willson, who had been brought up a Presbyterian, joined the Quaker society at Newmarket shortly after his arrival there in 1800. Coming from a section of New York State that would give rise to such unconventional religious systems as the Mormonism of Joseph Smith and the marital communism of John Humphrey Noyes, he took well to the society's denial of evangelical orthodoxy. Its subdued approach to worship was less to his taste, which ran to music, ceremony, and festival. In 1812 he broke away (or according to Quaker records was disowned) and persuaded a number of other society members to join him in forming the Children of Peace. Sharon Temple near Newmarket, constructed in the late 1820s for the celebration of festive occasions, still stands as a tourist attraction and as his monument. Despite some oddities, Willson was a man of wide-ranging vision who sought to combine the best elements of Judaism and Christianity in an all-embracing world-view with political as well as religious implications. To farmers in York County he offered the prospect of purposeful and disciplined, though not strictly communal, living, spiced with colourful ritual and larded with denunciations of the rich, the powerful, and the well educated.[9] His movement flourished while he lived, and the appeal of his teachings was attested by frequent invitations to speak in neighbouring communities. The movement never attained more than local importance, however, and no successful imitators appeared. Not in this way would Upper Canada secure the leaders to whom it would respond.

The limitations of the efforts from within the province made it clear that external initiative was necessary. Best placed to take that initiative effectively, to all appearance, was the Society for the Propagation of the Gospel, a voluntary Anglican agency that had been founded in 1701 to meet the needs of colonists and Indians in America and was able after the revolution to turn its attention to what remained of British North America. In pre-revolutionary days the society's missionaries had worked vigorously in the colonies, achieving enough success to worry Puritans who equated bishops with tyrannical government. Money was not lacking, for until 1815 clergy of the Church of England were paid by the Crown. By 1812, however, only six of the society's missionaries were at work in the province. All of them served parishes that had already been occupied in 1801, despite a rapid increase in population during the intervening decade.

The basic difficulty was the unwillingness of Anglican priests to serve in Upper Canada. In 1785 the society invited its missionaries who had been displaced by American independence to transfer to British North America, and the Maritimes thereby gained a fair supply of clergy. None chose Upper Canada except John Stuart, who had already followed his earlier parishioners there by a familiar wartime route. Of the missionaries who remained for significant periods only two, John Langhorn at Bath from 1787 and Robert Addison at Niagara from 1792, were recruited in Britain. George Okill Stuart followed his father John into the ministry, became rector of York in 1800, and succeeded his father at Kingston in 1812. John Strachan, a Scot of mixed Presbyterian-Episcopal parentage, arrived in Kingston in 1799. His immediate employment was as tutor to the children of two prominent families there; his ultimate ambition was to teach at an academy or college whose future establishment was vaguely hinted at. After applying for a Presbyterian congregation that did not fall vacant as expected, he settled the future direction of his life by accepting the rectorship of Cornwall in 1803. Richard Pollard, ordained for Sandwich in 1802, had been the local sheriff before his ordination and retained his offices as judge and magistrate until his death in 1824. Young British clerics evidently viewed emigration to Upper Canada not as an opportunity for advancement but as exile to a cold and backward region lacking even the strategic importance that might have appealed to patriotic sentiments. The secretaries of the society seem to have had little more conception of the needs of the province; they envisaged compact parishes served by cultured gentlemen of a type that was least likely to be attracted to the province. They also insisted that the clerics be British subjects, for understandable reasons but sometimes with inhibiting results.[10]

Given the scarcity of candidates, the society was probably as fortunate as could be expected in the quality of its missionaries. Most of them performed their duties conscientiously, some imaginatively. All of them ranged the neighbouring countryside in disregard of the society's instructions, and John Stuart may not have been exceptional in resolving to pay annual visits to all the townships east of Kingston. The two Stuarts were pastors of tact and understanding, perhaps somewhat lacking in initiative but popular even outside their own flocks. Some of Strachan's opinions would later be anathema to many Upper Canadians, but his ability, his vision, and his dedication to the task of building up his church were never in question. Under the circumstances, however, there could be no thought of stringent quality control. Langhorn was not only an advanced eccentric, but such a bigot that he offered to marry a couple who had been joined to other partners by the local Lutheran pastor, and such a stickler for form that he refused to recognize G.O. Stuart as a Church of England clergyman upon learning that he had omitted to wear a surplice at the burial of a soldier. Pollard was a rough diamond who doubtless satisfied his own constituency, but he was no advertisement to outsiders. He shocked John Stuart with his profanity even after ordination; but he resolved to do better and returned home, as Marion MacRae has suggested, 'determining to make his charges the finest damn parishes in all Upper Canada.'[11] John Bryan's lack of ordination went undetected for six years; Thomas Raddish used his brief ministry at York in 1796–7 mainly to gain possession of the parish's glebe lands.

The provision of Roman Catholic priests was the responsibility of the bishop of Quebec, which effectively meant Jean-François Hubert until 1797 and Joseph-Octave Plessis thereafter. In terms of population, Upper Canada constituted a small corner within a vast diocese that was already critically short of priests. Differences of language and culture, too, created difficulties for the Quebec bishops in communicating with colleagues who might have been able to spare English-speaking priests. In 1794 Edmund Burke, a dynamic Irish priest who felt that his talents were not being fully employed at the Quebec seminary, was able, through the support of the British governor, Lord Dorchester, to badger Hubert into appointing him vicar-general for Upper Canada. He frittered away the first three years in Michigan, where as a loyal British subject he sought to counteract the influence of a Dominican who was acting as a French agent. Then he turned to his main task, officiating where he could while making his headquarters at Newark (now Niagara-on-the Lake). Unfortunately, he was never able to achieve rapport with the ecclesiastical authorities at Quebec. They regarded him as an ambitious adventurer of a type only too familiar to them, and he complained of their lack of interest in Upper Canada. They might well have recognized his genuine zeal, while he had cause to be grateful that the Sulpicians assured continuity of care on the Detroit frontier and that the Scots of Glengarry had brought their own priests with them. The chief remaining problem was that of providing services to the scattered Irish who were beginning to arrive, and for that task he was unable to procure any clerical helpers prior to his hasty departure in 1801. During these years Roman Catholics suffered disappointment in another quarter. In 1793–4, and again in 1798, ambitious plans were laid for the settlement of a large number of French émigrés in Upper Canada. The first scheme called for the removal to Canada of thousands of French priests; the second failed to make provision for any. A historical plaque at Oak Ridges recalls the arrival of a greatly reduced number of well-born French colonists in 1798, but they provided Burke with no reinforcements.[12]

Alexander Macdonell, who became vicar-general in 1807, vividly described journeys even more arduous than Burke's:

For several years we had to travel over the whole Province from Lake Superior to the Province line of Lower Canada in the discharge of our pastoral duties carrying the Sacred Vestments, sometimes on horseback, sometimes on our own back & sometimes in small Indian birch canoes crossing the great Lakes and descending the rapids of the Ottawa, & St. Lawrence in those Miserable crafts living with the Savages and sleeping in the woods; nor were our fatigues and miseries more supportable in visiting the Miserable habitations of poor Irish emigrants whom Religious persecution, and oppression of their Landlords had driven from their Native Country & compelled to seek an asylum in the interminable forests of Upper Canada.[13]

Macdonell was able by such exertions to maintain many Catholics in the faith, but in 1812 the complement of priests remained much as it had been on his arrival.

The Baptists, despite their firm insistence on local autonomy, were more systematic than most in their cultivation of the field. The Shaftesbury Association of Vermont, which since its inception in 1780 had consciously identified itself as a missionary agency, was the virtual founder of the Baptist denomination in the province. In 1802 Caleb Blood, then its president, made an exploratory tour through western New York and into

Upper Canada as far as the Long Point area. He received a $30 advance for expenses, spent $22.34, and returned the rest to his association. He also took back a request for help that led to a series of official visits during the first decade of the century. The Baptists' main task, that of organizing churches, was complicated by the necessity of leaving to each congregation the ultimate responsibility for securing its minister. Since those chosen were usually local members with other means of livelihood, however, congregations did not need to be large or affluent in order to maintain themselves in accordance with Baptist principles. Despite the part-time nature of their service, such ministers as Peter Fairchild of Townsend and Titus Finch of Charlottesville combed the surrounding townships for converts. Official visits from the United States touched a limited portion of the province and were only briefly resumed after the War of 1812. Meanwhile, however, strong Baptist churches were permanently established in several counties north of Lake Erie.[14]

Of all the denominations, the Methodists were most successful in founding churches and providing them with ministerial leadership. So effective was their penetration, indeed, that this period more than any other may justly be regarded as one of Methodist ascendancy. In 1788 the veteran Methodist itinerant Freeborn Garrettson and twelve young assistants were assigned the task of planting Methodism in the upper Hudson Valley, where it had made little impression. Their work was fruitful, and resulted in the formation of nine new circuits by 1790. In his corner around Lake Champlain, however, William Losee found the response far from promising. Having relatives in Dundas County, and aware of his eligibility for a loyalist land grant, he took leave to visit Upper Canada. Enough Methodists were on hand to send him back with a petition for a preacher, and in 1791 he returned with a commission to organize a circuit. Within a month he was able to regularize the unofficial loyalist class in Augusta and to form two new ones on the Bay of Quinte. After that, each succeeding year seemed to bring a greater number of American itinerants across the border for annual or biennial stints. From the old loyalist area the preachers gradually pressed westward until Nathan Bangs reached the Detroit River in 1804. By 1812 the Methodists had the largest ministerial complement of any denomination in the province and by all odds the most widely distributed. Inevitably, their progress was sometimes slower in communities already served by other churches, but by 1801 they were holding services in York and by 1810 or 1811 had erected a church at Kingston. In many rural communities, especially ones settled by Americans, they were without rivals.[15]

This rapidity of advance was made possible in part by the efficiency and adaptability of the Methodist organization. Wesley had gradually worked out new methods because the urgency of the mission to which he felt himself called demanded greater flexibility than the rigid English parish structure allowed. Basic was the principle of itinerancy, whereby lay preachers were sent out to fulfil a round of engagements within a particular area or 'circuit.' In order that their message should remain fresh and vital, their assignments were made on an annual basis with the possibility in early days of no more than one renewal. Since the Methodist movement was at first essentially an extension of Wesley's own mission, he himself made the appointments. Procedures of consultation would later be devised, but direction from the centre continued to be an essential feature of Methodist polity. By the time of the Upper Canadian mission a very important development had occurred. Whereas Wesley's arrangements had had in mind lay preaching to voluntary societies, the itinerants of Upper Canada were ministers or 'elders' of the American Methodist Episcopal Church, ordained after a period of probation, who not only preached but administered the sacraments and provided a measure of pastoral care. The principle of flexibility in deployment remained unimpaired.

While they were often homespun, the early Methodist preachers were by no means 'self-appointed,' as some detractors suggested. Typically, the superintending minister in each locality was on the lookout for likely prospects. When he spotted a pious young man of promising talents, he might ask him to deliver an exhortation or appeal for decision at the conclusion of the Sunday preaching service. After his formal recognition as an exhorter, further steps would be a sermon at a small appointment, placement on the regular list of local preachers on the circuit, and finally a recommendation to the presiding elder or superintendent of the district. Reception into and continuance in the travelling ministry, which to the Methodists was ministry *par excellence*, was determined by the whole body of itinerants meeting in a regional conference. Assignments to particular posts were made by a bishop, who in those days read off before breakfast on the final day of the conference a list of appointments that were effective immediately.[16] Preachers without families to move found it prudent to set off for the conference with all of their worldly goods packed in their saddle-bags, for they might well leave it in an altogether different direction. Even then they could not be certain of their eventual postings, for the presiding elder of each district could alter appointments throughout the year as circumstances warranted.

A Methodist 'circuit' was a sequence of appointments that a preacher or pair of preachers was expected to cover in two weeks or a month by utilizing both Sundays and weekdays. Created not by voluntary local organization but by the bishop's fiat, it was subject in times of rapid expansion to constant division or rearrangement. Within it the superintending minister exercised authority as absolute as that of the bishop in his sphere. He determined the times and places of preaching and could make or terminate all appointments to local offices. He could not forget, however, that he and his fellow preachers were totally dependent on the people for support. Conference merely recommended a stipend, which at first was $80 annually for a single preacher, and $110 for a married man.[17] In practice, therefore, the superintendent had to take account of the opinions of resident superannuated ministers, local preachers, licensed exhorters, and class leaders who met groups of members weekly for counsel and spiritual growth, as well as of regular meetings of the circuit, its constituent societies, and leaders and stewards. Episcopal Methodism thus combined elements of autocracy and populist democracy.

The system demanded an amount of travel that would seem strenuous even in the automobile age. John Stuart took satisfaction in visiting all the townships in the lower end of the province annually, but some itinerants were expected to cover county-sized areas fortnightly. During the War of 1812, when American preachers were forced to withdraw, a single circuit extended from Lake Simcoe to Long Point on Lake Erie. Jacob Mountain, the Anglican bishop of Quebec, made eight visitations of his diocese in his episcopate of thirty-two years.[18] This was a creditable record for someone of his background and circumstances, but a Methodist presiding elder of this era was expected as a matter of course to attend meetings of every circuit in the province four times a year. This mobility made possible a degree of access to the people unapproached by other denominations.

Methodist preachers had some other advantages in the pioneer situation of Upper Canada. Mainly recruited from areas where living conditions were similar, they knew how to travel light and make do with primitive accommodation. They were familiar with the mentality of most of the settlers. They found active cells of their faith already in existence and were able to capitalize on the preparatory work of a Methodist loyalist, Major George Neal, who had been preaching in the Niagara area since 1786. Politics was another significant factor. Whereas American Baptists, Presbyterians, and Congregationalists were for the most part avid and outspoken republicans, Methodism discouraged its preachers from engaging in political controversy and retained close enough ties with Britain to attract ministerial candidates who could be reasonably at home in monarchical surroundings. Although the Methodist concentration on personal religion did not forestall charges of republicanism in some quarters, it minimized the offence of an American connection to loyalist sensitivities.

The Methodists were also fortunate in the timing of their entry into the province. In 1790, when Losee made his first exploratory trip, the only clerical representatives of the Protestant mainstream in the province were Bethune of the Presbyterians and John Stuart and Langhorn of the Church of England. In later years western New York, long known as the 'Burned-Over District' on account of successive fires of revival that swept over it, became a base from which religious propagandists of many kinds pressed into Upper Canada. When Losee entered the province, this region was still largely unsettled. Before the revolution it had been Iroquois territory, and for several years thereafter it was effectively closed by a territorial dispute between New York and Massachusetts. By the time it had become mature enough to export preachers, the Methodists were firmly in possession of many Upper Canadian communities. Finding the territory thus pre-empted, and generally preferring republican institutions, most of these evangelists remained in New York or sought out the Ohio or Illinois country. The priority in time thus secured by the Methodists may have precluded not only equal competition from other American churches but the emergence of a large-scale indigenous religious movement.

Despite their spectacular growth, the Methodists offered only one among a number or religious options available to early Upper Canadians. A careful though probably incomplete count indicates that, in addition to an undetermined number of authorized (though unpaid) Quaker ministers, the ordained clergy of all denominations numbered eight (plus one impostor) in 1790, twenty-five in 1800, and forty-four in 1812. Of these last, twelve were Methodist, nine Presbyterian or Reformed, six Church of England, six Baptist, five Roman Catholic, five Mennonite, and one Lutheran. The ratio of clergy was a little better than one to every two thousand inhabitants, less than adequate in view of the current state of communications but far from the state of spiritual destitution that has sometimes been portrayed. Occasional hints suggest, moreover, that a fair number of unrecorded evangelists may have found their way into the bush. In 1788 the ever-vigilant Langhorn reported the presence in his parish of both 'new lights' and 'enemies of the Christian Sabbath,' while in 1806 McDowall wrote: 'The Baptists frequently send missionaries through this country, and missionaries from Connecticut have lately visited these places.'[19]

The clergy were unevenly distributed through the province, however, in a manner that indicates patterns of settlement but suggests a significant time-lag in reaching new, small, and scattered communities. In 1791 Ernestown in Lennox and Addington County was the headquarters of Langhorn of the Church of England, and Carroll reported the presence there of a Lutheran minister whose name he rendered rather improbably as 'Scammerhorn.' A Methodist exhorter named Lyons had been preaching unofficially in the area since 1788, and so had James McCarty, an Irish Whitefieldian and probable instigator of the 'new lights' mentioned by

Langhorn, until his mysterious disappearance in 1790.[20] By 1791 Losee
was stationed at Kingston and was concentrating his efforts on the
surrounding countryside, not least Ernestown. Robert McDowall had paid
his first visit as a catechist in the previous year, and there were several
well-established Quaker meetings in the vicinity. Between Ernestown and
the border of Lower Canada six clergymen were at work. To the west there
was only François-Xavier Dufaux, a Roman Catholic priest who had been
stationed at Sandwich since 1785. Although both the Niagara and Detroit
frontiers had been scenes of modest loyalist settlement, the former was
without a resident missionary until 1792, and the latter received its first
Protestant minister only in 1802. By 1812 the balance was greatly
equalized, but some even of the indefatigable Methodists served circuits so
large that a fair number of people knew of them only by rumour.

Of the forty-four clergy identified as serving in Upper Canada in 1812,
nineteen had been recruited in the province. Five were either natives of
Lower Canada or had spent time there before moving to the upper
province. Three had come from England, four from Scotland, and one
from Wales. One, already in the province when he was received into the
ministry, had been born in Ireland. Among those whose provenance can be
determined, the remaining eleven were living in the United States when
they were engaged for work in Upper Canada. Twenty-two occupied their
posts as the result of initiative taken by a higher church authority or
missionary society, sixteen by congregational call or consensus. Five had
entered the province on their own, though in most cases their ministry had
been validated by formal appointment. One was in process of moving from
the Lutheran to the Anglican ministry. Since some of the categories
overlap, these figures are only approximate. In interpreting them one
should also bear in mind that nine of those reported as being already in the
province and called by congregations were Mennonites or Baptists, who in
the nature of the case were most unlikely to have been secured otherwise.
The great majority of these were of American origin, and some of them had
held similar posts in the United States before their arrival in the province.
By 1812 a majority even of Methodist itinerants had been recruited locally,
although most were of American birth or parentage. American background
and local experience thus stand out as conspicuous features of the religious
leadership of Upper Canada at the end of its first period of growth.

Assessing the quality of these missionaries is not easy, for contemporary
judgments were strongly coloured by denominational preference and
theological conviction. That most of them were sincere and conscientious
is beyond question, and many performed labours beyond the line of duty
for which they have not always received due credit. It is clear, however,
that congregations usually had to accept whatever ministers were available

and that the available ministers tended to be ones who lacked the qualifications or gifts to secure pastorates elsewhere. Even with respect to the Methodist itinerants, who were well above the average in piety and zeal and not so far below it in educational qualifications as has often been assumed, there are some indications that conferences found Canada a convenient dumping-ground for weaker preachers. Despite the occasional oddity, alcoholism, and forged papers, however, the wonder is that the province fared as well as it did.

From these data it is possible to draw some very broad conclusions about the manner in which the religious needs of the early population of Upper Canada were met. The process was greatly eased by homogeneity of settlement, especially when close contact was maintained with the sending area. Mennonites and Quakers, and to a considerable extent Scottish Highlanders, both Presbyterian and Roman Catholic, were closest to this happy situation. In the great majority of cases, where it was necessary to introduce a clergyman from without to a congregation without prior knowledge of him, a combination of external and internal effort seems to have been necessary. Congregations that were unable to gain the ear of supportive agencies outside the province either failed to secure pastors or had to make do with a haphazard and often unsatisfactory process of selection. The Presbyterians of Brockville, for example, made two unsuccessful attempts to call a minister, and Stamford had a record of short and sometimes disastrous pastorates. On its side, the supporting agency was helpless unless it could muster a measure of local support. In 1795 Bishop Hubert complained that the Roman Catholics of Kingston were clamouring for a priest but taking no measures to receive one.[21] The inability of the Dutch Reformed church to place ministers in the congregations organized by McDowall was certainly due to no lack of effort on its part, and the failure of Lutheran congregations to retain the ministers they had been sent spoke eloquently of the need for local support to complement interest from without.

By one means or another Upper Canada received by 1812 a supply of religious leaders that was not woefully incommensurate with its needs; but only the Methodists – and, on a smaller scale and for the time being, the Baptists – had come close to solving the problem of providing services to a scattered and heterogeneous population. They were able to do so because they combined vigorous external initiative with a method of creating effective local organization where none already existed. Churches of longer standing and set ways – the Church of England, the Presbyterians, and the Lutherans – were able neither to furnish adequate sustenance from without nor to mobilize local resources. Externally, the chief problem was a shortage of missionary zeal and of experience in efficient missionary organization. Protestants were still in the early stages of a missionary awakening that had begun with concern for the 'perishing heathen' rather than for neglected colonists. Among Roman Catholics the aggressive missionary spirit of the Counter-Reformation had been eroded by the eighteenth-century Enlightenment and crippled by the French Revolution and succeeding ripples of rebellion throughout Catholic Europe. Internally, the habit of reliance on outside help for clerical services was deeply ingrained not only among adherents of the old state churches of Europe but, to a lesser extent, among Congregationalists accustomed to the standing order of New England. Interestingly, Upper Canadians showed much more readiness to erect churches, even in the absence of any immediate prospect of ministerial supply, than to pay the clergy who would officiate in them. Wood was plentiful and money scarce, but there seems also to have been a feeling that buildings were communal assets that encouraged settlers and thus raised the price of land, while parsons promised no comparable tangible benefit.[22] This inability to match external initiative with local organization may not have had catastrophic results in relation to the needs of a small population, but it clearly needed to be overcome if an approaching wave of new immigrants was not to be left largely unchurched.

4 Varieties of Pioneer Religion

Providing leadership was only the first step toward eliciting religious commitment. John Stuart, on his appointment to Kingston, reported to the SPG that he was obliged to teach his parishioners 'the first principles of religion and morality' before pressing them to become members of his church. Strachan at York in 1812 came to the same conclusion: 'The majority had little or no sense of religion, the congregation must be made by the zeal and abilities of the clergyman.' Nor was the people's desire for such instruction by any means universal. William Case, carrying Methodism to the western section of the province in 1809, noted in his journal 'some outcast settlements, where they seldom hear preaching of any kind, & but few wish to.' William Bell, fresh out of Scotland a few years later, was shocked to find that 'so feebly were the restraints of the Law of God felt that many, when rebuked for swearing or Sabbath breaking, would boldly ask what harm was there in it.'[1]

To announce preaching was usually to draw a crowd, but for positive results it was necessary not only to attract but to convince. Besides the indifferent there were at first many in the province who declined to commit themselves to any particular denomination. Becoming a church member was regarded as a much more serious step then than it usually is now, and many people of sincere Christian conviction were held back by a sense of unworthiness. Others were troubled by sectarian competition or were simply disinclined to rule out any options. The diary of Ely Playter of York reveals a man who combined attachment to the pleasures of the day with desultory attendance at the services of various Protestant denominations until conversion to Methodism introduced the formula 'To meeting as usual.' Jesse Ketchum of the same town, who held a pew at Saint James's Church of England and taught in the Methodist Sunday school, extended his philanthropy to all evangelical denominations and donated portions of the block now occupied by Simpson's department store as sites for churches.[2] It is difficult to determine where his own denominational preference lay until a daughter's marriage to York's first Presbyterian minister turned his loyalty in that direction.

In this fluid situation, competition was limited only by the scarcity of preachers. Sometimes denominational positions were put to the test of formal public debate. One of the most celebrated of these intellectual duels, on the respective merits of Calvinism and Arminianism, pitted McDowall against the Methodist presiding elder Samuel Coate at well-churched Bath on 26 October 1804. The Methodists claimed victory when McDowall and his partisans departed after hearing only two hours' worth of Coate's argument. Langhorn, whose high churchmanship inclined him to Arminianism, commented more impartially: 'Both sides claimed the victory. The Methodists had a good cause, and did not defend it well. The Presbyterian preacher had a bad cause to uphold, and he maintained it as well as could be expected; but on the whole he did himself no good.'[3] Challenges to public debate would remain popular through much of the century. In 1819, for example, the Methodist itinerant Alvin Torry engaged in a series of skirmishes in the London area with representatives of Quakerism, one of whom was a woman.[4] Decisions were affected more frequently by inherited affiliations, by the persuasiveness of preachers, and not least by relative satisfaction or dissatisfaction with the state of society.

Although theological considerations were undoubtedly important to many Upper Canadians, their responses to religious stimuli often depended to an even greater extent on varying analyses of the problem of placing the province on a secure spiritual footing. To some the problem was essentially one of transplanting a traditional religious culture into a new setting, or at most of reconstituting it out of familiar elements. Others saw it, in more fundamental terms, as calling for a radical conversion that would establish provincial society on a new basis. How individual Upper Canadians analysed the situation was affected by both external and internal factors.

When Upper Canada was receiving its first white settlers, English-speaking countries were in the throes of a remarkable cultural transition. In the wake of the strife stirred by Puritanism in the seventeenth century, the British had sought tranquillity by renouncing fanaticism of all kinds, which they dismissed collectively as 'enthusiasm.' Socially the eighteenth century was the age of Sir Roger de Coverley, when squires both exploited and patronized their tenants. Politically it was dominated by the log-rolling of Sir Robert Walpole; ideologically it inspired Edmund Burke (the British political theorist, not the Roman Catholic vicar-general) to ascribe the superiority of the British constitution to the neat balance of forces that characterized it. The ideal life of the period, as modelled by the upper classes, was one of leisure and gentility though not of high culture. The onset of the industrial revolution, with its requirement of rapid capital formation, brought a new demand for application to business along with a social mobility that held out the promise of wealth to some, the threat of dislocation to others, and the possibility of failure to all. The ultimate result, generally known as Victorianism but in the making long before Victoria's accession to the throne, was an unaccustomed tautness and seriousness of purpose. The importance of being earnest was gradually superseding the necessity of being well bred.[5]

Significant religious changes accompanied these social developments, sometimes reflecting and sometimes furthering them. The dominant strain of eighteenth-century religion, represented by moderates in the Church of Scotland and the alliance of squire and parson in the Church of England, stressed the integration of religion into the social fabric. Relying on a perceived harmony of orthodox doctrine with the science and philosophy of the age, religious teachers devoted themselves to the inculcation of morality, loyalty, and acquiescence in the status quo. Already by the second quarter of the century, however, a number of evangelical movements were insisting on the necessity of a decisive reorientation of personal attitudes and on a heroic rather than a merely prudential morality. Each with their own particular emphases – Wesleyan Methodists, Scottish Seceders, evangelicals in the established Churches of England and Ireland, and the products of fervent Welsh revival – were calling for a religious earnestness that would complement and sometimes challenge the secular earnestness of manufacturers and upwardly mobile artisans and tradesmen.

Developments in America paralleled those in Britain, though with some unique manifestations. In America as in Britain commercial prosperity led to a cooling of zeal, and in New England to the virtual identification of religious and civic concerns. The task of occupying and organizing a continent, however, was one that demanded sobriety and concentration of effort, and especially after the attainment of independence nation-building and church extension tended to proceed together. From early days there developed a pattern, peculiar at first to America, of relying for evangelistic outreach largely on intense local campaigns, known as 'revivals,' in which individuals were pressed to make decisions for Christ. Revivalism was never primarily a phenomenon of the frontier; it drew its inspiration and financial support mainly from New York and other metropolitan centres. Its most florid expressions, however, appeared in marginal areas where institutions were least secure and the need for social integration was most urgent. Upper Canada before 1812 was distinctly marginal. Associated with revivalism, though to be distinguished from it, were revivals of religious interest that swept through large portions of the country. The first

'Great Awakening' was associated principally with missions conducted by George Whitefield in the middle of the eighteenth century. The second is usually dated from 1801, when simultaneous revivals broke out on the eastern seaboard and on the Kentucky frontier, although there is some justification for accepting Donald G. Mathews's suggestion that the expansive thrust of Methodism in the 1780s might be a more realistic starting-point.[6] It was already affecting the province before 1812. .

In Upper Canada there were those, mostly in positions of power or prestige, who saw in the transfer of British institutions to the province the only means of preventing it from breaking its ties with the motherland as other American colonies had done. Their ideal was a society of checks and balances to which royal absolutism and mob rule would be equally foreign but in which the prerogatives of respectable birth would be acknowledged. Many others, less securely placed, saw in this vision merely a self-serving attempt to retain a monopoly of influence. Few of them would have ventured to endorse democracy, which had shown its colours in the United States and France, but they believed strongly in equality of opportunity for advancement. As was only to be expected, there was considerable correlation between expectations of society and attitudes to religion. Those who favoured an aristocratic view of society leaned to a traditional, middle-of-the-road form of religion. Those to whom local aristocrats were merely oligarchs were more likely to prefer a clear-cut evangelicalism. One can trace other correlations, such as urban/British-born/traditional and rural/American-born/evangelical, which, though they have some validity, admit so many exceptions that they should be treated with extreme caution.

The distinction between evangelical and what the Scots aptly termed 'moderate' Christianity, which was never in any case absolute, did not neatly follow denominational lines. Presbyterians ran the gamut from the traditional Kirkman John Bethune through the Seceder William Smart, who eschewed revivalist techniques but is reputed to have organized the province's first Sunday school, to the fiery 'Calvinistic Methodist' Lewis Williams. Within the Church of England John Stuart maintained his popularity by catering to the expectations of evangelically minded parishioners. Although in a community of largely American population he did not scruple to own two black slaves, he put aside a flute when he was reprimanded for giving an impression of levity. When visiting the townships above Kingston he used extempore prayers and preached without notes; he reported that on this account he was well received.[7] Mennonites and Quakers belonged unequivocally to neither category, with the result that they would both subsequently suffer schism. In the Upper Canadian situation, however, the most obvious contrast was between the moderatism that generally characterized the Church of England and the evangelicalism of churches of American provenance.

The SPG missionary ideal was redolent of the eighteenth century in both its strengths and its weaknesses. The society expected a good deal of a missionary, and sought to reassure itself on 'His Prudence,' 'His Learning,' 'His Sober and Pious Conversation,' and 'His Zeal for the Christian Religion, and Diligence in His Holy Calling,' along with, inevitably, 'His Affection to the present Government' and 'His Conformity to the Doctrines and Discipline of the Church of England.' Once appointed, he was expected to take care in admitting adults to baptism and communion, to catechize and set up schools, to visit his parishioners regularly, and to seek to 'convince and reclaim' dissenters with a 'Spirit of Meakness and Gentleness.' Missionaries were also advised 'that the chief Subjects of their Sermons be the great Fundamental Principles of Christianity, and the Duties of a sober, righteous, and godly Life, as resulting from these Principles.' Interestingly, the society found it necessary to warn them against frequenting public houses and participating in gaming and 'all vain pastimes.'[8]

Stuart's rational religion, equidistant from enthusiasm and superstition, fitted the prescription neatly. Services in his parish church of Saint George in Kingston also illustrated, if under less than ideal conditions, many of the usual features of eighteenth-century worship. Bishop Jacob Mountain described the church itself as 'a long, low, blue, wooden building, with square windows and a little cupola or steeple, for the bell, like the thing on a brewery placed at the wrong end of the building.' Vestments and ornaments were notable for their scarcity. Hymnody would have been limited to the metrical psalter of Tate and Brady, along with a few supplementary hymns for festivals then bound with the Book of Common Prayer. A barrel organ provided a limited repertoire of tunes, and the parish clerk alone read the responses. Holy Communion took place only four times a year and attracted a handful of communicants. Lacking both the emotional impact of impromptu utterance and the appeal to the senses of colourful ritual, services conveyed a sense of moderation, stability, and predictability.

The rather perfunctory quality of early Anglican worship services implied no lack of dedication on the part of missionaries. Strachan visited the patients of the hospital at York at least twice a week, conversing with each one and then delivering a brief exhortation based on the church catechism. He catechized the children once a month, and reported that he was careful to make his sermons plain enough to be understood by all. Langhorn visited his extensive parish regularly on foot, catechized children at every service, and rigorously excluded 'evil livers' from communion.[9] While Langhorn was exceptional in his severity, Strachan also seems to have been more concerned to warn against unworthy reception of the elements than to encourage the dubious. Clearly, belonging to the Church of England was much more than a formality, and any latitude allowed to worldly amusements sprang not from a willingness to compromise with evil but from a conviction that a golden mean was the best rule of life.

This offshoot of Old World religion appealed to various segments of the population. To those raised as Episcopalians it had the attraction of familiarity, and to the few with memories of England that of nostalgia. In communities where troops were quartered, the parish church was the obvious choice for military parades that provided a colour otherwise lacking in services. At the centre of government it was a place for officials and social leaders to see and be seen; even a number of prominent Roman Catholics and dissenters found it strategic to rent pews at Saint James's. Those without other church connections found it natural to turn to the Church of England for such services as christenings, churchings, and funerals. At Kingston and York, where even many who disagreed with its doctrines and resented the claims of its clergy looked to it to provide a focus for community life, its Sunday services resembled general musters of the respectable portion of the population. Most of all, however, the rational religion of the Church of England appealed to genteel Upper Canadians for whom the social graces, cultural amenities, and religious traditions of the Old World constituted an inseparable unity.

Methodists, American Presbyterians, and Baptists were mainly instrumental in carrying the thrust of evangelical Christianity into Upper Canada. While they differed significantly and often vociferously in theology and polity, these denominations agreed on the necessity of a conscious personal conversion as the gateway to salvation. Presbyterians of the revivalist tradition, often Congregationalists in disguise, were the least insistent on denominational principles. Firsthand accounts of pre-war Presbyterian preaching in Upper Canada are not available, but a description of a protracted meeting in 1833 by William Proudfoot of the Scottish Secession suggests that Eastman at least was from that mould. Proudfoot was greatly impressed by Eastman's record of sacrificial and successful service in Canada, and in many ways by Eastman himself, whom he described as 'possessed of a splendid voice, some imagination, particularly in the use of descriptive words, great elasticity of body, and a zeal for souls that makes him sing at the top of his voice.' He was less impressed by his preaching, of which he wrote in his journal: 'Grammar, taste, logic, were all set by while he was making a push, firing (as he said) red hot balls at the conscience.' With his Scottish dedication to careful discipline and church order, Proudfoot was especially disturbed that those who had been awakened during the revival were immediately admitted to the Lord's table after only a cursory examination.[10]

Baptists, though no less fervent than Presbyterians in preaching to the unconverted, were more intent on propagating their distinctive principles. Wherever missionaries of the Shaftesbury Association went, the administration of the ordinance of believer's baptism was the climax of their efforts. Everywhere, one missionary observed, it created the most solemn impressions, though it also awakened great opposition. Congregations were formed on the basis of uncompromisingly Calvinistic church covenants, and applicants for membership and ministry were closely scrutinized. Procedures were meticulous if sometimes quaint. When Christopher Overholt intimated that he felt himself called to the ministry, the Beamsville congregation agreed to allow him to 'improve his gift' at a church meeting. The minutes tersely recorded their judgment: 'The Church met according to appointment. Meeting was opened by prayer and proceeded to business. We have heard Br. Overholt and do not think his Gift profitable therefore we desired him to stop and he likewise did. Meeting was concluded by prayer.'[11] Members were subject to a strict discipline. Some were constantly in and out, usually as the result of quarrels within the ranks. Even Peter Fairchild, the zealous founder of several churches, was eventually 'disfellowshipped' for marrying outside the church. Such carefulness made for tightly knit communities, but it must also have contributed an element of instability.

In Upper Canada the Methodists became the chief bearers of the Second Great Awakening. Reporting 2,550 'in society' by 1812, they had at this time by all odds the largest number of active members of any denomination. They were second to none in the urgency and passion of their calls to repentance and conversion, to the point where 'Canadian fire' gained a reputation in Methodist circles south of the line. As their name implied, they were also unusually pragmatic in adopting and adapting methods that promised results. Some means of grace, such as preaching and the sacraments, had been ordained by Christ himself. Others, such as the class meeting, were 'prudential,' but because of their proven efficacy essential to Methodism. Others again were 'extraordinary' in that they had demonstrated their usefulness in certain circumstances and might therefore legitimately be employed. Of these last the most widely used in early Upper Canada was the camp meeting, an open-air gathering that consisted of several days of intensive and virtually unceasing evangelism. The camp meeting was not a Methodist invention, though Methodist preachers took part in the first one held at Cane Ridge, Kentucky, in 1801. Its ultimate origin was in the Scottish long communion – Robert Burns's 'holy fair' –

which began with several days of religious exercises and reached its climax in the serving of the elements to successive 'tables' of communicants. Methodists systematized the camp meeting, took precautions against the disorders that inevitably accompanied it, and made it peculiarly their own. Their first use of this technique in Upper Canada seems to have been in a field near Dundas in 1805. They soon placed great reliance on it, though they made more sparing use of it than has sometimes been supposed.[12]

The stated purpose of Wesley's original mission, it may be remembered, had been to 'spread scriptural holiness over the land.' In their anxiety to rescue the multitudes who appeared to be headed for perdition, the first generation of circuit-riders in Upper Canada seem to have emphasized the necessity of the first step of conversion somewhat to the neglect of Christian perfection. They could never forget, however, that conversion was intended always to issue in holy living. Unlike most other evangelical denominations, Methodism demanded of candidates for membership not necessarily conversion but merely 'a desire to flee from the wrath to come and to be saved from their sins.' Once in the society, however, a Methodist was subject to rules, including 'avoiding evil of every kind' and 'doing good of every possible sort,' that seemed to assume that perfection had practically been attained already. Even if some itinerants laid relatively little stress on sanctification, compulsory membership in a class ensured that each week a Methodist would be examined on his or her spiritual progress and encouraged to seek further growth in grace. Some of the rules, such as that against ornaments (which led Christian Warner to refuse to wear suspenders until obesity compelled him), may seem picayune in retrospect, but at least they encouraged members to regard every detail of behaviour as important.[13]

Evangelism in a pioneer setting as conducted by preachers of American-based denominations had many of the features of a military campaign, including a considerable amount of incidental hubbub. So urgent was the necessity of conversion that proclamation of the message could not be limited to sacred times or places but must be carried into the camp of the enemy, in crowded taverns where profanity abounded or, if opportunity offered there, on a dock. Preaching in such circumstances often was accompanied by free-and-easy banter, with opportunities for sceptics to voice objections on the spot. Even when it took place in more decorous surroundings where a systematic presentation of doctrine was possible, the message was commonly pressed home with a rousing exhortation. Evangelism thus proceeded in an atmosphere of constant crisis. 'Smite him, my God!' an early Methodist preacher exclaimed when a mocker interrupted his meeting, and the man was soon writhing on the floor in agony.[14]

Since Upper Canada was then on the frontier of settlement, it was only natural that such relentless pressure would raise a fair head of emotional steam. The Methodist historian John Carroll, who was fond of dramatic incidents and doubtless made the most of them in description, told how the meticulous itinerant Darius Dunham, arriving in the midst of an unusually turbulent session, was brought groaning to his knees when his junior colleague Calvin Wooster repeatedly cried out 'Lord, bless Brother Dunham.' Similar if more edifying was the description by the Baptist missioner David Irish of a service at a certain Deacon Mabie's: 'Preacher and people could scarce conceal their passions. Heaven and hell appeared to be eternal realities. Saints were filled with extatic [sic] joy, while sinners in silent astonishment confessed that God was with us of a truth.'[15] It has customarily been argued that revival in Upper Canada was largely free of the abnormal psychic manifestations reported in the United States, but this judgment rests in large measure on exaggerated or one-sided accounts of happenings in Kentucky.

What relentless pressure such methods could impose on the unconverted becomes evident in Nathan Bangs's classic description of one of the first camp meetings to be held in Canada, a description especially revealing for its indications of constant interplay between the spontaneous and the carefully programmed:

At five o'clock Saturday morning a prayer-meeting was held, and at ten o'clock a sermon was preached on the words, 'My people are destroyed for lack of knowledge.' At this time the congregation had increased to perhaps twenty-five hundred, and the people of God were seated together on logs near the stand, while a crowd were standing in a semicircle around them. During the sermon I felt an unusual sense of the divine presence, and thought I could see a cloud of divine glory resting upon the congregation ... I ... descended from the stand among the hearers; the rest of the preachers spontaneously followed me, and we went among the people, exhorting the impenitent and comforting the distressed; for while Christians were filled with 'joy unspeakable and full of glory,' many a sinner was weeping and praying in the surrounding crowd. These we collected together in little groups, and exhorted God's people to join in prayer for them, and not to leave them until he should save their souls. O what a scene of tears and prayers was this! I suppose that not less than a dozen little praying circles were thus formed in the course of a few minutes. It was truly affecting to see parents, weeping over their children, neighbors exhorting their unconverted neighbors to repent, while all, old and young, were awe-struck. The wicked looked on with silent amazement while they beheld some of their companions struck down by the mighty power of God, and heard his poeple pray for them ... During this time some forty people were converted or sanctified.[16]

In view of the intensity of feelings aroused, it is scarcely surprising that this pioneer period was recalled as one marked by signs and wonders of divine grace. Missions were frequently accompanied by warnings and portents. After a prosperous man had turned Bangs out of his house, 'one untoward event after another occurred until he was a complete wreck, morally, mentally, socially, physically, as well as in his secular affairs.' In time he was deserted by his wife, reduced to dependence on charity, and allowed no peace even on his deathbed. Detroit likewise refused to receive Bangs, and within a few weeks it was reduced to ashes. Preachers on their rounds were frequently guided by 'impressions' to change well-laid plans and reported unexpected conversions as a result, though Bangs was warned of their fallibility after breaking a trail to a remote house in bitter winter weather only to find no one there. Yet Bangs was no naïve fanatic, but a future manager of the Methodist Book Room in New York. Methodists of a later generation, recalling the rapidity of their early growth, could only ascribe their entry into the province to the operation of divine providence.[17]

It has commonly been assumed that evangelical religion, and Methodism in particular, appealed specially to the poor. This was true only in the sense that outside a favoured circle few settlers had much ready cash. Most converts were from walks of life – farming, skilled labour, and retail trade – that offered considerable opportunity for upward mobility. Many of the drunkards whose conversion figured so prominently in contemporary accounts were probably of this class, failures in the pioneer setting only because of their addiction. Most readily identifiable as disadvantaged classes among those especially attracted were women and young people, who found in the sharing of testimonies a means of expression not readily available elsewhere. The rarest trophies, if we may judge from the interest their conversions aroused, were members of the social élite. To respectable people eager to make more of their lives than they had hitherto been able to do, evangelical Christianity offered the double support of rigid moral standards and the grace to maintain them. Methodism had the further advantage that its insistence on constant striving toward perfection fitted well with their aspirations for themselves.

To those affected by the evangelical spirit the religion of the golden mean seemed scandalously inadequate. Their objections had little to do with theology, on which Methodists were closer to the spiky Langhorn than to Presbyterians or Baptists. They complained, rather, of a lack of vital religion. By evangelical standards the missionaries of the SPG seemed lacking in seriousness of intent, in faith in the possibilities of grace, and above all in power to transform the lives of individuals. Ironically, in view of the pains they took to inculcate a sound morality, it was especially their deportment that failed to satisfy. Dancing, card-playing, and theatre-going, to the SPG innocent components of civilized living, were all on the evangelical list of cardinal sins. George Mountain, Bishop Jacob Mountain's son, summed up the problem neatly: 'The Americans expect a good deal of a clergyman, and it is useless for a man to go among them in that capacity who will not seem to be truly a man of God. A hypocrite may sometimes succeed with them. A careless worldly clergyman never can.'[18]

How readily a sincere representative of the old order could jar evangelical sensitivities can be strikingly illustrated from contemporary accounts of the ministry of Robert Addison, the SPG missionary at Niagara. Methodist itinerants seized on him as a glaring example of how ministry should not be exercised. Alvin Torry complained of an Anglican missionary, unmistakably Addison, who visited the Mohawks only once or twice a year, accompanied them on these occasions to horse-racing and card-playing, and was often intoxicated. Nathan Bangs, who lived for some time in the Niagara area, similarly described an Anglican minister nearby as 'a drunkard' who 'performed the liturgical service with indecent haste, following it with a brief, rapid, and vapid prelection.' From Addison's own writings, however, we receive the impression of a hard-working if sometimes querulous missionary. He reported to the SPG in 1797 that he had 'performed his duty with humble and conscientious assiduity,' making 'a circuit several times a year or more than 150 miles through a wild country.' Especially interesting, in view of Methodist criticisms, are his references to contacts with the Indians. He rejoiced that some of them had become candidates for baptism 'from a persuasion of the truth & value of our holy faith, without which he would not wish to baptize any of them.' It gave him special satisfaction that many among the Six Nations had left off 'the ruinous habit of drinking spirituous liquors.' On another occasion he noted the good reputation of his Presbyterian counterpart John Young as a preacher but lamented that he had become 'a slave of liquor.' Evidently, in an age when total abstinence was almost unknown, differences in the measure of imbibing could assume great significance. John Stuart, who was Mountain's commissary for Upper Canada, acknowledged that Addison was sensible, scholarly, and anxious to discharge his duty, but regretted that he was not popular at Niagara: 'For, amongst a mixed multitude of various Professions, a clergyman of very slender Talents, whose common Deportment is serious and solemn, and who seems impressed with the awful & important Truths, which he inculcates both from the Pulpit & by his own Example, will be more esteemed, and more useful, than one of much larger Information, without these Recommendations.'[19]

The Church of England bore the brunt of evangelical criticism, but other groups with traditions that antedated eighteenth-century revival were also vulnerable. The services of the Church of Scotland, though not read from a book like those of the Church of England, were no livelier and no less stereotyped. Congregations were expected to restrict their hymnody to the Scottish metrical version of the psalter, limited by custom and at one time by ecclesiastical legislation to a mere handful of tunes, and by all accounts few worshippers knew how to sing even these. Early Lutheran ministers, according to local tradition, were especially prone to drunkenness. Such scandals were rare among the peace groups, but Mennonites of this era were characterized less by religious fervour than by faithful adherence to inherited ways and by a determination to retain their German language. Innovation might be penalized by the 'ban,' which forbade the community to have any social intercourse with the excommunicated, while conformity would earn an honoured position in the community and perhaps election to one of its coveted offices. Even the Moravians of Fairfield drew from William Case the comment, 'In every respect they deserve the character of Gentlemen & Ladies, being strictly moral, & truly christian in their outward deportment, but as to any spiritual attainment I could not be satisfied that they had any.'[20] All of these religious bodies were protected to some extent by their ability to appeal to group or ethnic consciousness. Even so, none of them was exempt from strain and occasional defection. The disintegration of early Lutheran congregations was due in part to their inability to satisfy rising expectations of spiritual nurture; the formation of the Children of Peace can be regarded as a symptom of comparable tension among the Friends.

To the adherents of conventional religion, however, the direct approach of evangelical preachers represented the enthusiasm that had once involved England in civil war and now threatened to overturn public order. Evangelical moral demands struck them not only as ridiculously extreme but as destructive of many of the amenities that constituted civilized behaviour. Observing in many converts a sharpness in business practice that belied their profession, they were quick with accusations of hypocrisy. Most influential of all in determining their attitudes was the American origin of many preachers, which suggested to ultra-loyal minds an association between evangelical revival and republican subversion that remained long after most evangelical denominations had ceased to depend on the United States for ministers. Typical of their reaction, though from a somewhat later period, was John Howison's description of the Methodists of St Catharines:

Meetings are held at different houses, three or four times a week. At some of these I have seen degrees of fanaticism and extravagance exhibited, both by the preachers and congregation, which were degrading to human nature. Several of the inhabitants of the place, like most other people in Upper Canada, are fond of dancing and playing at cards; but the Methodists, of course, condemn these amusements, for they made it a general practice, to pray that those addicted to them might be converted, and that the Almighty would not let loose his wrath on the village of St Catharine's; while their own lives were, in many instances, one continued outrage against decency, decorum, and virtue.[21]

In their reaction against enthusiasm the defenders of moderation were not always above resorting to physical violence. As in eighteenth-century England, the toughs who scoffed at Methodist preachers were sometimes abetted by, and sometimes identical with, the respectable element that saw in their activities a threat to the established order. The most notorious case, even yet unclear in some of its details, was that of the Whitefieldian James McCarty. Condemned by the Kingston magistrates in 1790 for disturbing the peace, McCarty was ordered deported to Oswego and disappeared from sight amid rumours of foul play. Carroll described, with obvious relish and doubtless some embellishment, the reception given Case and Henry Ryan at Kingston in 1800 when they 'made a bold push to arouse the people': '[T]hey suffered no particular opposition, excepting a little annoyance from some of the baser sort, who sometimes tried to trip them off the butcher's block which constituted their rostrum; set fire to their hair, and then blow out their candle if it were in a night season. This was accomplished one evening by a wicked sailor, who then sung out, "Come on, boys, and see the Devil dance on a butcher's block!" Such opposition the preachers regarded [as] trivial, and held on.' When McDowall was similarly set upon by 'a gang of young bloods of the establishment,' he turned on his tormenters and proved himself the abler fighter.[22]

The religious differences that inspired such mutual hostility were real and significant, but we should be wary of accepting them as constituting the whole story. Whatever may have been the extravagances of pioneer evangelical preaching, its intention and ultimate result were to inspire the 'godly, righteous, and sober Lives' commended by the SPG. However ill adapted Anglican moral homilies may have been to the taste of some pioneers, they gradually nurtured their people into increased fervour. In worship, by modern standards, there was little to choose between the colloquial vulgarity of the one and the slipshod complacency of the other. Regardless of denomination, frequent coming and going during services testified to the absence of a developed sense of Victorian awe. Attempts have been made, notably by S.D. Clark, to apply Ernst Troeltsch's contrast of inclusive church and exclusive sect to the Upper Canadian situation.[23] Undeniably, evangelicals were reminiscent of Troeltsch's sect-type in the rigour of their moral demands. Far from withdrawing their adherents from community life, however, they were bringing communities into being. Subversive of public order as they may have seemed, they were preparing the way for an order that would rest on a broad base of popular support.

In fact, those who contended with one another for the religious allegiance of the pioneers had more in common than many of them would have been prepared to admit. Few Upper Canadians doubted the existence of a divine order to which, in the final analysis, individuals and societies had to conform or face the consequences. Neither was there much disagreement about the essentials of that order. God was recognized as sovereign, history as the unfolding of his purpose, Scripture as an infallible record shedding light on the future as surely as on the past and present. Human beings were without exception sinners by inheritance, incapable of saving themselves and therefore dependent on the saving work of Christ on the cross. If they responded to Christ in faith and obedience, they could look forward to an eternity of bliss in heaven. If they rebelled or neglected their duty, the certain consequence was unending torment. With rare exceptions, sinners were no more disposed than saints to question these verities. Frequently recognizing themselves as doomed to hell, they were likely when faced by death to suffer an extreme anxiety that made them vulnerable to appeals for repentance. As seriously as issues such as predestination and infant baptism were taken by the various churches, they represented merely disagreement on the details of an economy of salvation that was accepted in general outline by all but a handful of Upper Canadians.

This agreed theological structure rested on a rationally constructed philosophical base. In the early years of the nineteenth century British and American writers relied on evidence from the natural order to buttress the credibility of Christian revelation to critical readers; Bishop Butler's appeal to analogies from human experience and William Paley's catalogue of natural phenomena explicable only as expressions of creative purpose were special favourites. On this matter there was little disagreement along denominational lines. The SPG library for missionaries was well stocked with works of natural theology. Presbyterians, following Calvin, recognized a revelation in nature which, while insufficient in itself to lead to salvation, was so patent as to leave sinners without excuse. Wesley's intellectual point of departure had been John Locke's empirical philosophy; his followers, acknowledging right reason, in conjunction with Scripture, tradition, and experience, as a valid source of knowledge about God, relied consistently on Butler and Paley as guarantors of the reasonablenes of belief. Edmund Burke, who after his departure for Nova Scotia carried on a vigorous polemic against local Protestant divines, also published an apology for Christianity, based on natural theology, to which few Protestants of the time would have taken serious objection.[24] The light accessible to any rational being had to be supplemented by supernatural revelation, of course, and great emphasis was placed on the miracles and prophecies of Scripture both as proofs of its reliability and as pointers to its superiority over merely human speculation. It was generally agreed, however, that science properly understood could never be at variance with God's direct utterances in Scripture.

Based as it was on rational premises, Christian belief implied the necessity of moral behaviour. Although churches differed significantly in the details of their ethical demands, almost all agreed on the Ten Commandments and on the necessity of constant warnings against activities, such as sabbath-breaking and extramarital sex, that were especially difficult to control in a frontier setting. There was general agreement, too, both that Christian faith was credible only when expressed in moral living and that moral living was possible only through the sanctions provided by Christian faith. Preachers seldom distinguished between the wicked and the ungodly, and in frontier conditions the two categories may well have come close to coinciding. In this identification of Christianity with morality there was doubtless an element of expediency. To some extent Christianity was valued, even believed, because without it no stable social order could exist. Yet there was also a transcendent aspect that could come to the fore in unlikely settings. Attorney-General John White, mortally wounded in a duel with John Small at York in 1800, was careful to make his peace with God: 'Knowing his dissolution to be inevitable, he submitted to his fate with a pious & Christian resignation to the divine will & forgiveness to all his Enemies.'[25] That the sentiment was conventional is no reason to dismiss it as insincere.

The apprehension of reality as an ordered whole in which reason, faith, and morality were complementary to one another suggested the importance of education as a necessary auxiliary to religion, and the cultural backwardness of the province provided a further incentive to clerical initiative. Most of Upper Canada's earliest schools were founded by Anglican and Presbyterian ministers, who as a matter of course made religion an integral part of their curricula. Their theologies affected their educational approach, if sometimes indirectly: Episcopalians emphasized the classics, while Presbyterians leaned to the more philosophically and practically oriented schooling customary in Scotland. Yet Strachan, who established at Cornwall in 1803 a school that was soon reputed the finest in the province, favoured the Scottish system of practical education for the masses over the more aristocratic English tradition. Methodist itinerants, who had no time for schoolteaching, eked out their minimal salaries by selling, from their saddle-bags, books from their publishing house in New

York. These were the most accessible sources of enlightenment for many rural families who lacked ready access to bookstores but desired to broaden their horizons and had leisure in winter for reading. Carroll went so far as to claim that as a result of Methodist salesmanship Upper Canadians bought more and better books than in later years.[26]

Despite the keenness of denominational competition and the vigour of theological debate, agreement on basic principles pointed to the possibility of reaching a substantial measure of consensus on the place of religion in provincial life. Even at the time it ensured that religious animosity was not nearly so general as the rhetoric of eager partisans suggested. Instances of friendly contact across denominational lines were frequent. Joint church buildings were used to keep down expenses, though arrangements that were based on expediency tended eventually to fall apart amid hard feelings. So long as ministers were scarce, many people attended the services of other denominations; Burke had to reprimand Catholic officers at Niagara for parading soldiers of their faith to Protestant services in order to keep them out of local taverns. Any conscious ecumenism was still in the future, but a visiting Baptist minister was able to report in 1812 that bigotry was rare.[27]

5 *Atlantic Triangle*

The War of 1812, soon largely forgotton in other parts of Canada, left an indelible mark on the Upper Canadian mentality. Most immediately, it changed colonists' perceptions of the United States and thereby – by a peculiar but well-understood Canadian logic – their perceptions of themselves. The loyalists of an earlier era had abandoned their homes but not, at least in their own minds, their nationality.They were British Americans, Americans loyal to the Crown but none the less Americans. Those who had chosen the other side in the revolution were traitors and enemies, but it can seldom have occurred to the most loyal of loyalists to think of them as foreigners. The War of 1812 displayed citizens of the United States in a new role as invaders from without, and the result was to make possible a sentiment that was not merely anti-republican or anti-democratic but specifically anti-American. A positive sense of being Canadian would develop more slowly, but at least the war suggested to colonists the need of identifying themselves by nationality rather than merely by allegiance. The necessary process of myth-making was already under way in 1817 when John Strachan, in an exhortation for support of the Loyal and Patriotic Society of Upper Canada, expressed his confidence that future historians would record how 'the Province of Upper Canada, without the assistance of men or arms, except a handful of regular troops, repelled the invaders.'[1]

An important effect of the war was to engender a new confidence in the permanence of the province. Simcoe had dreamed of attracting a population of disaffected Americans who would make possible the undoing of the revolution, but almost no one anticipated that Upper Canada in its existing state could be held against a determined American attack. Constant alarms were the order of the day, and until the Peace of Amiens in 1802 the provincial militia were under arms more often than not. The war, while confirming the reality of the American threat, demonstrated that the province could be defended, and thus encouraged the construction of such major works as the Rideau and Welland canals. By putting a quietus to Simcoe's dream of reconquest, the war also showed that the province would have to live within its existing boundaries, and thus made more urgent the definition of its institutions and the formulation of its values.

Commercial growth was accompanied by massive changes in demography. The population of the British Isles had increased markedly since the onset of the industrial revolution. A prolonged depression that followed the end of the Napoleonic wars in 1815 inspired a widespread conviction that it had become too large, and Upper Canada now seemed a credible repository for the surplus. Many emigrants – even Canadians had not yet learned to call them 'immigrants' – were motivated by ambition, disillusionment with the slow progress of reform in Britain, or worry about their personal futures in a period of widespread pessimism. Others fled, or were pushed, from situations of actual want. They included culls from English poor-rolls, unemployed textile workers from the Scottish Lowlands, and Highland crofters displaced by the clearances. The Irish were by all odds the largest ethnic group, constituting at least a quarter of the province's population by 1842 and contributing a distinctive element to its character. Two-thirds of them were Protestant. Most of them came from the rural areas of the northern half of Ireland. Many had suffered from a slump in the domestic textile industry, but few of them were destitute. Immigrants from the United States were no longer encouraged, and in any case the frontier of settlement was moving westward. Many older settlements in eastern Ontario retained their loyalist character, but in the towns and in new backwoods settlements old-country elements came to predominate. By mid-century less than 10 per cent of the work force of Hamilton was Canadian-born; 79 per cent had come from the British Isles.[2] The total population grew to 236,702 in 1831 and 455,688 in 1841.

The war and the forces it set in motion also affected the religious development of the province. Denominations with American connections felt its consequences immediately. When the border was closed to American preachers, the Methodist cause was kept alive largely through the exertions of its presiding elder, Henry Ryan, who was able to claim British citizenship by virtue of his birth in Massachusetts before the revolution. Baptist congregations at Queenston and elsewhere were permanently dispersed, and Elijah Bentley of Markham was imprisoned for using seditious language in a sermon. Strachan, as rector of York, came to public prominence by virtually taking charge of the town when it was sacked by the Americans. Long-term effects were no less significant. Churches with

American associations were under constant pressure to demonstrate their loyalty, for this was an era in which 'to be popular in Canada one must show aversion to Jonathan.'[3] All churches had to cater to immigrants from the British Isles, whose religious tastes did not altogether coincide with those of the pre-war population. The rapid development of the province added an element of urgency, demanding a measure of missionary organization of which hitherto only the Methodists had shown themselves capable.

Forces were already operating that would provide a supply of missionaries to meet this rising demand. During the 1790s, in the wake of the evangelical revival of the century, there was a flurry of missionary organization among British Protestants. The Baptist Missionary Society, founded in 1792, was followed in 1795 by the non-denominational London Missionary Society and in 1799 by the evangelical Anglican Church Missionary Society. Such auxiliary institutions as the British and Foreign Bible Society and the Religious Tract Society attracted widespread support across denominational lines. Similar stirrings of missionary interest among Protestants of the United States and continental Europe soon gave rise to further constellations of institutions. Among Roman Catholics, reaction against the rationalism of the French Revolution set off a new wave of militant dedication to the propagation of the faith. New preaching orders sprang up in various parts of France, and the formation of the Society for the Propagation of the Faith at Lyon in 1822 provided a financial base for their overseas operations. By the 1820s the missionary impulse, at first confined within small circles of zealots, was gaining wide enough support in all churches to make expanded budgets possible. These were primarily intended for the conversion of non-Christians, but graphic accounts of the spiritual destitution of settlers in Upper Canada suggested the existence of a need that was almost as pressing. Further reminders were provided by emigration societies, which especially in Scotland owed their formation largely to religious motives.[4]

Like its population, the province's supply of missionaries multiplied several times in the decades following the war. It was drawn mainly from the same areas, and represented another aspect of the European outward thrust that continued throughout the nineteenth century. Anglican clergy other than military chaplains, 9 in 1819, became 30 in 1825, 44 in 1830, and 91 in 1840. Missionaries for the Church of Scotland were provided by the Glasgow Colonial Society, which was organized in 1825 by many of the same evangelicals who had been active in promoting emigration societies. In 1818 there was only one Kirk minister in the province; by 1840, thanks largely to the society, there were sixty.[5] The British Wesleyan Methodists entered the province in 1816, the Colonial Missionary

Society of the English Congregationalists in 1836; the Canada Baptist Missionary Society was organized in England in 1837. Roman Catholics, while they benefited from the financial aid of the Society for the Propagation of the Faith, were slower in devising effective methods of deploying personnel. Alexander Macdonell, who became an auxiliary bishop in 1820 and bishop of Kingston in 1826, had to depend for priests largely on cast-offs recommended by Irish bishops.

As Macdonell's experience showed, the process by which missionaries arrived in Upper Canada was still often haphazard and unsatisfactory. An official of the Glasgow Colonial Society pointed out tactfully, 'Young men of good principles & talents have of course the best chance of succeeding at home & they are usually unwilling to give up their prospects in this country.' The implications for a colony commonly associated in clerical minds with 'utter banishment' were obvious. An American Presbyterian missionary was informed by a member of a congregation in the Niagara area that their present minister was the 'best they ever had as a preacher, the only exception to him being that he had two wives living.' A number of ministers who arrived in the province as settlers rendered acceptable if not always distinguished service. One such was James Magrath, who emigrated from Ireland in 1827 at the age of fifty-eight, secured a bishop's licence, and served for some years in Toronto Township. Another was George Pashley, whose journal has preserved for us the recollections of one among many immigrant Methodist local preachers who continued to exercise their gifts in Upper Canada.[6]

As they sought to cope with 'destitute settlers' en masse, church authorities began to adopt more systematic and sometimes unaccustomed methods. In 1816–17 Charles Stewart, a well-connected Scot who was then employed as an Anglican travelling missionary, raised a building fund by appealing to British friends of the mission. This, along with a further appeal in 1823–4, contributed to the erection of sixty-eight early Ontario churches. In 1834, when he had become bishop, his nephew W.J.D. Waddilove set up the Upper Canadian Travelling Mission Fund so that others could emulate his earlier career. Under its terms, missionaries received three-year appointments to specified blocks of townships on the understanding that by the end of their tenure they would have carved out settled parishes. The Upper Canada Clergy Society, founded by evangelical laymen in southern England in 1837, operated on the same principle. In 1830 Stewart, with financial help from the Society for the Propagation of the Gospel, began to create a body of licensed catechists to alleviate the shortage of clergy. Both the Kirk and the United Secession also followed the pattern of appointing itinerant ministers for a limited period in the expectation, which was usually fulfilled, that they would organize congregations and then receive calls from them. They also sponsored missionary tours in search of clusters of Presbyterians, and the Kirk attempted to arrange supply for vacant congregations on a systematic basis. These innovations constituted a tacit admission that Methodism had benefited from the use of itinerant ministries. There was also a stiffening of educational requirements; in order to qualify for a Canadian posting one unfortunate candidate was required to preach twice before the directors of the Glasgow Colonial Society.[7] Despite constant complaints that population growth was outpacing missionary budgets, and despite the dispatch of some clerical misfits, British churches were increasingly able to offer acceptable ministerial leadership.

Upper Canada was still most readily accessible from the United States, and despite increased Canadian resistance American missionary efforts were resumed after the war. In 1819 the Dutch Reformed Church, sensing a preference for Scottish preachers, quietly withdrew from the province. Three years later, however, the Associate Synod of North America, the American counterpart of the Antiburgher wing of the Scottish Secession, entered the province inadvertently; a list of convenient stopping-places on the way to the home of a family that wanted a baby baptized was mistaken for suggested sites for churches. Swallowing their disappointment, the travellers remained to establish a mission that constituted for several years the chief Presbyterian presence west of the Niagara River. A more ambitious enterprise was that of the American Home Missionary Society (AHMS), founded in 1826 with support from both Congregationalists and Presbyterians. Attracted first to Lower Canada by the abundance of New England settlers in the Eastern Townships and by an evangelical abhorrence of popery, it began to support missionaries in Upper Canada in 1830 and by 1837 had six on its roll in the province. In 1833 the American Baptist Missionary Society reopened a connection across the border that had largely lapsed during the war. On the whole, these efforts seem to have represented responses to local appeals rather than deliberate attempts to gain footholds in Canada. The AHMS, which was more active than any other American society, advertised its aims in terms of national needs and seldom mentioned Canadian missions in its annual summaries. Meanwhile the American Methodists had repaired the damage inflicted by the war, and in 1817 rejoiced in their most successful revival yet. By 1824, approximately one-quarter of their itinerants were natives of British North America, and in succeeding years the great majority were called into the ministry in Upper Canada.[8]

As the more familiar churches, both British and American, sought to cope with the expanding population of Upper Canada, they were subjected to an onslaught by aggressive new religious groups. During the 1830s one such movement after another arrived on the scene, threatening to take the province by storm or merely gathering small groups of believers in scattered corners. Most of these movements were imports from the United States. The Disciples of Christ, who first appeared in western Upper Canada in 1830, were a product of the frontier. Their basic conviction, formulated by Alexander Campbell and his son Thomas, was that the purity and unity of the church could be restored only by following the clear directions of the New Testament. Although they rejected the exclusivism of the Scottish Secession, to which they had belonged, the Campbells owed their convictions in large measure to a strain within that body that emphasized strict conformity to Scripture. Similar in emphasis was the Christian Connection, whose members professed 'the Bible as their rule of faith and practice, with no name but *Christian* and no test of fellowship but Christian character.' The Christian Connection's work in the province, which was concentrated in the area immediately to the north and east of Toronto, began in 1821 as the result of a request for help from a local woman who had been a member in New York State. The Connection represented a fusion of several American movements, but the formulation of a church covenant by one of its earliest Upper Canadian congregations suggests a link with the particular emphases of Abner Jones, a former Baptist from Vermont. Universalists, who denied the possibility of eternal punishment but were still orthodox in most other respects, established their first congregation at London in 1831, but were most successful in rural areas. The Mormon leader Brigham Young and his brothers Joseph and Phineas actively propagandized the eastern part of the province in the early 1830s, and John E. Page was especially successful in the same area in 1836 and 1837. John Taylor, a convert from Toronto, was to become Young's successor. The Methodists around Toronto lost members to the movement, and in 1838 a shipload of 150 converts from Prescott and Brockville were reported on their way to the 'land of promise.'[9]

Europe also contributed, though more modestly, to the sectarian ferment. Of English background were the 'Irvingites' of the Catholic Apostolic Church, who offered an unlikely combination of elaborate liturgy and glossolalia. Introduced to the province in 1834 by William R. Caird, an evangelist who had been specially dispatched to Canada in order to gain a North American foothold, they were able in 1836 to establish congregations at Kingston and Toronto. Among their converts were George Ryerson, the eldest of a family of distinguished Methodist ministers (though himself only a probationer), and Adam Hood Burwell, an Anglican priest and a member of a prominent loyalist family. Such prizes gave the Irvingites an entrée into both Methodist and Anglican congregations that yielded an élite if never numerous following. The even more exotic doctrines of the Swedish visionary Emanuel Swedenborg were being disseminated, mainly in Lutheran circles, by 1830 at Markham and by 1833 at Berlin, now Kitchener.[10]

It seemed to representatives of orthodoxy that doctrines of almost unlimited variety were being propounded. Agents of Bishop Stewart's Travelling Missionary Fund, fresh from England or Ireland, larded their reports with lurid accounts of 'extravagances' they encountered. Typical was the complaint of William Bettridge: 'New denominations are continually claiming a portion of the public attention; and it is no easy thing to discover, for some time at least, what the character of the heresy may be which these new lights propound as the truth of God.' Although such reports indicate that these new movements were being propagated in immigrant areas, their chief impact seems to have been on the older American settlements. Methodism, which by its broad appeal had attracted zealots of all types, was especially vulnerable to their depredations. Among those who went over to the new sects were a disconcerting number of preachers and class leaders.[11] The doctrinal stability and tight discipline of the province's most actively evangelistic denomination may, however, actually have contributed to the failure of the new groups to secure followings as large as in many parts of the United States.

Almost every missionary report of the period suggests that until the arrival of its author entire townships were destitute of the gospel. After reading a number of such documents one is more likely to conclude that, by the 1830s at any rate, ministers were lurking behind every bush. In 1837 F.L. Osler observed that Newmarket lacked an Anglican clergyman but had Sunday preaching from eight different sects. Adam Elliot, an Anglican travelling missionary, described matter-of-factly how at Bowmanville a Methodist preacher stood aside for him and a Presbyterian then followed with a second sermon. Such incidents, which were by no means uncommon, lend credence to the contention of William Proudfoot that the province had fully as many ministers as it could support. Knowing (only because his wife collected his reminiscences) that David Marks of the Free Baptists paid at least ten visits to Upper Canada, one also wonders how many visiting missionaries have remained anonymous.[12]

Inevitably, ecclesiastical allegiances tended to instability as churches and societies jostled for position with each other and with new challengers. That clergy of each denomination would attempt to steal sheep from the others was generally taken for granted, and recognition of such mutual designs did not necessarily inhibit personal friendships or prevent co-operation in common causes. The rival claims of competing agencies within a single denomination or denominational family, however, were a source of conflict and recrimination. Some of these internecine quarrels were provoked by inherited theological differences, some by ethnic or national loyalties, a fair number by both. Almost all of them were complicated by involvement in provincial politics, which will be discussed in greater detail in the next chapter.

The Methodists provided a textbook example of internal conflict. Until after the War of 1812 Upper Canadian Methodists were a single body, part of the Methodist Episcopal Church of the United States and supplied by it with preachers. During the war the British Wesleyan Methodists, fearful of republican influence, installed themselves at Quebec and Montreal, and in 1816 they appointed preachers to Kingston, Cornwall, Stamford, and York. In 1820, when wartime passions had cooled, the British agreed to a compromise by which they would withdraw from the upper province. They came close to complying with that promise, retaining only the garrison town of Kingston where their adherents stoutly resisted any suggestion of being handed over to the Americans. By this time some Canadian Methodists themselves were embarrassed by a connection that offended their loyalist sentiments and left them open both to British competition and to suspicions of disloyalty. Henry Ryan, who had saved the movement from disintegration during the war of 1812, commenced an agitation that proved so popular that a visiting American delegation led by Bishop Elijah Hedding had little alternative but to promise sympathetic consideration of any Canadian proposal for a friendly separation.[13] In 1828 this came about, and William Case became the superintendent of an independent Canadian Methodist Episcopal Church.

One might suppose that this development would have avoided any further difficulty, but instead it subjected the main body to competition from two directions. Ryan had used such immoderate language in his campaign that in 1828 the conference declined to sustain his ministerial character. He immediately organized his followers into the Canadian Wesleyan Methodist Church, which made quite a stir for a few years. Then in 1832, to the dismay of the Canadians, the British Wesleyans announced that Canadian independence had abrogated the agreement of 1820, which had been with the American church, and that they intended to send missionaries to Upper Canada. We can readily understand Canadian resentment of this high-handed action, while reminding ourselves that as late as 1925 the United and Presbyterian churches divided between them the foreign missions of the former Presbyterian church without any thought of consulting the national churches involved.[14] That an imperial power should pay serious heed to colonial opinion was a thought slow in dawning.

Faced with the threat of British competition for a constituency increasingly made up of immigrants, and already in debt for a mission among the Indians of the province, the Canadians, at the urging of John and

Egerton Ryerson, determined to seek union with the British conference. The Wesleyans agreed, but insisted on terms that reserved to themselves the appointment of a president of conference and a superintendent of missions. In 1833 the Canadians thus became 'Wesleyan Methodists,' a name they would retain until 1874. The union did not work well. It had been hastily pushed through the Canadian conference with little regard for the strong reservations of many veterans, including Case, and it was coldly received by the members and ministers of the British societies that had already been established. Although the British conference demonstrated its good faith at the outset by transferring several leading opponents of union out of the province, the union foundered in 1840.[15]

The ostensible cause of this speedy abortion was the conservative Wesleyans' disapproval of the association of the Canadians with reform politics and especially of their insistence on equality before the law with the Church of England. Another major source of friction was described by Joseph Stinson, the British superintendent of missions, in a graphic portrait of the 'American Methodists' at Kingston: '[T]hey are violent Temperance men, they allow no person to be in Society who either drinks or *sells* ardent spirits, many of our British Methodists do both, & they are lampooned in no very measured terms by these long faced, half starved Yankees ... these very persons *eat* as much tobacco as would poison a pack of hounds & commit as many indecencies in the house of the Lord as would bring the exterminating Judgement upon the whole Province were He not merciful.'[16]

Frequent suggestions that the British missionaries were theologically more sophisticated than the Canadians cannot be sustained. Most of them were artisans, and the British conference established its first theological seminary only in 1834.[17] Differences in the pitch of evangelistic appeals, the subject of frequent Anglican comment, were at most a matter of degree. Egerton Ryerson, on a visit to England, found at a Wesleyan service 'no more decorum than in Canada, if as much.'[18] The two groups differed in their basic conception of Methodism. The British regarded themselves as a religious society, auxiliary and in some ways subsidiary to the Church of England. They thought of their ministers as essentially lay preachers who had been raised up to meet an extraordinary need; they began to ordain them with the laying on of hands only in 1836. The Canadians, by contrast, inherited the conviction of American Methodists that they constituted a church and were entitled to recognition as such.

Misunderstanding between the Canadians and the British was by no means the only source of Methodist disunity. In 1833 some dissatisfied members of the Canadian body, mainly in rural districts of early American settlement, set in motion the organization of a continuing Methodist Episcopal Church that grew steadily to become a formidable rival. When the main body attempted to discredit them as self-serving opportunists, they became all the more firmly attached to episcopacy and intent on establishing their credentials as a church. During the same decade English immigrants introduced several other variants of Methodism. The Methodist New Connexion, which had broken from the main body in 1797 in protest against the monopolizing of decision-making by preachers, absorbed Ryan's dwindling band of followers in 1841. It also offered a haven to Wesleyans who for one reason or another felt alienated from the conference. Two other groups had been products of regional movements of fervent revival that could not be contained within the increasingly cautious Wesleyan body. The Primitive Methodists, of self-consciously working-class orientation, entered the province in 1829 and were especially strong in the Toronto area. Bible Christians, who came exclusively from Cornwall and Devon, attained some local importance in the counties just east of Toronto. The smaller English groups differed from the Wesleyans in giving the laity a large part in their polity. They attracted many, both native and immigrant, who missed in the main body the simplicity and single-mindedness of early days. By 1840, as a result of these divisions and importations, the monolithic Methodism of the 1820s had been replaced by six jurisdictions that competed not only in the province as a whole but in many communities that could ill afford more than one church. The denomination had lost little of its early vigour, but many wondered about its future in the province.

Presbyterian dissensions were even more complex: controversies imported from Scotland were mingled with tensions between Old World and New World outlooks. In part, this complexity reflected a different model of organization. Whereas in Methodism ultimate power resided in a conference that delegated authority to districts and circuits, the higher Presbyterian church courts were constituted by the banding together of individual congregations. The first effective local court, the Presbytery of the Canadas, was formed in 1818 on the initiative of ministers of varied backgrounds, and without authorization by or association with any ecclesiastical body outside Canada. Most of its ministers had been connected with some branch of the Seceders, however, and the presbytery largely reflected their point of view. Throughout the 1820s, despite the abstention of Kirk ministers, it demonstrated a considerable willingness among Presbyterians to co-operate with one another. This situation changed in 1829, when missionaries of the Glasgow Colonial Society began to arrive. The society's stated policy was to avoid local competition whenever possible. It was also pledged to appoint only ministers of the established Church of Scotland, however, and these held aloof from the existing presbytery. Inevitably, the two bodies confronted each other as rivals, and in 1831 both organized synods. A broad hint from the colonial secretary, Sir George Murray, that government aid would be most readily available to a consolidated denomination suggested the desirability of a union between the two bodies.[19] Representatives of the Kirk delayed this for some years by insisting that Seceders could not be recognized as ministers of equal standing with them, but in 1840 the two bodies came together.

Despite these Scottish connections, Upper Canadian Presbyterianism during the 1820s and 1830s represented a congeries of disparate elements among which the American tended to predominate. In the United States, since the formulation of the Plan of Union in 1801, Congregationalists had left the planting of western missions largely to the Presbyterians. Most early American Presbyterian congregations in Upper Canada represented this 'Presbygational' strain in which authority was largely in lay hands. Some of their ministers participated in the Presbytery of the Canadas until it offended their voluntarist convictions by accepting public money. Appointees of the AHMS, who likewise reckoned themselves Presbyterians despite joint sponsorship by Congregationalists, also considered joining the presbytery despite reservations about its attitude to state aid. In the event, the issue was decided for them by the synod's refusal to allow the use of Isaac Watts's metrical version of the Psalms alongside the Scottish Psalter, and in 1833 they organized the separate Presbytery of Niagara.

With the exception of the Antiburghers of the Associate Synod of North America, who kept largely to themselves and were regarded by the most dogmatic members of other Presbyterian sects as excessively narrow, these American Presbyterians represented the revivalist tradition then current in almost all Protestant denominations in the United States. Scots arriving in increasing numbers did not take kindly to their accents, their emotionalism, or their casual attitude to Calvinist orthodoxy, and the result was a series of local struggles for ascendancy between representatives of the two traditions. Samuel Sessions, an AHMS missionary, wrote from Oakville in 1834 that he had been obliged to abandon his ministry among the Scots of Nassagaweya because they would hear of nothing but 'unconditional reprobation from eternity.' In 1836 his successor Joseph Marr complained that 'the Methodists and the Seceders, and the Kirk (consisting of old country people, Scotch chiefly) appear to have conspired against me, and have done their utmost to put me down.' The Americans hung in as well as they could, disgusted by the attendance of Kirk ministers at 'parties of pleasure and gaiety' and disillusioned with the compromises of the United Synod.[20] Gradually, however, they were being eased out of one community after another.

By the end of the 1830s, immigration, the heightened activity of Scottish churches, and the disruption of American work by the rebellion of 1837 were giving Canadian Presbyterianism a distinctly more Scottish cast. In 1831, when the United and Kirk synods were organized, the two were practically equal in membership. By 1840 the Kirk counted sixty against sixteen in the United Synod. Its progress entailed greater power for ministers and Kirk sessions, as well as greater emphasis on orthodox doctrine. A further Scottish entrant was the United Secession Church of Scotland (later the United Presbyterian Church), which in 1832 sent out three missionaries, of whom William Proudfoot was destined to leave the largest imprint on the religious life of the province. Their first thought was to ally themselves with the United Synod. During the 1820s, however, their parent church had decisively opted for the voluntary principle of church support, and they accordingly organized the Missionary Presbytery. Although it resembled the Americans in its warm evangelical theology and strict moralism, it rejected their revivalist techniques and deplored their relative indifference to theology. Yet the New England element, with its traditions of lay independence and activist pietism, did not disappear but was gradually absorbed into the Presbyterian mainstream. Proudfoot observed that at York 'independents' were numerous in the Kirk and United Synod congregations, and even in the Methodist churches.[21]

These developments help to account for the singular fact that although among early American settlers Congregationalists may well have outnumbered the adherents of any other denomination, no lasting church of their order was founded from the United States during this period. Instead, Congregationalism was given its real start in the province in 1819 by English immigrants, and came to depend for ministers on the Colonial Missionary Society, an affiliate of the Congregational Union of England and Wales. AHMS missionaries found their English counterparts strictly tied to denominational principles and unwilling to co-operate. Since Congregationalists in England were mainly well-established merchants and manufacturers with little tendency to emigrate, growth in the province was slow.[22] In Toronto, however, John Roaf of Zion Church was able to win back most of the 'independents' who had joined other churches.

Baptists had difficulty in creating effective organs of common action. Most Baptists in Upper Canada were inhabitants of rural townships in the southwestern peninsula. American in background, strongly Calvinistic in doctrine, and insistent on restricting communion to immersed believers, they were even more strongly attached than Congregationalists to the principle of local autonomy. From early days they organized themselves into regional associations, but these were strictly advisory and many congregations ignored them altogether. When the energetic and rather more liberal Baptists of Montreal undertook to provide an institutional framework for the denomination, resistance was inevitable. A college and a journal in Montreal attracted little Upper Canadian support. The Canada Baptist Missionary Society, formed in England on Montreal initiative, supported many missionaries in Upper Canada but was unable to bring the disparate elements together.

Montreal's failure to maintain its leadership was due in some measure to a change in orientation on the part of some Scottish Baptists who began to settle along the lower Ottawa in 1816. The piety of these settlers had been shaped largely in conventicles where the Seceders' quest for the restoration of New Testament discipline was taken with unusual seriousness; it was this quest that had ultimately led them to adopt Baptist principles. Their initial ties in Canada were largely with the Baptists of Montreal, many of whom were likewise Scottish. Two developments gradually brought them closer to other Upper Canadian Baptists. One was their acceptance of the practice of closed communion, which had been traditional in Scotland but which they had waived for a time in Canada in deference to the views of several ministers. The other, doubtless encouraged by memories of revivals in Scotland led by the brothers Robert and James Haldane, was their successful adoption in 1835 of American revivalist techniques. Although they never were numerous, the Ottawa Valley Scots eventually provided a remarkable proportion of the denomination's leaders. Churches organized by other Scotch Baptists who settled in the western part of the province generally held themselves aloof from denominational affairs, and some of them affiliated with the Disciples of Christ.[23]

During the 1820s and 1830s most smaller Protestant denominations were in a similar state of flux and tension. The Lutherans, despite their comparatively early start, had never been able to set up churches in proportion to their numbers. By 1840 even their existing congregations had dwindled, gone over to other denominations, or disappeared. In their place a new centre was taking shape in the Waterloo area, a centre based on direct immigration from south Germany and Alsace that began in the 1820s. Here the ministry of Friedrich Wilhelm Bindemann provoked dissension almost from the outset. Bindemann was able and energetic, but so liberal in his theology that Henry William Peterson, a lay pastor, refused to recognize him as a Lutheran. The Quakers were weakened by the Hicksite separation of 1829. Each party claimed to represent true Quakerism, which Hicksites identified with traditional practice and their opponents with evangelical doctrine. Both groups suffered in the long run. The traditionalists laid down rigid rules to which many young people were unwilling to conform, while the evangelicals were on a road to accommodation that ultimately left little reason for their separate existence. The province was still attracting

Mennonite settlers, notably the ultra-conservative Amish who began to arrive in 1824 from Germany and the United States. Within their community too, however, aggressive evangelical preaching was creating tensions and even fractures.[24]

One of the most spectacular disputes of the period convulsed the supposedly monolithic Roman Catholic Church. W.J. O'Grady, formerly a chaplain to Irish mercenaries who had settled in Brazil, came to Upper Canada in 1828 and made such a favourable impression that Macdonell appointed him parish priest of York and then vicar-general. At first, parish activities boomed, but O'Grady made enemies and in 1834 Macdonell informed him of his transfer to Prescott and Brockville. O'Grady not only refused to go, but managed with the aid of hand-picked churchwardens to retain possession of his church. Macdonell ultimately regained control, but not before O'Grady had demonstrated the appeal to many Irish immigrants of a brand of Roman Catholicism radically different from the bishop's. While O'Grady's intransigence undoubtedly embittered the contest, the arch-Tory Macdonell pointed to a deeper issue when he characterized O'Grady's sermons as 'democratical and demoralizing.'[25]

Although O'Grady demonstrated more ability than stability, the outbreak of similar troubles in several parishes signalled significant changes in the social composition, ethos, and public image of Roman Catholics in the province. Before the War of 1812 the church operated much as it had in feudal times, with gentry and commoners well aware of their unequal places. In Glengarry, which to Bishop Macdonell always represented the norm, the old system of clan loyalties carried over into the church. In the French settlements along the Detroit River the great fur-trading families conceived of themselves as *seigneurs* and patrons, though not without vigorous resistance from more egalitarian *habitants*. The rather sudden predominance of the Irish introduced a constituency of a very different temper. The immigrants, largely homogeneous in social class, had unfavourable memories of aristocrats and every expectation that priests would take the people's side as they normally had done in Ireland. The hostility to Macdonell that erupted in the O'Grady case was only too natural in the circumstances. Macdonell saw the coming of the Irish as imposing on him the painful necessity of 'tranquilizing and reducing them to order and regularity,' and his burden was not lightened by the presence of Whiteboys and Ribbonmen whom Peter Robinson had enticed to the province from some of the most politically unstable sections of Ireland.[26] To many of the Irish, in turn, Macdonell was a tyrant and collaborator with the governing Protestant clique. Immigration also had important effects on the way in which Roman Catholics were perceived by the Protestant majority. Even though their views on religion had been dismissed as misguided, they had hitherto enjoyed general acceptance as loyal, well-disposed citizens. Now, in part through the influence of the numerous Protestant Irish, Roman Catholicism came to be regarded in many quarters as socially unacceptable, vaguely subversive, and even threatening to British liberties.

Oddly, in view of subsequent developments and the current political state of the province, the Church of England exhibited fewer internal strains than almost any other denomination. Despite the appearance of unity, however, various hints suggest the presence of seeds of conflict. Divergent visions of the church were represented most conspicuously by Bishop Stewart and Archdeacon Strachan, both Scots but of very different backgrounds. Stewart, an aristocrat of ascetic habits, was a moderate evangelical who welcomed the co-operation of other ecclesiastical bodies. Strachan, an ambitious plebeian, was determined that the Church of England should be pre-eminent in the province. Clergymen supported by Stewart's fund for travelling missionaries were predominantly evangelicals by conviction. Scarcely by coincidence, Strachan was blamed for virtually bringing Stewart's plan to an end. Quite apart from party differences, some tensions were inherent in the attempt to integrate independent missionary societies into an episcopal polity. In the words of Richard Ruggle, 'The colonial clergy usually served two distant masters – their bishops, and the societies which supported them ... – as well as their congregations. And they often displayed a disregard for any master.'[27]

Despite constant complaints that neglected sheep were being snatched by sectarian wolves, Anglicans were more widely distributed than hitherto; in 1842 the first census indicating religious preference showed them in first place. No longer was Church of England support limited almost entirely to administrative, military, and commercial centres. Apart from a few well-born settlers, such as the Stricklands and the Moodies, who offered spontaneous support in the backwoods, however, the immigrants required careful cultivation. Typical were the parishioners of the fictional missionary Vernon described by W.S. Darling, who had to be taught what a surplice was but who gradually responded to the services of a church that vividly called up recollections of home. Some continuing leakage of immigrants' children to other denominations can be attributed not only to the shortage of clergy but to the lack of adaptability of such missionaries as Thomas Green, who complained of the indignity of having to cut his own firewood and of the difficulty of keeping a boy to groom his horse.[28]

While the various denominations were seeking to inculcate their particular tenets, some Upper Canadians found their own ways of providing themselves with religious facilities. On Monday, 12 July 1824, the foundation of a 'free church' at Ancaster, to be erected by community effort, was formally laid. On this occasion no clergy were reported in attendance, no prayers offered, no hymns sung. Under the foundation-stone were deposited a Masonic scroll, several British silver coins, and some current newspapers. After a dinner at which the first toast was to 'the King and Craft' and none was offered to any church or religious cause, 'national airs, songs and some fine sentiments were the order of the evening.' On the following evening the ballroom was opened for dancing. While presumably the church was intended to double as a Masonic hall, the presence on the board of managers of several Presbyterians and at least one prominent Methodist indicates the existence of elements of popular religion that would never be inferred from the missionary reports of the time. Unfortunately, the building – an impressive landmark with six turrets – proved to be a fertile source of contention.[29]

If the decades following the War of 1812 were notable for ecclesiastical confusion and conflict, there was taking shape by 1840 a religious pattern of which traces remain even today. Anglicans were becoming less an élite and more a cross-section, Roman Catholics less feudal and more populist. Tensions between British and American orientation were being resolved among Presbyterians and Congregationalists in favour of the former, among Baptists in favour of the latter, and among Methodists not at all. The Waterloo area was becoming a significant base for both Lutherans and Mennonites, though as yet it could claim a majority of neither. Quakers were already a fading but visible presence. Religious groups introduced during these decades, while conspicuous and apparently omnipresent, constituted at their end a small fraction of the provincial population. Time would confirm all of these trends.

A conspicuous feature of the religion of the period was a surge of Irish influence that affected Roman Catholicism most dramatically but had scarcely less far-reaching effects on several other denominations. Both lay and clerical Irish, mainly from what is now the republic, imparted a pronounced evangelical tint to the Anglicanism of the western part of the province and would in the later years of the century constitute the primary power base of the low church party. The Irish were also far more formative of Presbyterianism than later Presbyterians have been inclined to acknowledge. They furnished much of the constituency of the United Secession Church and came to dominate the United Synod in its later years; after 1838, when it established mutual relations with the Synod of Ulster, even the Church of Scotland admitted Irish ministers. Among the Methodists, Irish self-consciousness was an important factor in the Ryanite schism, and the Irish were increasingly represented in the membership and ministry of the main body.[30] In many areas of Protestant Irish settlement, meanwhile, King Billy became the focus of a mythology more familiar to many Upper

Canadians than most of the Bible or the creeds. The rites and ceremonies of the Loyal Orange Order did not claim religious status, but to deny them religious significance is to miss a vital element of folk piety.

In 1840 it would have occurred to few Upper Canadians that their religion might be considered in any sense indigenous. They asked of particular beliefs and practices not whether they were contextual but whether they were orthodox or scriptural. Yet it was quickly recognized that Upper Canadians had peculiar needs that could best be met by locally educated ministers. Mennonites and Quakers had no problems in this respect, and by the 1830s Methodists and Baptists were moving towards self-sufficiency. Strachan believed strongly in the superiority of local candidates and began soon after the War of 1812 to train some of them at his own expense.[31] A theological school established at Chambly in 1818 educated seven or eight Anglican priests who served in Upper Canada before 1840. Macdonell prepared forty priests at his home in Saint Raphael, though he complained at one time that all had disappointed him. The chief laggards were the Presbyterians, who cherished the ideal of a learned ministry. The United Presbytery attempted to found a seminary at Hillier in Prince Edward County, however, and several candidates of the Church of Scotland studied under local ministers at Hamilton and Streetsville.[32] Meanwhile, as they drew on the varied offerings of British and American agencies, Upper Canadians were beginning to establish religious institutions that fitted their situation.

6 Religion on the Hustings

A striking feature of Upper Canadian life prior to the War of 1812 was the virtual absence of political agitation or even political interest. There were a few individuals who held power, many who did not, and even a few outspoken critics of those in power; but occasional ripples of discontent did little to distract most inhabitants from the more urgent tasks of clearing the forest and establishing the basic structures of community life. As late as 1822 Robert Gourlay, who had managed to get himself thrown into jail for his caustic comments on the authorities, could write that politics were 'scarcely named or known' and that the population lacked enough cohesion to be 'agitated by parties.'[1] By the late 1820s no one could have written in such terms, for a rash of editorials, resolutions, and petitions betrayed a discontent that would culminate in 1837 in armed rebellion.

The relation of religion to public life underwent an equally striking change. Since we are not so naïve today as to suppose that the most avowedly neutral expressions of religion can be devoid of political content, we can recognize significant political implications even in the earliest Anglican and Methodist initiatives. The first settlers were largely unaware of such connections, but no such innocence was possible in later years. By the late 1820s religious issues provided much of the fuel of political controversy, and secular politics impinged on practically every aspect of religion. Every ecclesiastical union or division was subtly or not so subtly affected by politics. Every mission and every revival had political repercussions.

The basic source of contention was the existence of provisions, in some cases already embodied in the Constitutional Act of 1791 that created Upper Canada, for carrying over into the province certain aspects of the English religious establishment. Some of these provisions conferred a special status on the Church of England or reserved certain prerogatives to it. Among these was an act of the legislature in 1793 that bestowed on the

Anglican clergy the exclusive right to perform marriages. (A justice of the peace might substitute when the nearest clergyman lived more than eighteen miles away; the act also seemed to take for granted the eligibility of Roman Catholic priests, in consequence of guarantees given at the time of the conquest.) Although the Anglicans had no official monopoly of education, early provisions for grammar schools gave their clergy a controlling voice in the system. Besides these legal advantages, the Church of England received a number of special favours from the state. Until 1815 its clergy were appointed by the lieutenant-governor and paid out of provincial funds; after that time parliamentary grants to the SPG performed the same service indirectly. Governments provided additional assistance in the form of glebe lands, chaplaincies to supplement regular pay, and occasional contributions to building funds. Most valuable of all, in the long run, were the fruits of a provision of the Constitutional Act that land 'equal in Value to the Seventh Part' of that otherwise granted should be set aside for the 'Maintenance and Support of a Protestant Clergy' and for 'no other Use or Purpose whatever.'[2] These lands, which came to be known as the clergy reserves, would ultimately prove to be the most divisive of all the provisions made by government for the regulation or support of religion.

For the most part these provisions represented simply the extension of English laws and customs to new territories acquired by the Crown, and similar ones existed in colonies as diverse as Jamaica and Nova Scotia. Their application to the Canadas was actually softened through the intervention of Lord Dorchester, governor when the Constitutional Act was passed, who did not wish to alienate French-Canadian opinion by showing too obvious partiality to Protestantism. James J. Talman has argued convincingly that the Church of England was never actually established in Upper Canada, as it undoubtedly was in most other British possessions. Even the clergy reserves were in no respect innovative. Land was a customary means of endowing the church in England; it seemed even more appropriate in an undeveloped colony, where land was both plentiful and likely to increase in value. Similar reserves were set aside for education and for the general revenue of the Crown. Use of the land was seen by the authorities as imposing little hardship on the people, who had done nothing to produce it. Even the American government, as late as 1787, instructed the Ohio and Scioto companies to set aside land for religious purposes. The chequer-board pattern familiar in Upper Canada was usual for such reserves, and the proportion of one in seven not uncommon.[3] Tithes, which would have impinged on the population much more directly, were also envisaged in the Constitutional Act, but on the advice of John Strachan, the most persistent defender of the reserves, they were ruled out for Upper Canada.

Even thus attenuated, the privileged position of the Church of England was bound ultimately to be resented. Its adherents constituted a relatively small proportion of the population, and many Upper Canadians were of a New England stock that had traditionally associated Anglicanism with royal oppression. The province was governed in its early years by oligarchies at both the provincial and local levels.[4] Official favour to the Church of England promised a clerical oligarchy as well, and experience already indicated that it would collaborate closely with existing élites. Land, which was to be the mainstay of the church, was also the chief source of political patronage and breeder of political scandal. To complete an almost infallible recipe for discord, the Constitutional Act assigned responsibility for the implementation of its religious clauses to the local legislature, with the usual provision for final review in London.

Precedents for objecting to special favour to particular churches were numerous and becoming more so. The first amendment to the constitution of the United States forbade the national establishment of religion. In England, Catholic emancipation was enacted in 1829 as the culmination of a long agitation. Dissenters saw their worst disabilities removed at about the same time and immediately began a campaign to get rid of those that remained. In 1829 the Scottish Seceders came out for the voluntary principle, which decreed that members alone should be responsible for the upkeep of their churches, and English dissenters soon took it up. Radicals such as Joseph Hume lent their support, and the establishment seemed in great danger. Upper Canadians of various churches were mainly concerned to preserve their own vested interests or to dispose of provisions that discriminated against them, but they could not fail to be aware of unrest elsewhere and eagerly seized on the arguments of controversialists on either side.[5]

First to be challenged were restrictions on the activities of denominations other than the Church of England. Exclusion from the parish cemetery and the necessity of resorting to a strange pastor at one of life's most solemn moments were painful blows to denominational self-esteem. Some restrictions also had serious practical consequences. At a time when most ministers eked out a meagre living, the inability to preside at marriages cut off the most lucrative source of additional income available. Similarly, a lack of provision for the corporate holding of property by some denominations left them at the mercy of individuals who might dispose of the property in unwelcome ways. The authorities offered no systematic defence of such Anglican monopolies when they were challenged, but rather followed a British tradition of making exceptions to meet particular hardships while leaving the general principle intact. In 1798, under pressure, the legislature extended the privilege of performing marriages to Calvinist and Lutheran ministers. The alleged intention was to accommodate those who were 'members of an establishment elsewhere' and thus persons of 'sober & regulated modes of thinking,'[6] though the result was also to admit revivalist American Baptists and even Tunkers. A similar approach was taken to the peculiar problems of the peace churches. Under special arrangements the state was able to recognize Quaker marriages, dispense with the taking of oaths, and provide alternatives to military service, though it exacted fines and imposed some civil disabilities in return. The result of such concessions was to leave the Methodists conspicuous outsiders, discriminated against partly because their loyalty was suspect and partly because the authorities were reluctant to recognize their societies as regularly constituted churches. Their right to hold land for church building was conceded in 1828. Despite eight successive attempts in the legislature beginning in 1802, however, Methodist ministers secured the right to perform marriages only in 1831.

The assault on the clergy reserves began with little fanfare. A common complaint was that the chequer-board pattern in which the reserves were scattered throughout the province inhibited the formation of continuous settlements and forced settlers further into the bush. When Robert Gourlay conducted the province's first public-opinion survey in 1817, many respondents placed the pre-emption of desirable land high on their list of grievances. As yet, however, the clergy reserves attracted less attention than the disposal of large tracts of land to government favourites.[7] In that same year Colonel Robert Nichol, whom we should describe today as a large-scale developer, made the first public attack on the reserves, but he proposed nothing more radical than the sale of some land to expedite settlement and the use of the proceeds to build churches. By this time, Strachan was becoming a leading figure in the official group popularly known as the Family Compact, along with some former students of his Cornwall school.[8] His passionate defence of the reserves made them a convenient target for critics of the Compact. The bitterness that came to characterize the controversy was due in large measure to the association of the reserves with a privileged oligarchy, and much of the storm gathered over Strachan's head.

The first serious challenge to the Anglican monopoly had a different motive, however. In 1819 the Presbyterians of Niagara-on-the-Lake, whose church had been destroyed during the war, requested a grant from the reserves or some other fund on the basis of the establishment of the Church of Scotland in the homeland. Although there was little doubt that the term 'Protestant clergy' normally designated in law those of the Church of England, the Presbyterians pointed out that a possible application to other established clergy had been suggested in the debate preceding the

Constitutional Act. There were no immediate consequences, for Strachan saw to it that Canadians were not informed of a ruling of the Crown's legal advisers that some of the proceeds could be so allocated. Representatives of the Kirk continued to press the issue, however, and for several years the clergy reserves controversy was essentially a struggle between two churches claiming the privileges of establishment. The provincial authorities resisted any suggestion of co-establishment, even when made by the British government, but arranged in 1826 that as a condition of its charter the colonizing Canada Company should make annual grants to both the Kirk and the Roman Catholic Church. It was the existence of these grants, not shared with the United Presbytery, that suggested the formation of the Kirk and United synods in 1831 and led to their ultimate union in 1840.

Meanwhile, however, questions had been raised about the propriety of government aid to churches on any terms. In 1825 the legislative assembly urged that the revenues from the reserves be used for educational purposes, and thereafter it pressed repeatedly for some form of secularization. In 1825 Strachan used a sermon on the death of Bishop Jacob Mountain as an occasion for urging greater public support of the church and defending its monopoly of the reserves; he argued that otherwise its good work would be undone by 'numbers of uneducated itinerant preachers, who, leaving their steady employment, betake themselves to preaching the Gospel from idleness, or a zeal without knowledge, by which they are induced without any preparation to teach what they do not know and which ... they disdain to learn.' Egerton Ryerson, then the junior Methodist preacher at York, replied early in 1826, at the urging of colleagues who sensed that Strachan's reference was to them. Not content merely to defend the Methodist reputation, he went on to rehearse at length current English nonconformist arguments against church establishments.[9]

The debate heated up in 1827 with the publication in the province of a chart purporting to show the relative numbers of ministers of various denominations Strachan had prepared from memory in England to rebut the claims of the Church of Scotland. Ryerson then compiled a chart of his own, as did J.C. Grant of the Kirk. All three charts were significant less for their accuracy than for their revelation of varied perceptions of which ministers deserved to be counted. In 1828 the province elected an assembly pledged to reform. The name by which it came to be known, the 'Saddle-bag Parliament,' indicated the unaccustomed political awareness to which Methodists had been roused. There followed an intense season of agitation by self-constituted bodies bearing such names as the 'York Central Committee against the Exclusive Claims of the Church of England' and the 'Friends of Religious Liberty.' The former group ensured that Joseph Hume made its grievances known to the House of Commons.

By the end of the 1820s a formidable coalition was taking shape in opposition to the use of the reserves for ecclesiastical purposes. It could count on the support not only of secularly motivated Reformers but of Baptists, American Presbyterians, Congregationalists, and apparently the great mass of Methodists. Presbyterians of the United Presbytery were also unhappy about the reserves, if only because they resented their exclusion from the proceeds. Nor did the campaign for secularization represent merely a ganging up on the Church of England, for such Anglican Reformers as Robert Baldwin played an essential role in it. During the 1830s this opposition would be substantially reinforced by the formation of the Seceders' Missionary Synod and the continuing Methodist Episcopal Church, and by the appearance of new immigrant Methodist bodies, all of which were committed to the voluntary principle. On its side, the British government was aware that it could not hold Upper Canada indefinitely in defiance of public opinion there. In 1828 a select committee of the House of Commons condemned the clergy reserve system, and the accession of the Whigs to power in 1830 boded further trouble for its defenders.

As if the reserves were not enough, another contentious issue was now before the province. In 1827 Strachan fulfilled a dream of long standing by securing a royal charter for a provincial university at York to be known as King's College. By the standards of the time its terms were liberal. Only Anglicans could be professors or members of the college council, but – well in advance of English practice – non-Anglicans could be students in arts though not in divinity. In Upper Canada, however, the prospect of a state-supported university under Anglican control stirred predictable indignation, which was not lessened by a provision that the rector of York should ex officio be president. Restrictions on enrolment in divinity in an era when candidates for the ministry made up a large proportion of the students of most universities was a further source of dissatisfaction. Debate would have been even more acrimonious if any immediate action had been taken to implement Strachan's charter. Instead Sir John Colborne, who became lieutenant-governor in 1829, diverted the available money to the foundation of Upper Canada College, which attracted mainly Anglican students but was not officially linked with the Church of England. The intrusion of the university question had the immediate effect of providing opponents of the reserves with one more grievance. In the long run it would help to demonstrate the existence of a remarkable diversity of interest among religious groups.

This diversity was not long in appearing, and with it evidence of the instability of the united front against the reserves. The steady expansion of the Kirk during the 1830s reinforced the ranks of the friends of establishment, and the hope of sharing in the reserves brought around most of the ministers of the old United Presbytery. Still upholding the principle of co-establishment, the Kirk now began to press for the appointment of an additional professor of divinity at King's College for Presbyterian students. Bishop Macdonell, who was both ideologically and temperamentally close to those in positions of power, had no desire for secularization so long as his church received its share of government subsidies. It was the promise of a government grant, likewise, that persuaded the British Wesleyans to return to the province in 1832. The extension of government largesse to denominations other than the Church of England was making them, in effect, friends of the system.[10]

After the union of 1833 a cooling of enthusiasm for reform among the Canadian Wesleyans, or at least among some of their most articulate leaders, was also distinctly noticeable. This was due in part to the direct influence of the British Wesleyans, who objected to agitation against the reserves in the columns of the *Christian Guardian*, a periodical that had been founded by the local Methodist Conference in 1829. In part it came about because Egerton Ryerson discovered on a trip to England that Hume and other radicals were not particularly friendly to revealed religion, and passed on his impressions in the *Guardian*. Mostly, however, it was the unintended result of Methodist involvement in the university question. In 1830 the Methodist conference resolved to found a seminary, Upper Canada Academy, that would be free both from sectarian teaching and from the élitism of Upper Canada College.[11] They commenced the project in a spirit of high idealism, and Reformers were prominent among those who rushed to offer their subscriptions. A belated realization that through its Wesleyan connection the conference was now receiving government money, along with widespread disapproval of the conservative trend of the leadership, caused a drying up of contributions that forced Ryerson in 1836 to seek a government grant. Of course, this grant was to be used for educational rather than religious purposes, but both friends and foes interpreted the application as evidence that the main Methodist body had abandoned its earlier voluntarism.

While individuals and groups moved to various middle positions, the extremes became more extreme. To William Lyon Mackenzie, who patronized various denominations but had all the marks of a Seceder, any deviation from strict voluntarism constituted a betrayal of the people. His campaign for secularization of the reserves reached its high-water mark in 1835 when a committee of the legislature under his chairmanship published the *Seventh Report on Grievances*, which castigated all denominations caught enjoying government bounty. The campaign was showing signs of running down when renewed government favour to the Church of England came to Mackenzie's rescue. In 1832 the British House of Commons, seeking to meet Hume's criticism, announced that parliamentary grants to the SPG would be phased out over a four-year period. The clergy reserves became more important than ever to the colonial church, but their revenues were not sufficient to prevent a reduction in the salaries of existing missionaries at a time when the expansion of the population was calling for the appointment of many more. As his term of office was closing in 1836, Colborne sought at least to secure some revenues to existing parishes by setting up fifty-seven rectories, of which only forty-four were ready for signing. He had had this action in mind for several years, and believed himself to be acting within the instructions he had received from the colonial office. In England, induction as a rector conveyed ecclesiastical jurisdiction over the population of a parish. Colborne insisted, despite contrary advice from the executive council, that the rectories should consist only of endowed glebe lands, some taken from the clergy reserves, and thus should give their incumbents no jurisdiction over non-Anglicans. In the province's excited state, however, his action suggested not only the compounding of unequal treatment but the imminent danger of a clerically dominated society. As the threat of bishops had been a major factor in precipitating the American Revolution, so, in the opinion of Lord Durham, was that of rectors in inducing in radical reformers the desperation of 1837.[12]

The rebellion and the bitterness that followed it had disastrous effects on church life in many parts of the province. A posse of loyalists sacked the peaceful Quaker settlement of Yarmouth in revenge for the involvement of a few inhabitants in the uprising. John Roaf, the pastor of Zion Congregational Church in Toronto, reported that his 'radical chapel' had been 'shaken to the very centre.' Several prominent Methodist Episcopals, including a son of Bishop John Reynolds, were arrested for complicity, and some of their ministers fled the province. Even among the Canadian Wesleyans, few of whom had been involved in the rebellion, a number were so discouraged by the atmosphere of repression that followed its defeat that they organized the Mississippi Emigration Society to encourage settlement in Iowa. The York congregation did not recover from this exodus for some years, and even the dissolution of the union with the British could be regarded as a by-product of the rebellion. American Presbyterian missions were temporarily broken up, and at least a few prominent lay members followed their pastors out of the province. Strachan reported more cheerfully in 1841 that a new mood of loyalism assured Anglican priests of a welcome where previously they had found it scarcely safe to visit.[13]

Surprisingly, compromises that previously had seemed impossible were brought to fruition during these years of extreme polarization. Amendments to the charter of King's College by the provincial legislature in 1837 reduced the measure of Anglican control and removed all religious tests, except in divinity, beyond an affirmation of the Trinity. They satisfied few Reformers, but at least made possible the erection of a building in 1842 and the commencement of classes in 1843. Proposals for breaking the long-standing deadlock on the clergy reserves were also beginning to circulate. By the middle of the 1830s Methodists, Roman Catholics, and two brands of Presbyterians were all receiving government aid, though from the casual and territorial revenue of the province rather than from the clergy reserves. If some means could be found to satisfy these groups, the voluntarist denominations would be hopelessly outnumbered. The willingness of the Roman Catholics and the two major Presbyterian bodies was well known, and in 1837 the Wesleyan Conference intimated that despite some unhappiness about the principle of government aid it had no desire to be left out of a division. William Bettridge and Benjamin Cronyn, Anglican clergymen on a money-raising tour in England, proposed unofficially in that year that the Churches of England and Scotland should have a prior claim on the reserves and that the remainder should be divided among the other denominations.[14] The authorities did not thank them for their effort, but in the wake of disturbances in Upper Canada the new governor-general, Charles P. Thomson, made a similar proposal. It was acceptable only to the denominations already mentioned, but in 1840 it was enacted into law.

Returning to Cobourg from a missionary anniversary at Kingston in February 1842, Egerton Ryerson discovered that one of his fellow passengers on the coach was John Strachan, now bishop of Toronto. Ryerson wrote of his old antagonist, whom he had not previously met, that one could not 'desire to meet with a more affable, agreeable man.' The Methodists had recently succeeded in securing legislation transforming Upper Canada Academy into Victoria College, and Ryerson had been named its first principal. One of the topics that came up for discussion on the long coach ride was the college's financial state, which was bad. Strachan had some practical advice to offer. An annual grant would give the institution insufficient security. Instead, since the Methodists now 'had as much right to a portion of the Clergy lands as the Church of England' and did not wish to have government support for their ministers, they should go after such support for the college. After parting with his new friend, Ryerson reflected that 'the settlement of the Clergy Reserve Question had annihilated the principal causes of difference between those individuals and bodies in the Province who had been most hostile to each other.'[15]

In fact, the 'Clergy Reserve Question' was not settled, nor was the question of the university. There would have to be one more series of convulsions before the churches could settle down to their normal pursuits. Already, however, several views of the proper relations of church and state had been set before the people of Upper Canada. At one extreme were the advocates of the official establishment of a particular form of religion, which should be ensured the privileges and perquisites that would make its role clearly visible to all. At the other were the voluntarists, who insisted that it was improper for the state to subsidize any religious organization under any circumstances. In between were those who might occasionally use the language of separation but whose chief concern was that their own denomination should be treated equitably. While in public debate the advocates of various positions commonly relied on legal and expedient arguments,[16] statements were made in the course of controversy that offer significant insights into the religious and ideological attitudes that underlay them.

Among the propositions so vigorously argued in the early nineteenth century, the one that an Ontarian of the late twentieth century is likely to find most dificult to take seriously is that which held that the state ought to choose one or more churches for special recognition. Today it seems so evidently wrong that our natural tendency is to assume that those who advocated it in early years did so from blind prejudice or (to adopt a favourite twentieth-century explanation) in the hope of personal gain. Prejudice and self-interest undoubtedly played their parts, but it is also clear that to its advocates the concept of church establishment was logically compelling. If only because its arguments have long since ceased to persuade, this is the position that most urgently calls for elucidation.

Belief in some form of religious establishment came naturally to those who retained something of the older organic view of society. For a millennium and a half it had been assumed that the states of Europe were Christian, and in a Christian state it was natural both for a monarch to promote the welfare of the church and for a bishop to inculcate loyalty to the state. In England, where the established church could not rest its claims on the unanimity that had been assumed during the Middle Ages, there were special reasons for valuing its presence. Its freedom from papal authority, which since Elizabethan times had been associated with the threat of foreign conquest, enabled it to be a rallying-point for national sentiment. At the same time its decency and good order interposed a barrier against the 'enthusiasm' which since the Puritan ascendancy had threatened to overturn the foundations of English society. To a great many of its members and especially of its clergy, indeed, any other system was scarcely conceivable. Accordingly there was a deeply ingrained conviction that an Anglican minister was a 'parson' in a sense that a dissenting preacher could never be, and was therefore entitled to a competency that would enable him to uphold the dignity of his office. Though he saw no objection to pew-rents, William Bettridge was sure that no self-respecting clergyman would want 'a yearly or half-yearly *begging sheet* going round among his people.'[17]

State endowment could also be urged as a necessary resource for missionary outreach. Even if a voluntary system was preferable in theory, supporters argued, it would inevitably fail in Upper Canada until provincial society reached a more advanced stage of development. They were convinced that it had already failed in the United States, with a result described by one writer as 'the almost total extinction of Christianity.' If the provision of government aid could not be shown to have produced much better results in Canada, this was because it had been given on too niggardly a scale. In such circumstances the provision of the facilities of a national church was a matter of sacred duty to the poor, whose claims on the mother country were all the greater since their removal to Upper Canada had in many cases relieved English taxpayers of the burden of their support. The clincher in this line of argument was a reminder that clergy of the Church of England were supported out of imperial funds and thus cost Canadians nothing beyond the expense of maintaining church buildings.[18]

Seen in such terms, the establishment principle could be defended by people who had been deeply affected by the evangelical and missionary spirit of the age. Thomas Chalmers, the leader of the evangelical party in the Church of Scotland, upheld it with such vigour that in 1838 he was invited to England to defend the establishment there against tractarian attacks. Many of his arguments were identical with those used by Strachan, who had been a boyhood friend and continued to correspond with him regularly. 'Free enterprise' in religion was doomed to failure, he insisted, because religion is not a natural taste and therefore needs to be stimulated from without. In a Christian society this responsibility devolves on the state, which would be remiss if it failed to put its resources at God's disposal. We even find in Chalmers the assurance, often ridiculed when urged by Strachan in the Upper Canadian setting, that the ministrations of a state church had only to be provided in order to be welcomed.[19]

Such arguments might serve the advocates of establishment with more or less plausibility, but a more urgent consideration was the contribution establishment could make to keeping Upper Canada in British hands. Strachan and the former students who surrounded him had devoted themselves without stint to the defence of the province during the War of 1812, and they did not propose to see it lost because disaffected preachers were allowed to sow seeds of sedition unchecked. Without the steadying influence of the Church of England, Strachan wrote, the province was 'certain to become a moral waste and a hotbed of sedition and discontent.'

To those imbued with the traditions of Christendom the issue of loyalty was not merely political but had transcendent implications. George Petrie reported a widespread impression that 'preachers who disseminate Disaffection to the British Crown, cannot be well affected to the throne of Him "by whom Kings reign and Princes decree Judgment."'[20]

Whereas virtually the entire Anglican clergy would have endorsed the foregoing arguments, another factor gave a particular edge to the advocacy of such as Strachan. During much of the eighteenth century the Church of England, despite its social conservatism, had been unpopular not only with the common people but with many of the privileged. Only in later years, especially after the American and French revolutions, was it able to forge alliances with the aristocracy and gentry and with the wealthier segment of the professional and business classes. The resulting conviction that the well-being of society depended on the co-operation of recognized élites in both church and state was still novel enough to inspire intense commitment among true believers. Simcoe was one of these, but his regime was brief. Sustained agitation began only in the 1820s when, in collaboration with Lieutenant-Governor Sir Peregrine Maitland, who was another true believer, Strachan was able to replace an earlier Kirk majority on the executive council with a solidly Anglican one. Among people of this mentality the prevalence of dissent, with its threat of democratic levelling, induced a sense of crisis that made them seem more conservative than they really were. They were also capable of interpreting their vision in messianic terms. Let the state provide adequate support for the church in Upper Canada, Strachan urged, and the ultimate blessings would extend far beyond its borders and 'the whole earth become the garden of the Lord.'[21]

Voluntarism was a natural stance for religious bodies that had to depend on their own resources, but it took a long time to emerge as a systematically formulated program. Early English dissenters, regarding themselves as witnesses against a false church, had hoped for national recognition and under Oliver Cromwell had briefly received it. Their immediate successors were content to minister to a limited constituency, the 'dissenting interest,' while leaving larger issues to the national church. Even the Wesleyan Methodists regarded themselves at first as essentially an auxiliary of the Church of England and accordingly welcomed state aid in Upper Canada and New South Wales alike. With the fading of the perception of Christendom as a seamless whole – an end dramatically signalled by the American and French revolutions – new approaches became possible and even inescapable. The state was increasingly perceived as essentially profane, as resting on a social contract rather than on divine institution. Religion, as a corollary, was left in almost undisputed possession of the realm of private belief and behaviour. That advocates of official neutrality in religious matters were often individuals of exemplary piety was no coincidence. Hostility to any suggestion of collaboration between church and state was especially strong among the laity, many of whom were quick to suspect the motives of clergy who sought favours from the state. Upper Canadians showed little inclination to pay decent stipends to their ministers, but were overcome with righteous indignation when those ministers sullied their hands with government money. In 1835 Edward Marsh of the American Home Missionary Society reported (with some glee, one senses) that several ministers of the United Synod had been driven from their pulpits after accepting state aid.[22] The drying up of grassroots support for Upper Canada Academy after Ryerson's break with the radical Reformers indicates the presence of similar feelings among Methodists, and O'Grady's collaboration with these Reformers suggests that many Roman Catholics also inclined to voluntarism.

Despite the poverty or parsimony of Upper Canadian congregations, voluntarism owed much of its credibility to growing evidence that people were prepared to give generously if their imaginations were stirred. Just when the establishment principle seemed to have exhausted its vitality, there was a great outburst of voluntary religious activity. Its expressions will be examined in greater detail in the next chapter, but references to the explosion of missionary activity in the early nineteenth century have already suggested the magnitude of its impact. Within Protestantism such activism was largely a product of evangelical revival. Though some evangelicals of Chalmers's stature could continue to defend establishment, therefore, the weight of the movement was against it if only because it was demonstrating so dramatically the possibilities of voluntary action.

To strict voluntarists the right path was obvious; one should 'render to Caesar the things that are Caesar's, and to God the things that are God's.' In 1835 a Seceder gave unambiguous expression to a conviction that would command broader consent today than it did then: 'Let the magistrate protect the natural & civil rights of the subject – let him defend every person in the due exercise of his religion – let him maintain the rights of conscience – and we may conceive that he has discharged his duty as far as he is concerned with religious affairs in his official capacity.' Yet this apparently clear-cut statement raised a question that has still not been answered to everyone's satisfaction: precisely how and where does one draw the line between the realms of Caesar and God? In the early nineteenth century it occurred to few Upper Canadians that official neutrality in religious matters might imply the removal of the Bible from school curricula or indifference to Sabbath observance on the part of the state. In 1824 the legislature allocated £150 to establish Sunday schools in indigent settlements, and ten years later it authorized not only a chaplain for the penitentiary at Kingston but a Bible for each prisoner there.[23] The demarcation of such debatable areas as education and social welfare would not easily be achieved.

Advocates of the middle road of shared government bounty represented a wide range of points of view. Those seeking special recognition for their own churches shared many attitudes current in the Church of England, and pleaded their own eligibility for support on similar grounds. Representatives of the Kirk claimed that their establishment north of the Tweed entitled them to co-establishment in a province that was British rather than English, and Macdonell once described Roman Catholicism as the 'established religion of the Country' in view of its recognition at the time of the conquest. Both were careful to remind the government of their proved loyalty. Even when such arguments were not readily available, churches without settled conscientious objections tended to look to the state when funds ran low. The most unlikely candidate for such help was David Willson, who informed the legislative assembly of his prayers for 'the conversion of the members of the Church of England and the Kirk of Scotland' and went on to request five hundred pounds for the completion of his temple in view of the inadequacy of private donations. Perhaps the most revealing sign of the times, however, was an increasing tendency to insist that no favours were being asked that would not willingly be conceded to all.[24] Whatever theories of church and state might be proposed, it was becoming evident that most Upper Canadians thought of their churches as having equal rights to existence and support.

Any appraisal of the effects of the controversies of the 1820s and 1830s on the religion of Ontarians must at this stage be tentative. Some of the sharpest exchanges were still to come. Many new proposals would have to be made, and some dramatic changes of position take place, before anything like a permanent settlement could be arranged. Nevertheless, the period would be remembered as one that embroiled the various religious groups in issues on which they would ultimately have to come to some mutual understanding. Most significantly, it raised questions that would have to be answered in terms not only of political solutions but of the implications of religious belief for participation in the broader life of society.

That the religious controversies of this period played a formative role in the politics of the province is beyond question. No one familiar with party alignments was unaware that Baptists could be counted on to vote the Reform ticket or that defenders of Anglican privileges were almost uniformly Tory. This state of affairs came about not only because the platforms of these parties appealed to members of various religious denominations but also because the interplay of religious interests helped to bring the parties themselves into existence. By the same token, denominations that divided on the religious issue tended to be split in their party allegiance. One must be careful not to overstate the case. The frequent alternation between Tory and Reform majorities in the legislature indicated that many Upper Canadians had not yet arrived at settled views on such questions as the clergy reserves, or else that secular issues were decisive in determining their votes. It is clear, too, that the rank and file of such denominations as the Methodists did not always follow the advice of their leaders on political matters. The basic point remains valid: party structures rested on religious bases. Issues and alignments would change, but their religious underpinnings would remain significant even into the twentieth century.

The effects of the controversy on religion were more subtle, and even more difficult to measure. On balance, it probably strengthened the religious bodies that maintained an unambiguously voluntarist position. A number of their supporters left Upper Canada both before and after the rebellion because of what they saw as an oppressive political climate, and the extremism of their attacks on constituted authority alienated others. The voluntarist Methodist Episcopals gained steadily at the expense of the compromising Wesleyans, however, and a remarkable Baptist ingathering of members was reported to have commenced in 1838.[25] Otherwise, these denominations were probably least affected by the controversy. They went into it with their minds made up, and nothing in the course of it suggested any reason to change them. The necessity of emphasizing the separateness of church and state, however, may well have made them more reticent on public issues that could not be described in clear moral terms. Certainly, their publications of the period expressed little interest in the general development of the province.

Anglicans experienced the controversy as a drain on energy that failed to yield commensurate rewards. Virtually their entire clergy agreed that state aid to the church was both legitimate and desirable. Many became increasingly unhappy with the high line taken by Strachan and his associates, however, for they recognized that it was bringing the church into disrepute. John Leeds, an SPG missionary at Fort Erie, wrote in 1828, 'The very anxiety of the authorities to promote the Church in the Province seems to defeat its own end by strengthening a suspicion that prevails that it is an Instrument in the hands of the Government.' In East Flamborough agitators who raised the cry of 'Tithes! Tithes! Rates! Rates!' in opposition to the holding of Anglican services made the same point less elegantly. However reluctantly, Anglicans were beginning to suspect that eventually they would have to operate as voluntarists. Strachan, despite his dogged advocacy of establishment, was one of the first to do so. As early as 1832 he was exploring the possibility of involving the laity in money-raising and thus in decision-making.[26]

For those occupying a middle position, and for none more than the Canadian Wesleyans, the period was one of heart-searching. Most members were embarrassed by the government grant that came to their church as an unanticipated by-product of their union with the British. Almost all were embarrassed that Methodists should be concerned with politics at all, for in their view, expressed by Egerton Ryerson himself in the course of his controversy with Strachan, 'those divines who are constantly dabbling in politics are a disgrace to the church and a pestilence to their parishioners.' Edwy Ryerson expressed the matter even more succinctly in a letter to his brother: 'politics run high, and religion low.'[27] Unlike most other denominations, the Methodists had inherited no fixed principles on the legitimacy of state support for religion. Their roots in the American Methodist Episcopal church made them suspicious of it, but John Wesley had given no clear guidance and the British saw no harm in it. By 1840 the Canadian Wesleyans were content, for the most part, to leave the issue to others.

Perhaps the most enduring legacy of the period was a mythology that became deeply embedded in the Ontario consciousness and helped to shape the images that various denominations projected to themselves and others. In this mythology the central figures were John Strachan and Egerton Ryerson. Strachan was essentially what he was remembered as being, an uncompromising advocate of Anglican ascendancy, though the myth-makers commonly forgot his amiability and his generosity when a matter of principle was not at stake. Ryerson probably always was a voluntarist of sorts, but along the way he made compromises that alienated thorough-going reformers and shocked many of his fellow Methodists. No matter; what was remembered was the debate of 1826 in which an iconoclastic probationer for the ministry had bearded the venerable archdeacon of York. Methodists continued to think of themselves as giant-killers long after they had become the province's wealthiest religious community. Anglicans were apologetic in public for Strachan's arrogance toward other denominations, but inwardly they knew that he had merely been tactless in expressing an obvious truth.

7 New Measures

While political parsons were wrangling over the clergy reserves, the religious life of Upper Canada was showing signs of considerable maturity and sophistication. In townships back of Lake Ontario and in the Huron tract, to be sure, pioneer conditions persisted into the 1830s and beyond; writing from one of the newer settlements, Featherstone Lake Osler graphically described a service held in a barn where accommodation was so limited that many worshippers could follow the proceedings only by peeking through cracks in the hayloft. Older sections of the province, some of which had been settled fifty or even eighty years previously, had shed most of their frontier characteristics. Anson Green, a prominent Methodist minister, observed in 1829 that roads had improved to the point where his colleagues were beginning to secure buggies and sleighs, and in 1836 that those in circuits around the Bay of Quinte were driving gigs.[1]

The most visible evidence of change was the appearance of more numerous and imposing church buildings. A natural process whereby pioneers provided themselves with successively more substantial homes was hastened in the case of churches, which first appeared near the international boundary, by the destruction wrought by the War of 1812. Throughout the 1820s newspapers carried frequent reports of dedications, and some of the churches built during the 1830s were very substantial. The first Methodist meeting-house in York, erected in 1819, was recalled by John Carroll as 'then without a fence around it – unpainted – and stood up from the ground on some blocks which supplied the place of foundations, while the wind whistled and howled beneath.'[2] Its successor, erected on Adelaide Street in 1832, not only seated a thousand people but incorporated a kitchen, an infants' room, and several meeting rooms. Even so, it had to share pride of place with Saint James's Episcopal, Saint Andrew's Kirk, and Saint Paul's Roman Catholic.

With increased prosperity came also a desire for elegance. Most pioneer structures were starkly utilitarian, though builders commonly incorporated remembered features of churches elsewhere. A number of architects entered the province after the war, and even in their absence pattern-books were often available to builders. Episcopalians at first favoured the Georgian style of the homeland as illustrating an attitude to religion at once familiar and respectful. Saint Andrew's Kirk at Williamstown, begun in 1812, was predominantly in the same tradition. A few congregations, such as Saint Andrew's Presbyterian at Niagara-on-the-Lake, imported the Greek Revival style popular across the border. Roman Catholics preferred gilt and gingerbread, at least in areas where Macdonell's influence prevailed. By the 1830s, however, the upward lift of Gothic was almost universally favoured. Many rural congregations, less affluent than those in the towns, began their building projects just in time to be caught up in the vogue for it.[3]

Worship generally followed familiar patterns, though few congregations would have tolerated the disorders common in earlier years. William Lyon Mackenzie, attending a Methodist service at York, observed with evident surprise that 'none of those indecorous interruptions for which Methodists are, (as we think, *justly*) blamed, ever occurred.' In almost every denomination the sermon was the *pièce de résistance*. If we may judge from published examples, the usual production of the time would be regarded today as unacceptably ponderous and disappointingly short on illustration. Although Anglicans were sometimes accused of short-changing their congregations, Osler estimated that his sermons ran on the average to two and a half hours. Methodists were distinguished mainly by the urgency of their appeals; one service drew from Green the approving comment 'not a moment lost.' In the absence of many competing attractions, preachers were heard with both delight and discrimination; even Protestants are said to have flocked to hear O'Grady.[4] Outside the Roman Catholic Church, sacramental services were infrequent occasions. Some Presbyterians of Scottish background carried over the tradition of a prolonged annual communion. Otherwise, quarterly administration of the eucharist was usual, and a few Anglicans and Methodists were moving to a monthly observance.

The most striking developments were in music. Choirs (then often called bands) were becoming general in most denominations, despite objections from some Scots, and a few congregations employed singing masters. The first denominationally approved tune-book, the Methodists' *Sacred Harmony,* was published by Alexander Davidson in the midst of the turmoil that followed the rebellion. Its contents, though not all of the highest musical quality, reflected the respectable taste of the period. Singing schools, which operated beyond church walls but concentrated on sacred music, drilled enthusiastic members in arrangements of a difficulty that few congregations would attempt today. Musical instruments were welcomed by congregations that could afford them, Scottish Presbyterians again excepted. Flutes, flageolets, and melodeons were among those used; the designation 'Kirk fiddle' saved the bass viol from the opprobrium associated with the variety that set the feet moving. The Children of Peace were the first to commission the building of a pipe-organ.[5]

Churches were providing themselves with many of the appurtenances to which we are now accustomed. Sunday schools were becoming usual, midweek groups familiar, and social gatherings increasingly popular. A well-stocked library was part of the essential equipment of the Sunday school; its books circulated among adults and children alike. As late as 1859 Sunday school libraries were five times as numerous as all others combined and contained more than triple the number of volumes. The books were largely imported, but Upper Canadians gradually came to feel a need for literature with local content. In 1819–20 Strachan issued the province's first religious periodical, the *Christian Recorder*, taking such an irenic line that a correspondent wondered whether the editor was really an Anglican. The next and most successful journal was the *Christian Guardian*, founded in 1829 as one of the first undertakings of the independent Canadian Methodist church. Comparable in importance to the paper itself, in the long run, were the books and tracts that were printed on the press secured for it. During the 1830s religious journals were attempted by almost every denomination of any size. Most of them soon ceased publication, leaving few traces in the provincial memory, but some represented considerable effort on the part of spare-time editors and demanded an impressive level of theological literacy from their readers. The same decade saw the chartering in 1836 of the Methodists' Upper Canada Academy, which forswore the imparting of any system of theology but hoped to cultivate leaders of 'virtuous principle and Christian morals.'[6] In 1838 the Roman Catholics laid the foundation of what would become Regiopolis College in Kingston, and in 1841 the Kirk compensated for its failure to secure a chair of divinity at King's College by setting up Queen's University.

Consciences were slowly being awakened to the needs of an emerging class of urban poor. Protestants, while acknowledging aid to the unfortunate as a Christian duty, generally assumed that responsibility for it belonged to the community at large. Most charities of the time were designed to meet the immediate needs of immigrants, many of whom arrived in distressing circumstances. Clergy were usually prominent on the charities' committees, which were often constituted with a view to denominational balance. The Kingston Compassionate Committee, formed in 1817, was a representative body chaired by G. O. Stuart, the local Anglican rector. The Society for the Relief of Strangers in Distress, founded at York in the same year, was set up on a similar basis although with less prominent clerical representation. When cholera struck in 1832, it was Strachan who organized the Society for the Relief of the Orphan, Widow, and Fatherless. Like other such agencies, this was not intended for the relief of the able-bodied, who were assumed to have both the obligation and the ability to fend for themselves. Its chief activity was the binding out of orphans as servants and apprentices; 'in this manner,' Strachan piously suggested, 'much of the bitterness of this sad dispensation would be removed by Christian love.'[7]

These and other signs of aggressive religious activity, in part natural results of the growing wealth and maturity of the province, also reflected, as in so many other cases, the reception of new impulses from without. By the early nineteenth century, evangelicalism had become a well-organized movement that was vigorously promoting a comprehensive program in all English-speaking countries. Its appeal, especially to those well situated in society and government, had been greatly enhanced by the French Revolution, which seemed to place in jeopardy the often neglected religious values on which British society was believed to rest. It took shape mainly in Britain, and its ambitious design was further developed in the United States and gradually percolated into Upper Canada. Leaders on both sides of the Atlantic maintained regular contact with one another, and information about effective methods and materials passed readily across national borders.[8]

Central to the evangelical program was the cultivation of a conversion experience by which individuals would be brought, consciously and usually instantaneously, into an assurance of faith in Christ. Evangelicals might call themselves Calvinists or Arminians, but almost without exception they were convinced that appropriate means might help to induce conversion, and they moved heaven and earth to promote those means. A favourite method was the dissemination of literature – Bibles, manuals of devotion, and tracts with urgent and usually pathetic messages – that would awaken a hunger for salvation. More direct pressure could be applied in prayer meetings and rallies, where the example and influence of those already converted could be brought into play. The Sunday school, at first mainly a vehicle of working-class education, was gradually infiltrated and turned to evangelical purposes. Supporters, many of them women, were gathered into auxiliary societies and set to work raising money or distributing tracts. Evangelicals were remarkably innovative in their methods, and introduced techniques that have been adopted almost universally by voluntary organizations and in some cases by businesses:

the every-person canvass, the well-planned convention, the personalizing of appeals by the use of anecdotes, and perhaps above all the mass production of printed materials at low, fixed prices. For the most part these enterprises were kept free from direct control by the churches. Although churches reaped the benefits, the leadership was predominantly lay and the approach deliberately non-sectarian.

While individual conversion was the immediate aim, the ultimate hope was for the renovation of society on a Christian basis. Vices, especially the more blatant ones, were singled out for spccial attack. Every effort was made to relieve those, whether blacks, prisoners, or factory hands, who were subjected to intolerable hardships. Nor were the benefits of the program to be limited to Christendom, for the missionary dimension of the movement pointed to the creation of a new world order. By the end of the period, indeed, the outward thrust of evangelical Christianity was raising hopes that history was about to reach its culmination in the return of Christ to earth to inaugurate his millennial reign. In other respects the vision was more limited. A happy death or resigning oneself to untoward circum-stances was the solution to the problems of the poor suggested in tract after tract.

Relying heavily at first on British literature and experience, American evangelicals gradually introduced significant innovations. Charles G. Finney, drawing on earlier revivalist experience, systematized methods of direct approach, such as house-to-house visitation, concerted prayer for specific individuals, and the anxious bench in front of the preacher's podium for inquirers, into what came to be known as 'new measures' of evangelism. He also helped to popularize opposition to alcoholic bever-ages – a particularly American emphasis – by encouraging abstinence as a helpful step towards conversion and insisting on it as a test of genuine commitment. Programs of evangelism and of related 'benevolences' were pressed by non-sectarian agencies that expanded from bases in Boston, New York, or Philadelphia to become national organizations. The largest of these – the AHMS, the American Bible Society, and the American Sunday School Union – pioneered the use of itinerant paid agents, a large proportion of whom were deployed in what was regarded as the immensely strategic western hinterland. Having reached the height of its influence during the early 1830s, this ambitious co-operative effort virtually collapsed in 1837 when the Tappan brothers of New York, who had been its leading organizers and backers, suffered heavy losses in a financial crash.

Upper Canada, which before the War of 1812 had already been caught up in an earlier phase of evangelical revival through the efforts of Methodist itinerants and other American preachers, began to be affected by the movement's later manifestations after the war's close. The British origins of this new wave of evangelicalism were reflected in the spurt of missionary initiative that resulted in the entry of the British Wesleyans, the Glasgow Colonial Society, the Bishop of Quebec's Travelling Missionary Fund, the Upper Canada Clergy Society, the Colonial Missionary Society of the Congregational Union, and the Canada Baptist Missionary Society. Its American aspect was represented most conspicuously by the AHMS. Local activities and attitudes were affected by both British and American influences, but most dramatically by revivalist techniques that readily made their way across the border.

Upper Canadians were applying many of the American new measures well before Finney systematized them. Methodists singled out individuals for prayer at a major revival at Elizabethtown in 1817, and in 1824 their newly constituted conference called on itinerants to observe a monthly day of prayer and fasting. AHMS missionaries imported the whole package, and others followed their example. In 1832 the mourner's bench was in use at a Primitive Methodist watch-night service, and in 1835 a concert of prayer for revival, house-to-house visitation, and particular attention to individuals helped to promote a revival at Normandale. The measure that made the most lasting impression in Upper Canada was the protracted meeting, originally a four-day affair but eventually continued as long as interest could be sustained 'in order never to let the fire go out.'[9] For several decades a staple of evangelistic outreach, it had the particular advantage in the Ontario climate of extending the benefits of the camp meeting over the entire year.

Fervent revival has commonly been regarded as a frontier phenomenon that subsided or retreated to the backwoods as society settled down, but it has recently been argued that evangelists were just hitting their stride in the 1830s. During that decade the Wesleyan Methodists reported more successful evangelistic campaigns than ever before, though they were also losing members at an unprecedented rate through controversy and schism. The first large-scale revival under Baptist auspices, described as 'one of the best,' occurred only in 1836. When old-timers looked back in nostalgia, they complained of a loss not of fervour but of simplicity and close fellowship. 'Paroxysms' of ecstasy reported at a protracted meeting near Belleville recalled the first raptures of the 1790s, and outbursts of tears at a similar gathering in Brockville anticipated a typically Victorian way of showing emotion.[10]

The direct approach to the unconverted was supplemented by well-tried aids to evangelism. Bible societies, of which the province's first was formed at Niagara in 1816, initially concentrated on the provision of the Scriptures in Gaelic and German and on translation into Indian languages.

The Upper Canada Bible Society also placed Bibles in the local jail, while laying down stringent provisions for securing them against theft. For the dissemination of other literature, almost every religious organization promoted the formation of libraries attached to churches, voluntary societies, or Sunday schools. The literature thus made available had little secular content, but consisted mainly of denominational materials and tracts from the evangelical mill. In 1822 the Methodists founded the first local missionary society,[11] and other denominations soon followed their example. Missionary annual meetings or 'anniversaries' became highly publicized occasions that called for the most eminent speakers. On a less formal basis, tea meetings combined social fellowship with appeals for the missionary cause.

The centrepiece of the evangelical program was the Sunday school. Having originated in Britain as a charitable endeavour to provide elementary schooling for slum children, it was rapidly transformed in North America into a means of bringing together children of all social classes for religious instruction. At first it was regarded as an institution distinct from the churches, and this pattern was carried over into Upper Canada; by 1826 Norfolk had a county-wide non-denominational society for founding Sunday schools and supplying them with books. Methods suggesting a Pavlovian system of rewards and punishments were designed to drive home religious lessons. At Vittoria each child in attendance had the privilege of borrowing for a week a tract 'selected not only with a view to the instruction of the child but also with a reference to the circumstances, the character or the vices of the parents.' Promptness and memory work were rewarded with tickets that could be exchanged for 'useful little books' that would drum in still further the lessons learned in class. The seriousness with which such instruction was taken is indicated by the rules of the York Methodist Episcopal Sunday School, which provided that volunteer teachers could be fined for missing sessions and expelled for three absences. By 1832 an estimated ten thousand pupils were enrolled in some 350 schools in Upper Canada.[12]

The Sunday school soon proved itself too useful to be confined within the mould of non-sectarian evangelicalism. At Kingston and York Anglicans and Methodists maintained separate schools from the outset, though at York the practice of holding common examinations and occasional joint sessions recalled the extra-ecclesial origin of the institution. In 1829 the Roman Catholics of the Gore of Toronto organized a Sunday school, and in 1840 the Mennonites set up near Hespeler their first Sunday school in North America. Isaac Fidler, who resided briefly in Upper Canada during 1832, reported that denominations maintained their own schools except where population was sparse. As late as 1867, however, 216 of 721 schools reported to the Wesleyan Methodist conference were still being run on union lines.[13] Evidently the older tradition of lay-operated union schools lingered on, and one may fairly surmise that the older evangelicalism lingered on in them.

In both Britain and the United States, evangelicals of the early nineteenth century launched campaigns against almost every conceivable sin. With one exception, these causes failed to generate great excitement in Upper Canada before the 1840s. Occasional anathemas were directed against Sunday mails, stage plays, and Freemasonry, but usually from the pulpit rather than from the public platform. Simcoe took the first steps toward the elimination of slavery from the province, and Bishop Stewart substituted maple for cane sugar to avoid supporting it. Most Upper Canadians condemned slavery, but little public agitation ensued. When Luther Lee, a prominent American Methodist abolitionist, visited the Canadian Wesleyan conference of 1838, the conference invited him to speak but declined to accept his credentials as a delegate of the Utica Anti-Slavery Convention, which another American visitor described as 'illegitimate and revolutionary in its tendency.' Lee claimed that the Canadians sympathized with his position, but an English abolitionist journal accused Ryerson in 1840 of systematically excluding discussion of slavery from the *Christian Guardian* in order not to offend the American church.[14] However sympathetic Canadian Wesleyans may have been to the cause, they had particular reason to avoid giving offence at a time when they were contending with the continuing Methodist Episcopals for recognition by the parent church. A few Upper Canadians were more outspoken, but most Protestant churches were reluctant to break relations with supportive American bodies.

The notable exception to this inactivity on the social front was the battle against strong drink. Upper Canada's first temperance society was founded in 1828 in Leeds County, and by 1832 about one hundred local societies were recorded. Originally, temperance organizations had represented an exercise in self-help by workingmen who wanted to break a debilitating habit, and in a society where the reduction of drinking had obvious social utility, economic and medical arguments continued to be stressed. By the time the movement reached Upper Canada from the United States, however, Finney and Lyman Beecher had co-opted it for the evangelical crusade. Canadian temperance organizations drew their membership mainly from the respectable elements of society, and stressed the religious aspects of the movement. The Methodist Episcopal Conference organized itself into a temperance society in 1830, and several Presbyterian congregations of American background adopted total abstinence as a condition of membership. What has been called 'the coercion of

voluntarism' was sometimes in evidence, as at Brockville where Anson
Green and William Smart inveigled a local merchant into the chair of a
temperance meeting and then succeeded in placing him in a position where
he was practically dragooned into forswearing the sale of liquor.[15]

The campaign against alcohol embraced two distinct but overlapping
stages. The original pledge exacted abstinence only from 'ardent spirits,'
which Wesley had condemned but which most early preachers of all
denominations were accustomed to imbibe. Even after the inception of the
temperance crusade, a pious Methodist merchant received an apology for
the quality of the beer supplied by his wholesaler. By the mid-1830s,
however, a teetotal pledge was being widely demanded, and there was
even 'interference, in some places, with the vinous beverage of the Lord's
Supper.' In western New York the result of this thoroughness was an
estimated loss of 40 per cent of the membership of temperance societies,
and Upper Canadians seem to have been similarly unwilling to accept
draconian measures. There was, however, a perceptible tightening of
licensing laws.[16]

The evangelical vision pointed beyond the spiritual and moral renewal of
Christendom to the conversion of the 'perishing heathen.' Upper Canadians were not ready to contemplate the sponsorship of foreign missions, but
the local Indian population offered a ready-made field. The Delawares of
Fairfield, the Mohawks, and some others at the Grand River were already
Christian when they arrived in the province, and Moravians and Methodists had made a few inconclusive early contacts with the as yet unconverted
Ojibwas. Only with the spread of missionary interest in the 1820s,
however, was conversion significantly forwarded. In 1823 William Case,
the most active organizer of the local Methodist missionary society,
arranged that Alvin Torry should give part of his time to the Iroquois and
Delawares of the Grand River. In the following year Mary Brant and her
brother Peter Jones, mixed-blood children of one of the province's busiest
surveyors, were converted at a camp meeting at Ancaster. Peter, who had
spent his early years with his Mississauga mother, became the first of many
Indians who actively propagated their newly adopted faith among their
people. Case's leadership and Jones's preaching were instrumental in
bringing into Methodism the bulk of the Mississaugas of southern Ontario,
whose land had largely been pre-empted by white settlers and who seemed
on the verge of extinction as the result of alcoholism and general despair.
Other native missionaries carried the message into the territory that is now
Michigan and Wisconsin.[17]

Humanitarians of the period were convinced that aboriginal races could
survive European contact only by adopting European ways, and it was
generally believed that they were unlikely to embrace Christianity until

they had done so. Although the Methodists found acculturation unnecessary as a means to christianization, they assumed, like others, that conversion would be incomplete without it. At the Credit River and on Grape Island in the Bay of Quinte they were soon supervising model villages where schooling was central and where community life was regulated by a strict discipline. The rapidity with which Indians were converted and the ensuing improvement in their circumstances seemed, to Methodists and others alike, striking confirmation of the effectiveness of these methods. Grape Island was so successful, indeed, that it attracted many admiring visitors from the United States.

Other denominations were soon in the field. In 1830, on Colborne's initiative, the Anglicans of York set up the Society for Converting and Civilizing the Indians. Although much of its energy was soon diverted to 'destitute settlers,' it sponsored at Sault Ste Marie the first Anglican mission to the Indians of northern Ontario. In 1827 the New England Company, a non-denominational society of Puritan origin, began to support the Anglican mission on the Grand River. The Mohawk Institute, which it founded, can be regarded as the Canadian prototype of the Indian residential school. Already in 1820 Sir Peregrine Maitland had proposed the formation of model Indian villages in which missionaries would head up teams of varying expertise. He was forestalled in this plan by the Methodists, but in 1838, after a delay due to Lieutenant-Governor Sir Francis Bond Head's scepticism about missions, such a project was launched for the northern Indians on Manitoulin Island. Meanwhile, Bishop Macdonell had placed a missionary among the Roman Catholic Indians who had settled there, and the Anglican mission was never able to overcome this head start. Native converts were responsible for the initiation of Baptist work at the Grand River and on Lake Superior. Except for the Mohawks, however, a majority of the Iroquois of the Grand continued to adhere to the Good Message of Ganiodaio, and Christianity had as yet scarcely touched the Crees north of the Hudson Bay watershed.[18]

There was not the same eagerness to provide religious services to the American blacks who began to enter the province in limited numbers during the 1820s. Most Upper Canadians were proud to offer a refuge from slavery, but especially in the southwestern peninsula, where most blacks settled, many had inherited American inhibitions against accepting them as equals or mingling with them socially. Some Methodist and Baptist churches received blacks into their membership and even their governing boards, but the Methodists were handicapped by their silence on slavery, and the Baptists had only spotty success. Beginning in 1820, when they formed Salem Chapel at St Catharines, blacks gravitated for the most part to churches of their own founding, where they could worship in accustomed ways and not be confined to back galleries.[19]

While some aspects of the evangelical program commanded more general commitment than others, all were expected to mesh together in the common cause. Revival meetings promoted abstinence, and temperance societies offered conversion as the prime remedy for drunkenness. Parents were urged to send their children to Sunday school, and the children were sent home with tracts specially selected to wean parents from their vices. The various denominations were also expected to work together for the promotion of efforts in which all who had been truly converted were assumed to have a stake. Attempts to organize missionary outreach on a non-sectarian basis had little success, but such auxiliaries as Bible and tract societies, temperance societies, and Sunday school associations brought evangelicals of various churches together in common action.

Although laymen may not have been as prominent in the leadership of evangelical institutions in Upper Canada as in either Britain or the United States, their financial contributions gave them a major voice in voluntary associations. Women were seldom admitted to positions of power, but were given unprecedented opportunities for participation. From the outset they constituted a large proportion of Sunday school teachers; each clause in the rules of the York Methodist Episcopal Sunday School meticulously applied to teachers and pupils the pronouns 'his or her.' Women also formed auxiliaries to the York Methodist Missionary Society and the Upper Canada Bible Society, though the latter had disbanded by 1837. Finney scandalized the eastern establishment by encouraging women to offer prayer in public. References to preaching by women in Upper Canada during this period, while scattered, are not rare. Eliza Barnes, an American volunteer for Indian work who later married Case, was reported to have drawn crowds and to have begun at least one revival. Bible Christians and Primitive Methodists admitted women to the ordained ministry: Elizabeth Dart was one of the pioneer Bible Christian missionaries, and the Primitive Methodist Jane Woodill Wilson was in constant demand as a preacher. Similar openness existed among the more liberal Quakers and Universalists.[20]

The activist temper of the era was epitomized most vividly and consistently in the person and career of Thaddeus Osgood. Ordained by Congregationalists in Massachusetts in 1806 as an evangelist, Osgood spent most of the years from 1808 to 1859 in Canada representing several societies or attempting, with varying degrees of success, to found new ones. It is difficult to leaf through a major collection of religious papers of the period without coming upon a reference to his seeking Anglican orders, requesting a grant from the English Wesleyans, or merely introducing his latest project to someone in authority. In 1808 he founded a tract society to which Strachan contributed. In 1811 he travelled widely in both Canada and the United States. During the early 1820s he visited almost every settled township of Upper Canada as an agent of the Sunday School Union Society of Canada, founding schools and setting them on a union basis whenever possible. Then he became interested in education for Indians, blacks, and the poor. From 1835, when he settled in Montreal, his efforts were largely concentrated on social welfare there. In the end he ran foul of intensifying denominationalism, and most of his schemes failed. In his heyday, however, he was backed by the force of a powerfully felt impulse: 'Newspaper editors gave him space, clergymen allowed him to use their churches, steamboat captains gave him free passage, and the laity gave their shillings.'[21]

The seeds of the newer crusading evangelism were sown from abroad, but they required prepared soil in order to take firm root locally. This was provided not by the continuance of pioneer conditions but by their passing. Converts at Canadian revivals of the 1830s were described by the *Christian Advocate* of New York as being predominantly from 'the middle and more opulent' classes. They represented the emergence of a growing middle class, largely independent of the official oligarchy, who took pride in seeing industrial, commercial, and educational progress, and who liked to think that the province was beginning to take its place in Western civilization. Perhaps not by coincidence, importers and wholesalers were prominent sponsors of American evangelicalism and promoters of Toronto's temperance society. Such people were anxious to do away with lingering reminders of frontier roughness, and their readiness to make use of strong emotions for this purpose did not then detract from their respectability. Already in most cases convinced Christians, they believed that material prosperity would prove a blessing only if turned to higher ends. This was the Jacksonian era in the United States, when rising classes outside the old eastern establishments were asserting their right to a place in the sun. Scholars have linked the evangelical offensive both with the Jacksonian spirit and with a fear of where it might lead if unchecked. There is probably truth in both analyses.[22]

In the United States, it is generally agreed, the concerted evangelical drive of the early nineteenth century was decisive in shaping the national ethos. To it are attributed, rightly or wrongly, a narrow moralism, a suspicion of intellectuals, a distaste for subtle distinctions, a fear of alien contamination, and even a sense of national destiny, all of which show few signs of losing their currency. Its influence is still felt in Ontario as well, but it would be difficult to maintain that it was ever determinative of the provincial character to the same degree. Here and there its effects may be seen in purest form, but domination of provincial life has always – if sometimes only just – eluded it. Penetration may never have been quite so thorough as it was in many American states. In the United States Presbyterians and Congregationalists always dominated evangelical coalitions, though Methodists and Baptists were allowed subordinate roles in them. The AHMS carried their program into Upper Canada, requiring its missionaries to report not only on church membership but on enrolment in Sunday schools, Bible classes, and temperance societies; but by the late 1830s its thrust had been blunted by financial reverses, Scottish stubbornness, and loyalist reaction to the rebellion. Suspicion that the Presbyterians were using allegedly non-sectarian institutions for their own purposes eventually led in the United States to the setting up of separate Methodist and Baptist agencies, and some of this suspicion may have carried over into Upper Canada. Canadian Methodists were sympathetic to the aims of the movement and active in organizations promoting various aspects of it, but their strong connexional-ism inclined them to concentrate on their own programs. We hear little in this period of the joint evangelistic campaigns common in the United States, and in 1827 the Methodist Conference set up its own Sabbath school society.

More seriously, resistance to the evangelical program itself was relatively stronger in Upper Canada than in the United States. To Anglicans of the classical tradition its emphases smacked of the enthusiasm from which they recoiled, and its professed non-sectarianism was subversive of loyalty to the church. Despite Strachan's earlier contribution to Osgood's tract society, the SPG insisted that the Society for Promoting Christian Knowledge, a cognate Anglican organization, should be its exclusive literary arm. At Niagara in 1816 and at York in the following year, societies were founded that had as objects the distribution of both the Bible and the Book of Common Prayer. Strachan, belying his reputation for exclusiveness, arranged for the division of the York society into separate bodies for promoting Bibles and prayer-books in order to make possible the participation of members of other denominations in the former group. The experiment attracted few non-Anglicans, however, and in 1828 the British and Foreign Bible Society organized a new auxiliary on a more inclusive basis. Neither were the authorities of the Church of England keen on independent temperance societies. Recalling that the formation of voluntary organizations had started the Methodists on a course that eventually led them out of the church, they saw in the scripture readings and prayers common at temperance meetings the threat of a possible substitute for the church. The same fear led Bishop Mountain to refuse a request for a prayer-book that was to be used in house meetings.[23] Anglican evangelicals, whose numbers were constantly being swelled by Irish immigration, figured prominently in transdenominational organizations. One of the province's major churches, however, was far from unanimous in its support.

In 1820 and 1821 the British and Foreign Bible Society presented Bibles to Roman Catholic priests for distribution among their people. Macdonell was not greatly displeased. Some of the Bibles were in Gaelic and French, and met a need beyond his immediate resources; in these versions he found little of which to complain. The child of a Protestant mother, he had more than once received generous help from Upper Canadian Protestants when his own people had been unable or unwilling to provide it. Roman Catholics soon found reasons for caution in dealing with evangelical agencies, however, for the identification of the pope as Antichrist and predictions of the imminent end of his reign were staples of the evangelical literature of the time. Soon there were complaints that Protestants were circulating not only a bad version of the Bible but pamphlets pitilessly attacking Roman Catholics. Worse still, evangelicals were using 'insidious methods' to entice children of poor Irish Catholics into 'their Sunday schools and screaming conventicles.'[24] Roman Catholicism, more deeply rooted in Upper Canada than in neighbouring states, would be another obstacle to evangelical consensus.

Aggressive evangelicalism, with its relentless desire to make everyone conform to a single pattern, also created problems for minority groups with distinctive traditions, such as Quakers and Mennonites. Its preference for faith over forms and its strict enforcement of congenial moral standards were attractive to both groups. Its busy activism wreaked havoc with their carefully preserved structures of community life, however, and its insistence on the necessity of conversion undermined their efforts to preserve the continuity of their witness to distinctive values. The intrusion of evangelical ideas among the Quakers was responsible for the disastrous Hicksite schism. The receptivity of the main body of Mennonites to Sunday schools and prayer meetings eventually led to the separation of several groups that either disapproved of change altogether or thought its pace too slow. It is ironic that many Mennonites today have opted for a style of evangelicalism that has largely been abandoned by the denominations from which they originally absorbed it with such hesitation.

While the sectarian movements of the period were predominantly evangelical in background and general orientation, their rise was due in part to a dissatisfaction with some aspects of the evangelical united front. The appearance of a number of so-called anti-missionary churches on the American frontier was prompted not so much by opposition to foreign missions as by resentment of the high-handedness of the AHMS in pushing college-trained ministers in competition with their own homegrown preachers. The appearance in Upper Canada during the 1830s of the Disciples of Christ, the Mormons, and the Catholic Apostolic Church could be regarded, in one aspect, as a sign of a similar discontent with the concentration and entrenchment of power that marked this phase of the evangelical enterprise. Caird of the Catholic Apostolic Church was particularly outspoken in his denunciation of what the *Christian Guardian* described as 'those blessed institutions, founded and reared by men whom we had ignorantly thought wise and holy, Missionary, Bible, Tract, Peace, Temperance Societies, and all the other parts of the machinery employed by the world's improvers.'[25] Although Upper Canada had no evangelical cliques comparable to those of Britain or the United States, the involvement of religious leaders in political agitation similarly frustrated those people who were more concerned for the salvation of their souls.

One can sense also a more basic source of dissatisfaction. The predominant evangelicalism of the period was essentially one-dimensional, offering a tried-and-true formula of conversion, moral conformity, and satisfaction with one's station in life. Disciples of Christ rejected the formula for its admission of religious experience as a supplement to Scripture. 'We place our hopes and rest our joys,' wrote their leading Canadian apologist David Oliphant, 'upon faith and the meaning and power of facts rather than ... upon opinions, feelings, phantoms and dream-begotten notions.' Others of a more Gothic spirit aspired to new, more metaphysical, and sometimes esoteric revelations. Irvingites offered divinely inspired glossolalia, Mormons divinely revealed tablets of gold. Most esoteric of all was the Swedenborgians' mystical vision of the New Jerusalem. In fact, most of the seeming novelties of the 1830s, such as the dating of the millennium, the identification of the ten lost tribes of Israel, and the ultimate place of Israel in the divine dispensation, had long been matters of speculation among reputable divines, but to those jaded by evangelical certainties the promise of 'songs that never were sung, nor committed to the world since the sun rose from the mighty deep' was clearly alluring.[26]

Searching could also lead in a quite different though no less Gothic direction. In 1833 the Honourable John Elmsley, the son of a former chief justice of Upper Canada and hitherto a regular attendant at Saint James's Church of England, announced his conversion to Roman Catholicism. His change of religion caused a considerable stir, and provoked Strachan to write an acerbic response.[27] Elmsley had recently married a Roman Catholic, but his conversion was too obviously the result of conviction to be dismissed as a mere case of 'turning' to keep the family together. Although a Roman Catholic priest had presided at the wedding, Elmsley had insisted as a matter of conscience on having Strachan remarry them. Elmsley's conversion, which he attributed to private reading, coincided to the year with the beginning of a movement in the Church of England that would lead to the defection to Rome of John Henry Newman and many of his followers. It also coincided with the height of the O'Grady agitation, when prudence would have suggested hesitation.

Although Elmsley's shift of allegiance attracted few imitators, parallels in the province were not altogether lacking. S.G. Lynn was another prominent Anglican convert to Roman Catholicism. The Irvingites, who probably owed most of their following to their cultivation of millennial expectations and to the charismatic appeal of revived glossolalia, called themselves the 'Catholic Apostolic church' and held 'high' views of liturgy and ministerial office. In the first flush of conversion to their views, George Ryerson wrote to Egerton: 'The Papists amidst much rubbish have retained the whole truth; Protestants have horribly marred it in their fear of retaining any of the rust.' The taking of Anglican orders by three Methodist itinerants in 1839 was not unusual in itself and was probably precipitated mainly by the internal troubles of their denomination, but a yearning for a greater measure of ecclesiastical order and solemnity seems to have been present in their case as well.[28]

Despite these movements and counter-movements, one might easily conclude from travellers' reports and clerical jeremiads that little had changed since pioneer days. Visitors continued to report the prevalence of drunkenness, ignorance, and crass materialism. An English Congregational delegation estimated in 1836 that less than half of the population of Toronto attended church services, and described 'the great majority of the settlers' as 'indifferent on the subject of religion.' Thomas Green of the Stewart Missions asserted in 1840 that the chief problem was no longer competition from dissent but 'an Ignorance and utter Indifference to the very spirit of Christianity.' W.S. Darling complained that young people were 'uppity' and had 'a passion for long hair!! the yellower and lankier and more unmanageable it is, the longer they delight to wear it.' Conscientious ministers recognized the precariousness of the situation in the urgency of their appeals. Osler distributed tracts even at weddings, and at funerals it was a common practice to 'improve the death' by enlarging on the virtues or vices of the deceased in order to move the living.[29]

Such comments, while indicating that religious fervour was far from universal, may tell us more about the expectations of the writers than about the actual state of religion. Especially in the older sections of the province, a mood of religious seriousness was beginning to take hold. Anson Green, who moved to well-cultivated Prince Edward County in 1823, wrote: 'In many respects Canada compares favourably with New York State; the people, as a whole, are more religious and manifest more veneration for divine things ... You can scarcely find a man who does not profess to belong to some form of religion; hence there is much less scoffing at sacred things.' Torry noted, more practically, that Upper Canadians treated their ministers more generously than Americans and kept up their superannuation allowances. Anglicans reported increasing attendance at communion, Presbyterians more regular attention to family worship. Osler, who tended to pessimism in his assessments, was deeply moved when a cavalcade of 110 vehicles saw him off on a visit to England. David Wilkie painted an idyllic, and doubtless somewhat romanticized, picture of a Presbyterian congregation during the 1830s: 'The farmers as they arrived, some from many miles distance, threw the bridles of their horses over a convenient stump or branch at the door, quaffed a bowl of water from a pailful placed at the roadside, on the root of a fallen tree, and then, Bible in hand, slipped into their places with all the unobtrusive simplicity of the covenanters of old.'[30] Despite occasional gloomy appraisals of the state of religion, a generation or two of preaching and pastoral care had left their mark on the province. Increasingly, the chief barrier to involvement in religious activity was not hostility, or even indifference, but merely preoccupation with secular affairs. Upper Canada had not yet entered an era when it was almost unthinkable not to be religious, but it was closer to it than its worried clergy would have dared to hope.

8 *Echoes of Europe*

What is the theological basis of authority in the church, and by whom is it legitimately exercised? Such questions, which have always lurked beneath the surface of ecclesiastical controversies, had not been examined systematically for many centuries. In the 1830s they were suddenly thrust into prominence throughout western Christendom by three apparently unrelated movements: ultramontanism in the Roman Catholic Church, the Oxford or Tractarian Movement in the Church of England, and a militant Scottish evangelicalism that ultimately led to the disruption of the national church and the formation of the Free Church of Scotland. Not long thereafter, the mass of Christians began to be aware of developments in historical criticism and natural science that raised questions about the authority of the Bible and ultimately about the validity of Christianity itself.

During the 1820s and 1830s, Upper Canadians were largely preoccupied with problems arising from their own situation. The provision of church services, the determination of the relations of the churches to one another and to the state, and the weaving of Christian influences into the social fabric of the province were the religious issues that attracted the greatest attention. Upper Canada had always been open to outside influences, however, and by the 1830s immigration, improved communications, and the proliferation of local journals were awakening greater interest in developments beyond the provincial borders. After 1841, when the union of the Canadas officially transformed Upper Canada into Canada West, its inhabitants resonated increasingly with ideas emanating from the metropolitan centres of Christendom.

Since medieval times the Roman Catholic Church had been torn between two contrasting tendencies. One, generally called 'Gallican' because of a long association with France, favoured autonomy for national segments of the church and usually a measure of royal control as a guarantee of this autonomy. The other, ultramontanism, exalted the prerogatives of the pope 'over the mountains' as a symbol of the universality of the church. Gallicanism predominated during the post-Reformation era, when prelates looked to increasingly powerful monarchies for support in their struggles against Protestantism and in their attempts to rid the church of inherited abuses. It was seriously discredited in 1790, however, when a majority of the French clergy accepted a settlement that virtually incorporated the church into the machinery of government. Reaction against revolutionary excess inspired a Catholic revival, which took an ultramontane direction almost from the start. For a brief period it seemed that the papacy might ally itself with popular movements, but such a development was ruled out by the church's unhappy memories of revolution and by the anti-clericalism of most European liberals. In 1832 Pope Gregory XVI condemned Félicité de Lamennais's journal *L'Avenir*, which had advocated this policy, and during the long pontificate of Pius IX (1846–78) deference to the papacy and hostility to political liberalism became inseparably linked as tests of fidelity to the church.

Whereas ultramontanism came to dominate the church in French Canada only after considerable public controversy, its progress in Upper Canada was quiet but thorough. Alexander Macdonell, the province's first bishop, represented the end of a long Gallican tradition in his careful cultivation of the local authorities and the class from which they were drawn. A different outlook can be discerned in Rémi Gaulin, his successor at Kingston, and subsequent appointments continued the trend. The ultramontane program was most consistently pressed by Armand de Charbonnel, a French aristocrat who as bishop of Toronto from 1850 to 1860 constantly urged it on the faithful and enforced it with uncompromising rigour. The appeal of ultramontanism was furthered by parallel developments in Ireland, the source of most of the Roman Catholic population, clergy, and bishops, during the long tenure of Cardinal Paul Cullen as archbishop of Dublin. A dramatic shift in the orientation of the Irish church from Gallican to ultramontane was accompanied by a 'devotional revolution' that within fifty years increased the weekly attendance at mass from 33 per cent to 90 per cent of the population.[1]

The transformation of the Roman Catholic Church in the province from a rudimentary mission held together by episcopal correspondence and visits into a highly efficient and well-disciplined organization, in part a natural evolution, was greatly furthered by instructions emanating from an increasingly aggressive curia. Macdonell and his immediate successors had had to keep refractory priests in line by the exercise of peremptory and often arbitrary personal authority. Later bishops evolved systems of intermediate supervision through archdeacons and rural deans, a code of ecclesiastical jurisprudence with tribunals to enforce it, and a system of careful accounting at all levels. In 1846 Bishop Michael Power of Toronto forbade priests to accept chaplaincies or other government appointments without episcopal permission, a practice that in his view had led to 'a spirit of independence and insubordination.' Claims to local autonomy, which had given so much trouble to Macdonell at York, were met with the denial of any right of the laity to 'interfere' in the temporal or spiritual government of the church, though lay complaints against parish priests usually received prompt episcopal attention.

To promote and consolidate this program of renewal, bishops looked to the religious orders, which were relatively invulnerable to lay pressure, accustomed to strict internal discipline, and usually active in promoting current developments in spirituality. In 1841 Gaulin brought three nuns from Montreal to open a girls' school at Kingston, and in 1843 Power persuaded French Jesuits to take over the Indian missions of his diocese.[2] English-speaking dioceses looked mainly to Ireland for the nuclei of new foundations. Except for a few francophone communities that continued to recruit personnel in Quebec, these religious orders owed their survival and growth to their ability to attract novices locally. Within a few years they made possible greatly expanded programs of education and social work.

The effects of ultramontane revival extended beyond formal structures to the popular practice of religion. Until the Second Vatican Council, much of what was expected of pious Catholics had been normative outside Italy only since the middle of the nineteenth century. In general, a pattern prevailed that left little power to the laity but gave them plenty to do. A good Catholic was expected to belong to a confraternity or sodality devoted to a pious cause such as the promotion of temperance or the extension of the faith, and a plethora of newly introduced 'paraliturgical' devotions supplemented the familiar sacraments. Corporate devotions, such as the Benediction of the Blessed Sacrament, novenas, Forty Hours' devotions, pilgrimages, and processions, were conducted with deliberate pomp in imposing settings. Churches were provided with such practical appurtenances as Stations of the Cross and with ornamental decoration in romantic profusion. Other devotions, privately performed, emphasized the particular blessings granted to supplicants by Jesus, Mary, and the saints.

The promotion and practice of ultramontane piety called for tracts, guides to devotion, and cult objects such as rosaries, medals, and scapulars. The confessional was used more systematically than before, and every officially authorized act of piety was rewarded with an appropriate indulgence to mitigate the trials of purgatory. Promotional material customarily accentuated the positive; in its manual the Archconfraternity of the Most Holy and Immaculate Heart of Mary, which Gaulin directed to be established in every parish of his diocese, assured the prospective member that 'the obligations of this Association are very light indeed and the advantages to himself and to his neighbours immense.' The trump card of the promoters of renewal was the parish mission: over a period of two weeks or longer a team of visiting preachers from the Redemptorists or another order would urge penitents to confession, encourage regular attendance at the sacraments, drum up membership in parish organizations, promote a favoured devotion, advertise religious books and objects, call the faithful to a renewal of vows, and if possible attract non-Catholics. Through such means some lapsed Catholics were restored to the fold, but more frequently those who had been practising Catholics all along were introduced to a type of spirituality with which they had not previously been familiar.[3]

Like the Church of Rome, the Church of England had long oscillated between two contrasting tendencies. The 'high church' party emphasized the more 'Catholic' elements that had been retained despite the break with Rome; the 'low' held fast to the Protestant principles which it saw enshrined in the Thirty-nine Articles and the Book of Common Prayer. The low church party, somewhat on the defensive after the rejection of the Puritan commonwealth in the seventeenth century, was revitalized by the religious revivals of the eighteenth and took on a new 'evangelical' identity. By 1800 it was pre-eminent in philanthropic and missionary endeavour. In succeeding years its vitality was sapped by rigid insistence on conformity to a particular pattern of Christian experience, and the rationalism and moralism of an earlier age reasserted themselves. Some people began to ask whether the Church of England had anything to offer, beyond an increasingly ambivalent connection with the state, that was not available in dissenting chapels. The first alarm was sounded at Oxford by John Keble in an assize sermon in 1830. A succeeding series of 'Tracts for the Times,' inspired and largely written by the Oriel College trio of Keble, John Henry Newman, and E.B. Pusey, hammered home the thesis that the Church of England with its apostolic succession of bishops was a legitimate branch of the church parallel with the Roman Catholic and Greek Orthodox, and downgraded the Protestant Reformation as an aberration of limited value. During the same period the Cambridge Camden Society championed Gothic architecture, and the Alcuin Club ransacked ecclesiastical archives for usable liturgical materials from medieval England. Later Anglo-Catholicism resulted from the convergence of these movements, although those in search of 'advanced' models of worship found current Roman Catholic usages more accessible than the Sarum Missal and other antiquarian materials.

The ideals of the Oxford Movement were introduced into Canada West from a variety of sources. Some of the clergy had been affected by it in England, while a few imported organists were enthusiasts for liturgical innovation. A large proportion of the clergy who were considered high church during the middle years of the century, however, had imbibed their principles within the province: at Toronto, under the personal instruction of John Strachan; at a seminary in Cobourg which he entrusted to his protégé A.N. Bethune; or later at Trinity College, which he founded. Strachan was attracted by the arguments of the 'Tracts for the Times,' which he saw as vindicating his own attitude to dissent and as validating the position of the Church of England against Roman claims. He could pick and choose among the motifs of the movement, however, and became distinctly cautious in his attitude to it even before Newman's defection to Rome in 1845. In fact, Strachan did not need the Oxford Movement to form his opinions; he made use of it mainly to confirm the beliefs that he already held. He owed more to his friend John Henry Hobart, the Episcopal bishop of New York, who envisaged his church as a body at once apostolic in faith and practice, evangelical in its adherence to the principles of the Protestant Reformation, and capable of adapting itself to the requirements of self-reliance in the New World. Anglo-Catholicism of the English type also gradually made its way into the province, though it never eclipsed the more cautious local model.[4]

Anglo-Catholics attached great theological importance to bishops, but their chief practical concern was to ensure that the Church of England should be able to arrange its own affairs without undue interference from the state. Strachan had long hoped to introduce organs of self-government into the church in Upper Canada. In 1842 he set up a church society for outreach to new areas of his diocese, and in 1851 he transformed it, at first unofficially, into a diocesan synod with lay representation and legislative powers. For this institution, then unknown in England, he drew on precedents in the United States and the maritime provinces rather than directly on tractarian inspiration. Yet these and some other measures, such as the local election of bishops on Strachan's insistence, the formation in 1861 of a provincial synod of Canada, and the maintenance in the diocese of Toronto of episcopal appointment of parish priests, were supported almost exclusively by adherents of the high church party. Another conspicuous initiative from this direction was a resolution of the provincial synod in 1865 that led to the calling of the first international conference of Anglican bishops at Lambeth in 1867.[5]

Anglo-Catholic devotional practices were at first largely limited to parishes served by known sympathizers: Saint Peter's, Cobourg, where Bethune was rector; Saint Philip's, Weston, under W.A. Johnson; and among Toronto churches most conspicuously Holy Trinity, whose rector,

W.S. Darling, would eventually find Roman Catholicism more congenial. A full choral service was first reported at Cobourg in 1848, daily Holy Week services at Holy Trinity in 1857, and a choral eucharist at Trinity College Chapel in 1866. The use of *Hymns Ancient and Modern* (1861), which ran more to the medieval, was sufficient proof of the Anglo-Catholicism of a parish. Innovation was inhibited by widespread congregational resistance, by the increasing opposition of an organized party, and by Strachan's reluctance to admit divisive extremes. The traditional combination of morning prayer, litany, and antecommunion held its place as the normal Sunday service through the 1850s and 1860s, and the metrical psalter of Tate and Brady was still widely used. The pace of change then quickened, especially in the diocese of Toronto when Bethune succeeded upon Strachan's death in 1867, but surpliced choirs and the decoration of altars with cross and candlesticks were still widely regarded as dubious innovations. The Church of England presented a picture of liturgical variety that would have been inconceivable in denominations theoretically more hospitable to congregational autonomy. Yet certain trends reflecting Anglo-Catholic influence were fairly general. The celebration of Holy Communion became more frequent; in the diocese of Toronto, where more than half of the parishes had from four to six communions in 1863, monthly communion was the norm by 1874, and a few parishes were moving to weekly and even weekday celebrations. Greater frequency of services was accompanied by an increase in the number of communicants, and both trends accelerated in succeeding years.[6] Patterns of Anglican spirituality were changing, however slowly and unevenly.

The Church of Scotland too was marked by contrasting tendencies, represented in its case by moderate and evangelical parties. The Moderates, who controlled the Kirk's general assembly throughout the eighteenth and well into the nineteenth century, derived their name from their efforts to moderate the theological quarrels that had distracted the country since the Reformation. Emphasizing the rational foundations and moral implications of Christianity, they owed their power largely to a system, inaugurated by parliamentary act in 1712, that left clerical appointments in the hands of wealthy lay patrons. Evangelicals placed more emphasis on personal piety and upheld traditional Calvinism in all its rigour. The common people preferred them, and they in turn supported the traditional right of congregations to call their own ministers. The United Presbyterians, who represented the coming together of several groups of Seceders, were the successors of early evangelicals who had left the Kirk over the patronage issue.

Evangelicals who remained within the national church gradually gained strength, especially when the accession to their ranks of the outstanding scholar-preacher Thomas Chalmers gave them an intellectual stature they had hitherto lacked. After gaining a majority in the assembly in 1833, they proceeded to legislate a congregational veto of appointments by patrons and to consolidate their grip on power by giving legal standing to unofficial chapels that had sprung up, mainly under evangelical auspices, to serve the needs of unchurched city dwellers. What had the appearance of a successful ecclesiastical revolution was quickly undone, however, when the civil courts declared its major achievements ultra vires. In 1843 a large proportion of its most dedicated clergy and laity left the Kirk to form the Free Church of Scotland, claiming that by accepting dictation from the state the old church had forfeited its spiritual prerogatives to the new.

Many in Canada West who found themselves on opposite sides of the controversy neither wanted a split in the provincial body nor expected it to be necessary. To enthusiasts who habitually described what had happened in Scotland as a 'glorious disruption,' however, any reluctance to break fellowship with the 'residual' church was tantamount to compromise with the Devil. Free Church sympathizers in Canada West felt in duty bound to separate from a synod that refused to drop from its name the phrase 'in connection with the Church of Scotland' even while they admitted that the connection implied no limitations on local freedom. The Free Church had a ready-made fifth column in the province. Many local ministers of the Kirk had been appointed through the offices of the Glasgow Colonial Society, a body composed largely of evangelicals. Robert Burns, secretary of the society for some years and thus Canadians' chief contact with Scotland, led a Free Church deputation to North America that spent two weeks in Canada West, and he soon settled in Toronto as minister of Knox Church. Recent immigrants who had followed the struggle in Scotland were another source of support. Showing an unflagging interest in the province, the Free Church sent a series of deputations between 1844 and 1848 to press ministers and funds on congregations. Its success can be measured by the increase in its ministerial complement from 20 in 1844 to 129 in 1861.[7] The Church of Scotland showed no corresponding energy. It had no surplus of ministers to dispose of, but rather a shortage that attracted many of its remaining colonial clergy back to Scotland.

Although it introduced no radically unfamiliar forms of spiritual expression, the incursion of the Free Church had a significant impact on the balance of religious forces in the province. Prior to the disruption, the largest and fastest-growing segment of Presbyterianism had been the Church of Scotland. Despite its strong evangelical element, the Kirk had perceived itself as a correlate to the Church of England, responsible for the

Scottish population as the latter was for those of English origin. After the disruption the Free Church gradually took over its pre-eminent position, setting what would be the tone of local Presbyterianism in the years to come. Its place in society was closer to that of Wesleyan Methodism than to that formerly occupied by the Kirk, however, and with some reluctance it came to acknowledge this. This development had been foreshadowed, indeed, by the welcome extended to Free Church delegations in the pulpits of Protestant churches without traditions of establishment. The Free Church attracted a disproportionate share of Presbyterians of American and Ulster background and gradually absorbed the remnants of the American-based presbytery of Niagara; it inherited their suspicion of clerical leadership and in practice allowed authority to pass mainly to its congregations. The resulting body was oriented less to the preservation of the status quo than to its transformation, though along lines of aggressive evangelism and rigid moralism rather than of social and economic reorganization. Strongly activist in outlook, it was less inhibited in its advocacy of current causes than the somewhat self-contained Wesleyans and brought to them greater resources than smaller denominations such as the Baptists and the Methodist splinter groups. Canada West would have to take notice of it.

While readers will recognize a number of parallels between ultramontanism and Anglo-Catholicism, resemblances between their emphases and the convictions that prompted the formation of the Free Church are far from obvious. Ultramontanism and Anglo-Catholicism represented a reassertion of traditional Catholicism, with considerable concentration on precisely those aspects of medieval practice to which the Protestant Reformers had most vigorously objected. The founders of the Free Church were uncompromising in their Calvinism and alarmist in their response to 'Catholicizing' tendencies. To ultramontanes and tractarians the modern world was suspect; Free Church supporters welcomed every advance in engineering or communication. In the heyday of these movements, however, Thomas Arnold lumped them all together as threats to the tradition of royal supremacy, which he regarded as a necessary safeguard against clerical domination of the church. In 1917 Harold J. Laski linked them again in a more sustained analysis entitled *Studies in the Problem of Sovereignty*. While recognizing radical differences among them, he saw them all as denials of the modern state's claim that it represents the whole of society and is thus entitled to unlimited sovereignty.[8] One might add that all three, as much as the older evangelicalism, represented reactions of Victorian seriousness against the routine quality of much eighteenth-century religion. All, moreover, shared a romantic interest in heroic traditions, whether of Knox and Melville, the martyred King Charles, or a more remote crusading past of 'mighty acts of God through the French.'

These movements, which originated in Europe in response to circumstances there, were imported into Canada not because they met local needs but because the natural flow of ideas was from metropolis to hinterland. They struck the province with particular force at this time because of the presence of an unusually large number of relative newcomers from the British Isles who still thought largely in Old World terms. They resonated sufficiently with the concerns of many Upper Canadians, however, to suggest specific and sometimes novel applications to local circumstances.

Immigrants from Ireland who brought about a quadrupling of the Roman Catholic population between 1842 and 1861,[9] though for the most part warmly attached to their church, habitually neglected its requirements and seldom troubled to distinguish its teachings from traditional beliefs in leprechauns and banshees. Already disoriented by experiences of famine, epidemic, and separation from friends and kinfolk when they arrived in the province, they found in shebeens and street brawls ready means of socialization in a hostile environment. Protestants actively sought converts among them, and many immigrants were not immune to their arguments and inducements. The round of pious activities associated with the ultramontane pattern, along with money-raising social events such as picnics and raffles, provided the church with means to assume direction of the Irish Catholic community and divert its energies into acceptable channels.[10] To the French Canadians settling in the lower Ottawa Valley, meanwhile, churches offering a round of pious devotions became natural centres of ethnic consciousness and helped to promote a sense of ethnic destiny.

One of the difficulties of the Church of England overseas was that the traditions of English law made no place for its existence. When the appointment of colonial bishops was first mooted, no one was quite sure how it could legally be brought about. Even when some had been appointed, popular prejudice insisted that the only real bishops were those who sat in the House of Lords. Colonial bishops came in some shadowy way under the jurisdiction of the archbishop of Canterbury. More practically, they were expected to carry out the policies of the Society for the Propagation of the Gospel and other missionary agencies, whether or not these seemed appropriate to their situation. The Oxford movement, with its insistence on consecration within the apostolic succession rather than appointment by the state as the criterion of a true bishop, served to validate the colonial episcopate and to bolster its authority. Such considerations doubtless had a special attraction for bishops. Others who wished the church to put down local roots might be attracted to tractarianism, however, because its emphasis on apostolicity indirectly bestowed a heightened dignity on the colonial church and provided a rationale for its existence that would endure even if state endowment were to come to an end.[11]

Of the various European movements under discussion, that which tore asunder the Church of Scotland was apparently imported with the least justification. In Canada West the freedom of the church was not abridged by the civil courts, nor was there any reason to think that it might be. The compromise offered by Kirk supporters – that of affirming the spiritual independence of the Canadian body without breaking communion with the mother church – was one that would have seemed reasonable in most circumstances. Yet there is more to be said. Many lay members of the Kirk, having no desire to be part of a quasi-establishment, resented the eagerness with which their ministers sought government subsidies. A brand was touched to this smouldering straw in 1843 by the introduction of a temporalities bill that would have vested church property in a centralized legal corporation rather than in congregations. Meetings of protest were convened at Toronto and Scarborough, and Peter and George Brown attacked the bill vigorously in the *Banner*. This local threat to lay liberties may have been more potent than the tyranny of distant British courts in inducing some Upper Canadians to opt for the Free Church.[12]

The incursion of these militant religious ideologies was bound to aggravate existing tensions. Most conspicuously, they seemed to confirm latent Protestant suspicions of all forms of Catholicism. Anti-Catholicism in Canada West was a generalized but also complex phenomenon. Most Britishers had long regarded Roman Catholicism as superstitious and foreign and therefore as vaguely disreputable. The Orange Order added imported Irish animosities, though it generally pressed political rather than religious objections to an ecclesiastical system it regarded as inherently disloyal. The new factor introduced in the 1840s was a deep sense of insecurity on both sides. Protestants denounced a world-wide papal conspiracy of which Anglo-Catholicism was seen as an integral part, while Roman Catholics warned the faithful against a great coalition of unbelief. The master-minds of intrigue were Jesuits on the one side and Freemasons on the other; opponents could not conceive of the possibility of exaggerating the watchfulness, the ingenuity, or the lack of scruple of either. Nor was either side motivated entirely by irrational bigotry, for Roman Catholics and Protestants alike made no secret of their desire to convert the world to their beliefs. In 1846 the Roman Catholics of Toronto offered special prayers for the return of England to the faith of the 'Fathers,' while in the following year the students' missionary society of Knox College sponsored its first graduate, John Black, as a missionary to French

Canadians.[13] The act of 'papal aggression' in 1850 by which the Roman Catholic Church re-established its hierarchy in England after three centuries stirred up a further wave of indignation that lasted through the 1850s.

The Church of England suffered from severe internal strains, for the main line of tension bisected its ranks. As often happens, the taking of sides was considerably influenced by non-theological factors. Clergy anxious to 'improve' worship tended to the Anglo-Catholic party, while lay leaders who resented clerical dictation came to reckon themselves evangelicals. Cultural and ethnic differences also played a part; children of the Church of Ireland inherited a horror of possible Roman infection that seemed excessive to many of English origin. Since the issues at stake were seen by both sides as affecting eternal destiny, however, compromise even on apparently trifling matters became a betrayal of principle. Every proposal for innovation in liturgical procedure or church furnishing called both camps into action. Almost every episcopal election, beginning with that of the evangelical Benjamin Cronyn to the new diocese of Huron in 1857, was fought on party lines. The autonomy of the Canadian church, sought by Anglo-Catholics as essential to its freedom, was resisted by evangelicals as a threat to its dependence on a monarchy of guaranteed Protestantism. Most contentious of all was the education of the clergy, for on them the future of the church depended. In 1852 Strachan installed George Whitaker, who considered himself a moderate churchman, as provost of his newly founded Trinity College. Simmering discontent among evangelicals came to a head in 1863 when Cronyn was goaded into a public attack on Whitaker's teaching.[14] Later that year, after failing to secure satisfaction from his fellow bishops, Cronyn founded Huron College as a bastion of evangelical truth. Eventually, the church had not only rival theological colleges and private schools but competing missionary societies, hymn-books, and even Sunday school lessons.

Religious polarization had the effect not only of hardening positions but of intensifying differences. Within Roman Catholicism, rigorism became more pronounced. Rules of abstinence that had originally been designed as disciplines to make better Catholics were increasingly also badges of distinction from Protestantism. The reading even of approved translations of the Bible was restricted to those for whom it was judged unlikely to be prejudicial,[15] and Protestant stories of priests who forbade the book altogether to their parishioners were not completely without foundation. Strictness applied especially to marriage. For Catholics to be married by a Protestant minister was a mortal sin, and episcopal dispensations for mixed marriages were given grudgingly if at all. An old accommodation by which sons took the faith of their fathers and daughters that of their mothers was no longer acceptable.

Protestants accentuated their differences not only from Roman Catholics but more especially from high Anglicans. In earlier times there had often been complaints that read prayers were unspiritual, congregational responses mechanical, and bishops unscriptural, but it had not ordinarily been suggested that any of them were popish. And if we rarely hear of pulpit gowns or surplices among the accoutrements of Methodist circuit riders, their absence was due chiefly to the limited capacity of saddle-bags and the limited resources of the preachers. By the 1840s 'sacramentalism' and 'sacerdotalism' were emerging as bugaboo words in Protestant polemic, and beliefs or practices that suggested a possible association with them were automatically suspect. Encouragement of frequent communion, pioneered by Wesleyans and evangelical Anglicans, was suddenly a dangerous ritualistic innovation.[16] Increasingly, Protestantism came to be defined in terms of what might not be believed or practised.

Developments that aggravated some tensions brought Protestants of various denominations closer together. Enough of the spirit of the earlier evangelical coalition persisted in the province that denominations sometimes encouraged one another in good works. At the 1842 missionary anniversary of the English Wesleyans of Toronto, for example, the customary resolution calling for aid to the parent society was moved by William Rintoul, the Kirk minister of Streetsville. Such co-operation received further encouragement in 1846, when, on the initiative of some Anglican evangelicals and Free Church Scots, a well-attended international conference on Protestant unity inaugurated the Evangelical Alliance. The immediate occasion for action was a government grant to the Roman Catholic college at Maynooth in Ireland, the larger motive a more general fear of what Anson Green described as 'the cunning of Jesuits, the ravages of Antichrist, and the alarming defection of Tractarians.'[17] Whereas the earlier impulse to common action had reached Upper Canada largely from the United States, American objections to the strong anti-slavery stance of the Alliance now left the initiative almost entirely in British hands. Despite its initially negative motivation, the Alliance inspired a genuine desire for Christian unity and was one of the significant precursors of the twentieth-century ecumenical movement.

Anticipating the formation of the Alliance, a number of Toronto ministers of various denominations offered a series of 'evangelical' or 'Protestant' lectures in 1845. 'Schism: Its Nature, Causes and Remedy' was the unaccustomed title of another lecture delivered by Methodist editor George Playter in 1846. A correspondent of the *Christian Guardian* who took the expansive pseudonym 'Cosmos' proposed that Protestants should unite 'under one general government' as the only credible alternative to Rome, and his was not the only suggestion for an ambitious scheme of union. The tangible results of this burst of ecumenical enthusiasm were not impressive, although Canadian and English Wesleyans credited the Evangelical Alliance and the fear of tractarianism that had inspired it with helping to bring about their reunion in 1847.[18] Mutual recrimination among Protestant bodies, and especially among closely related Protestant bodies, continued to take up space even in journals that used adjacent columns to laud unitive efforts.

From this time forward, however, unity would be a recurrent subject for discussion among Canadian Protestants. From 1854 to 1857 Robert Dick, a Free Baptist minister, published the *Gospel Tribune* at Toronto with the stated purpose of promoting ecumenical endeavours. He was eclectic in his approach to the subject, and featured stories on topics as diverse as current proposals for reducing the number of Presbyterian and Methodist splinter groups, the advocacy of open communion in his own denomination, the Young Men's Christian Association, and coeducation. In 1865 Richard West called for the publication of a 'Christian Union' journal whose profits would help to promote a 'Protestant Mission Fund.' His approach was more pragmatic, his main argument for union being 'It will pay!' Perhaps the most significant contribution of these early discussions was the formulation of a rhetoric, in which Jesus' prayer for his disciples 'that they all may be one' figured prominently, that could be called into play whenever a new step toward Protestant consolidation was proposed.[19] Since there was no consensus on the ultimate goal of ecumenism, whether organic union, federation, or merely informal co-operation based on a sense of spiritual kinship, both advocates and opponents of the twentieth-century union that gave birth to the United Church of Canada were able to draw on elements of this rhetoric.

While some movements from abroad were encouraging Christians to seek renewal in neglected traditions, others were calling all traditional interpretations of Christianity into question. A fertile source of disturbance was Germany, where the practice of educating theological students in state universities left their professors free to engage in almost unlimited speculation. During most of the eighteenth century, through the influence of English and French deism, Christianity was in general disrepute among German intellectuals. Late in that century and into the next, strenuous attempts were made to rehabilitate it: by Immanuel Kant as the source of a moral imperative, by G.W.F. Hegel as the basis of a satisfying philosophy of history, and by Friedrich Schleiermacher as the fulfilment of an emotional necessity. In contrast with Wilhelm Wrede, who had dismissed the Jesus of the gospels as a deluded visionary, D.F. Strauss in his *Life of Jesus* (1835) found great spiritual meaning in the gospel record at the cost of reducing to insignificance the historical existence of Jesus. Before 1840 English-speaking Protestants had been almost totally unaware of German developments, and even thereafter increasing knowledge of them was limited almost entirely at first to a small group of intellectuals. Within the churches there prevailed a conservative view of the Bible and of Christian doctrine to which even the more positive German thought of the nineteenth century was bound to be profoundly unsettling. In 1860 a group of English scholars opened this Pandora's box in a collection entitled *Essays and Reviews,* which commended the critical study of the Bible and contained essays questioning the eternal damnation of non-Christians, the historicity of the Creation stories, and the usefulness of such external evidences as miracles. Conservatives exploded in indignation, and could scarcely contain themselves two years later when J.W. Colenso, an Anglican bishop (if only a colonial one), used his *Introduction to the Pentateuch and the Book of Joshua* to deny the factual accuracy of much of their content.

English theologians had long enjoyed a fairly comfortable relation with scientists, owing to Sir Francis Bacon's restriction of the pretensions of science to the establishment of empirical facts and Sir Isaac Newton's convincing demonstration of the marvellous order of the universe. During the nineteenth century this longstanding friendship gradually broke down as the result of difficulties in reconciling scientific discoveries with the traditional view of the Bible. In 1830 Sir Charles Lyell classified rock strata according to periods of a much greater span of time than the biblical narrative readily allowed. Then in 1859 came Charles Darwin's *On the Origin of Species,* which argued not only that species are subject to change but that such changes result from purely natural processes. The early response to Darwin was relatively unemotional in comparison with that which greeted *Essays and Reviews.* The English were accustomed to dealing with scientific questions, and the earlier theory of purposive evolution set forth by Charles's grandfather Erasmus Darwin was fairly well known. With the appearance in 1870 of *The Descent of Man,* which was interpreted as suggesting that respectable Britons had apes for ancestors, the argument would heat up.

As yet the new ideas scarcely affected English-speaking Roman Catholics, who regarded them simply as further manifestations of a liberalism that everywhere threatened the truth. For the Protestants of Canada West, as of English-speaking countries generally, they raised two distinct but inseparable issues. One of these was the authority of the Bible. Since the immediate post-Reformation era, when medieval scholastic methods had regained much of their lost prestige, Protestant scholars had assumed that any scriptural passage could be cited as authoritative evidence in any field of study. The main question raised by nineteenth-century criticism, therefore, was not the validity of particular doctrines but the reliability of the entire Bible on historical and scientific as much as on theological questions. On this point there was a striking difference between Germany and English-speaking countries. In the former, contention focused on substantive issues of Christian belief such as the reality of the Resurrection and the historical existence of Jesus. In the latter, more attention was paid to items less crucial in content but especially vulnerable to attack, such as the chronology of the Pentateuch and, later, the digestibility of Jonah. Yet, as Anson Green recognized, German criticism also carried a fair load of philosophical freight. What he called the 'pantheistic idealism' of Germany would ultimately prove difficult for Protestant orthodoxy to absorb.[20]

In Canada West, where criticism was known largely through British sources, initial reactions to it were predictably negative. The Free Church's Knox College, which from the outset maintained close relations with the ultra-orthodox Princeton Seminary, was one of the first to sound the alarm. As early as 1848 Professor Michael Willis warned against a 'torrent of wild and licentious criticism, as well as philosophy, which threatened to sap the foundations of Christianity.' Anglican response to *Essays and Reviews* was much as in England. In 1863 the clergy of the diocese of Toronto aligned themselves with Strachan's denunciation of Colenso and the essayists. In the following year the bishops and clergy of the province of Canada signed the Oxford Declaration, which not only condemned the essayists but placed the signatories on record as maintaining 'without reserve or qualification, the inspiration and the Divine authority of the whole canonical Scriptures, as not only containing, but being the Word of God.'[21]

Less laden with emotion than the issue of the historical and scientific reliability of the biblical record, but of comparable significance, was that of the intellectual grounding of Christian belief. Theologians of all schools agreed that faith could never be at odds with reason rightly understood. In the eighteenth century public confidence in this coherence had been badly shaken by the scepticism of David Hume and the deism of French encyclopedists. In 1843, however, Adam Lillie of the Congregational Academy of Upper Canada was able to write: 'Look back fifty years, and what do we find? The most highly esteemed philosophers of the day arrayed against the truths of revelation. But how stands it now? Sir, the very lights of science are now the pioneers of revelation.' For this brightening of outlook two developments had been mainly responsible. One was the rise of the Scottish philosophy of 'common sense,' a term which in this context implied not the level-headedness of its adherents but the ordering of our minds in such a way that certain ideas will carry conviction to any rational, unprejudiced person. Conveniently for Christian apologists, these 'innate ideas' were commonly understood as including belief in God, immortality, and moral obligation. Oddly, in view of its popularity with evangelicals, common-sense philosophy was a product of Scottish moderatism. Further underpinning for Christian belief was provided by the *Christian Evidences* of William Paley, who sought to demonstrate by a multiplicity of examples that the intricate order of nature pointed to a shaping mind. At the time when Lillie expressed his optimism, and to an even greater extent by mid-century, both Paley and common sense had become staples of provincial college curricula.[22]

Amateur scientists abounded in Canada West as in other parts of British North America. They were not theorists but naturalists of the Baconian tradition who studied rocks or flowers in order to identify and classify them. Almost all of them were religious, and a fair number were clergymen. To them the examination of nature was a means of attaining greater understanding of God's design, and they found there – doubtless with help from Paley – remarkable evidence of its intricacy, beauty, and ingenious adaptation to human requirements. Along with providing assurance that God was in his heaven, moreover, this exploration of the harmonies of the natural order confirmed their belief that the universe was unfolding as it should and that the British Empire rested on a solid foundation.

The extended time-lines of geology and evolution raised questions about Paley's careful arguments from design, and Darwin's principle of natural selection negated them outright. Common-sense philosophy was less directly challenged, but its picture of reality was similarly static and depended for its credibility on the existence of minds specially created to recognize innate ideas. Understandably, the initial local reaction to Darwin's *Origin of Species* was negative. Academic reviewers recognized his contributions to knowledge, but rejected his theory as resting on an unproved hypothesis and as involving the denial of providential design. To J. William Dawson, the principal of McGill University and by general consent Canada's foremost scientist, the existence of divine purpose and the validity of the Mosaic cosmology were inextricably linked. As a geologist he readily conceded the necessity of interpreting the chronology of Genesis with some latitude, but as a Christian he felt obliged to dissect the theory of evolution in one book after another. While universities gradually incorporated evolutionary biology into their curricula, amateur naturalists for the most part continued their researches in the assurance that Dawson had verified their premises.[23]

Here and there the new ideas received a cautious welcome. Daniel Wilson, the evangelical president of the University of Toronto, saw difficulties in Darwin's theory but reflected that 'in the conflict – whatever dust and heat arise – the inevitable destruction of some long cherished error is of itself a clear gain.' Some Methodists, convinced that their grip on 'the inner assurance of faith' left them little to fear from the honest investigation of external facts, exhibited a similar freedom from defensiveness. As early as 1853 Principal S.S. Nelles of Victoria College laid down the principle: 'Study without prayer is arrogance, prayer without study is fanaticism.' His successor Nathanael Burwash, who served an apprenticeship in science while awaiting the establishment of a chair of theology, advised his students to hold fast to faith but to be open to scientific thinking even when the two could not easily be reconciled.[24] At most, however, the debates of the 1850s and 1860s represented preliminary skirmishes over issues in which the mass of Ontario churchgoers took little interest. Serious wrestling with the implications of the critical scholarship of the nineteenth century would occupy the churches throughout the rest of the century and beyond.

The infusion of metropolitan ideas that marked the generation prior to Confederation introduced Upper Canadians to international discussions in which they were at first essentially receivers rather than contributors. On the one hand, this preoccupation with European issues threatened the imposition in Procrustean fashion of programs that had been inspired by needs perceived in England, Scotland, or Italy. On the other hand, it represented a raising of the theological horizon that was necessary if the province was to take its place in the mainstream of religious discussion. The price for paying too exclusive attention to local problems had been provincialism, with characters on a narrow stage seeming more important than they really were. Meanwhile, unfinished business had to be dealt with locally, and in settling it Upper Canadians showed themselves capable of adapting metropolitan solutions to their own particular circumstances.

9 Affairs of State

By 1840, to all appearances, tolerable compromises had brought an end to ill-tempered controversies over the clergy reserves and the provincial university that had distracted Upper Canada for more than a decade. No one was satisfied with the terms of those compromises, but arguments too often repeated had grown wearisome, and the province needed time to recover from the wounds of 1837. Besides, the balance of forces that had already compelled mutual concession seemed unlikely to be upset quickly. The Church of England had too few adherents in Upper Canada to give it a credible claim to exclusive recognition. The uncompromisingly voluntarist denominations, though vehement in argument, likewise lacked the numbers to back up their arguments with votes. Those who belonged to churches with intermediate positions – Kirk, Roman Catholic, and Wesleyan – were too numerous to be ignored and too diverse in their interests to make a radical solution feasible. So, at least, matters seemed to stand.

Appearances proved deceptive. Strachan and Ryerson might regard the clergy reserves issue as settled, and Morris of the Kirk might shrink from reopening 'this tiresome subject,'[1] but Upper Canadians were by no means finished with it or with the related question of the provincial university. The renewal of controversy was inevitable, not so much because of considerations of abstract justice as because the social framework presupposed by existing arrangements was everywhere under severe strain. In Europe an epidemic of revolutions in 1848 served notice that the secular state had arrived. Locally, the apportionment of government favour did not correspond to the religious preferences of the majority of the people. While weariness might bring about a lull in controversy, therefore, the dynamics of the situation called for readjustment. In varied ways the movements described in the previous chapter helped to bring about the realignment of forces that determined the results of this readjustment.

Ultramontanism was associated in Europe with reaction against every form of political liberalism. Its effects were similar in Canada East, where clerical zealots denounced a vote for the *rouges* as mortal sin. The situation in Canada West was different. Here conservatism, locally understood as adherence to the value system of the official oligarchy, was associated with the Gallicanism of Alexander Macdonell. As the O'Grady affair indicated, Irish Catholics were not prepared to go along with Macdonell's dependence on the good will of the governor's set. Reform attacks on their bishop and church could provoke their indignation, as was shown by their prominence on the Tory side in riots at York in 1832,[2] but they also found it natural to identify Anglican privilege in Upper Canada with the 'Protestant ascendancy' they had so detested in Ireland. The frequency with which Reformers were elected in Glengarry suggests that Macdonell was unsuccessful in convincing even his clansmen that their religion required them to support the powers that were. His successors were scarcely political radicals, but they coveted equal recognition for their church and sympathized with the desire of their people for equal access to the provincial university. By distancing themselves from the governing clique, moreover, they made it easier for Reformers to cultivate Roman Catholic support.

The political significance of tractarianism lay less in the support it attracted than in the opposition it aroused. Earlier critics of Anglican privilege had denounced it mainly for its inequity, often urging as a clinching argument the relative ineffectiveness of church missionaries in meeting the religious needs of the people. Now they could also point to the scandal of favouring a church that was engaged in spreading doctrines not far removed from popery. Dissenting ministers from Britain, where Anglo-Catholicism stirred even deeper emotions, were especially prominent in the struggle against ecclesiastical endowments. The situation within the Church of England itself was more complex. Association with the British Crown, since 1689 by definition Protestant, had a symbolic value for evangelicals that it did not have for tractarians. Few of the evangelical clergy objected to government grants, and their party resisted all moves toward self-government that might weaken the imperial connection. By contrast, many evangelical laymen, most notably members of some prominent families of Irish background such as the Baldwins and Cawthras, were avid Reformers. Their opposition to the state endowment of religion antedated tractarianism and reflected other concerns, but horror at any suggestion of subsidizing popish aberrations gave it a keener edge. Their leadership would be an important factor in undermining the privileged status of the Church of England.

The most telling blow of all to the continued association of church and state was the entry into Canada West of the Free Church of Scotland. There was no theoretical reason why this should have been so. Thomas Chalmers, the leading founder of the Free Church and a close friend of Strachan, had scandalized the Kirk leaders of the province by suggesting that they should make no objection to the establishment of the Church of England there. Even at the time of the disruption he insisted, 'Though we quit the Establishment, we go out on the Establishment principle.'[3] In Canada West the attachment of some ministers to this principle was strong enough to constitute a significant obstacle to later proposals of union with voluntarist bodies. At first, indeed, the Free Church saw no reason to object to the clergy reserves, and in October 1844, it applied unsuccessfully for a share of their proceeds.

Four years later, upon discovering that the reserve fund had accumulated an unappropriated surplus, the authorities made a belated offer to the Free Church. After lengthy debate the synod rejected it: 'However justifiable the retention of endowments under different circumstances may be ... the Synod is of opinion that it would be deeply injurious to the interests of the Presbyterian Church of Canada and to the cause of the Redeemer in this land, to accept, in present circumstances, of any grant of public money from Government.' It further prohibited individual ministers and congregations from applying for government aid. This change of mind did not in itself represent a repudiation of the establishment principle. The Free Church believed that 'nations, as such, are bound to honour God and support His cause,' but was offended by the government's offer of endowments 'without reference to the distinction between truth and error.' It had in mind not only the continuance of grants to the residuary Kirk but also grants to a Church of England now tinged with tractarianism and, even worse, to the Roman Catholic Church. It broke new ground, however, when it referred to 'the strong feeling which prevails throughout the Church that their acceptance would tend to diminish the usefulness of ministers and the liberality of the people,' for in so doing it committed itself in practice to the voluntarism it rejected in principle. In coming to this position it reflected the sentiments of most of its people. A major factor in provoking change, however, was the conversion to the expediency of voluntarism of Peter Brown of the *Banner* and his son George of the *Globe,* and their tireless promotion of their new-found conviction.[4]

It would be difficult to exaggerate the importance of the Free Church to the later stages of the debate over the reserves and the university. Its leaders were prominent on the platform of every voluntarist rally and active in the formation of societies dedicated to the eradication of ecclesiastical privilege. They were not more thoroughly committed to the cause than their counterparts in more traditionally voluntarist denominations. R.A.

Fyfe and other Baptist participants in the debate enjoyed greater prominence at the time than later historians have accorded them, and the
Canadian Independent later singled out John Roaf of Zion Congregational
Church, Toronto, as having done the most to remove 'the incubus of a state
church' from Canada West. Nevertheless, the Free Church made three very
important contributions. It secured for the voluntarist position the adhesion
of a considerable segment of the population that had not previously been
committed to it. It brought the special zeal of the newly converted. And,
not least important, its unofficial organ the *Globe* became a potent vehicle
for mobilizing voluntarist sentiments throughout the southwestern peninsula. Meanwhile, the Kirk pressed for further endowment on the plea that
'the prevalence of democratic principles and of Arminian and Pelagian
opinions was bound to create hostility to a church holding Establishment
principles and Calvinistic doctrine.'[5]

The Canadian Wesleyan Methodists, despite Egerton Ryerson's early
and well-remembered challenge to Strachan, were relatively quiescent in
the later stages of debate. They were not satisfied with the share of funds
from the reserves that was allotted to them in 1840 and said so at their
conference in 1841, but for several reasons they were reluctant to press the
issue.[6] The break with the English Wesleyans in 1840 allowed the
Canadians to speak out more freely on political issues, but also resulted in
the withholding from both parties of the annual government grant on which
the Indian work depended. Although the deficiency in missionary funds
was quickly made up, a preoccupation with the tasks of reorganizing the
circuits after the separation, countering competition from both the English
and the Methodist Episcopals, and putting finances back into shape left
little leisure for political agitation and added lustre to the prospect of
receiving even half a loaf in government subventions. The ambitious step
of transforming Upper Canada Academy in 1841 into Victoria College,
with responsibility for teaching at the university level, added to the
financial burden and thus to the reasons for caution, and a series of
difficulties in securing adequate leadership for the newly upgraded
institution constituted a further distraction.

Then in 1844, when Governor Sir Charles Metcalfe dissolved the
assembly in protest against the actions of its Reform majority, Ryerson
accused the outgoing administration of unconstitutional procedure and
called for support of the Tories in the forthcoming election. Wesleyans
immediately felt the repercussions. In 1845 a group of dissatisfied
members launched a short-lived publication, the *Toronto Periodical
Journal*, with no other purpose than to counter Ryerson. Membership in
the Wesleyan societies, which had increased by five thousand in the three
years after the break with the English, declined by more than two thousand

in the next two as the result of massive desertions to the New Connexion, the Methodist Episcopals, and the Primitive Methodists.[7] Many who remained in the fold were distinctly uncomfortable with the turn of events. Reunion with the English was in the air, however, and conference leaders were reluctant to dampen the prospects for it by taking radical stands on issues of church and state.

Neither the Wesleyan conference nor the *Christian Guardian* desisted from opposition to what all Methodists regarded as an unfair settlement of the reserves question or to the Anglicans' virtual control of the provincial university, but during the late 1840s many Wesleyans were showing signs of reverting to their traditional pietism. In their view, politics was at best trifling in importance when weighed against the salvation of souls, and in all probability a serious distraction from it. The same line of argument suggested that when involvement in political matters could not be avoided, the part of wisdom was to favour policies that would conduce to the encouragement of vital religion. Wesleyan ministers retained for the time being their determination not to accept a penny of money towards their own salaries. Support for Indian missions or Victoria College was not necessarily in the same category.[8]

Rather improbably, the first person to revive serious agitation on the clergy reserves was John Strachan. The Church of England had little reason, apart from the conviction of some of its leaders that it was entitled to the entire endowment, to complain of a distribution of funds that still left it the lion's share. Its problem was that the legislature was much more concerned to open the reserved lands for settlement than to provide revenue for the churches, and had offered terms highly favourable to lessees and squatters. Strachan saw a danger that a finite and irreplaceable asset might be sold at bargain-basement prices, with little advantage to the intended beneficiaries. The solution that he either proposed or quickly endorsed was to vest the administration of the Church of England portion in the church society of his diocese, presumably leaving other denominations free to make similar requests. The problem he addressed was a practical one, for the need for clergy was growing much more rapidly than the resources available to meet it. The mood of the province, even after the election of Metcalfe's Tory legislature in 1844, made his solution politically impossible. The net result of his initiative, apart from some minor improvements in administration that were generally admitted to be necessary, was to keep the issue before the public.[9]

What ultimately doomed the reserves was their belated success in producing surplus revenue. The division worked out in 1840 had been conditional on the availability of revenue in excess of that needed to meet existing commitments. Receipts on old sales were to be divided between the Churches of England and Scotland in the ratio of two to one, an arrangement that was to prove an unexpected windfall for the Kirk when the disruption abruptly reduced its commitments. Other denominations were to benefit only from new sales, and from them only when existing charges had been met. These conditions were fulfilled in 1848, when a laconic notice in the official *Canada Gazette* of 29 January announced the existence of a surplus already amounting to £1,800 and invited churches that had hitherto been overlooked to apply for a share. Denominations with an outright commitment to voluntarism did not apply; the Baptists and the United Presbyterians, however, took advantage of the invitation to reaffirm their conviction that the money should be used for general education. The Free Church declined the proffered gift as inexpedient. Requests from Lutherans and Moravians reflected the state-church tradition of Germany. Despite the original designation of the reserves for 'a Protestant clergy,' Roman Catholics were similarly uninhibited by a voluntarist tradition. The Wesleyan Methodists, once again a combined English-Canadian body, asked for money not only for their educational projects but, in a break with precedent, for 'distressed parsonages.'[10]

This reminder that the reserves involved not merely tokens of privilege but actual cash set off a spate of agitation. Already in late 1848 editorials were being written and resolutions passed in favour of the complete abolition of religious endowment. A more vigorous campaign against the reserves was inaugurated in 1850 with the formation of the Anti-Clergy Reserves Association, later renamed the Anti-State Church Association. The holding of its organizational meeting at Knox Church, Toronto, signalled the growing importance of the Free Church in the movement, though the speakers represented the whole spectrum of voluntarist denominations. In 1851 the Baptists sponsored a series of meetings that featured speakers from both sides. Their own contention, like that of voluntarists generally, was not that the reserves should be equitably divided but that their very existence was 'at variance with Christianity as revealed in the Bible, and unjust to non-professing members of the civil government.'[11] Meanwhile, Strachan drummed up pro-church rallies and counter-petitions. He was seconded by William Morris of the Kirk, which had objected to the settlement of 1840 but was now doing well out of it, as well as by Roman Catholics who, despite their earlier support for the Reformers, found it natural to associate George Brown's attacks on the reserves with his repeated denunciation of their church.

As the controversy proceeded, Strachan found himself increasingly isolated. In 1851 the Wesleyan conference, torn between the need to hold together a still fragile union and the convictions of most of its members, broke its silence so far as to make known that while it regarded the matter as essentially one for the imperial Parliament, its own preference was for a voluntarist solution. Even within churches favouring the reserves there was a growing inclination to adapt as quickly as possible to the inevitable result. The mind of the province was no longer in doubt. The process of legal enactment took a little while, for legislators had other matters to consider and personal interests to further. By the time they were ready to act, a convenient change of government in Britain had brought the necessary consent of the colonial office to a local decision. In 1854 the Conservative administration of John A. Macdonald voted the clergy reserves out of existence, subject to provision for vested interests. The proceeds were not applied to education but assigned for general purposes to the municipalities, many of which lost their shares during the financial panic of 1857.

Unlike the compromise of 1840 on the reserves, the 1837 amendments to the University Act that provided for a reduced measure of Anglican control never had even the appearance of permanence. The realities of the situation became evident in 1843 when it was observed that only Anglicans participated in the official opening of King's College.[12] The college became in practice a Church of England institution, teaching Anglican divinity and using the Book of Common Prayer in its chapel. Throughout the 1840s, therefore, the legislature wrestled with the problem of devising a solution to the university question that would be acceptable to all parties. The problem was particularly intractable because of the existence of several vested interests. The Wesleyans had Victoria College, the Kirk Queen's University, and the Roman Catholics Regiopolis College, none of which would willingly be surrendered without compensation. The Church of England, if it should lose King's College, would be bereft of any institution of higher learning. The voluntarist denominations had no arts colleges and no desire to establish them, but hoped instead to be able to set up theological halls under the wing of a neutral provincial institution. It was in this expectation, indeed, that the Free Church commenced theological classes in Toronto in 1844. Throughout the decade a succession of university bills followed one another into legislative oblivion, more than once carrying with them the sponsoring administration. These bills all sought to broaden the range of government support while taking some cognizance of existing denominational interests. Two of them provided for the amalgamation of existing arts colleges, while allowing them some continued existence as theological halls as well as some financial support. A third called for Anglican retention of King's College along with the division of its endowment. They received varying degrees of favour from denominations already in the field of higher education; their provisions for continued support to sectarian colleges were uniformly attacked by the rest.

The bill that finally passed, sponsored in 1849 by the Reform administration of Robert Baldwin, was more radical than any of the others. It provided for a single secular university at Toronto, with no aid to denominational teaching and only token representation for existing colleges on the university senate. The voluntarist groups and the Free Church welcomed it wholeheartedly. They were joined in their support not only by a number of dissident Wesleyans and Anglicans but by the bulk of Roman Catholics, who valued equal access to a neutral university more than any prospect of government aid to their feeble college at Kingston. Even the ultramontane Armand de Charbonnel, recently arrived in Toronto, could see little wrong with Baldwin's bill.[13] On the other hand, the act's provision for the concentration of higher education in a single non-sectarian university struck supporters of Victoria and Queen's as a death sentence for their institutions. It was a crushing blow to Strachan, who was left without even an impoverished college. With an energy that showed his indomitable will to advantage as never before, he was able by canvassing English friends to have a voluntarily supported replacement, Trinity College, in operation by 1851.

In the long run these bold decisions to cut all ties between church and state proved, in the case of the reserves and the university alike, to mark less than complete breaks with the past. To the great indignation of voluntarists, the act secularizing the reserves contained a provision for respecting the vested rights of existing claimants. In order to get the issue off the provincial agenda the government encouraged the commutation of claims on the future, both individual and corporate, into lump-sum payments. Individual members of the clergy were persuaded (some after a little arm-twisting) to make over their allotments to their respective denominations. Of a total of £381,971, 65 per cent went to the Church of England, 28 per cent to the Church of Scotland, 5.4 per cent to the Roman Catholics, and 2.6 per cent to the Wesleyan Methodists. To the first two bodies the sums represented a considerable endowment, though much of the Kirk's portion would disappear in the failure of the Commercial Bank in 1867. The rectories, equally scandalous to voluntarists, survived an attempt at secularization by George Brown that came within five votes of success in the legislative assembly. In a separate transaction the annual imperial grant to the Wesleyans for Indian missions was commuted in 1855 and taken back to England.[14]

Baldwin's University Act allowed no such exceptions, but it was not permitted to stand unaltered for long. Within a year he was compelled to introduce a declaratory act reassuring Upper Canadians of the Christian character of their provincial university. In 1853 a further bill, introduced by Francis Hincks and passed almost unanimously, reduced the university to an examining body and left teaching to affiliated colleges. The denominational colleges were invited to affiliate, and the teaching faculty of the university was reconstituted as University College. Aid to the denominational colleges was part of the original intention of the bill. All that was enacted in the end was a vague provision that any surplus income from the university endowment might be appropriated from time to time by the legislature for 'Academic Education in Upper Canada,'[15] and an astute university senate made sure that no surplus was ever allowed to accumulate. Annual grants eased some of the financial strain on the denominational colleges until the newly constituted Ontario legislature cut off the funds in 1868.

Looking back, one has the impression that the secularization of the clergy reserves was final but not complete, that of the provincial university complete but not final. The financial legacy of the reserves and other direct subsidies to the churches was considerable and at the time seemed a serious limitation on the separation of church and state for which voluntarists had struggled so long. Psychologically, however, the effects of secularization were decisive, and led Ontarians to take for granted henceforth that the state had no business in the sanctuaries of the province. This assumption was confirmed in 1866 by a court ruling that the Church of England had no special legal status or privilege, and no one has shown any disposition to argue otherwise. Despite the inability of the denominational colleges to secure any portion of the university endowment, Baldwin's University Act did not succeed in its aim of expunging denominationalism from higher education. Victoria and Queen's survived, and by their survival deprived the government of any excuse for denying a charter to Trinity. A number of new colleges were founded, several by denominations that had been among the most vociferous advocates of secularization. The University of Toronto, deprived of expected support, looked at times suspiciously like a preparatory school for theologues bound for Knox. An assumption persisted, to bear fruit only in the twentieth century, that governments might legitimately subsidize denominational colleges so long as they did so with an even hand.

While these hoary issues were moving toward temporary or permanent resolution, another issue was emerging that would eventually stir up a comparable amount of contention. At the university level, it now appeared, denominational education would be countenanced but not funded by the state. But what provision, if any, would be made for it in elementary and secondary schools?

Prior to the Act of Union in 1841, Upper Canada had had no more than the rudiments of a school system. An act of 1807 provided for the establishment of 'grammar schools' under teachers who were to receive a stipend of £100. Accusations that these rather élitist institutions were controlled by the Church of England were never entirely justified, although an official concern for loyalty ensured that a fair proportion of teachers would be ministers of the two national churches. Strachan was largely instrumental in drafting and securing the passage of the first Common School Act in 1816.[16] The act left the initiative in establishing elementary schools to the parents of children of school age, any twenty of whom might elect trustees, set up a school, and hire teachers; it also provided for a provincial subsidy that was too small to attract many competent teachers. Official efforts were supplemented by private initiative. A few teachers tried to eke out a living from the fees of pupils, and many of the clergy assumed that their vocation carried with it an obligation to set up schools. With education provided in such diverse ways, the question of religious content usually settled itself. When the clergy founded schools, they taught their own brand of religion in them. When parents took the initiative, they were the ones to be satisfied. Strife occurred only when parents failed to agree or when teachers were unusually stubborn, and in fact it was seldom reported.

The first attempt to set up a coherent system of elementary education was Charles Day's Common School Act of 1841, which proved to be provisional in many respects but set important precedents for the treatment of religion in the schools. Earlier school legislation in Upper Canada had made no mention of religion, though the King James version of the Bible had a place in the curriculum and was sometimes supplemented by the Anglican or Westminster catechism.[17] Significantly, the act was intended to apply throughout the newly united province of Canada, and was passed, like its successors until 1867, by a legislature that represented both Canada West and Canada East. Its first draft made no mention of religion; but after receiving petitions from Strachan and the Roman Catholic bishops of Quebec and Kingston the legislature referred the question of religious instruction to a special committee of twenty-three, of whom fifteen were from Canada East. The result was a clause allowing minorities of any denomination to set up their own schools. Members from Canada East, accustomed to a situation in which all schools were explicitly Roman Catholic or Protestant, found it natural to assume that the schools of Canada West were similarly confessional and that fairness demanded exemption for minorities. Provision for separate schools was carried over into Hincks' Act of 1843, which was intended for Canada West alone. Among several changes affecting religion, the most significant limited the right to establish separate schools to Roman Catholic or combined Protestant minorities. None of these provisions provoked much controversy at the time.

As all who operate within it seem to be aware even today, the Ontario school system began to assume its classical shape with the appointment of Egerton Ryerson as deputy superintendent of education in 1844 and superintendent in 1846. The choice of a minister of the much-maligned Methodists for such a post was a startling departure from precedent and, in view of Ryerson's electioneering for Metcalfe, smacked strongly of patronage. The appointment had, however, been intended by the reform-minded governor Sydenham, was ratified by his Tory successor Metcalfe, and was continued despite personal antagonisms by a succession of administrations. Ryerson's general philosophy of education was one then becoming current throughout Western society. He believed that the state had a responsibility for the formation of its citizens that could not be left to the vagaries of parental guidance. Education needed, therefore, to be practical, value-informed, and preferably compulsory.

Ryerson's view of the place of religion in schooling was similar to that of Horace Mann and other leading educators of the time. It also reflected his Methodist background and was identical with that set forth in the initial advertisement for Upper Canada Academy. Public education should not be sectarian, but should take account of all shades of provincial opinion. It should, nevertheless, be unmistakably Christian in content, for no one doubted the Christian basis of Upper Canadian society. Equally significant was Ryerson's conviction that morality, the inculcation of which he regarded as a special obligation of the schools, could only be grounded in Christianity. This conviction he enshrined in his *First Lessons in Christian Morals*, which he published in 1871 specifically for use in Ontario schools. The *Lessons* began with a creed, outlined the duties required by Scripture, contained a section on the sacraments, and even included a defence of miracles. Although he might have been content to assume that his readers would accept the necessity of this grounding, he took pains to demonstrate that the light of nature was insufficient as a basis for morality and that further illumination must be sought in Scripture.[18]

Eager to secure the co-operation of all religious groups, Ryerson assembled a widely representative board of education in 1846 and persuaded Michael Power, the Roman Catholic bishop of Toronto, to chair it.[19] But what, then, would be the place of the separate schools already sanctioned by law? Ryerson was too much a realist to demand their abolition. He was convinced, however, and would remain convinced with apparent reason for many years, that the superior resources of the common schools would limit their number and even lead to their eventual disappearance. He also believed that there was no valid reason for even Roman Catholics to object to the inclusion of non-sectarian Christianity in the curriculum. His concept of 'common Christianity' was, however, to be challenged from two directions.

Sometimes it was objected that Ryerson's common Christianity was not common enough. At first the chief ground urged for permission to establish separate schools was the possibility that Roman Catholic children might be exposed to Protestant propaganda or embarrassed by having attention called to their oddity if they declined to take part in Protestant exercises (or vice versa, for in the 1840s there were more Protestant than Roman Catholic separate schools). Power claimed no more, and his position had support in high places; for some time the Sacred Congregation for the Propagation of the Faith permitted Catholic participation in the non-sectarian national schools of Ireland so long as no taint of heresy was injected. Armand de Charbonnel, Power's ultramontane successor, used the same argument in a more acerbic way, complaining to Ryerson that the school system was open to 'a quaker book abusing baptism, a methodist book abusing the high church, a presbyterian book abusing the trinity of persons in God, a socinian book abusing all mysteries,' etc.[20] While this description was highly exaggerated, Ryerson's common Christianity was in fact so distinctly an evangelical Protestant version of the faith as to alienate Roman Catholics and to create serious difficulties for high Anglicans.

This argument for separate education would have lost its force if the common schools actually had been religiously neutral. Some outright voluntarists, especially Baptists and United Presbyterians, would have liked to see them so. Although he admitted that 'there is a knowledge and principle necessary to man's acting his part as a rational and accountable being,' William Proudfoot argued that teaching it was not the business of the common schools. This position was unacceptable to the great majority of Protestants, and William Morris was not the only one prepared to pay the price: 'If the use, by Protestants, of the Holy Scriptures in their schools, is so objectionable to our fellow-subjects of that other faith, the children of both religious persuasions must be educated apart; for Protestants never can yield to that point, and, therefore, if it is insisted that the Scriptures shall not be a class-book in schools, we must part in peace, and conduct the education of the respective Bodies according to our sense of what is right.'[21] Roman Catholics had great difficulty with this point. Although today scholars have found it relatively easy to devise a translation of the Bible acceptable to Roman Catholics and Protestants alike, it was then considered improper for Catholic children to remain in a room where the Protestant Bible was read or a version of the Lord's Prayer only slightly different from their own was recited.

A contrasting objection was that Ryerson's Christianity was *too* common, and failed to include the distinctive teachings without which its impact would be seriously blunted. Strachan made this point repeatedly over many years; he maintained that non-sectarian schools could teach at best a watered-down version of Christianity. Like-minded Anglicans backed him in various ways. In 1845 the periodical *Church* protested the 'virtual exclusion' of the Bible from the schools, and twenty years later C.E. Thompson of Fergus was still arguing that 'neither piety nor morality' could be cultivated without distinctive religious teaching. Adam Townley, a former Methodist preacher turned high Anglican, proposed that any denomination be allowed to sponsor its own schools.[22]

During the 1850s Charbonnel began to make use of this line of argument, insisting that to ensure the proper education of their children Roman Catholics could be content with nothing less than the complete control of their schools. He had considerable precedent for his stand. From Macdonell's time the bishops of the province, convinced that education proceeded best in a totally Catholic ambience, had attached a high priority to the foundation of schools. The rising tide of ultramontanism would have intensified pressure for Catholic education even if Charbonnel had never entered the province.[23] Yet it was of great practical importance that Roman Catholic demands for separate schools had been put forward at first on the very different ground of affording protection to the sensitivities of a minority. Ryerson's attitude to the question, in particular, would always be coloured by his recollection of Power's co-operative spirit.

Anglican objections were at first the most worrisome to the promoters of a unified system. Strachan was assiduous in applying pressure from 1841 almost until his death in 1867, and no one doubted that he was a formidable opponent. Yet it was symptomatic of changing times that even while on traditional issues of church and state he was still defending the most favoured position of the Church of England, he was reduced on this newer one to basing his claim on the right of a minority to fair treatment. His demands were rejected in the end not because they were less reasonable than those of Roman Catholics but because politicians knew that they would gain no votes by conceding them. Most Anglicans were content with the common schools, and proposals such as Townley's for extending the privilege of separate schools to all denominations were frightening to ratepayers who recoiled even from the cost of a single system. Roman Catholics insisted on separate facilities, and not only because Charbonnel condemned support or patronage of mixed schools as a mortal sin. As an underprivileged minority they were comfortable in sending children to schools where, in the company of their own kind, they would learn to respect themselves for what they were. In Hamilton, at least, the establishment of separate schools led to a large increase in the attendance of Catholic children.[24] Meanwhile, concerned Anglicans founded private schools, sometimes as much for social as for religious reasons.

The pattern of separate education familiar to Ontarians of the twentieth century was the product of a long and complicated process: moves and counter-moves, amendments in committee and changes in regulations, lofty episcopal pronouncements and ringing denunciations of them in the *Globe*, a series of elections fought ostensibly on the issue, and always anxious log-rolling by Ryerson and his successors in the Department of Education. The basic direction of events can, however, be described fairly briefly. What began as an assortment of individual schools to accommodate local minorities, both Roman Catholic and Protestant, eventually became a full-fledged separate school system integrated into the total public system in some respects and isolated from it in others. To secure this result Roman Catholic bishops had applied constant pressure. Charbonnel's approach was through imperious demands and public agitation. John Joseph Lynch, his successor as bishop of Toronto, preferred to negotiate with politicians behind the scenes. Both methods were effective. Most legislative gains were won in the pre-Confederation period, when the union of provinces enabled French Canadians to participate in the process. The British North America Act confirmed those gains, ensuring to the Roman Catholics of Ontario the rights to their own schools enjoyed by the Protestants of Quebec. Yet suggestions that the Confederation bargain imposed on Ontario a system disliked by most of its citizens are only partially correct, for the major expansion of separate school enrolment occurred after 1867. On the eve of Confederation the *Globe* foresaw no danger of any extension of sectarian influence in the schools; but on this occasion Brown was mistaken.[25]

The emergence of a separate school system was, indeed, encouraged by factors beyond episcopal pressure and the support of French-Canadian legislators. It can, for example, be regarded as a counterpart to the centralization that Ryerson tirelessly promoted for the common schools. So long as responsibility for elementary schooling devolved largely on local ratepayers, it was natural to think of separate schools as local phenomena and to justify their establishment in the context of local circumstances. As the schools of the province gradually coalesced into a system, there was a corresponding tendency to think of separate schools as constituting another system within or even apart from it. Rivalry between the two was further stimulated by a trend toward longer schooling in preference to outside employment, which led in the 1850s to a multiplication of common schools and made the defence of Roman Catholic rights seem more urgent.[26] Even so, the hopes of the bishops could scarcely have been fulfilled had it not been for the availability of teachers from the religious orders. The separate schools were never as well funded as the common, and depended largely for their effective operation on services made available at bargain rates by members of religious orders who had taken vows of poverty.

The fruits of continued agitation satisfied neither side. To opponents of separate schools each concession represented yet another nail in the coffin of the public system. To supporters, it constituted a grudging recognition of injustice but never went far enough to redress an unfavourable balance. This difference in judgment reflected a difference in perception of the nature of public schools. Most Protestants thought of them as non-sectarian and therefore regarded exemption from their support as a special privilege allowed to only one denomination. Roman Catholics thought of public schools as Protestant and therefore regarded equal provision for their own schools as a requirement of simple justice. Misunderstanding was compounded by the views that most nineteenth-century Ontarians entertained of one another's religions. Separate schools were part of the papal plot to which knowing Protestants were wise; public schools were nests of infidelity, and even the morals of Roman Catholic children were not safe in them.[27] Hysterical exaggerations aside, there was a measure of truth in each perception.

Essentially a product of the nineteenth century, the Ontario school system came to embody some assumptions that have proved to be distinctly time-bound. While rejecting any preference for one sectarian view of Christianity over another, legislators had no qualms about accepting into the educational curriculum a 'common Christianity' that can be recognized in retrospect as having pertained to a particular time and a particular constellation of Protestant sects. They also did not hesitate, despite the pleas of Strachan and others, to determine that some sectarian differences were significant enough to justify separate schools and that others were not. Their classification of Ontario children as either little Protestants or little Catholics accurately reflected the perceptions of the time, but it no longer corresponds very closely to the realities of an increasingly secular and pluralistic society.

One cannot fail to be struck, moreover, by the application of different criteria to the place of religion in elementary, secondary, and higher education. The result cannot be justified in terms of logical symmetry, but there were historical reasons for it. Roman Catholics wanted elementary schools to maintain their faith, as well as universities to ensure an educated priesthood and to hold the gifted children of their élite members. Between these two levels they inherited a distinctive tradition, that of 'little seminaries' that concentrated on classical and philosophical studies. They did not require more of these than the teaching orders could provide, for a working-class constituency furnished few candidates for them. Archbishop Lynch, the one person who might have lobbied successfully for Roman

Catholic secondary schools, never overcame a suspicion that too much education was likely to detach Catholics from their faith. He therefore allowed Ryerson to put a single system into place without serious protest.[28]

Along with some direct and immediate effects on Ontario law and administration, these varied encounters of church and state had repercussions and implications that were both significant and ambiguous. Even before the province had decided that support of churches was not its concern, it had discovered that the religious interests of its people extended to fields, such as education, to which it could not be indifferent. It also learned that while it might officially ignore churches as such it could not ignore the constituencies they represented. The resulting approach had the merit of recognizing, in Laski's terms, that the total community must take account of particular communities within it. Its great drawback has been that the relation of denominational institutions to the state has been determined more often by trade-offs among interested parties than by rational argument. Pragmatism has been a useful hedge against the too easy assumption that the things of Caesar can be distinguished neatly from the things of God, but it has also injected a large element of expediency into the determination of the line between them.

On their side, the churches had to learn to adapt to a new situation as Old World dichotomies of church and dissent dissolved into a New World continuum of officially equal denominations. As the state learned that it was not thereby absolved from considering the interests of religious communities, so the churches discovered that they could not ignore social and economic developments within provincial society. The voluntarist denominations, despite their protestations of neutrality, found themselves concerned with many of the matters with which legislatures dealt; they then applied to them political techniques they had learned in resisting Anglican privilege. The Church of England, whose expectations of preferment had been unceremoniously dashed, made the transition with remarkable grace. Freed from the 'abominable incubus' of its pretensions to establishment, it could now begin the painful process of seeking to resolve its own internal differences.[29]

This process of adjustment set in motion new jockeyings for position that related to different attitudes to denominational education rather than unequal access to endowments, and brought about a few remarkable realignments. Among those forming part of Strachan's long funeral cortège on 5 November 1867 were a group of Victoria College students from Cobourg, the more conspicuous because of the absence of a delegation from nearby Knox College. Along with some losses there had been significant gains for all. Those who had supported and opposed state endowment could now combine to fulfil, albeit with different emphases, the role of custodians of the provincial conscience.[30] In the process, despite the appearance of new lines of theological cleavage, they would become more similar in parish programs and social function. The shadow of a legal establishment had been exchanged for the substance of an unofficial but highly effective moral wardship.

10 *Mission Accomplished*

By 1867 Ontario had many of the attributes of a mature society. Railways now ran where stage-coaches had bumped along rutted roads. A network of telegraph lines spanning the continent had just been connected with Europe by submarine cable, and daily newspapers relayed its messages to the public without delay. Wheat farming, increasingly efficient technologically, was nevertheless being challenged by manufacturing as the province's economic mainstay. Entrenched privilege had given way to state-assisted enterprise, alarms of rebellion to the respectable banalities of responsible government. Surplus wealth was accumulating, and with it greater attention was being paid to literature and the arts; employers and workers alike listened avidly to informative lectures on an astonishing range of subjects. Except in the north, which would reach maturity only in the twentieth century, 'new settlements' were restricted to marginal areas. For the rest of the century population growth would depend on natural increase, and the largely British population that had already arrived would lose by westward emigration more than it would gain by immigration from abroad.

The growth of the churches had outstripped even that of the province. For almost a century after the arrival of the loyalists their chief preoccupation, when they were not engaged in political battles, had been the provision of religious institutions and the incorporation into them of the indifferent, the careless, and the uncommitted. By the time of Confederation this initial mission could be regarded as substantially accomplished. Between 1842 and 1871, when population slightly more than tripled, the increase in Anglican and Wesleyan ministers, for whom figures are most readily available, was at least fourfold. The census of 1871 noted 4,094 church buildings of all denominations, as against only 1,474 in 1851. These structures, now mostly of brick and stone, clustered at rural crossroads, measured the importance of ambitious towns, and dominated the Toronto skyline. They accommodated not only Sunday services but prayer meetings, Bible classes, and an abundance of midweek services. The great majority of Protestant children were enrolled in Sunday schools, and an increasing number of Roman Catholic confraternities and sodalities catered to the faithful of various ages and both sexes. In 1860 the Free Church synod was still lamenting 'much worldliness and immorality' and 'much indifference and apathy among the professed followers of the Saviour,' but progress was evident in the reduction of the proportion of the population expressing no religious preference from 16.7 per cent in 1842 to the negligible figure of 0.9 per cent in 1871.[1]

Ontarians were not entirely dependent for spiritual nourishment on the churches. The Young Men's Christian Association, under lay leadership but with an aggressively evangelistic program, opened its first local branch at Toronto in 1853 and was entering many smaller communities by the 1860s.[2] Bible and tract societies commanded followings difficult to imagine today, and temperance organizations normally opened their proceedings with worship. Fraternal lodges provided a relaxed social atmosphere, especially welcome to men, that contrasted with the starchy moralism of the churches. Many Protestants treasured Masonic rituals of a formality they would not have tolerated in their own churches, and Orangemen were never unmindful of the theological commitments of their order. Yet, while members of such extra-ecclesial organizations might at times compare them favourably with the churches, they would have found it almost unthinkable not to·have church connections as well.

Participation in church-sponsored activities and organizations was important to individual Ontarians in a variety of ways. Affiliation with a particular church was a major factor in establishing a sense of identity in relation to others. It was a prime source of social contacts, which were especially important if the denomination insisted that its members should 'marry in.' Church picnics, teas, and bazaars, and for that matter revival meetings and sermons, constituted a large proportion of the available entertainment. Official positions in religious societies offered, even in the major centres, some of the most prestigious public roles. Above all, church affiliation provided a system of beliefs and a world-view that enabled adherents to make coherent sense of daily events. In a province where money-making sometimes seemed all-important, it pointed to values that both undergirded and transcended secular enterprises.[3] How far individual understanding coincided with that offered in sermons is impossible to measure, for both Protestants and Roman Catholics mixed their ecclesiastical dogmas with a stock of folk wisdom and superstition which they freely shared. Family worship was common, however, and grace at meals seems to have been almost universal.

Religion was also a major factor in shaping community life. Special services and Sunday school rallies were significant events, and were reported at length in the local newspaper. Members of the cloth, including by this time even representatives of the more obscure branches of Methodism, ranked as leading citizens. A number were active boosters of their communities, promoting such enterprises as mechanics' institutes, public libraries, agricultural societies, and even factories. Some demonstrated modern methods of farming, collected botanical specimens, or investigated the geological formations of their neighbourhoods.[4] Most conspicuously, the churches set the moral tone of their communities, forming a public opinion that would not have tolerated hanging washing on the line on Sunday. If they were not always able to determine actual behaviour, they were increasingly able to determine acceptable behaviour.

Religious influence was not confined to the local scene. Parents looked mainly to denominational colleges for the higher education of their children. Methodist Victoria College, Presbyterian Queen's, and nine of the ten arts colleges founded in the 1850s were denominational in orientation. Young women, excluded from all but Albert College by the prevalent feeling that co-education was inappropriate in institutions offering university degrees, were served by a plethora of privately operated 'ladies' colleges' that almost always featured a protective religious atmosphere. A fair proportion of the periodical press was denominationally sponsored or undertook to speak for a particular religious constituency. The Methodist Book Room was issuing an expanding list of Sunday school materials, and was beginning to take a conscious interest in the elevation of literary taste. The promoters of a proposed Montreal newspaper, the *Daily Review*, testified to the public interest in religion by stating their intention 'to have a special staff of reporters' at the synod of the Canada Presbyterian Church in order to cover such 'vital questions' as Presbyterian union, a proposed hymn-book, and the use of instrumental music.[5]

The churches, not content to rest on their laurels, were aggressively propagating their doctrines. Theological students used their spare time to distribute tracts from door to door, and in 1856 the Free Church reported that its colporteurs had visited thousands of families and held 'religious conversations' with most. At Victoria College, where 'professors' of religion were said at one time to be almost extinct, a remarkable revival occurred during the 1853–4 session as the result of a series of prayer meetings. Before the year was out the godly 'plugs,' overwhelmingly outnumbered at first, had utterly routed the worldly 'bloods.' A continent-wide revival in 1857–8 resulted in unprecedented if often temporary accessions to the membership of more than one Canadian Methodist body, and indeed had been anticipated by a successful series of revival meetings conducted by James Caughey at Toronto and Phoebe and Walter Palmer at

Hamilton. Such results were not limited to denominations ordinarily associated with revivalism. John Bayne of Knox Church, Galt, whose sermons were regularly punctuated by 'deep sighs and groans,' saw his earnestness rewarded when a memorable revival broke out in 1869. Roman Catholics reported responses to parish missions reminiscent of early camp meetings: 'Even the most urgent work of harvesting was left undone. People seemed insensible to hunger, thirst, and rest.'[6]

By 1867 virtually no section of the present province of Ontario was altogether unreached by the churches. In the Queen's Woods and the Bruce Peninsula their activities were still in the pioneer stage that had long been outgrown elsewhere. The miners of Algoma were of special concern to Strachan, who despite his advancing years paid the district seven episcopal visits. The plight of the shantymen of the Ottawa Valley, who were cut off from regular church services for months at a time, roused even the sluggish Church of Scotland to action in 1868. Over the years, however, they were most consistently served by priests of the Oblate order who began an apostolate among them in 1845. J.-N. Laverlochère, another Oblate who built on earlier Sulpician efforts on the upper Ottawa, pushed a line of Indian missions from Timiskaming to Abitibi and by 1847 to Fort Albany on James Bay. In 1840 the British Wesleyan Methodists sent George Barnley to Moose Factory, and the Ojibwa missionary Peter Jacobs competed for many years with the local *midewiwin* at the present Fort Frances. After Barnley's withdrawal from Moose Factory in 1847 the Church Missionary Society appointed John Horden, who as bishop of Moosonee from 1872 to 1893 gradually built up a staff of largely native clergy. Already, however, the excitement once generated by Indian missions in the southern part of the province had largely dissipated, and the paternalism of while missionaries was displacing the earlier spirit of interracial co-operation. Among the Iroquois of the Grand River energetic Christian proselytizing had reduced the Longhouse proportion to 23 per cent, but this fraction resolutely resisted Christianization and acculturation.[7]

A trickle of black immigrants became a steady flow after 1850, when the Fugitive Slave Act made the northern states unsafe for runaways and free blacks alike. By 1860 an estimated forty thousand were resident in Canada West. Well-intentioned whites, of various denominations and several nationalities, undertook to assist their settlement and improvement. The most successful of these projects was the Buxton colony near Chatham, founded in 1849 by William King with the blessing of the Free Church and the backing of a non-sectarian board of directors. It succeeded mainly because King was able both to maintain a measure of paternal control and to encourage self-reliance on the part of the community. Yet the decisive factor in shaping the religion of the blacks of the province was not white philanthropy but the formation of their own churches, under the guidance of preachers who understood their emotional needs and did not attempt to conform them to alien moulds. Almost without exception these churches were Baptist or Methodist, like those to which evangelists had converted slaves on southern plantations. Although black Baptists sometimes linked themselves with existing associations, the formation of the Amherstburg Baptist Association in 1841 gave them a voice uniquely their own. Black Methodists, coldly received in white congregations, turned mainly to the African Methodist Episcopal church, which entered the province officially in 1838. By 1840 there was an Upper Canadian conference, by 1856 a separate British Methodist Episcopal Church. Black congregations were often confused and divided by the conflicting claims of white agencies to represent their interests, but they were also determined to maintain the freedom for the sake of which they had made their exodus.[8] By the time of Confederation, however, a reverse exodus to the freed soil of the United States was already depleting the ranks of the province's black churches.

By 1867 Ontario churches had gone far along the road to self-reliance. The urgency of raising up a local clergy had been conceded from the outset, for imports had been difficult to secure, expensive, and not always well suited to the country. There might be a lingering feeling that important positions such as bishoprics and professorships at Queen's University would best be supplied 'from home,' but the chief obstacles were a shortage of local facilities for theological education and a constantly increasing demand for clergy. By 1861, however, Knox College counted eighty-six theological graduates and Trinity College thirty-two. In its first quarter-century, by contrast, Queen's of the Kirk conferred only fifteen degrees in theology, and immigrant priests still predominated in the Roman Catholic church.[9]

Financial self-support depended partly on the means of local inhabitants, but by mid-century more on their generosity. Accepting missionary aid easily became a debilitating habit, prompting J.L. Poore to complain in 1865 of 'a want of vigorous life' in Congregational churches 'better off, *apparently*, than many of those who in England help to provide the funds.' By this time, however, external aid was directed mainly to new settlements, which in view of their predominantly emigrant population were regarded as a British responsibility. The Society for Promoting Christian Knowledge helped to build forty churches in the Anglican diocese of Huron, and into the 1870s the Colonial Committee of the Church of Scotland was supporting new missions.[10] Congregations in more settled areas generally accepted responsibility for ministerial upkeep, though they did not always deliver even the pittances they promised.

Progress toward self-sufficiency had brought varying degrees of autonomy as each denomination sought to balance its desire to meet local challenges against its fear of becoming isolated from the nerve-centres of its communion. To Roman Catholics independence from Rome would have been unthinkable, but the elevation of Toronto in 1870 into an archepiscopal see independent of Quebec made possible greater freedom of action. Anglican relations with the mother church were inextricably linked with relations to the state. The formation of a diocesan synod provided both a locally based power structure and a potential replacement for the supporting hand of the state. The first local episcopal election in 1857 was followed in 1862 by the first local consecration and in 1867 by the first election without confirming letters patent from the Crown.[11] Most Protestant churches received as much autonomy as they were able and willing to pay for; some of them hesitated to weaken external links for fear of furnishing excuses for the cutting off of financial grants. After mid-century, however, most British churches were so reluctant to accept additional financial burdens that they seldom intervened forcefully in Canadian affairs.

Despite inhibitions resulting from a lingering sense of dependence, Ontario churches were cautiously beginning to reach out beyond the provincial borders. The Free Church, always prone to identify the pope with Antichrist, took a special interest in missions to French Canadians. In 1851, forty years after the first request from Selkirk colonists for Presbyterian services, its local synod appointed James Black to the Red River. In 1854 the Canada conference took over the British Wesleyan missions among the Indians of Rupert's Land, and in 1866 the Canada Presbyterian church opened its first Indian mission at Prince Albert. By the time of Confederation both Methodists and Presbyterians had representatives in British Columbia. Anglicans learning to live without government subventions and Roman Catholics endeavouring to cope with an influx of famine Irish were still content to leave western missions to European agencies. For ventures even further afield few Ontarians were yet ready. During the late 1850s the Free Church and the Kirk briefly sponsored missionaries overseas, but otherwise provincial participation was limited to modest contributions to British or American societies.[12]

Confederation presented to the churches of Canada's most populous province new challenges and opportunities to which, in time, they would respond in various ways. They did comparatively little directly to bring it about. That churches should not involve themselves in purely political matters was a commonplace of the time, and the project of Confederation was so entangled with issues of defence and railway-building as to appear largely in a political light. When church leaders and religious editors intervened in discussions or negotiations, they usually concerned themselves with aspects of the proposed federation that directly impinged on their interests. The *Canadian Baptist* wanted a settlement that would 'secure the Protestant population of Upper Canada from the domination of the priests and Frenchmen of Lower Canada,' while the Roman Catholic hierarchy sent Archbishop Thomas Connolly of Halifax to London to make sure that the rights of separate schools would be safeguarded. Yet it counted for something that the articulate responses of church leaders to the idea of Confederation were almost uniformly favourable. Apart from the *Canadian Baptist*, the entire Protestant press was cautiously supportive. After some hesitation the Roman Catholic bishops also favoured the scheme, and Bishop E.J. Horan of Kingston toured the maritime provinces in 1865 at John A. Macdonald's request to bring around recalcitrant Roman Catholics there.[13] Roman Catholics favoured Confederation mainly as an alternative to the secularization they foresaw as the inevitable result of annexation to the United States or of representation by population in the united province of Canada. Presbyterians and Methodists, who welcomed most warmly the prospect of a single nation from sea to sea, were, significantly, the only religious bodies in the province with western missions.

Apart from disruptions and consolidations within denominational families, patterns of ecclesiastical allegiance had become fairly stable. Denominations prominent in 1841 continued to dominate the scene in 1867, though with significant changes in relative position. Methodists of all kinds, preferred by 28.5 per cent of the population according to the 1871 census, were now in first place. Presbyterians followed them with 22 per cent. Anglicans, third in denominational standing with 20.4 per cent, nevertheless constituted the largest single ecclesiastical organization. Roman Catholics reached their peak of the century in 1861 with 18.5 per cent as a result of Irish immigration, then slipped back to 16.9 per cent in 1871. Baptists, despite rapid growth, still accounted in 1871 for only 5.3 per cent of the population.

The Wesleyans, who were reunited with their former British partners in 1847, accounted for almost two-thirds of the Methodist total. Egerton Ryerson later reckoned the decades from 1849 to 1869 to have been the brightest in Methodist history,[14] but the price of this prosperity was a rather myopic concern for institutional growth. Only the appointment as president in 1868 of W. Morley Punshon, a prominent English preacher, would rouse the denomination from its provincialism. The Methodist Episcopals, about a third as numerous as the Wesleyans, had more members than all of the other smaller Methodist bodies combined. Less successful than the Wesleyans in appealing to British immigrants, they had steadily gained support in older areas of loyalist and American settlement. Each group had its distinctive emphases. The authority of conference was especially important to Wesleyans, ministerial order to Episcopals, and lay representation to those of English origin. Acrimonious debates were not uncommon, but once the settlement of the clergy reserves question had removed the main source of political contention these differences came to seem less important. Young people tended to join the branch of Methodism by whose agency they happened to have been converted.

Presbyterianism, by contrast, was well on the way toward consolidation. From the time of its formation the Free Church, benefiting from active Scottish support and from the appeal of its principles to a reform-minded constituency, had proved to be a catalyst for mobilizing Presbyterian energies. Attracting at first a minority of Kirk supporters, it overtook the older body in the 1850s. Remnants of the presbytery of Niagara, which after the rebellion never overcame the stigma of Americanism, gradually drifted into it. Leaders of the United Presbyterian synod, sensing the presence of too strong a competitor, immediately made overtures for union. Its achievement was delayed for years by the attachment of one body to a claim for the lordship of Christ in society of and the other to voluntarism, a conflict of principles that had no practical bearing on the Canadian situation but meant a great deal to transplanted Scots. When union finally took place in 1861, the resulting Canada Presbyterian Church immediately became the main Presbyterian body. In the southwestern part of the province where United Presbyterian congregations had been concentrated and where recent immigrants retained memories of the Scottish church struggle, it carried everything before it. The Auld Kirk would have been reduced to insignificance but for a solid base in earlier settlements east of the Bay of Quinte.[15] To those uncomfortable with the rigid dogmatism and narrow moralism of the Canada Presbyterians, however, it represented an attractive alternative.

Despite its failure to maintain its hold on the perquisites of establishment, the Church of England retained enough of its patina to attract a number of Methodists on the rise. With the eclipse of the Family Compact and the virtual disappearance of the military, however, it had ceased to be predominantly a church of the privileged and instead catered mainly to first- and second-generation immigrants from Ireland and England. In Hamilton by mid-century its members were less affluent, on the average, than either long-settled Wesleyan Methodists or aggressive Free Church Presbyterians.[16] Proportionately, Anglicans were most numerous in the cities and towns, though not to the extent they had once been or would be again. Distracted by internal strife, they intervened less vigorously in provincial affairs than some denominations that professed aloofness to politics.

The Roman Catholic population had undergone one shift in ethnic composition and was in process of undergoing another. The massive immigration of the 1840s and 1850s had made it preponderantly Irish, overshadowing the Scots of Glengarry and the French Canadians around Windsor who had given it much of its earlier character. From 1844, however, other French Canadians began to fill the vacant lands of the lower Ottawa Valley. Although most of them were economically motivated, their settlements were sponsored and virtually directed by Catholic zealots who envisaged nothing less than 'la conquête catholique de la Vallée de l'Ottawa.' The diocese of Ottawa, founded in 1847, had a colonization society in operation by 1849. According to a partisan historian, this advance was one that only God could have accomplished 'parce que seul il est tout-puissant.' Although francophones were destined to remain a minority in Ontario, they represented by 1871 more than a quarter of the Roman Catholic population. Irish and French Catholics, while united in defence of their minority rights, constituted two solitudes that never really understood each other. Franco-Ontarians were faithful attendants at mass and catechism, but they did not take so readily to the parish organizations conspicuous in Irish areas. Germans and Alsatians who settled in Waterloo and Bruce counties added another, more relaxed element. At Saint Jerome's College, founded by the Community of the Resurrection in 1865, German and Irish did not always mingle amicably but between them would soon provide, at last, an adequate supply of native-born priests.[17]

Despite great obstacles, the Baptists had finally surmounted the most paralysing of their organizational difficulties. A mounting Upper Canadian resistance to initiatives from Montreal had resulted by 1850 in the collapse of the denominational college and journal there. A major source of contention was a suspicion on the part of Upper Canadian Baptists that the Montrealers were sympathetic to open communion. In fact, they seem not to have practised it, but they maintained close ties with open communion English Baptists and were reluctant to allow the issue to divide the denomination. Rural suspicions of metropolitan leadership may have been an even more significant factor in souring relations. Several efforts during the 1840s to find alternate bases of association had been no more successful. In 1851, however, the formation of the Regular Baptist Missionary Society of Upper Canada provided Baptists with their first effective denominational organization. It purged the open communionists, and in 1858 the Baptists east of Kingston set up a separate society.[18] The Baptist Convention of Ontario and Quebec is a lineal descendant of these societies.

Among the Lutherans, now increasingly concentrated in the Waterloo area, imported theological disputes continued to cause division. In 1842

F.W. Bindemann organized a non-denominational 'free church,' and several ministers eventually embraced Swedenborgianism or Universalism. Those who professed an unadulterated Lutheranism were served mainly by the missionary-minded Pittsburgh Synod, which gave way in 1861 to the Evangelical Lutheran Synod of Canada. Those for whom even these bodies were too liberal welcomed the intensely confessional Missouri Synod, which began to send missionaries in 1854 and eventually overtook its rival. Dissatisfaction with some of the early Lutheran ministers also encouraged the entry of the Evangelical Association and the United Brethren in Christ, German-speaking bodies that had originated on the American frontier as the result of Methodist preaching and that resembled the Methodists in theology and polity. Of the two the Evangelicals made the greater impact on the province, sending their first missionaries in 1836 and organizing a conference in 1864.[19] Other Protestant groups had varying fortunes. While Mennonites and Quakers sought to maintain the integrity of their witness in an increasingly open society, Congregationalists resorted to popular and occasionally sensational preaching to attract the uncommitted.

New religious movements continued to proliferate, seldom attracting stable followings but laying foundations for future variants. During the early 1840s William Miller, a Baptist preacher from Vermont, gave shape to a general mood of expectancy by announcing, on the basis of calculations from Scripture, that Christ would return in 1843. His followers, numerous in the province, remained for a time in the churches but were alienated by the scepticism that greeted them there. Although the failure of Christ to appear in 1843 – or 1844, as a revised calculation suggested – led to widespread disillusionment, knots of persevering believers ultimately coalesced into several more stable groups, among which the Seventh-Day Adventists would become most numerous. Spiritualism came into sudden prominence in 1848, when the Fox sisters of Hydesville, New York, claimed to receive messages from the spirits of the dead through 'rappings' uncaused by living agents. Their family had recently moved from Belleville, and Susanna Moodie, initially sceptical, was convinced of the possibility of communication with the dead by demonstrations given by Kate Fox on a visit to her home town. In 1867 sects emanating from Boston that professed belief in 'soul-unconsciousness' or the annihilation or restoration of the wicked after death seemed sufficiently menacing to inspire several long editorials in the *Christian Guardian*. Most troublesome to the more conventional churches in the long run, however, were the Plymouth Brethren. Between 1862 and 1877 John Nelson Darby, an Englishman who became their most zealous propagandist, paid regular visits to Ontario where each summer a large conference was held at Guelph.[20] The Brethren, who stemmed from the evangelical wing of the Church of England and quickly divided into warring fragments, mapped out a scheme of divine dispensations that would culminate in the winding up of history. Decrying denominationalism, they were adept at infiltrating existing churches and had an especially profound effect on some of the more conservative Baptists.

Since one of the chief attractions of a new religious movement is that it claims to offer a unique key to an understanding of the cosmos, the identification of general trends in the mentality of sectarianism from one period to another is inevitably difficult. Fringe movements of the mid-nineteenth century, like those of almost any other era, ran the gamut from the occult wisdom represented by the Swedenborgians to the scriptural literalism of the Adventists and the Plymouth Brethren. Perhaps, however, one can detect a movement away from special revelations granted to inspired leaders to the careful if not always sophisticated examination of evidence, whether from Scripture, observed phenomena, or the exploration of the mind itself. The sectarianism of the 1860s was much less flamboyant than that of the 1830s, more at home in the study-group or the séance than on the rostrum. Basic to it was an assumption that amateur theologians might discern truths hidden from or suppressed by the authorized representatives of traditional churches.

That religion in Ontario could mean only Christianity was still generally assumed, although many people would have denied the Christian label to the Unitarians and Universalists who maintained a handful of struggling causes. To the followers of Ganiodaio on the Grand River, however, there had now been added another inconspicuous exception. Early in the 1840s a few Jewish merchants from Germany joined a handful of pioneers of their faith already in the province. By 1849 there was a large enough community in Toronto to establish a cemetery. In 1856 the cemetery was followed by a synagogue, later known as Holy Blossom. In 1863 the first Reformed congregation, Anshe Sholom, was organized at Hamilton.[21] Numbering only 518 in 1871, Jews were at first generally welcomed in Ontario in so far as they were noticed at all. Largely of English background and culture, they fitted readily into a society dominated by Bible-reading evangelical Protestants. As yet Ontarians had no suspicion that they might be forerunners of a religious pluralism to which they were totally unaccustomed.

In the Ontario of 1867 religious observance was in most obvious respects what it had always been, though more widely distributed and adapted somewhat to the needs of a more sophisticated society. Worship, whether austere or hearty in performance, was relatively unadorned. Church of England services, outside a few 'advanced' congregations, followed the prayer-book without ceremonial elaboration, and the Lord's Prayer and the Ten Commandments were the most common interior decorations. In the Roman Catholic Church, despite the introduction of a few paraliturgical devotions, a mumbled low mass was still usual on Sunday mornings. The *Christian Guardian* reported in 1864 that Canadian Methodists had always been accustomed to extemporary worship and that kneeling for prayer was universal. Most Presbyterian congregations, especially ones of Free Church background, insisted on the lining out of metrical psalms by a precentor with a tuning-fork. At Zorra, admittedly a bastion of conservatism, the session recorded in 1867 its conviction that only the psalms of David, being inspired by the Holy Ghost, should find a place in public worship. It would accept hymns only in 1894, and an organ in the sanctuary not until 1900. Presbyterians of all varieties continued to shun popish festival days; in 1872 a committee of the Kirk synod was called to begin its sessions on Christmas eve, and no out-of-town members objected. Ontarians clung even to some of the least attractive features of the past. Many churches were disfigured by large family pews, which at Richmond Street Methodist Church in Toronto occupied the centre of the main floor. The practice of coming and going during services was only gradually dying out and taking on new life in the Sunday school.[22]

Sermons had undergone even less change. Contemporary movements had added some new emphases, and a few younger ministers were nibbling at the edges of orthodox systems, but most preachers were still concentrating on the traditional scheme of salvation. John Bayne's contribution to a volume of sermons by prominent Presbyterian ministers began with a reminder of the shortness and uncertainty of life and reaches its climax in an evocation of 'the everlasting torments of hell' awaiting the impenitent. Morley Punshon maintained his reputation as one of the leading preachers of the day with such appeals as the following: 'Do you believe that just beyond you, very near you, there is a heaven of blessedness and a hell of death ... that the rupture of a small air-like vessel, attenuated as the web of a spider, may at any moment call you into the one or plunge you into the doom of the other? And yet you are only almost persuaded to escape the one and to secure the other! In all solemnity, in all earnestness I ask you to come to Jesus today!'[23] Old-timers could not complain of any watering down of traditional warnings and promises.

In denominations accustomed to direct evangelism, time-honoured methods, often identified in popular memory with the frontier era, continued to be applied with success in a more settled society. After a period of neglect during the 1840s camp meetings were vigorously promoted in the following decade, and big-time evangelists from the United States included the chief towns of Canada West in their itineraries.

James Caughey, a dynamic Irish-American who campaigned successfully for some years in England, visited the province several times after returning to North America in 1847. At London in 1855 he reported hundreds converted and scores sanctified, and in Toronto Wesleyan membership increased by almost 80 per cent during his visits there. It was in the old Methodist heartland and the southwestern peninsula, however, that evangelism continued to bring its greatest rewards. Phoebe Palmer, whose weekly Tuesday meetings in New York had made personal holiness a live issue in all evangelical churches, regularly made the summer circuit of camp meetings with her husband Walter. Despite the Palmers' prominence, many revivals were promoted and led locally. That the emotional temperature was still high is indicated by a report of a camp meeting in the Kingston district in 1856: 'The vast multitude fell prostrate on their knees, as the forest sometimes falls before the raging tempest; and the exclamation might be heard from many a trembling penitent, "God be merciful to me a sinner" ... while many others prostrate under the power of God could only exclaim "Glory! Glory!"' Results were considerably less spectacular during the 1860s; still, scarcely an issue of the *Christian Guardian* lacked references to successful camp or protracted meetings. Among the Primitive Methodists, who had introduced camp meetings to England, such gatherings were hitting their stride in Canada West only in the 1850s.[24]

Churches continued to uphold familiar norms of behaviour. In 1844 the Kirk of Smiths Falls barred employees of the Rideau Canal from church privileges for working the locks on the sabbath, even while admitting that they had no choice if they were to keep their jobs, and in 1867 the *Christian Guardian* required few words to record its judgment on novel-reading: 'Sow fiction, reap fiction.' The campaign against alcohol retained its central place. After some falling off in the late 1830s it gathered steam again in 1845 when the Congregationalist layman John Dougall founded the Montreal *Witness* to promote a variety of religious and moral causes. In that same year a group of Congregationalists circularized the churches in favour of the use of unfermented grape juice in the Lord's Supper, with little initial success. The leadership of the Sons of Temperance and the Independent Order of Good Templars, active in the province by 1848 and 1854 respectively, was predominantly lay. These organizations stressed expedient arguments, but they did not hesitate to urge abstinence as the only course consistent with Christian profession. The Roman Catholic clergy, distressed by the prevalence of drunkenness among Irish immigrants, initiated an active temperance movement of their own. After a tour of the United States in 1849 by Theobald Mathew, the Irish 'apostle of temperance,' Thomas Fitzhenry of Saint Paul's Church, Toronto, collected enough pledges to gain a comparable local reputation.[25]

Along with much that was familiar, however, there were also intrusions of novelty into religious life. Some innovations slipped in almost unnoticed; others provoked more controversy than their intrinsic importance seemed to warrant. The form of worship was a particularly sensitive area. Tractarianism aroused such deep suspicions within the Church of England that any departure from existing practice, however innocent in its motivation, was a signal for bitter and often prolonged wrangling. To many watchful Scottish, and sometimes Irish, Presbyterians the choirs and organs then beginning to appear in urban churches were interruptions of direct communication between the congregation and God and hence symptoms of encroaching priestcraft. Along with the use of paraphrases and hymns to supplement the original psalms of David as preserved without distortion in the Scottish Psalter of 1650, they stood under the further condemnation of lacking scriptural warrant.[26] So poor was Presbyterian singing and so listless were many Anglican responses, however, that dogged resistance could merely delay innovation. Anglican evangelicals gradually learned Merbecke settings, and Presbyterian congregations founded to resist organs soon installed them.

Evangelism, while still promoted by time-honoured methods, was increasingly being directed to a different constituency. Although rallies seemed in most respects as successful as ever, the complaint began to be heard that those in attendance were seldom treated any longer to the startling conversions of notorious sinners that had been such a prominent feature of pioneer revivals. It was noted internationally, indeed, that revivals had little effect on either the fashionable or the down-and-out but were directed increasingly toward the urban middle class. Many who responded to altar calls seem to have been recycled from previous revivals. Concurrent with this change was a downward trend in the age of converts. Youth had always dominated their ranks, but now conversion was increasingly a rite of passage for adolescents and even pre-adolescents. Church leaders, observing the susceptibility of children to evangelistic appeals and the greater perseverance of those who had known Christ from childhood, encouraged this trend and fashioned Sunday school curricula designed to culminate in decision for Christ. The thrust of evangelism also underwent a subtle change. It had always been assumed that a converted Christian would behave morally, but now the promotion of programs of moral reform sometimes seemed to be the chief purpose of evangelism.[27]

These changes were encouraged by the holiness movement with which the Palmers were associated, and which they and Caughey were chiefly instrumental in introducing to the province. Wesley, who defined entire sanctification as abstention from any conscious sin, had seen it not as the culmination of religious experience but as a gateway to greater understanding and growth in grace. Phoebe Palmer, while remaining largely within this tradition, freely used language suggesting that perfection could be grasped by a simple act of human will. Some others went a good deal further, and denigrated any conversion that did not lead to perfection to the point where in effect one was offered a choice of 'holiness or hell.'[28] Whereas Wesley's emphasis on sanctification had been linked with a vigorous program of evangelizing the unchurched, the emphases of the later movement were calculated to appeal more strongly to impressionable youth and to church members who were dissatisfied with the level of their spiritual experience. They also contributed significantly to the rather legalistic moralism of the age, for adherence to conventional prohibitions was the readiest test of sanctity. The initial vogue of holiness revival in the province was relatively brief, but it left a permanent impress on Ontario Methodism.

While the churches were maintaining familiar stands on moral and social issues, they were also supplementing persuasion with attempts to secure the co-operation of the state. In 1851 the state of Maine prohibited the manufacture and sale of alcoholic beverages. From that time forth the enactment of similar legislation became for Protestant temperance advocates the ideal solution to the alcohol problem. In Canada West their first major success was the institution of local option by the Dunkin Act of 1864. Alarmed by the sailing of mail packets, the running of trains, and even the delivery of mail of Sunday, Protestant churches also began to press during the 1850s for laws in defence of the Lord's day. Slavery in the United States, though no longer an issue in 1867, had awakened a great deal of indignation after the passage of the Fugitive Slave Law in 1850. Ministers of several denominations were prominent among those who in 1851 organized the Anti-Slavery Society of Canada,[29] and several churches in the province virtually broke off relations with American counterparts that failed to take a decisive stand on the issue.

This shift of emphasis from direct attempts to convert the ungodly to measures of consolidation and promotion has often been interpreted as evidence of a cooling of religious fervour and further linked with the transition from a frontier to a settled economy. It might more realistically be regarded as an inevitable result of the success of the churches in bringing the bulk of the population within their pastoral care. Their initial mission of reaching the unchurched accomplished, they had little alternative but to set new and more ambitious goals for themselves. A wider view would also recognize that what was happening in Ontario was a local example of a much more general phenomenon. Similar campaigns of evangelism had been taking place in almost every Western country, Protestant and Roman Catholic, and everywhere the eventual result was a movement beyond direct assaults on readily accessible unbelievers to programs of religious nurture, social penetration, and geographical extension. To most Christians of the time the prominence of these activities signalled not decline but the prospect of further advance, and they found it natural to read further signs of a favouring Providence into such contemporary secular developments as the spectacular extension of European colonization and conquest, a dazzling succession of useful technical inventions, and the rise of a well-informed middle class.

John Roaf, Toronto's most prominent Congregational minister, gave eloquent expression to this mood of religious optimism in a series of lectures originally delivered as an antidote to Millerism and published as *Lectures on the Millennium* in 1844. Miller's followers professed a premillennial theology, which expected history to reach a catastrophic climax in the sudden return of Christ to earth to institute his reign of a thousand years. Roaf set forth an alternative 'postmillennial' vision according to which Christ would return physically only at the end of the millennium, which would come as the culmination of a gradual process marked by signs visible to the discerning. He believed that the advent of the Kingdom was imminent, and he systematically enumerated the signs that led him to this conclusion. We have already encountered most of them: the progress of foreign missions, enlightenment both secular and sacred, growth in holiness, harmony among nations and churches, prosperity understood not merely as the increase of wealth but also as its more general distribution.[30] This postmillennial view was by no means novel, having dominated North American Protestantism since its adoption by Jonathan Edwards in the middle of the eighteenth century. Neither was its ideological content new; it was essentially a summary of the program of the old evangelical united front. What makes Roaf's obscure tract interesting today is the almost uncanny precision with which his signs of the end prefigured the major interests of Canadian Protestants throughout the nineteenth century and well beyond it. One might almost suggest that the United Church of Canada came into existence to implement it.

Even as the churches set before themselves this optimistic vision, however, their very success was creating obstacles to its realization. One of the reasons they had been able to speak with such assurance in earlier days was their consistent upholding of standards that shamed a worldly population and made membership a badge of achievement. By 1867 church and world were virtually identical in composition, and traditional means of discipline became increasingly difficult to enforce. Earlier in the century, Baptist churches had regularly meted out suspensions or expulsions from membership for offences ranging from fornication to scurrilous gossip. By 1867 references to occasions for discipline other than non-attendance at church ordinances were becoming rare. In earlier days the class meeting had been Methodism's chief means of preserving the cohesion of local societies. During the early 1850s its requirement as a condition of church membership came under fire from Egerton Ryerson, who painted a lurid picture of the difficulties encountered by young people catapulted from Sunday school into a gathering dominated by the reminiscences of nostalgic greybeards. Although the class meeting retained more vitality than he was prepared to admit, he was not mistaken in identifying an institution under stress.[31]

As the gap between church and world narrowed, that between clergy and laity was becoming more prominent. Increasingly complex programs created a demand for a more professional style of ordained ministry. The Wesleyan Methodists, who had long examined probationers on a course of required reading, decided in 1852 that candidates should be able to demonstrate proficiency in grammar as well. Formal theological education, already available to Anglicans and Presbyterians in the 1840s, quickly spread to other denominations. In 1851 Victoria College instituted classes in theology, though at first these were regarded mainly as remedial provisions for ineffective preachers. Local Baptists, traditionally suspicious of an educated ministry, helped to fund the establishment of Rochester Theological Seminary in 1850 and were represented on its sponsoring body. By 1860 they were offering theological classes, somewhat less academic in approach, at their own Canadian Literary Institute at Woodstock. This increasing emphasis on clerical competence sometimes led to a displacement of female and lay leadership. After 1840 women preachers were seldom heard outside Primitive Methodist churches.[32] Sunday school superintendents and teachers continued to be predominantly lay, but the increasing involvement of the churches was restricting their autonomy and gradually wresting leadership from local union committees. It was also forcing out of existence the union congregations common in earlier years. This pressure on the laity has been recognized as a major factor in 'high-low' disputes within the Church of England. It was equally important in rallying lay support for the Free Church, and it was a significant element in the appeal of the Plymouth Brethren. Militant anti-clericalism of the European type did not develop in Ontario; nevertheless, the clergy would have to reckon henceforth with a simmering distrust of their leadership.

As the churches laid plans for further advance, developments were brewing that would threaten the gains they had already made. The first thrusts of Darwin and the biblical critics had been parried, but their arguments would compel much more careful attention in the future. As demands for more interesting services of worship indicated, the churches were beginning to face competition for the control of leisure time that would only increase with the years. They would also have to contend, as the churches of Europe and the United States were already contending, with the peculiar problems of a society of megalopolitan scale. These challenges were little in evidence in 1867, and unusual prescience would have been required to foresee them. For the moment, Ontario had all the marks of an increasingly Christian and moral province.

11 *The Activist Temper*

One of the most conspicuous features of Ontario religious life during the last decades of the nineteenth century was the multiplication of voluntary organizations fostering particular interests or catering to particular segments of the population. Religious institutions subsidiary to or even independent of formal church structures were, of course, by no means novel. The evangelical coalitions of the early nineteenth century had found their most effective instruments in 'benevolences' such as temperance and missionary societies, and ultramontane confraternities and Anglo-Catholic guilds were already familiar in the province by mid-century. During the late nineteenth century, however, there was a veritable epidemic of voluntary activity that permanently altered the institutional shape of religion in Ontario.

Such activities proliferated in major urban centres, which had the population and resources to sustain them, but they caught on in communities of every size. In 1887 Saint George's Church in Guelph reported a literary association, a branch of the Church of England Temperance Society, a 'Band of Hope and Ministering Children's League,' and a Sunday school with about five hundred scholars and a branch with one hundred, along with two missions in town and two in the country. In the French-Canadian parish of Saint-François in Ottawa the program was different but no less comprehensive. Besides daily catechism the parish in 1902 sponsored la Congrégation de Notre-Dame-des-Anges for young girls, les Enfants de Marie for older ones, la Société de Saint-Louis for boys, and the Third Order of Saint Francis for adults; unhappily (and not untypically of all denominations), a society of young men under the patronage of Saint-Antoine de Padoue was reported defunct. Country churches adopted such aspects of the new programs as their resources allowed. W.H. Withrow, describing the experiences of a 'progressive' Methodist minister in a rural pastorate, suggested that they might even have a special significance there: 'The meeting fulfils an important place in the social economy of the backwoods of Canada. Amid the isolation of their solitary farm life the people – the female portion of the household especially – see little of each other except at these weekly and fortnightly gatherings.'[1]

The Sunday school, already well established, was still the centrepiece of auxiliary programming, and by the later years of the century was regarded as an indispensable adjunct of a Protestant congregation. Even denominations that insisted on the necessity of a definite experience of conversion increasingly looked to it as the agency most likely to induce one. The proportion of new Methodist members reported as coming through Sunday schools, only 3 per cent in 1862, rose to 19 per cent by 1894 and to 60 per cent in the early twentieth century. Evangelists, far from being jealous of this success, were among the principal promoters of Sunday schools. Early in the 1870s, at the instigation of Dwight L. Moody, a lay-dominated group in the United States organized the International Sunday School Association to promote interest and effective teaching; the association gave initial direction to the movement and sponsored mammoth international conventions. Although the use of the word 'international' was designed to encourage Canadian participation, interest in Ontario reached its peak only in the 1890s. George C. Pidgeon, later the first moderator of the United Church of Canada, recalled enthusiastic Sunday school conventions in Peel County as the most exciting feature of his pastorate at Streetsville during this decade.[2] Roman Catholics looked to their expanding separate school system for similar benefits.

Supplementing the Sunday school, and for the most part new in this period, were a number of societies designed to keep graduates involved with their churches. Usually these societies were expected to perform some educational functions, but their emphasis was on bringing together young people of both sexes for social and cultural activities in a protected setting and a devotional atmosphere. Christian Endeavour, the pioneer of church-centred programming for young people, was an American import that swept the province in the 1880s. Its formula for success was the provision of busy-work; each member was expected to participate in every meeting, if only by reciting a Bible verse. By the 1890s the denominations were setting up their own organizations to promote loyalty to themselves and to inject greater intellectual (and in some cases Canadian) content. There were Epworth Leagues for Methodists, Westminster Guilds for Presbyterians, Baptist Young People's Unions, King's Daughters and Sons for Anglicans, and Jügendbunde for Lutherans. Several of these incorporated Christian Endeavour within their programs. Roman Catholics had confraternities, such as those already noted at Saint-François, for both children and youth. Many Irish Catholic parishes, eager to improve the communication skills of a predominantly working-class constituency, sponsored literary and debating societies.[3]

Although missionary societies had existed within a few Protestant congregations since pioneer times, they came into prominence during the last quarter of the nineteenth century. They were organized, in almost every case, by women. The steps leading to this multiplication of effort were remarkably similar in all major denominations. First, a group of dedicated women in a large urban centre would form a local missionary society. This would then set itself up as a national organization, which in turn would encourage the formation of local auxiliaries throughout the country. Nor did the process stop there, for local auxiliaries were encouraged to organize young women into mission circles and children of both sexes into mission bands. The existence of similar models in the United States was no doubt largely responsible for this remarkable uniformity. The Canadian precedent was set in 1876 by the Presbyterian Woman's Foreign Missionary Society (Western Section), which was formed at the request of the church's foreign mission committee, and was soon followed by practically every Protestant denomination. By the end of the century these networks were establishing units in communities of every size.[4]

Other organizations, more varied in design, concentrated on service to the parish or the community. Great dependence was placed on Ladies' Aids, long common in Protestant and now also in Roman Catholic parishes, for maintaining the furnishings of churches and parsonages. Through their efforts and those of other organizations within the churches there was a great profusion of teas, bazaars, Sunday school and parish picnics, and, in denominations without moral scruples against them, concerts, dances, and lotteries. Organizations to serve the general community had a greater appeal for men. The Society of Saint Vincent de Paul, which enjoyed great prestige with the Roman Catholic Church, offered anonymous help to the needy regardless of religious affiliation as well as spiritual encouragement to its Catholic clients. Benevolent associations also multiplied within the Jewish community. Women were at least as active as men in charitable projects, either in auxiliaries to male societies or in organizations of their own. Roman Catholic women did a great deal of hospital visiting, and the Ladies' Montefiore Hebrew Benevolent Society of Toronto gradually extended its support from needy Jews to many public institutions.[5]

Protestant benevolence, carried on at first chiefly through secular agencies, created a burgeoning battery of institutions after 1867. They resulted more often from individual than from ecclesiastical initiative, although some congregations rented halls in the hope of reaching classes of persons that were not attracted by their regular services. As late as 1893 B.E. Bull lamented that the churches left slum work largely to 'independent missionary enterprise,' and identified the Toronto Mission Union, a project of the reforming mayor William Howland, as the most extensive in Toronto. Already, however, a Sunday school organized for slum boys by Isabella Alexander had become, under the ministry of D.J. Macdonnell of Saint Andrew's Presbyterian Church, the nucleus of an expanding program of outreach to the poor. Eventually this developed into an institute with its own building, which in addition to a gymnasium and swimming-pool contained a library, a savings bank, and rooms for instruction, reading, and relaxation.[6] In all of these institutions religious inspiration and moral advice were considered to be at least as important as material aid, and the aid was sometimes conditional on the reception of the inspiration and advice.

Supplementing the work of church societies were a number of organizations independent of any particular denomination. Their leadership was overwhelmingly lay, and at first almost uniformly evangelical in conviction. It would be difficult to exaggerate the importance of the Young Men's Christian Association, originally introduced to Toronto in 1853 and more solidly established in 1863. In its initial rush of enthusiasm the YMCA had set up branches in a number of middle-sized communities, but it found its ultimate niche in serving a few large urban centres. During the nineteenth century it took very seriously the word 'Christian' in its name, and concentrated its efforts on evangelism and the cultivation of the devotional life. Although its original intention was to promote the evangelization of underprivileged youth, the YMCA achieved its chief significance as a catalyst in the religious development of respectable young people with church backgrounds. After entering the student field with a branch at University College, Toronto, in 1873, it adopted in the next decade a policy of cultivating campus leaders that would eventually issue in the formation of the Student Christian Movement of Canada. Its programs for boys, worked out mainly in the 1890s, laid the foundations of Protestant approaches to adolescents in the twentieth century. YMCA leaders, a number of whom were prominent in business and public life, formed part of an evangelical network whose names would appear again and again on the boards of societies dedicated to missionary and philanthropic causes.[7]

The Young Women's Christian Association, despite the similarity of its name and underlying purpose, evolved independently out of various impulses from Britain and the United States. In line with current ideas of decorum, the Toronto YWCA was governed by a male board. It was essentially a protective agency, and operated a hostel for young working women newly exposed to the temptations of the big city. Committee members led the 'inmates' in prayer meetings and packed them off to church at least once on Sunday.[8] To many public-spirited wives of prosperous men, the YWCA provided opportunities for developing skills of leadership, as well as glimpses of the problems of the less affluent. It did not involve them in agitation for change, and in the long run its chief contribution was to religious programming for young women and adolescent girls.

More activist was the Women's Christian Temperance Union, which was founded in 1874 in the United States and provincially organized by Letitia Youmans in 1877. The WCTU came into being to discourage the use of alcoholic beverages, which it regarded as the most serious of all social evils, and never forgot its primary purpose. Under the prodding of its founder, Frances Willard, however, it soon added other planks to its platform. It pressed for greater power for women, including the franchise, on the ground that they were more committed than men to the preservation of the rising generation. It also began to seek other reforms, such as the deliverance of women from restrictive garments and greater recognition of the rights of labour. Like women's missionary societies, it set up an organization for children, the Band of Hope, in order to ensure continuity of interest.[9]

This burst of religious activity gave a prominence to the church that was made visible in the dominance of the Ontario landscape by church buildings and church-related institutions. At the end of the nineteenth century Toronto's tallest structure was not a bank headquarters or a communications tower but the spire of Saint James's Cathedral. The most imposing of these edifices, if not always the most charming, had been erected during the last third of the century. They were the pride of their communities, and no civic prospectus was complete without laudatory references to them. In rural districts, and even in cities such as Kingston where they have not yet been obscured by high-rises, they still serve as reminders of the extraordinary visibility of religion in the late nineteenth century. While they were intended primarily for the worship of God, the churches of the era also reflected the activist and optimistic temper of the time and usually included facilities for Sunday schools and other auxiliary programs.

Already in 1868 Centenary Church in Hamilton set a precedent for Wesleyan concentration on large and expensive 'central' churches in key cities, the culmination of which was the completion of a 'national' church in Ottawa in 1876. Metropolitan Church in Toronto, built between 1870 and 1872, is said to have been at the time the largest Methodist church in the world. Its dedication, marked like that of other churches of the period by special services with prominent preachers, gathered in offerings totalling thirty thousand dollars. Those who built so lavishly were not troubled by the sense of guilt for spending money on real estate that surfaced in the 1960s. 'These temples of God are the outward signs of a christian country and show to all the community that the christianity of Canada is not a barren sentiment,' the Wesleyan conference asserted in 1866. In Toronto, the erection of Jarvis Street Baptist Church was hailed as a sign of final triumph over the Family Compact.[10]

The clergy maintained an equally high profile. During the spring of 1891 the *Toronto Daily Mail*, seeking to boost its circulation, ran a contest to determine Canada's most popular preacher. The prize was to be a return ticket to England for the winning entrant. For a month and a half each issue of the newspaper contained a coupon, and the number of entries was limited only by the number of copies sold. Despite its theoretically national nature the competition was restricted in practice to Ontario, and the leading contenders were all located in Toronto. Each day the papers published returns, along with numerous letters from the supporters of the various candidates. During the opening weeks the lead changed hands several times, but a last-minute torrent of entries placed Joseph Wild of Bond Street Congregational Church far ahead with 160,494 votes to 139,553 for D.J. Macdonnell and slightly fewer for A.H. Baldwin of All Saints' Anglican Church. Obviously, it would be hazardous to attempt too precise an analysis of a competition that depended on the circulation of a highly partisan newspaper; still, several features stand out as significant. One is the similarity of the terms in which correspondents touted their favourite candidates to those associated in more recent years with celebrities in sport and entertainment; another is the choice of the clergy as suitable figures with which to launch this type of competition; the third, even more striking, was the apparent success of the contest in selling newspapers. The *Mail* was sufficiently encouraged by the results to conduct similar polls for such representative figures as military officers and aldermen, but without arousing comparable excitement.[11] The parson was, evidently, the person par excellence of late nineteenth-century Ontario.

The impulse that led to the proliferation of programs, the ostentation of buildings, and the lionization of clergy also inspired a demand for the best that money could buy. Church buildings not only had to be big but had to meet the specifications of soaring Gothic or the more massive Romanesque that followed it in the 1880s, and these only architects of standing could provide. Even denominations suspicious of ritualism began to 'improve' the worship that took place inside them by dignifying the setting and enhancing the quality of the music. Macdonnell urged on Presbyterians the adoption of norms of ordered worship then being advocated in Scotland by the Church Service Society, and during the 1890s the *Westminster* ran a regular column on church music. Trained organists were in demand, and some churches began to employ salaried singers. The same desiderata applied even more obviously to preachers, who were increasingly expected to have acquired a college education, even in denominations that had traditionally relied on natural gifts. Filling churches, especially in the cities, called for the 'most gifted pulpit orators,' and for those who aspired to such success the Neff School of Oratory offered well-advertised summer courses at the University of Toronto. When churches began to place more emphasis on service to the needy, it was natural that they should set up training schools for professional deaconesses. Even Sunday school teaching, that most amateur of all occupations, was encouraged toward efficiency through training institutes pioneered by John H. Vincent of the American Methodist Episcopal Church. It was the boast of Sunday school teachers that they had appropriated the most advanced methods in use in public schools.[12]

'Quality' implied a considerable measure of standardization. Denominations began to send out an expanding supply of program materials for use in city and country churches alike. By the 1880s, in practically all of them, common hymnals had replaced the congregational collections once in use. In 1895 the Presbyterian general assembly even appointed a committee on 'Uniformity in Public Worship,' although significant results would follow only after many years and the selection of a less threatening name for the committee. The most pervasive influence for standardization, however, was the system of International Uniform Sunday School Lessons that Vincent introduced as another of his projects in 1872. Consisting in skeleton of a curriculum of Bible passages chosen by a committee for simultaneous use in all schools and with all age groups, the lessons became the basis of teachers' books and students' leaflets, syndicated columns in the daily press, and innumerable series of sermons. Ideally, their use called for a standard physical layout, the 'Akron plan,' that consisted of an auditorium around which classes met in partitioned alcoves under the eye of a superintendent who sat at a desk on stage, from which he could intervene to maintain order or sum up the session. The result of these varied pressures was to bring about not only an unprecedented homogenization of local units within each denomination but a remarkable uniformity among Protestant denominations. By the end of the century one was almost as likely to find a Christian Endeavour society, a mission band, or the uniform lessons among Quakers, Disciples of Christ, or Universalists as among Methodists or Presbyterians.[13] Patterns of organization in synagogues such as Holy Blossom in Toronto or Anshe Sholom in Hamilton bore a distinct family resemblance.

Among the resources required for expanding programs, none was more vital than the printed word. Sunday schools created a demand for curricular materials, along with story papers to sustain youthful interest. Missionary and temperance societies had their own specific needs, and inspirational literature undergirded the entire operation. Much material in all categories was imported from the United States or Britain, according to the attachments of the various churches. Some local booksellers specialized in supplying the needs of particular denominations. Others, such as the evangelical and prohibitionist Toronto Willard Tract Depository, represented special party interests. Among local religious publications the family-oriented general periodical had the longest history. No denomination felt secure without a church paper, although it was often necessary to depend on private initiative to provide one. The Methodist Book Room, able to draw on the profits of commercial printing contracts, far outdid others in the provision of local backing for its Sunday school and other activities.

A spate of variegated programs usually gives rise, sooner or later, to a bureaucratic structure. Such systems would come to maturity only in the twentieth century, but in the last decades of the nineteenth they were already beginning to appear in embryo. Additions to the list of officials usually came about piecemeal as newly recognized needs gave rise to committees or societies and as these, after depending for a time on voluntary help, decided that only full-time staff could do justice to emerging opportunities. The most common additions in the late nineteenth century were secretaries and superintendents to promote missions in Ontario, French Canada, the west, and abroad. By 1886 the Methodists, with the most centralized polity, had full-time officials in charge of missions, superannuation funds, and education, along with a growing staff in the publishing house. The Presbyterians, by contrast, still directed such important enterprises as the office of the clerk of their general assembly out of the studies of pastors or college professors. Pressure for further appointments was mounting in all denominations.

Although the bill for paid officials was still moderate, the money required for the expanding activities of the churches was far beyond what Ontarians had been accustomed to pay. The increase came, moreover, at a time when subsidies from abroad were declining or ceasing. In the past, churches had raised their revenues through a variety of expedients: pew-rents, annual subscription lists, Christmas and Easter offerings, and fees for various services. These were intended merely to provide for clerical salaries, the maintenance of the fabric, and incidental expenses, and as local expenditures mounted it was increasingly necessary to have recourse to bazaars and other special events. 'Schemes' beyond the local church – colleges, missions, Bible societies, aid to small congregations – depended on special collections, which became increasingly unpopular as they became increasingly numerous. Charbonnel's solution, which was not very popular either, was to require each parish to forward one-tenth of its revenue to a central diocesan fund. The system increasingly favoured in Protestant churches was the institution of a weekly offering during the Sunday service, a distinct innovation and suspect in some circles as being high church. At first this offering was usually devoted to missions, and special envelopes were introduced to distinguish it. Later, when its usefulness for local purposes was recognized, the envelopes became duplex. Weekly offerings, which had been known in the United States since 1843, made their way into Ontario mainly during the 1870s and would not altogether supersede pew-rents for several decades. During this period the promotion of systematic and proportional giving became something of a sacred cause. The Anglican *Canadian Church Magazine and Mission News* identified it as the periodical's major reason for existence (though one would not have thought it promising bait to attract subscriptions), and called on readers 'to honor the Lord with the *firstfruits* of every cheque received and of every month's pay or quarter's salary.'[14] As in some other matters, women's missionary societies were well in advance of others. Eschewing bake sales and garden parties, they raised substantial sums out of regular contributions from household money.

Despite such efforts the ventures of the period severely strained the resources of the small ecclesiastical units into which, at the time of Confederation, most denominational families of the province were still divided. Groups rural in orientation were especially hard pressed, since they lacked the financial base represented by large city churches and were suffering a steady drain of members to the cities and the west. The resulting pressures, compounded by overbuilding in a period of relatively static population, encouraged various measures of denominational consolidation. Union between the Free Church and the United Presbyterians in 1861 was followed in 1875 by the amalgamation of all of the substantial Presbyterian bodies in Canada. In 1874 the Wesleyans of the central and Atlantic provinces united with the Methodist New Connexion, and ten years later the great majority of Methodists were in one fold.[15] The Church of England, envied by others for its unity after the formation of the provincial synod of (eastern) Canada in 1858, achieved a general synod only in 1893 and a missionary arm, the Missionary Society of the Canadian Church, in 1902. The two Baptist conventions in central Canada united in 1888, but, despite the strenuous efforts of Senator William A. McMaster, a dominion board founded in 1886 lasted only a year. The Roman Catholic Church was an exception to this tendency toward centralization, for the separation from

Quebec of the ecclesiastical province of Toronto in 1870 and of Saint Boniface in 1871 delayed for many years the emergence of national institutions. These measures of consolidation served to confirm the existing concentration of the population within a few ecclesiastical families and to sharpen the contrast between large and small denominations. The Presbyterians, from a rather amorphous collection of diverse fragments, became within two decades a powerful national body. The Methodists increased their membership by 38 per cent in the six years after their union in 1884.[16]

Despite their national scope, these changes had some specific implications for Ontario. Most of them resulted from initiatives taken in the province, although Montreal and Halifax contributed significantly to them.[17] Attitudes in Ontario, by virtue of the province's size and central position, were usually decisive in setting the terms of consolidation and determining its success. Nation-wide organization involved, officially for Methodists and less directly for others, a loosening of ties with mother churches in Britain. In the case of Protestant churches, they brought the whole of Canada within the range of religious influences from Ontario. Embryonic national headquarters almost inevitably gravitated to Toronto, from which programs and ideas were disseminated to local congregations from coast to coast. Methodist strength had always been concentrated in Ontario. Among Presbyterians and Anglicans, Montreal gradually declined in influence as Toronto gained.

From these varied developments the churches emerged as larger, more powerful, and more imposing institutions, while the prestige and influence of their clerical leaders grew. Church headquarters, which were still small in scale, not only encouraged and co-ordinated parish programs but provided much of their content. This expansion was possible, however, only because of an explosion in the growth of lay activity. Sunday schools were staffed by a multitude of anonymous volunteers, and numerous groups of dedicated women engaged in study or money-raising. Many of the province's most prominent citizens gave high priority to religious activities. Expansive projects and programs called for more money than could be provided even by new schemes of regular giving, and many of the wealthy responded generously. The Massey family was notable for consistent and usually spontaneous giving. They helped to maintain Metropolitan Methodist Church and to establish new congregations, founded the Fred Victor Mission in downtown Toronto, sponsored the Methodist deaconess order, boosted the church's Twentieth Century Fund, and made more large contributions than can be listed here to Methodist colleges and other institutions. Among the Baptists Senator William A. McMaster was a powerhouse in himself; he made possible not only the foundation of the university later named after him but the building of Jarvis Street Baptist Church and the extension of Baptist mission work.

The contributions of the prominent were not limited to money. Many of them spared time and energy to sit on church sessions and vestries, represent their congregations in the higher courts of their churches, and spend hours each week in committee work. In 1876, not an exceptional year, Premier Oliver Mowat was the president of the Evangelical Alliance, President Daniel Wilson of the University of Toronto chaired the board of the YMCA, and the Honourable G.W. Allan was secretary of the Bible Society. Some religious zealots invested a remarkable amount of energy in their favourite causes. Newton W. Rowell, a liberal (and Liberal) Methodist politician in the making, was the guiding spirit of the Epworth League and later of the Layman's Missionary Movement; he found time also to take part in the program of the Fred Victor Mission and to serve occasionally as a lay preacher. S.H. Blake, a leading Anglican lawyer who was as conservative theologically as Rowell was liberal, was active in the YMCA and the YWCA, shared with W.H. Howland in the leadership of the Toronto Mission Union, was probably the most influential of the founders of Wycliffe College, and took a keen interest in the China Inland Mission.[18]

Between the expanded role of the clergy and the heightened involvement of the laity there was no incompatibility in principle. The clergy actively encouraged lay participation, and the laity wanted the clergy to be better equipped for new tasks. Many lay volunteers were able to participate in the programs of their churches only because helpful materials were available from the centre; conversely, those materials would have gone unused if they had not met felt needs. A large proportion of the philanthropy of the period was channelled through the churches, and the clergy depended on it for the success of their programs. Clerical and lay interests did not always coincide, however, and significant differences in outlook occasionally surfaced. When the lay persons involved were leaders in business or politics, the likelihood of collision was even greater. In 1874, when laymen were first admitted to the conference of the Methodist Church of Canada, Anson Green observed that 'with trifling exceptions' they behaved with 'becoming humility and respect.'[19] His sense of relief is almost audible, and was occasioned less by the humility of leading Methodist laymen than by the position of entrenched power they had already achieved unofficially. Some other denominations, with less homogeneous roots in the province, found lay energies more difficult to contain.

That paths could diverge somewhat even when interests and sympathies largely coincided was indicated by the experience of women's missionary societies. Their leaders were at first reluctant to assert themselves, fearing to be seen as unwomanly. Several of their societies were formed at the request of male officials, and their early statements indicated a desire to defer to male direction. The Presbyterian Woman's Foreign Missionary Society expressed at the outset its intention of confining its activities to the raising of money which the church's foreign mission committee could spend at its discretion and the recruitment of workers whom it would deploy. Before the end of the century, when it was contributing more than two-thirds of the support of its church's Indian work, officials of the society had little hesitation in setting their male counterparts straight. By 1886 the Methodist wms, which had begun with similar protestations, had its own separate organization and was capable of holding property.[20] Although it has been suggested that the formation of separate institutions isolated them from the main power centres of their denominations, churchwomen were creating formidable power bases of their own. It was not without significance that their organizations, national in scope, paralleled the structures of their denominations from central executives right through to local units. It is notable too that church-sponsored deaconess orders attracted less qualified women as employees than the more autonomous missionary societies.[21]

Institutions soliciting support across denominational lines were even more likely to develop their own independent agenda. The Sabbath School Association of Ontario, while mainly engaged in promoting the work of denominational schools, set the lines of program development on its own terms. City missions sponsored by individuals or independent coalitions did not always relate easily to the existing churches. Under William Howland's leadership the Toronto Mission Union took on some of the characteristics of a separate denomination. The ymca, which counted many prominent evangelicals among its sponsors, was a prime example of an organization that regarded itself as auxiliary to the churches but resolved to be completely independent of them. When an attempt was made to place the ymca under church direction, an early chronicler of the movement reported that 'some speakers went so far as to say that the churches had wholly failed, that their divisions had put it out of their power to evangelize the world, and that the Association had, therefore, been raised up to do this work in their stead.'[22] Some ministers regarded the ymca as a competitor rather than an ally, and certainly its emphasis on central planning enabled it to provide attractive alternatives to church programs.

In meetings of the ymca, Christian Endeavour, and other non-denominational organizations there was gradually taking shape a sort of lay religion that diverged increasingly from that customarily found in the churches. In theology it tended to a rather simplistic biblicism tinged with contempt for the dogmas that distinguished the various denominations. In religious approach it reflected the confidence of American holiness advocates in the ability of the human will to make an act of total consecration to Christ. In social outlook it was sympathetic to the poor, but inclined to seek the solution of their problems through conversion and moral reformation rather than any radical change in economic arrangements. In style its practitioners preferred hearty informality, warming up audiences with humorous anecdotes before driving home their message with pithy illustrations from life. Settings, comfortable or otherwise as seemed appropriate to the social situation of the clientele, were uniformly devoid of traditional religious symbolism. Contrasts with churchly religion were nowhere more striking than in hymnody. While official committees sought through denominational hymnals to make available the classics of the ages, YMCA and Christian Endeavour leaders preferred what an unsympathetic contemporary described as 'sentimental songs and drivelling ditties.'[23] One of the most popular began, 'Come to Jesus, come to Jesus, come to Jesus just now, just now come to Jesus, come to Jesus just now,' and varied the other stanzas by substituting 'He will save you' and 'I believe it.' This pattern of simple choruses was derived ultimately from camp-meeting practice, although the hymns noted in firsthand accounts of early Upper Canadian examples were largely drawn from the standard repertoire. It gained more general currency when adopted for use in temperance and missionary rallies, but it was the YMCA that did most to popularize it. Such songs had the advantage of popular appeal, but the pioneer Upper Canadians who patronized singing schools would have found them distinctly insipid.

Professional evangelists, some of whom were immensely popular, both represented and encouraged the unsophisticated theology and informal style that typified one aspect of the religion of the era. Dwight L. Moody, who drew half the population of Toronto to a three-day campaign in 1884, set the tone for others. His approach was down-to-earth and business-like: it was geared to elicit decisions rather than displays of emotion, and called for adherence to a simple moral code. He also inaugurated the custom of pairing a preacher and a popular singer, in his case Ira D. Sankey. A number of Canadian teams, several consisting of women, followed the same general pattern. The best known was that of Hugh T. Crossley and John D. Hunter, Methodists who began campaigning in the fall of 1884. Their most sensational success was in 1888, 'when, in answer to an appeal by Mr. Hunter, that all who wished to become Christians and desired the prayers of the audience would stand up, the premier of the Dominion [Sir John A. Macdonald], whose name has so long been the synonym of iniquity to many worthy grit minds, arose with his wife.' During the last decades of the century virtually all denominations sponsored special evangelistic services. The rise of the evangelical party in the Church of England, for example, was significantly furthered by a mission conducted in 1883 by W.S. Rainsford at Saint James's Cathedral, Toronto.[24] Enthusiasm cooled, however, when it was observed that few converts continued to attend churches where the tone and setting of the services were far removed from those of revival meetings.

Stiff and formal as they might seem to those accustomed to young people's assemblies or evangelistic rallies, churches found themselves obliged to respond to popular tastes. To penetrate beyond an impressive Gothic exterior was often to be confronted by an auditorium theatrical in style. A young Presbyterian scholar commented in 1895, 'The church building itself has almost gone, for it is almost beyond courtesy to call the music halls now in vogue, churches.' Sermons were commonly reported at length in the press and tended, in consequence, to eschew doctrine and exegesis in favour of topicality. Elizabeth Smith, a young Anglican of refined sensibility, complained of a common type of preacher who 'must need try his powers of imitation in trying to be a Beecher, or a Talmage until this present generation finds itself acting a continued farce.' Difficult to exceed in originality was Amos Campbell, a Methodist Episcopal presiding elder, who 'once got into a basket and was drawn up by rope and pulley to a high platform from which to preach.'[25]

Under such pressures venerable institutions gave way or changed almost beyond recognition. The hostility of Presbyterian church courts to organs proved so ineffective in the face of popular demand that in 1872 the Canada Presbyterian Church conceded that congregations might decide the question for themselves. John Thompson of Sarnia lamented the passing of another Presbyterian tradition, that of testing family members on their theological knowledge by 'catechizing' them in their homes. He saw the result as neglect of the Bible and the *Shorter Catechism,* and laid a good deal of blame on the International Lessons. Among the Baptists, preachers of the 'sinfulness of sin' were said to have lost their popularity, and cases of individual discipline were seldom reported. Methodist class meetings were moving toward extinction, and conferences were increasingly hospitable to requests from circuits for ministers of their choice. Especially striking was the transformation of the camp meeting after the example of the American holiness movement. Campgrounds at Grimsby and in the Thousand Islands doubled as family resorts, complete with cottages and hotels, where urbanites could blend spiritual nourishment with recreational and cultural activity.[26]

Tensions between élite and popular religion were less apparent in the Roman Catholic Church because its authorities patronized both without embarrassment. While Rome urged the superiority of Gregorian chant, urban churches in Ontario featured 'grand vespers' with flamboyant musical accompaniment. With the encouragement of Archbishop Joseph-Thomas Duhamel, French-Canadian priests along the Ottawa River publicized officially sanctioned devotions and miracles in order to strengthen the faith of their parishioners. Archbishop Lynch was tireless in promoting the miraculous powers of plaster from the shrine of Our Lady of Knock in Ireland, testimonies to which in the Roman Catholic press bore a distinct resemblance to claims for patent medicines in adjoining columns. There were, however, limits. Francis McSpiritt, a priest whose piercing eyes suggest hypnotic power even in a photograph, was so prodigal with cures that it was found necessary to transfer him on several occasions so as to restrain the growth of devotion to his person.[27]

The surge of religious and religiously motivated activity that was such a conspicuous feature of Ontario life in the late nineteenth century drew its inspiration, as on many earlier occasions, from the metropolitan centres of Christendom. Its most visible expressions – monumental church buildings, expanded facilities, and networks of voluntary organizations – can be traced to prototypes in Britain and especially in the United States. The innovative programs to which it gave rise would scarcely have been possible apart from the availability of materials produced for a market continental in scale. Ontarians would not have been so deeply affected by this impulse if it had not resonated with local circumstances, however, and by the late decades of the century these were distinctly favourable to it. Several cities were now large enough to provide support and leadership for what was essentially an urban-based program; even a city the size of Brantford was able to support a Baptist congregation of metropolitan proportions. Industry was yielding sufficient wealth that profits did not all have to be ploughed back but could be put to other uses. Social changes concurrent with these developments, such as the growth of privacy within the family circle and the emergence of a class of women with considerable leisure time, provided both a clientele and a pool of available leaders for new voluntary organizations. As time would prove, numbers, wealth, and leisure could be put to secular as readily as to religious uses. Given the extent to which religious institutions had already shaped the provincial mentality, however, it was natural that religious undertakings should have first claim on newly released energies.

If the initial effect of urbanization was to quicken the pace of religious activity, it also brought about a subtle transformation in the ways in which Ontarians conceived this activity. A cursory survey of the trends of the period suggests anomalies and contradictions. The era of the construction of monumental churches was also that of the multiplication of small groups. Impressive improvements in the aesthetic quality of church architecture and worship coexisted with the most flagrant displays of sensationalism and bad taste. Even as professional evangelists were at the peak of their popularity, the Sunday school was becoming the normal channel of recruitment for church membership. Masked by this mixture of signals, however, a profound change was taking place in the way in which people related to their churches. Traditionally, the church had been perceived as a source of authoritative teaching, as the locus of common worship, or as a fellowship of believers, categories not mutually exclusive. Voluntary efforts in diverse religious causes had always been encouraged, but as projects of societies or religious orders rather than as functions of the church itself. Now many Ontarians, following a pattern more familiar in North America than in Europe, were coming to think of the church as the hub of a round of religious activities or as an umbrella under which a number of subsidiary organizations could take shelter. A fair number looked to these organizations, which were commonly segregated along lines of age, sex, or interest, as the chief outlets for their religious energy and the primary objects of their institutional loyalty. Even independent agencies such as YMCAs and city missions easily stepped into roles once reserved for the churches, and churches came to be regarded widely as voluntary agencies.

Some implications went beyond practical ecclesiology. The traditional view of the cosmos, to which almost all Ontarians had once adhered, placed God at the centre of historical events. Belief in the necessity of depending on God's initiative did not excuse humans from participation in religious and moral activities, but rather encouraged an intensity of commitment to them. Yet human activity could never substitute for divine initiative, and the service of worship owed its privileged position to an expectation that God's presence would be manifested there with peculiar power. Few Ontarians at the end of the nineteenth century would have queried this ordering of priorities, but words and actions often belied it. The new-born babe increasingly came to be seen not as a worm who could be saved only by amazing grace but as essentially a *tabula rasa* on which character could be etched by nurture. Young people learned from the YMCA to evaluate their intellectual, physical, devotional, and social growth in order to cultivate the balanced development of their faculties.[28] Adults banded together in efforts of extraordinary multiplicity in the confident expectation that as a result a thousand flowers would bloom. In an increasingly industrial society where improvements in technique so often seemed the key to progress, it seemed natural to apply a similar logic to religion.

12 *The Beckoning Vision*

The multifarious group programs that appeared toward the end of the nineteenth century were intended not merely to provide work for idle hands, or even to sustain youthful interest, but to mobilize all sorts and conditions of persons for concerted action to transform the province, the nation, and ultimately the world. Mission bands, which some Ontarians will still recall as among the more innocuous exposures of childhood, were part of a general thrust to convert the world to Christ. Sunday schools following the International Lessons devoted one Sunday in each quarter to missions and another to temperance; the latter sometimes served as an occasion for urging the pledge upon students and teachers alike. Rowell made the Epworth League a vehicle for evangelism and social action, and YMCA boys' parliaments cultivated qualities designed to Christianize the statesmanship of the next generation. Support for these and other causes of the era was also urged repeatedly in sermons and in the denominational press. Even the Gothic architecture of the period was intended not as mere decoration but as an affirmation of 'the presence, the reality, and the independence of the sacred in Victorian society.'[1] Inevitably, aims varied from denomination to denomination and even within denominations. A number of them commanded such widespread support within the Protestant churches that dominated the religious life of the province as to call for somewhat extended consideration.

The ultimate goal, to which specific efforts were expected to contribute, was the establishment of the sway of Jesus Christ over the entire globe. In 1872 the Wesleyan Methodists, disappointed when the purchase of the Hudson's Bay Company territories naturalized what had been their only foreign enterprise, opened in Japan the first Ontario-based mission abroad. In 1891 they followed it with another in west China that would eventually become the world's largest single Protestant mission. Early apologists for foreign missions had to contend with a good deal of indifference and scepticism.[2] By the end of the century, with virtually all doubters silenced, it had become *de rigueur* for each denomination to be represented in at least one 'heathen' country: Presbyterians in India, China, Taiwan, and Korea; Baptists in India and Bolivia; Anglicans in Japan; and Congregationalists in Angola. Their missionaries made converts, though not so many as they wished. They also affected significantly the educational and social development of the countries in which they worked, and their children, the 'mish kids,' would contribute to twentieth-century Canada a special sensitivity to Third World aspirations.

The main impetus in missionary expansion came not from church assemblies or denominational headquarters but from the dedication of volunteers who were seized by the urgency of the task. Within the churches themselves a great deal of both initiative and support was provided by women, whose societies were soon sponsoring missions of their own. University students were another prime source of recruits and recruiters; the formation in 1888 of the international Student Volunteer Movement, an outgrowth of Moody's revival movement, was followed by a quantum leap in the magnitude of the Protestant enterprise. In Ontario much of the initiative was taken by student YMCAs. Beginning with University College, Toronto, in 1883, they organized on almost every campus missionary associations that provided much of the overseas staff of the next generation. Sometimes the initiative was taken by individuals under the pressure of an irresistible sense of special vocation; the most reckless of these was Susy Rijnhart of the Disciples of Christ, who, contrary to all advice, insisted on venturing into Tibet on an ill-prepared expedition in which her husband and small child perished. The whole mission operation was made vividly real to groups and societies at home through missionary letters that kept them informed of developments abroad and solicited their interest, their prayers, and their financial support. 'Tomorrow there is a feast in honor of the Goddess of Mercy, and placards have informed us that we are to be killed then,' Virgil C. Hart of China informed well-wishers at the time of the Boxer rebellion. The Canadians of the denominational missions escaped with their lives on this occasion, but two persons employed by the China Inland Mission were killed at their posts.

By the 1890s Toronto was one of the foremost centres of missionary activity. In 1894 it was the site of a world missionary convention that attracted more than three thousand participants. In 1895 Dr F.C. Stephenson, a Methodist with a flair for colourful visual aids and a wife who kept him supplied with ideas, founded the Young People's Forward Movement for Missions and thereby set a precedent that would be followed in Britain and the United States. Toronto was for a time the North American headquarters of Hudson Taylor's China Inland Mission, the prototype of later faith missions. It was also the original and long-time centre of Rowland V. Bingham's Sudan Interior Mission, which was later estimated to be the world's largest Protestant missionary organization.[3] Candidates for both of these, who seldom met the educational requirements for admission to theological colleges, had available to them the facilities of the Toronto Bible Training School (now the Ontario Bible College), founded for this purpose by Elmore Harris of Walmer Road Baptist Church in 1894.

To most Ontarians the mention of missions conjured up visions of distant lands, but the northward progress of settlement within the province and the opening of the Canadian west called for an energetic program of home missions. The response was uneven. Anglicans set up the diocese of Algoma in 1873, mostly with English money, and used their commitments there as an excuse for leaving the west to the initiative of English societies. In northern Ontario, however, they outdid other Protestants. Presbyterians made use there mainly of the summer services of theological students, and even in 1900 other denominations were represented only by a few intrepid individuals. The Protestantism of Ontario was propagated in the west mainly by Presbyterians and Methodists, although Baptists and some smaller denominations did their best under severe organizational handicaps. Most successful in church extension was the Presbyterian superintendent of missions, James Robertson, who combined the rugged Scottish piety of his native Zorra with business methods learned in the United States. Able and energetic, he was also aided by the predominance among Ontario settlers in the west of Presbyterians from some of the stonier sections of the province.[4]

Robertson sought mainly 'visibility and permanence' for Presbyterianism in western Canada, and competition for strategic sites was intense; but from the outset Protestant leaders placed equal stress on the transplantation of the Victorian moral values that had become normative in Ontario. A policy of indoctrinating newcomers into these values would emerge only in the twentieth century when immigrants from continental Europe began to arrive in significant numbers, but already there was a sense that the annexation of the west heightened the stakes in a contest for the Canadian soul. 'A nation to be great must have great thoughts; must be inspired with lofty ideals, and must have men and women willing to work and wait and war for an idea,' wrote Principal George Monro Grant of Queen's University.[5] The sentiment, though scarcely original, expressed an idealism rare among Canadian public figures in the 1880s. The occasion that inspired it was Grant's participation in Sandford Fleming's pioneer survey of western Canada. Its realization, in Grant's opinion and that of other Protestant leaders, demanded the establishment of churches and religious institutions in time to shape the values of the new settlements before they could harden into a different mould. These were gradually provided, and were staffed mainly from Ontario. Meanwhile, the tone of the mainline Protestant churches of the rural west was set largely by theological students and recent graduates who were better equipped to transplant current enthusiasms than the inherited traditions of their churches.

If Ontario was to be a beacon of light to the world, it was essential that its social fabric should be penetrated more securely by Christian values. The first requirement was the shaping of character, for without virtue there could be no possibility of significant reform. That sobriety and diligence were cornerstones of Christian morality had long been as much an evangelical as a capitalist truism, and Protestants of the period showed little inclination to countenance levity. Denouncing card games at a session of the presbytery of London, J. Allister Murray 'associated them with pistols, daggers, bloodshed, and the gallows.' The same meeting concluded a resolution on the subject more soothingly, but perhaps not reassuringly to pleasure-seekers: 'While not condemning all amusements, the Presbytery earnestly recommends only those which are truly recreative, such as music, sprightly and improving conversation, and all that large class of lawful amusements which bring pleasure to the home, intelligence to the mind, purity to the heart, and benefit to society.' The Methodists, always thorough, added a note to their rules in 1886 that forbade, *inter alia,* 'dancing, playing at games of chance, encouraging lotteries, attending theatres, horse races, circuses, dancing parties, attending dancing schools.'[6]

To such moral suasion Protestant leaders added a remarkable confidence in the efficacy of compulsion to raise the tone of society. Various efforts had already been made to enact moral legislation in the province, but only in the last years of the century did Ontarians come under serious pressure to conform to the moral virtues we recall as Victorian.[7] The incentive to intensified effort was provided by a growing belief in the importance of environmental factors; it was felt that by controlling them one could ultimately affect not merely behaviour but inclination. Inspired by the optimism thus generated, reformers launched a co-ordinated attack on vice, with emphasis on overt forms of behaviour that could be identified as undesirable: political corruption, gambling and indeed all contact with playing-cards, prostitution, dancing, the theatre, and all forms of 'trashy' literature. The two chief targets were sabbath-breaking and booze.

While Sunday rest was a boon to workers and sedulously promoted as such, the observance of the Lord's day was of special significance to Protestants as the most conspicuous behavioural pattern by which the province symbolized its recognition of God's dominion over it. The institution was not unique to Ontario, but citizens viewed with satisfaction the contrast between Toronto and wide-open American cities. The clergy, especially the Presbyterian clergy and above all those of Free Church background, were especially vigilant in its defence. During the middle years of the century the improvement of communications had chipped away at the sanctity of the day. Then in 1888 a proposal that Toronto streetcars be allowed to run on Sunday precipitated a struggle in which Principal William Caven of Knox College was the leading strategist of the defence. The clergy lost this round, but in 1906 they succeeded in securing the enactment of a federal Lord's day act of sorts.[8]

For the most part, mid-century attacks on drink had been mounted not by the churches but by prominent laymen who were scandalized by drunkenness and disorder among the working classes. A Presbyterian minister, stung by charges of clerical inaction, complained of 'a cloud of itinerant temperance lecturers, some of whom made it their special business to attack ministers and Churches in a manner that would not be tolerated at a meeting of licensed victuallers.' Yet WCTU members and most temperance lecturers regarded their cause as essentially a Christian one, and a conviction that resort to liquor interfered with the self-control required for the shaping of a new age gradually roused the churches to more vigorous action. Legislative prohibition was the preferred route; despite the impossibility of securing the compliance of the Church of England, and despite the dissent of such Presbyterians of Kirk background as Grant and Macdonnell, most Protestant assemblies vociferously and persistently demanded it. The passage in 1878 of the Canada Temperance Act, which provided for local option, was a signal for vigorous and largely successful campaigns to secure positive votes. After 1888, when a broadening of the franchise led to a wave of repeal, the churches pressed for province- or dominion-wide prohibition. Plebiscites in Ontario in 1894 and the whole of Canada in 1898 yielded majorities favouring prohibition, but no action. Such frustrations merely whetted an appetite for reform that would become even more aggressive and achieve temporary success after the turn of the century.[9]

If, as W.H. Withrow asserted in a plea for prohibition, it was 'the duty of the Government to extend the Ægis of its protection over the people, to shield them from injury or wrong,' was similar intervention desirable in order to alleviate slum conditions or even to dismantle the economic system that fostered them? Protestants were at first reluctant to contemplate such a possibility, partly because of an ingrained belief that the universe is so ordered that diligence will normally bring economic rewards, and partly because recognition of divergent class interests was repugnant to their vision of a future society in which all would work together harmoniously. In 1893 Edward Barrass was of the opinion that 'much of the suffering among the poor [was] self-inflicted and might be greatly lessened by the adoption of total abstinence from intoxicating liquors and tobacco.' Labour militancy he denounced as evidence of a lack of Christian love: 'When all classes act according to the Golden Rule, strikes will be abolished, and the chasm between capital and labour will be greatly reduced.' Two years later the Methodist Toronto Conference assured its constituency that 'society as a whole can never be any better than are the individual members of which it is composed, and that individual character cannot be regenerated merely by changing its material and social condition.'[10]

Especially during the years of depression that stretched from the late 1880s into the 1890s, however, the churches were coming to take a more sympathetic view of the situation of the poor. Greater firsthand experience was one of the fruits of the activism of the period. A member of Metropolitan Methodist Church who established a Sunday school for street urchins was so shocked by her discovery of the plight of homeless men that she inspired the founding, with Massey family backing, of the Fred Victor Mission. The Presbyterians followed in 1899 with Evangelica, Toronto's first settlement house. Moral crusades raised storms of righteous indignation against the commercial interests that were increasingly identified as culprits, and incidentally inspired a rhetoric that could be turned against capitalism in general. Even the arch-conservative S.H. Blake was moved during a rally against Sunday streetcars to describe the battle as one 'fought shoulder to shoulder with the masses against the classes ... shoulder to shoulder against a grinding monopoly.' The first committee on sociological questions of the Methodist church, reporting in 1894, used even more heady language: 'as a church our sympathies are with the struggling masses everywhere, and we stand ready to aid to the utmost in ameliorating their conditions.'[11]

A fair number of writers in the religious press were prepared to move beyond band-aid remedies and expressions of solidarity to a search for long-term solutions. Specific proposals for reform, such as Henry George's Single Tax movement and various suggestions for altering the monetary system, excited some apprehension but also attracted considerable support. Socialism in various forms had a thorough airing. Most appraisals were negative; the editor of the *Canada Presbyterian* had to reach for such phrases as 'low moanings,' 'wild shrieks,' and 'sanguinary crimes' to describe it. Even sympathizers tended to take refuge in a 'higher socialism' that consisted in the main of applying the Golden Rule to social and economic relations. Legislation to ameliorate the condition of disadvantaged classes received wider support. E.W. Dadson, in a brief tenure as editor of the *Canadian Baptist,* stood up for trade unionism, shorter working hours, and even the right to strike. Perhaps the most significant step was a widespread admission that the churches had been remiss in neglecting economic issues. William Frizzell, in a fairly typical statement, identified the problem as concentration on the soul to the exclusion of the body.[12]

Such vague sentiments raised few hackles; more venturesome proposals were left to radical coteries that sprang up here and there during the 1890s. Social statements were also heavily laced with the moralism that had chiefly inspired them. Such enthusiasms of a later period as the achievement of social justice and the liberation of the oppressed were distinctly subordinate to the establishment of conditions making for righteousness. Significantly, however, even the radicals of the time made the teachings of Jesus the basis of their hopes for a transformed society, and depended on the support of maverick clergy and church youth organizations for much of their impact on public opinion.[13] Their twentieth-century successors would pay unconscious tribute to clerical distaste for class conflict by identifying their goal as a 'co-operative commonwealth.'

Most religious reformers favoured the extension of the rights of women. J.R. Jaques of Albert College urged as the clinching argument for woman suffrage the simple demands of justice, but other considerations usually weighed more heavily. Women, concerned for the stability of their homes and the future of their children, were dependable allies in campaigns for prohibition and other moral reforms. They favoured harmonious solutions in cases where men easily gave way to aggressive instincts. Their money, personnel, and administrative skills were becoming indispensable to missionary operations. Jaques himself, not entirely trusting the efficacy of the argument from equity, pointed to benefits that might be expected from the participation of women in public life: 'The Divine side of humanity, which is brightest and best in woman, is needed in our legislation to save us from atheistical darkness. If there were more of woman's voting in our legislative halls, there would be less of woman's wailing in our desolate homes.'[14]

This glorification of womanhood could cut two ways, for the special contribution of women would be endangered if they should cease to be womanly. '"Women's rights" could become "baby's wrongs",' John Thompson warned. As a counterpoint to the idealization of womanhood there emerged an emphasis on 'manliness' as the quality to be desired above others in men. Protestant churches generally favoured woman suffrage, and expected women to vote in favour of the causes to which the churches were committed. They urged the improvement of working conditions for women, even equal pay for equal work, hoping thereby to ensure the health and vigour of future generations. They were not ready to admit women to the governing bodies of the churches; the Methodist general conference, which alone gave the possibility serious consideration, consistently ruled against it despite the belated advocacy of several regional conferences.[15] On balance, however, the religious activism of the period advanced the position of women, who shared increasingly in the leadership of church programs and took advantage of the skills thus acquired to press for further opportunities.

Christian penetration of society would manifestly be incomplete unless it affected the cultural life of the province. The moral scruples of evangelical Protestants ruled out art forms, such as theatre and the dance, that involved questionable language or sexual stimulation. Even opera, so respectable today, had a prominence on Victorian lists of forbidden pleasures that can be explained only partially by the prominence of melodrama and farce in local opera programs.[16] The visual arts were unobjectionable in themselves if properly censored, but reeked of idolatry when brought into close association with worship. Apart from architecture, they received virtually no direct encouragement from Protestant churches. By the late nineteenth century, however, ecclesiastical patronage of sacred music was an established tradition, and church organists were largely responsible for cultivating a popular taste for the performance of choral classics that has continued into the twentieth century. Probably the most significant change was in attitudes to literature. Encouraged by the high seriousness of many Victorian writers, leading Protestants were ready to welcome even fiction so long as it could be made wholesome and improving. Withrow's *Canadian Methodist Magazine,* launched in 1875 amid many misgivings within his denomination, sought from the outset to provide varied fare for discriminating readers. As the editor of his church's Sunday school publications Withrow also encouraged Canadian writers to contribute stories, and after the appointment of William Briggs as book steward in 1879 the Methodist Book Room greatly broadened the range of its general publishing. In 1896 James A. Macdonald, later the editor of the *Globe,* introduced the *Westminster* as an unofficial Presbyterian literary magazine. For a time, writers of religious bent would dominate the local literary scene.

While most of the concerns that agitated local Protestants were current in all English-speaking countries, representatives of various traditions borrowed most readily from sources they found especially congenial. Baptists looked to the early American social gospel. Methodists were inspired by Hugh Price Hughes's London West Central Mission, where social service was combined with fervent evangelism. Presbyterians of Free Church background were most open to Thomas Chalmers's policy of encouraging the poor to help themselves. Congregationalists helped to make Ontarians aware of the 'nonconformist conscience' that had become a powerful moral watchdog in late Victorian England. An influential circle around Principal Grant and the philosopher John Watson at Queen's introduced a strong tincture of German idealism, with its emphasis on purposive social development, as mediated through such British interpreters as Edward Caird and T.H. Green. A tendency to eclecticism was apparent in the masthead of the *Canadian Methodist Quarterly,* a publication of the theological unions of the Methodist colleges, which promised a review devoted to 'Theology, Philosophy, Sociology, Science and Education.' Common to all of these manifestations was the suggestion that collectivities required attention as much as individuals.

Those caught up in one of the enthusiasms of the era might be lukewarm or hostile to others. Sessions of the Presbyterian general assembly sometimes seemed to be offered two distinct versions of social Christianity. D.H. MacVicar of Montreal regarded prohibition as the keystone of the entire program, whereas G.M. Grant had no faith in it and preferred a broadly educational approach to social questions.[17] By and large, however, evangelicals regarded these enterprises as aspects of a single program, and commitment to one aspect usually carried over to others. Legislation would make Ontarians abstemious, and abstemious people would pass good laws. Christian influence would sanctify the Western cultural inheritance, and missions would pass on the benefits to nations ignorant of Handel's *Messiah.* All were implications of conversion; all aids to evangelization. The unity of the program was not fortuitous, but reflected a unitive view of the cosmos itself. The goal, increasingly identified as the Kingdom of God, was a state of affairs in which social harmony would be buttressed by the solidity of individual character. What economic and political arrangements would prevail in this blessed society was as yet by no means clear, for a coherent social program would take shape only in the twentieth century. Already in the 1890s, however, there was a widespread conviction that something very big was impending. Whatever it might turn out to be, it would represent the fulfilment of a purpose in God's mind since the foundation of the world, and meanwhile called for intense human striving.

This vision of an ultimate unity suggested a final plank in the evangelical platform. If all were to be one in the Kingdom of God, why was the church divided into denominational fragments now? Christian union promised benefits of two kinds. A pooling of resources would make possible more effective mobilization on various fronts, and union itself would be a foretaste of the ultimate unity that God intends. At a meeting of the Evangelical Alliance at Montreal in 1874 Grant set forth an ambitious, if scarcely immediately practical, vision of a single Canadian church in which even Roman Catholics would find a place. Although his proposal created few immediate ripples, successive unions of branches of Presbyterianism and Methodism provoked discussion of possible further consolidation across denominational lines. An official Anglican invitation led to a conference on union in 1889 with Presbyterians and Methodists. All three churches saw difficulties in the way, but each church considered the issue sufficiently urgent to require a careful review of its own position.[18]

Organic union was an idea whose time had not yet come. Many who deplored unseemly rivalry looked for its solution merely to the association of like-minded Christians in enterprises transcending denominational divisions. S.G. Phillips spoke for many when he likened the various denominations to so many regiments in an army, adding, with a dizzying change of metaphor, 'if one ship sinks, God has others.' Like their successors today, such people saw the way to closer relations among the churches in 'a great outpouring of the Spirit' rather than in a 'union of names and machinery.' The 1889 conference seemed to have no immediate result beyond confirming its participants in their respective principles, but the idea of union was now in the air. In 1898 Herbert Symonds took the lead in founding the Canadian Society of Christian Unity, with a largely Anglican membership. Anglican participation raised special problems, however, and attention was shifting to proposals that would involve only non-episcopal churches. In 1899 Alfred Gandier, who later became prominent in the union movement, noted 'whispers ... of possible organic union in the near future between Presbyterians and Congregationalists, Presbyterians and Methodists,' and predicted with what proved to be unwarranted optimism, 'Without any undue pressure, but in the most natural way, such unions will come about during the next few years.'[19] At century's end the exhilaration and pain of the long road to the fulfilment of Gandier's dream were still in the future, but within two years the proposal that issued in the formation of the United Church of Canada would be presented to the churches.

Despite the apparent optimism and general aggressiveness of their promoters, these varied attempts to extend Christian influence have commonly been interpreted as defensive reactions to social and intellectual changes that threatened the hegemony of evangelical Protestantism. S.D. Clark helped to set the pattern by emphasizing sectarian inroads into the constituencies of the traditional churches. Neil Semple's appraisal of Methodism from 1854 to 1884, though positive in tone, stresses the role of the urbanization of the province in compelling the reappraisal of traditional means of grace. Christopher Armstrong and H.V. Nelles, who recognize the orientation of the churches to aggressive action, nevertheless leave with the reader of their account of the controversy over Sunday streetcars the impression of the an embattled establishment seeking to hold on to the remnants of a declining influence. Such typical judgments as that of Carol Lee Bacchi that churches were suffering from a distinct falling off in urban attendance and in candidates for the ministry suggest a general mood of pessimism. In *The Regenerators*, a searching examination of varied and hitherto largely unstudied reformers who derived much of their inspiration from religious sources, Ramsay Cook traces the spate of reformist activities in the late nineteenth century not so much to local challenges as to a 'religious crisis provoked by Darwinian science and historical criticism of the Bible' that 'led religious people to attempt to salvage Christianity by transforming it into an essentially social religion.' The result, he claims, was 'the substitution of theology, the science of religion, with sociology, the science of society.'[20]

That the churches were subject to stresses that belied their triumphal language is beyond doubt. Despite their omnipresence in the province, there were significant gaps in their hold on its population. Complaints of the difficulty of reaching the working class and retaining the young were endemic, and the initial success of the Salvation Army in reaching unchurched city-dwellers set off a wave of self-examination among Methodists. In fact, most churches were having difficulty not merely in reaching the working class but in rousing themselves to serious efforts to do so. The migration of urban churches to the suburbs left the inner city increasingly neglected, and congregations that remained there were tempted to depend on pulpit stars to draw members from a distance. The dream of Sunday schools equal in effectiveness even to the public schools of the time was seldom realized, and reports on young people's societies revealed a tendency to decline almost from the time of their foundation. New styles of evangelism owed their popularity, at least in part, to the failure or exhaustion of older methods. That they in turn were unequal to the problem of reaching city-dwellers would become evident by the early years of the twentieth century.[21]

Meanwhile, a rapidly urbanizing society was increasingly asserting its ability to manage itself without help or advice from the churches. A case in point was the controlling board of the public schools, hitherto a preserve of the clergy, which after 1874 was dominated by political appointees. That the same process of secularization was casting into question the traditional right of the churches to set the moral standards of the community was evidenced by the eventual defeat of their efforts to prevent the running of Sunday streetcars. Even their own constituencies were not immune to the temptations of a more open urban society. The cynical C.S. Clark struck a sensitive nerve in asking how many members the evangelical churches would retain 'if they expelled from their communion those who dance, play cards, and attend operas,' and the evangelist Ralph Horner referred darkly to 'Methodist dances' in remote rooms to which guests gradually slipped away from ultra-respectable parlours.[22] The vogue of church-sponsored activities was certainly motivated in part by the increased difficulty of controlling leisure time and preventing it from being used in disapproved ways. The churches were also subjected to intellectual challenges, to be considered in the next chapter, that sent many of the clergy scurrying for new formulations of Christianity that would be less vulnerable than traditional beliefs to the attacks of sceptics.

There are cogent reasons, however, for taking seriously the expansive rhetoric of the energetic campaigners of the period and regarding them as actors rather than merely as reactors. For one thing, suggestions that the influence of religious leaders was declining are difficult to substantiate. In 1882, and again in 1896, the *Globe* conducted a survey of church attendance in Toronto on a chosen Sunday, estimating on each occasion that roughly 45 per cent of the total population attended church at least once. This proportion is likely to seem impressively high to some and unexpectedly low to others, but no significant decline in church-going seems to have taken place in the intervening fourteen years. In 1836 a visiting delegation had reported, admittedly on the basis of impressions and hearsay, that less than half of the Toronto population attended church. Significantly, too, the ratio of Protestant churchgoers to adherents was highest in denominations emphasizing evangelism – in 1896, 75.2 per cent of Methodists, 62.3 per cent of Presbyterians, and 31.7 per cent of Anglicans. The Anglicans, who do not show up well in these statistics, were able to build seventy-five new churches in the diocese of Toronto alone in the decade from 1879 to 1889.[23] Contemporary complaints of the loss of young people seem rather unconvincing in the light of these figures, and evidently the unreached workers were not increasing at a rate higher than the general population.

Other indicators were similarly positive. The clergy were still prime candidates for university presidencies and membership on university boards. C.S. Clark's assertion that aspiring politicians used offices in the church as ammunition in election campaigns, though intended pejoratively, suggests that such positions counted for something in the public estimation. The Consumers' Gas Company and several banks found it advantageous to hold pews in Metropolitan Methodist Church, much as firms today reserve blocks of seats at Maple Leaf Gardens. On the moral front, on the whole, Protestant crusaders could still claim progress. If they suffered some setbacks on Lord's day observance, the temperance cause was still making headway. In 1874 Torontonians had available to them one tavern for each 220 inhabitants; by 1911 the ratio had fallen to one per

14,091.[24] Individual conversions, on which moral and social progress were generally held to depend, had never been more in evidence. One could argue that religion, though perhaps not more pervasive than at the time of Confederation, achieved its greatest impact on the province only toward the close of the century.

To explain the enthusiasms of the late nineteenth century simply as responses to the social and intellectual challenges of the period is to treat them as greater novelties than they were. Reformers did not have to invent a program *de novo*; they merely dusted off and updated a long-familiar one. Practically all of it had already been prefigured in the signs of the millennium identified by John Roaf in his 1844 lectures. His millennium had become the Kingdom of God. Missions, which he had hailed as the going forth of the first angel of the Apocalypse, had gained more general acceptance since his time. Enlightenment was coming about through the sponsorship of culture, as well as in the Sunday school. Holiness as he described it, at least in its external aspects, was being taken up in moral campaigns. Harmony could be related to the prospect of church union, prosperity to growing interest in economic issues. For that matter, the later package of reforms was strongly reminiscent of the benevolences sponsored by the evangelical united front of the early years of the century. Locally, the Free Church had contributed its concern for the headship of Christ over society, and loyalism had brought with it a fondness for public order.

In the final analysis, recognizing elements of both initiative and response in late-century movements of reform involves no contradiction. The quest for righteousness, individual and social, was one in which religious leaders had long been engaged. Aware of past success and present strength, they were confident of their ability to shape the future. They expected opposition, for the spectre of Antichrist lurked not far below the level of consciousness of the most liberal evangelical. They did not fear it, knowing from the Bible that Antichrist was doomed to ultimate defeat. None the less, there were elements of real novelty in the situation of the late nineteenth century. Neither the world nor the evidence was as hospitable to traditional formulations of Christianity as before. Religious leaders on their side were beginning to diagnose elements of systemic evil in society which these traditional formulations did not seem adequately to address. It was not strange that they rushed to update their message while holding fast to Victorian moral verities. It was not strange, either, that some of the more venturesome found the pace of change among the mass of the clergy so slow that they struck out on paths of their own. As the aftermath of the Second Vatican Council demonstrated, nothing is so productive of dissatisfaction as the raising of hopes that cannot immediately be fulfilled.

Consideration of the efficacy of the reform program raises other questions. Did the manner in which many Protestants responded to nineteenth-century challenges result, as Cook has suggested, 'in Christianity becoming less rather than more relevant'? If so, the fault can scarcely have been in the extension of their range of interest to include the well-being of society as well as that of the individual. Such Old Testament prophets as Amos and Micah, who came to be widely read during this period, gave social justice a central place in their proclamation of God's judgments.[25] In any event, to have continued to urge the transformation of a highly industrialized society through individual improvement alone would have been to have asked the waves to stand back. It would also have been to define religion in terms especially appealing to those who had reason to be content with the status quo. More questionable was the widespread if often unacknowledged confidence of the age, as represented by evangelists, program planners, and social reformers alike, that in order to effect spiritual results it was necessary only to manipulate the right levers. Integral to the Judaeo-Christian tradition has been the belief that God both transcends the world's categories and is immanent in its processes, a belief that God invites humans to share in the fulfilment of divine purpose but is not reduceable to the sum of their efforts. Immanence received much more than its share of attention in the late nineteenth century, with the result that the Kingdom of God sometimes seemed to be little more than a program of human devising. Such a reduction was as yet seldom countenanced by church leaders, but the balance was tilting dangerously toward it.

To turn to the Roman Catholicism of the era is to encounter many of the same concerns. Both the Jesuits and the Oblates founded missions in northern Ontario among the native population, and the Oblates were especially active among French Canadians who were beginning to move into the area around Lake Timiskaming. Jean-Marie Nedelec, an Oblate who peregrinated from his base at Mattawa as far as James Bay each summer during a pastorate that extended from 1869 to 1891, was outstanding as an example of sacrificial devotion. Although the Catholicism of western Canada was largely shaped in France, John Joseph Lynch zealously promoted for several years a projected Irish settlement in Manitoba. Needs at home were still too pressing to allow for involvement abroad, but in 1902 John M. Fraser would begin a long missionary career in the Orient. Roman Catholic temperance societies were even more closely associated with churches than were similar Protestant societies. Both as bishop of London and as archbishop of Toronto, John Walsh required of all children he confirmed a pledge of abstinence until the age of majority; Lynch exacted a similar promise from priests with drinking problems.

Catholics were free of some of the taboos general among Protestants, such as those against dancing, small-scale gambling, and the theatre, but French-Canadian priests took an especially strict view of contacts between the sexes. Duhamel forbade males and females to mingle as actors in theatrical performances or in promenades on snowshoes, and even the *Irish Canadian* noted with evident approval a circular of the coadjutor bishop of Cincinnati insisting that in church functions 'there must be no dancing after dark and no round dancing at any time.'[26] If Protestants sometimes thought Roman Catholics lax in their moral demands, Catholics were not slow to return the compliment.

In dealings with trade unions the Roman Catholic Church had a distinct advantage. Protestants who interested themselves in labour problems were, with rare exceptions, middle-class well-wishers with little experience of the realities of industrial conflict. Roman Catholic priests knew workers and their problems from daily contacts with their parishioners. A number of early unions ran foul of ecclesiastical law by exacting quasi-religious secret oaths from their members. When the Knights of Labour entered Canada in the 1880s with high-flown rhetoric but a moderate program, however, Lynch went along with the American hierarchy in recognizing it. Even when Archbishop Elzéar Taschereau of Quebec secured a condemnation from the Holy Office, Lynch refused to act on it on the canonically proper ground that he had received no official notification.[27] In philanthropy too Roman Catholics had the advantage of closer acquaintance with the needy. Partly because of a desire to protect their people from Protestant proselytizers, and partly because of a long tradition that made charity a peculiar responsibility of the church, they usually insisted on maintaining their own institutions.

Missing among Roman Catholics, however, were the social utopianism and the commitment to absolute measures so conspicuous in many Protestants of the era. Few of them supported the prohibition of alcoholic beverages. Lynch opposed even the Scott Act of 1878 with its provision for local option, despite its sponsorship by a Roman Catholic, and encouraged the establishment of bars as a preferable alternative to drinking in the home. Walsh favoured Sunday streetcars as helpful in getting people to church, and despite the support of the Roman Catholic labour leader Daniel O'Donoghue the defenders of Sunday quiet recognized that the Catholic vote was almost solidly against them. The *Catholic Weekly Review* attacked woman suffrage as a threat to the survival of the family, and the *Catholic Register* characterized socialism as a 'product of the alcohol-steeped brains of the effete capitals of Europe.' Even Henry George's Single Tax proposal, which Cardinal Gibbons of Baltimore was prepared to tolerate as a permissible aberration, was assailed by Lynch as revolutionary.[28]

The publication by Pope Leo XIII in 1891 of the encyclical *Rerum novarum*, which condemned both socialism and the excesses of capitalism and encouraged the formation of Catholic unions, provided a basis for systematic social thought. Walsh cited it in support of the rights of workers while calling on them to act responsibly and discouraging them from striking except as a last resort. A hierarchy that still consisted mainly of natives of rural Ireland, however, did not easily master the intricacies of labour relations. Only with the appointment of Henry Somerville as editor of the *Catholic Register* in 1933 would the church in Ontario begin to develop a sophisticated social philosophy.[29]

A major reason for the comparative modesty of their social program was the minority status of Roman Catholics in the province. In Quebec ultramontanism inspired agitation for reforms comparable in range, though not identical in content, with those urged by English-speaking Protestants. In Ontario similar reforms were imposed on Roman Catholics from without, and human nature demanded that they be resisted. Roman Catholics do not seem to have been singled out in Ontario as targets of sabbatarian and prohibitory laws;[30] but they could scarcely be unaware that in the United States much of the impetus for comparable measures came from a desire to make Irish immigrants behave. Many Catholic statements of the period were, accordingly, defensive in tone. Roman Catholics saw themselves as cheated in provisions for their school system, largely excluded from government jobs, and subject to harassment by the police. Proselytizing efforts by representatives of Protestant charitable agencies were a source of special worry, and recalled charges of similar Protestant efforts in Ireland among victims of famine during the 1840s. Such perceptions of danger to the faith led to suspicion of measures proposed by Protestants and encouraged the development of 'safe' Catholic contacts. The *Catholic Register* warned: 'The culture that should be the object and aim of a Catholic Club is not culture in general or any kind of culture; it is emphatically Catholic culture ... Modern culture is not Catholic.'[31]

Roman Catholic social expectations differed from those of Protestant evangelicals on theological grounds as well. Protestants, whether or not they looked to a literal millennium, tended to think of the Kingdom of God as an ideal order that would be revealed in its fullness only at some time in the future. To Roman Catholics, following Saint Augustine, the city of God was an eternal reality always in process of actualization in human society but, on account of the limitations imposed by original sin, never completely fulfilled within time. They were thus saddened but not greatly surprised when parishioners became involved in street brawls or when priests succumbed to alcoholism. Nor were they without recourse, for the sacraments were available to afford the remedy of supernatural grace for the inevitable lapses of the faithful. This realism about human nature made Catholics wary of the once-for-all solutions to which evangelicals were often attracted. They did not expect legislation to usher in a new age, or even to ensure the existence of a moral society.

Roman Catholics were not without their own brand of utopianism, however. Catholic theology was the only true basis of social order, the Church its natural custodian, the clergy its appointed interpreters. Only in a Catholic society could ambition and insubordination be held in check so that classes might harmoniously fulfil their appropriate roles. The conversion of the world became immensely important, therefore, not only for the salvation of individual souls, which was by no means to be despised, but also because only thus could justice and stability be assured. Notable conversions around the world were faithfully reported in the local Catholic press. No mission was complete without a call for converts, and Lynch's weekly lectures were credited with securing a large number. Questionnaires sent to parishes included an inevitable question on conversions, although their scarcity suggests that matrimony was usually the decisive factor. Franco-Ontarians believed themselves chosen to out-populate the heretics, while Lynch saw the vocation of the Irish as the conversion of North America. Among the Irish, however, who as a 'double minority' in church and society desired to be both good Catholics and respectable Ontarians, this messianism was necessarily muted. The role of the church has been described as that of creating a Catholic 'subculture,' and the choice of wording is significant.[32] Securing a fair share of government patronage was a more realistic objective than attaching Ontario to the Holy See.

Anglo-Catholic social thought had a flavour of its own. Strong stands on issues of personal deportment were seldom deemed necessary, perhaps because of the gentility of much of the constituency. A writer in Trinity College's *Rouge et Noir* took note of prohibition only to dismiss it as impracticable; another objected to the fanaticism of those who condemned the moderate drinker as 'a worthless outcast.' When a tobacconist presented a supply of cigarettes to the college, students agreed that they had never tasted better. Moderation in such matters was always advocated and often assumed. Anglo-Catholics were, however, much more open than evangelicals within their church to the possibility of applying Christianity to the ordering of society. On the one hand, the Oxford Movement had begun as a protest against interference with vested rights, and probably most Anglo-Catholics were always reasonably well satisfied with existing social arrangements. On the other hand, the romantic medievalism associated with the movement was inhospitable to the individualism and gigantism of modern capitalism and encouraged sympathy for labour unions as the nearest existing equivalent of the earlier guilds. Moreover, the difficulty experienced in England by the Anglo-Catholic clergy in securing desirable livings raised up a generation of slum priests who proved receptive to the Christian socialism pioneered by F.D. Maurice and Charles Kingsley and founded the Guild of Saint Matthew to propagate it. Their influence was as yet barely perceptible in Ontario. Christian socialism was favourably noticed in *Rouge et Noir*, but more widely acceptable was a tradition of dedication to the service of the poor that found notable expression in the formation of the Sisterhood of Saint John the Divine in 1874.[33]

Anglo-Catholics also had a vision of unity. Christ had founded one church, they believed, and provided it with the beginning of a succession of bishops as guarantors of its visible unity and continuity. The vicissitudes of history might wound its unity but never irretrievably destroy it; any break in communion among Christians was an anomaly and a scandal. Anglo-Catholics were mainly responsible for placing union firmly on the Anglican agenda at the Lambeth conferences and thus ultimately at the interdenominational meeting held in 1889. Insistence on the necessity of preserving the episcopal succession also compelled them to place repeated stumbling-blocks in the way of union, but despite the embarrassment this caused them they could neither surrender their convictions nor abandon the quest for union.

13 *Strains in the Fabric*

Contention over religious issues had been a constant feature of Ontario life from the earliest days of settlement, witnessing to the importance of religion to the inhabitants of the province but also souring relations among and sometimes within ecclesiastical bodies, complicating politics, and occasionally erupting into violence. By the end of the nineteenth century the obsolescence of some of these quarrels was making possible a large measure of practical co-operation and even talk of union among the Protestant churches that dominated the province. At the same time, resistance to social and theological innovation was opening up new areas of disagreement. Strains in the religious fabric of late nineteenth-century Ontario were in some cases inherited, in others special to the period and destined to fade in the twentieth century, and in still others as yet almost imperceptible but pregnant with future controversy.

That Protestantism and Roman Catholicism represented radically incompatible forms of Christianity had always been an Ontario axiom, and nothing happened in the nineteenth century to call it into question. To a general Protestant antipathy to popery various groups added specific grievances. Anglicans were particularly offended by Roman claims to a monopoly of catholicity. To many evangelical Protestants, who inherited a deep-rooted belief that the pope was the Antichrist predicted in the book of Revelation, Roman Catholicism constituted an idolatrous system to be rooted out with reforming zeal. Ultramontane interventions in Quebec politics, duly reported in the Ontario press, confirmed widespread Protestant suspicions of Roman Catholic political designs. Albert Carman and George Douglas, both prominent Methodists, objected vociferously when Sir John Thompson, a Methodist convert to Roman Catholicism, was chosen prime minister. John Joseph Lynch, aware that his people were a vulnerable minority, would have preferred peaceful coexistence but was drawn into prolonged controversies with Arthur Sweatman and John

Langtry of the Church of England and with James Gardiner Robb, the minister of a Presbyterian congregation that was composed largely of immigrants from Ulster.[1] The clergy on each side felt it part of their duty to warn their flocks of the menacing presence of the other.

An emotional tinder so carefully kept dry required only a small spark to burst into flame, and sparks were in ready supply. A parade on the seventeenth of March or the twelfth of July, a provocative statement by a Quebec bishop, or a visit to Ontario by Charles Chiniquy, a former Roman Catholic priest and temperance lecturer turned Presbyterian, could easily lead to broken noses or even to loss of life. In 1875 Lynch announced an indulgence to anyone who would mark a year of jubilee by going on pilgrimage fifteen times to four local churches. The climax to what had been a peaceful series of pious acts was reached in the autumn when, on two successive Sundays, large groups of pilgrims made the rounds. Protestant mobs gathered on both occasions, stoning not only the pilgrims but the police who were sent to protect them. Violence was less in evidence after this time, but Ontarians were regularly reminded of their differences. Protestant demands for the execution of Louis Riel provided one such occasion; although the hostility was directed primarily against French-Canadians, memories of Riel's execution of the Orangeman Thomas Scott in 1870 injected a religious note. In 1889 the refusal of the federal government to disallow a Quebec act compensating the Jesuits for the forfeiture of their pre-conquest estates provoked the formation of the Equal Rights Association, which was chaired by William Caven and backed by many influential members of the business community. In 1890 the Protestant Protective Association, an offshoot of an American nativist organization, entered the province with a call for a general boycott of Roman Catholics in both politics and business. Most Protestant leaders were not prepared to support such measures, and the association had to be content with a failed Knox alumnus as president. Nevertheless, it captured enough seats in the provincial election of 1894 to demonstrate that the pope did not yet have Ontario in his pocket.[2]

The relation of the Roman Catholic Church to public education, which had attracted relatively little attention in the years immediately after Confederation, suddenly became a contentious issue in 1884. Before approving a set of selected Bible readings for use in the public schools, Premier Oliver Mowat, a Liberal, secured the consent of representative religious leaders. The fact that Lynch was one of these, and that Mowat was correctly suspected of sounding out his opinion frequently, brought charges from W.R. Meredith, the Conservative leader, that the government was under Roman Catholic domination. The *Toronto Daily Mail* far outdid Meredith in attacks on the church, and one outraged Protestant demanded 'the whole d—d Bible, and nothing but the Bible.'[3] Perhaps not altogether by coincidence, 1884 was also the year in which James G. Blaine campaigned for the American presidency against 'rum, romanism, and rebellion.' At Meredith's insistence, Roman Catholic education became a prominent issue in the provincial elections of 1886, 1890, and 1894. The decision of the Manitoba government in 1890 to replace that province's Protestant and Roman Catholic schools with a single non-denominational system also provoked great excitement in the province when Roman Catholic demands for redress from the federal government made the issue a national one.

Religious bigotry, an ugly reality in nineteenth-century Ontario, subjected Roman Catholics to various forms of petty persecution and disgusted those of good will on both sides. Except when particular issues roused intense feelings or when old-country feuds were imported into the province, however, that bigotry does not seem to have prevented Ontarians from living together in relative harmony. Legends of priests mingling in Orange parades or even being invited to ride King William's white horse are sufficiently numerous to indicate, at any rate, a widespread view of what ought to have happened. Indeed, the Orange Order, which always insisted that its objection was to the political activities rather than the religious beliefs of Roman Catholics, could at times be a moderating force. Undoubtedly, many Orangemen voted for candidates of the Protestant Protective Association, but their leaders were cool to fanatical ideas that could only discredit militant Protestantism. Meanwhile the Protestant horse had a way of stumbling on the way to the polls; it failed to deliver a single election victory to Meredith. In general, the conflict served more to rally forces on either side than to do great damage to the other. The imagined threat of papal domination, at a time when the Catholic proportion of the population was actually declining, helped to mobilize Protestants to common action and served as an effective argument in promoting several church unions. In return, the experience of living in the shadow of a hostile Protestant majority stiffened Roman Catholic resistance to assimilation. Not all Ontarians were taken in by their own rhetoric. 'There is a wonderful periodicity in these perturbations and subsidences, not less marked and mysterious than the ebb and flow of ocean tides, or the approach and retreat of the flaming comets,' the *Christian Guardian* once observed of anti-Catholic polemics.[4]

If to many Protestants the Roman church seemed so monolithic that 'the whole weight of her vast machinery [could] be hurled in an hour for or against those who aid or oppose her,' Catholics knew better. A notable source of internal strife was a growing alienation between French and Irish Catholics. Although mutual admiration among ethnic groups had often been lacking from earliest days, the bishops of Upper Canada until about 1860 made a point of learning French. With the massive immigration of 'famine Irish' into the province and the far from negligible influx of French Canadians into the lower Ottawa Valley, however, relations began to deteriorate. Considerable indignation was stirred during the 1850s when Armand de Charbonnel, scandalized by what he regarded as the disorderly behaviour of many of the older Irish priests, replaced them with imports from France and Germany.[5] Pierre-Adolphe Pinsoneault, the first bishop in western Ontario, established his episcopal see at the bilingual town of Windsor. John Walsh, his anglophone successor, almost immediately removed it to London.

The centre of conflict was the diocese of Ottawa, which straddled the provincial boundary and formed part of the ecclesiastical province of Quebec. Along with an increasing French-Canadian population, it included a sizeable and vocal Irish element. Much of the controversy was local, issuing in an English-language University of Ottawa (until 1901) and distinct separate school boards for French and Irish. The predominantly Irish hierarchy of the province also took a hand, proposing in 1875 the division of the diocese and the inclusion of its Ontario portion within the archdiocesan jurisdiction of Toronto. When this failed, they were able to secure in 1890 the carving out of Kingston of a tiny, Scottish-dominated diocese based on Alexandria in Glengarry; it was hoped that its obvious lack of resources would provide leverage for annexing to it the predominantly francophone counties of Prescott and Russell along the Ottawa. Meanwhile, however, Archibishop Joseph-Thomas Duhamel had succeeded in 1882 in securing the erection of the upper, largely English-speaking portion of his diocese into a new vicariate apostolic of Pontiac (later the diocese of Pembroke), which also straddled the provincial border, and in 1886 Ottawa became an archbishopric.[6] Traces of these and other manoeuvres can still be detected on the ecclesiastical map of Ontario.

Ethnic conflict within religious communities is not uncommon; practically every Protestant denomination suffered from it so long as Upper Canada had a predominantly immigrant population. Although its manifestations can be ugly, such conflict ordinarily reflects not merely irrational prejudice but a significant incompatibility in religious mentality. There were no doctrinal differences between French and Irish Catholics, and the two could stand shoulder to shoulder when their common interests were threatened. Yet each had a conception of how Catholicism ought to operate that rendered the other's expression of the faith suspect. A grave curé in a soutane guiding his flock from a presbytery in the centre of his parish and protecting them from external infection represented one point of view. An extroverted pastor sharing the life of his parishioners, mingling at their picnics, and sometimes bullying them into salvation typified the other.The existence of incompatible visions of the future was a further divisive factor. French Canadians relied for the future of Catholicism on the extension of their language and culture into new areas. Irish Catholics found this vision distasteful both as anglophones and as citizens of Ontario.[7] They also regarded it as impossible; in Ontario one spoke English, and attempting to propagate the faith in any other language would be counter-productive.

If Irish Catholics were capable of united action in defence of their nationality, they had their share of donnybrooks among themselves. Differences arose among the bishops, and sometimes rankled. When a long-standing dispute over the claims of dioceses carved out of Kingston to a share of its original endowment was resolved in favour of Kingston, Bishop J.V. Cleary was warned that Lynch would never forgive him. Relations were not improved by complaints of other bishops that Lynch was giving too much away in his dealings with Mowat; a letter Cleary had received from Lynch contains a marginal jotting: 'Evasive.' Bishops also had problems with their people, for the desire for a lay voice in parish affairs that had flared up in O'Grady's day was by no means dead. In a province where Roman Catholics were not easily elected to public office, positions on separate school boards and on the executives of Catholic societies were important outlets for ambition. They also furnished strategic platforms from which to promote such favourite causes as Irish nationalism. Those who held them, often persons of independent spirit, soon discovered that the bishops expected them to uphold official policies. In the archdiocese of Toronto they also learned that they were expected to avoid statements that might jeopardize relations with the state.

Conflict was especially open and bitter in the last years of Lynch's episcopate. In 1888, for example, he issued a circular to the Catholics of Toronto condemning trustees who pressed Irish nationalism, refused to go in procession on the queen's jubilee, or demanded the secret ballot in separate school elections. He did not hesitate to reprimand and even suspend priests who showed sympathy with the opposition. Ill feeling over the ballot issue was strong, especially when the Orange Order offered its support to the trustees. Lynch was able to stem the tide within his lifetime, but after his death in 1888 the ballot was soon conceded. Although such dissent was usually reported in publications that few Protestants read, the lockstep uniformity of the Roman Catholic Church was indeed a figment of the Protestant imagination. Meetings of separate school trustees sometimes broke up in disorder, and complaints of the inefficiency of teaching orders reached such a pitch that for several years the Brothers of the Christian Schools abandoned the province.[8]

The Church of England's internal Protestant-Catholic conflict reached its height during the 1870s. Strachan's policy had been to appoint high church clergy to parishes east of Toronto while allowing evangelicals to predominate in the west, thus determining the future orientation of the dioceses of Ontario and Huron. While strife raged in all parts of the province, Toronto, as debatable ground, became the main bone of contention. So long as Strachan lived, his prestige and formidable presence held opposition in check. The lid blew off with the accession in 1867 of his protégé and former pupil A.N. Bethune, who was as stubborn as Strachan and less conciliatory to opponents. Distressed by Bethune's willingness to tolerate and even encourage ritualistic innovations, a lay-dominated group organized the Evangelical Association in 1869 to press for congregational participation in clerical appointments. So intense was feeling during the next few years that the credentials of lay delegates to the diocesan synod were challenged as systematically as the rota of a criminal jury. In 1873, after suffering a crushing defeat in synod, the evangelicals formed the more tightly organized Church Association. Having failed to capture the machinery of the synod, they now adopted the strategy of setting up institutions independent of it: Wycliffe College (at first the Protestant Episcopal Divinity School) in 1877, Wycliffe missions, endowed Wycliffe parishes, the *Evangelical Churchman,* and even a fund for the widows and orphans of their own clergy. When Bethune died in 1879, S.H. Blake is reported to have given thanks in a prayer at a Wycliffe College anniversary. The two parties then worked out a compromise, with the high church agreeing to the election as bishop of an evangelical, Arthur Sweatman, on condition that the Church Association be disbanded. Despite an assertion that 'perfect peace and harmony' had resulted, the truce was at best uneasy. Although the evangelicals had attained a fair number of their objectives, parallel high and low church structures remained in place. Some discontented evangelicals, notably at Ottawa in 1874 and Toronto in 1893, withdrew from the church altogether to form congregations of the American-based Reformed Episcopal Church. These breakaway groups, launched with considerable fanfare, were destined to gradual extinction.[9] Other discontented Anglicans found homes elsewhere, especially among the Methodists.

Various correlations have been suggested for high-low orientations within the Church of England. The evangelical agitation has been described as a 'struggle for the rights of the laity,' and there can be no gainsaying the prominence of influential laymen in the leadership of the evangelical party and of clergymen in the promotion of Anglo-Catholic practices. High and low church supporters have been identified as representing mainly old and new families respectively; with some plausibility, the diocese of Toronto in the 1870s might be regarded as the last bastion of the Family Compact. One can easily identify an ethnic factor as well. Trinity College graduates and English imports were conspicuous in the Anglo-Catholic party, and Bishop Isaac Hellmuth's recommendation that the diocese of Huron should adopt the canons of the Church of Ireland was a significant indicator of the orientation of the other.[10] It was also significant, however, that each party represented a movement of reform within the church. Evangelicals were caught up in the late-century drive to purify society; Anglo-Catholics sought to restore a sense of distinctive identity to a church that had come largely to embody national values. This sense of mission on both sides had the effect of hardening attitudes, with a resulting danger of paralysis by compromise.

Internal conflict within the Church of England complicated its relations with denominations of unambiguously Protestant orientation. By the time of Confederation the settlement of the clergy reserves issue had rendered many old grounds of contention obsolete, and Anglican and other churches became increasingly similar in appearance, social composition, and program. During the later decades of the century, however, the Anglo-Catholic unwillingness to recognize the equal standing of non-episcopal churches became a major source of irritation. In 1876 the *Dominion Churchman,* after condemning Rome and infidelity, referred to 'a sectarianism, which in some cases means well, but which involves a principle much to be deplored.' Some twenty-five years later the *Canadian Churchman* was horrified to learn that Anglican clergymen had preached regularly in a Presbyterian church that served an isolated summer resort, thus suggesting that '"one church is as good as another." one set of shepherds as fully authorized as others.'[11] This lack of reciprocity came prominently to light in union conversations, and soured the relations they were designed to improve. A fear of Anglo-Catholicism also induced in non-episcopal churches a nervousness about ritual that sometimes expressed itself in strangely inconsistent ways. Gothic architecture and vested choirs were acceptable in Methodist churches long before ministers dared to appear gowned in their pulpits.

While Anglicans and Roman Catholics were trying to patch up their internal quarrels, the cohesion of the main body of evangelical Protestants was showing unaccustomed signs of strain. These had little to do with competition among denominations which, though sometimes intense, did not prevent them from working together ever more closely in a variety of projects and, in some cases, even discussing union. They were signalled, instead, by the appearance of disruptive new movements and by a growing divergence of attitudes within denominations. Signs of a fading of consensus were concentrated on three issues: the methods and aims of evangelism, the nature and limits of the authority of the Bible, and expectations for the future.

Personal holiness, a matter of widespread concern throughout much of the nineteenth century, received renewed attention in its last decades in both Britain and North America. Although its promotion ran the gamut from ultra-respectable interest in the 'higher life' to emotional camp meeting appeals, two features were common to many of its later manifestations. One was a tendency to think of holiness not in Wesley's terms, as a springboard for further growth, but as an experience that paralleled, completed, or even replaced conversion. The other was a widespread hunger for special blessings, especially divine healing, that the more conventional churches failed to offer. Holiness had some well-placed advocates in the province's churches, such as the one-time *Christian Guardian* editor E.H. Dewart. It could not always be contained comfortably within them.

A version of holiness close to the traditional Wesleyan model was the banner under which soldiers of William Booth's Salvation Army, originally an offshoot of the Methodist New Connexion in England, appeared on the streets of Toronto and London in 1882. The Army was noisy, aggressive, opportunistic in its methods, and at first frankly competitive with the churches. It spread rapidly, not only attracting a following in working-class districts but setting up detachments in many smaller centres. While its well-advertised trophies were rescued drunkards, its dependable supporters were mainly earnest young Christians who failed to find satisfying outlets for their energies in the regular churches. Much of its success, indeed, was due to its ability to put converts quickly to work gaining others. It was especially attractive for this reason to women, who soon constituted the bulk of its corps of officers. Within a decade, however, the Army was in trouble. The membership of many outposts was below the critical mass for survival, and in the upper echelons there were serious factional quarrels. The Booths had no knack for delegating authority, and some of the enthusiasts attracted to the movement were not temperamentally inclined to submit to a quasi-military discipline. The most serious and only permanent split, precipitated by P.W. Philpott in 1891 in opposition to uncritical glorification of the Army, led to the formation of several congregations of the rival Gospel Workers in Toronto. After these setbacks the Army was able to resume its growth, though not at the spectacular rate of early days. To the public it was increasingly known for the uncontroversial social work it undertook through a separate branch set up in 1896.[12]

Whereas the Salvation Army was British in origin and direction, other newly emerging groups owed more to local initiative. The most flamboyant of these resulted from the revivalist preaching of Ralph Horner in east central Ontario. After experiencing an emotional conversion at a Methodist camp meeting in 1872, Horner soon felt called to the work of an evangelist. Two years of study at Victoria College and, as he always emphasized, the attainment of a B.O. from the National School of Oratory at Philadelphia, were followed by ordination to the Methodist ministry in 1887. Unhappily, there was misunderstanding from the outset between a conference that counted on the availability of its members for appointment and an individualist who expected freedom to preach where and as he was led, and in 1894 he was deposed from the ministry. Horner's preaching, which reflected both the emotional abandon of a 'crisis convert' and the deliberate technique of a graduate orator, frequently left listeners swooning on the floor. He claimed a 'third blessing,' beyond justification and sanctification, that endowed him with 'cyclones of power' irresistible by all but the most hardened church members, and called successfully for definite acts of commitment, of which the most colourful was the 'stripping room' wherein converts divested themselves of jewellery and other ornaments. In 1895 he organized his followers into a separate denomination, chartered in 1900 as the Holiness Movement Church of Canada. In western Ontario a more sophisticated Methodist minister, Nelson Burns, was deposed in the same year as Horner for his extreme expressions of holiness doctrine. Other bodies of holiness orientation were the Free Methodists, who entered the province after the Methodist union of 1874 on the invitation of unhappy members of the Methodist New Connexion and added to their numbers in 1884 through similar accessions from the Primitive Methodists, and the Mennonite Brethren in Christ (now the United Missionary Church), who represented the union in 1883 of several groups in the United States and Canada who had seceded from the main Mennonite body.[13]

Despite the attention they received, none of these movements achieved spectacular growth. In 1891 adherents of the Salvation Army constituted 0.5 per cent of the provincial population, by 1901 only 0.3 per cent. The census category of 'other' rose more impressively from 0.7 per cent in 1881 to 1.6 per cent in 1901, but it included more than the holiness bodies. Horner's converts were overwhelmingly rural. Contrary to a general impression, even Salvation Army adherents constituted as large a proportion of the population of the whole of Ontario as of its cities.[14] The holiness denominations seem to have appealed chiefly to people who yearned for the simplicities of a remembered past or who felt ill at ease when catapulted by union into a large denomination. Accepting and even intensifying the behavioural requirements of evangelical Protestants of the time, they assigned a special prominence on their list of sins to 'worldliness.' Avoidance of defilement by the world meant plainness, but not necessarily poverty. It precluded efforts to cure systemic social ills, but not the use of the most effective means of publicity available.

Ontarians, dimly aware by the middle of the nineteenth century that daring scientific and historical studies had raised important questions about the formation of the Bible and hence about its authority for Christians, were fully alert well before its close to the urgency of answering them. Concern was natural in view of the exalted status that Protestants attached to the book, and was heightened by the manner in which they had been accustomed to use it. Since the seventeenth century they had regarded it, in scholastic fashion, as a source of indubitable propositions that could be used to prove other propositions, although by the nineteenth century they preferred to speak in Baconian terms of facts that could be arranged to form systems. Biblical critics undermined the foundations of this approach by noting inconsistencies and identifying successive layers of tradition, geologists by calling for a time-line much longer than the letter of Scripture allowed. Apologists had pointed to miracles and fulfilled prophecies as compelling evidence of the truth of Christianity. Critics, applying to the narratives of Scripture the criteria they had long regarded as appropriate to other historical documents, denied the credibility of the miracles and the intention of the prophets to predict the coming of Jesus. William Paley had accumulated examples of adaptation in nature to demonstrate the existence of a divine purpose, and now Darwin proposed to explain them by random mutations.

When the new interpretations were introduced to the province, they encountered predictable resistance. George Workman of Victoria University, after returning in 1887 from study undertaken in Germany under the university's sponsorship, denied in a public lecture that Old Testament prophecies could legitimately be used as predictions of the coming of Christ. His basic contention was that the prophets' words should not be interpreted in a 'double sense' but taken to mean simply what the authors intended. In 1891, at the urging of such Methodist leaders as Dewart and General Superintendent Albert Carman, the Victoria board of regents responded by restricting Workman's teaching to the arts faculty. He thereupon resigned in protest. Ironically, he would set forth his ideas most systematically in a book designed to counter an attack on the authority of the Old Testament by Goldwin Smith, a former Regius professor at Oxford who was now a considerable intellectual lion in Toronto. Smith, with a streak of conservatism not uncommon in those who wish to justify their scepticism, claimed that 'those who have given up the authenticity of Genesis ... must apparently give up the Fall, the Redemption, and the Incarnation.' Workman insisted that, on the contrary, 'there is nothing about the Old Testament that needs to be renounced but a traditional view of its origin and structure, and also that there is nothing about it that needs to be modified but an erroneous theory of the inspiration of its authors and an irrational method of interpreting its books.'[15]

Workman proved to be Ontario's only martyr for biblical criticism in the nineteenth century, though others would suffer in the twentieth. By the century's end, a contemporary wrote, some of the more cautious conclusions of the higher critics had become 'by an almost unconscious process' practically the common property of the educated portion of the clergy. Before the next century was well under way, most Protestant colleges were taking them for granted as ingredients of their curricula. It was no longer those who had been accused of heresy but their accusers who were beginning to have a sense of estrangement from their churches. This result was made possible, in large measure, by the 'proven piety and good sense' of those who introduced the critical view to the province.[16] Those who sought enlightenment in Germany to prepare themselves for teaching careers most commonly frequented the Leipzig lectures of Franz Delitzsch, a believing Christian who avoided extreme positions. Their students, on graduation, seldom intruded critical expertise into their sermons.

Many Ontarians remained unpersuaded that the finality of scriptural assertions in any branch of knowledge, history or science as much as theology, could be denied without ultimately fatal results for Christian faith. They were handicapped by the fact that Protestants, while agreeing on the inspiration and centrality of the Bible, had never canonized any particular view of the authority of individual texts. Benjamin B. Warfield of Princeton Seminary filled the void by insisting, in words accepted by most later conservative evangelicals, that the Scriptures are the 'book of God, of which God is the author in the sense that every one of its affirmations, of whatever kind, is to be esteemed as the utterance of God, of infallible truth and authority.' Driven to acknowledge that imperfections may have crept into the text in transmission, A.A. Hodge retreated to the inerrancy of the 'original autographs.' Knox College maintained close relations with Princeton, and Principal William MacLaren faithfully passed on the Princeton theology to his students until his retirement in 1908.[17]

In 1968 Ernest R. Sandeen called attention to the prominence in the late nineteenth century of a third issue, the nature of the Christian's hope for the future. Social gospellers looked to the establishment of the Kingdom of God of earth. Although they did not envisage it in strictly millennial terms as a thousand-year reign of Christ on earth, their expectation that its advent would be the culmination of a process of gradual amelioration was strongly reminiscent of the postmillennialism represented in an earlier period by John Roaf. The premillennial alternative, which anticipated from history only increasing woes from which the faithful would be delivered by direct divine intervention, has until recently received much less attention from historians. It did not die out, however, but always retained some currency even in the major churches. During the last decades of the century it gained new support. The appearance of Seventh-Day Adventists and Jehovah's Witnesses in the province was evidence of this interest, but such incursions were only the tip of an iceberg.[18]

Most influential in the revival of premillennialism was the version proposed by John Nelson Darby, the founder of the Plymouth Brethren. Darby posited, in line with what was already a hoary tradition among millenarians, the division of history into periods marked by successive divine dispensations or programs for human society. His most distinctive thesis was that the refusal of the Jews to accept Christ interrupted this progression, which will be resumed at some time without warning. Dramatic events will then follow in rapid succession. A great tribulation will precede the final judgment and the millennial reign of Christ, but meanwhile the faithful will have been snatched from the earth to meet their saviour in the air. Relatively few Ontarians joined the Plymouth Brethren, but Darby's dispensationalism was espoused by such clerical leaders as Elmore Harris, Bishop Maurice Baldwin of Huron, and H.M. Parsons of Knox Presbyterian Church, as well as an even more formidable array of prominent laymen that included Mayor William Howland. The Toronto Willard Tract Depository under S.R. Briggs issued a stream of propagandist materials, leaders of the movement were regularly invited from the United States, and Ontarians were active participants in a series of annual Bible study meetings and prophecy conferences held at Niagara-on-the-Lake from 1882 to 1897.[19]

Various combinations of views on holiness, biblical authority, and eschatology were theoretically possible; positions taken with respect to them showed enough correlation in practice, however, to suggest the existence of two diverging tendencies. One tendency combined a readiness to promote environmental as well as individual change, a developmental view of the historical process, and an openness to the modification of traditional approaches to the Bible. The combination did not originate in Ontario, but gained currency in the province through personal contacts and published materials. Locally, it was promoted most effectively by several unusually able university teachers. George Paxton Young of University College, where Knox and Wycliffe students normally did their undergraduate work, took them in his lectures through the successive stages of a pilgrimage from Scottish common sense to the idealism of T.H. Green. John Watson of Queen's University submitted the presuppositions of his students to relentless cross-examination in order to compel them to think for themselves. Nathanael Burwash of Victoria University challenged his students in gentler fashion to learn from both science and revelation in the confidence that, whatever the apparent contradictions, 'all truth is sacred and harmonious.'[20] All accepted the critical approach to the Bible, and all insisted on the primacy of the spiritual over the material.

Such ideas were not presented to unresponsive listeners. Victorians were convinced, by and large, not only that change is inevitable but that to a considerable extent it can be controlled to human advantage. To many minds that were tuned to such assumptions, traditional beliefs in the eternal punishment of the wicked and predestination before birth had come to seem excessively rigid, and conversion more a process than an event. Prospective ministers were aware of scientific and critical challenges and often unsure of their ability to counter them. When they entered university, therefore, they were not entirely unprepared to hear Christianity described as an ideal principle rather than as a credal system or to have values emphasized more than miracles as arguments for belief. The suggestion of limits to biblical infallibility was shocking at first, but the view of revelation as progressive was one they found congenial. The resulting syntheses were not always logically consistent and sometimes neglected significant elements of Christian tradition, but they helped many young Ontarians over crises of faith and enabled them to preach with strengthened conviction. By the end of the century these syntheses had vocal advocates in all the major Protestant churches, although in the Church of England they were received more sympathetically in high than in low church circles.

During the late nineteenth century there also emerged a remarkably cohesive alliance of Ontarians, often in prominent positions, who 'constituted a proto-fundamentalist movement' opting for precisely the opposite set of alternatives. Like those who moved in the other direction, they professed an assortment of beliefs that did not all readily cohere. Most of them were premillennialists, and those already mentioned in this connection were their outstanding representatives. They were overwhelmingly of Calvinistic background – Presbyterians, Baptists, or evangelical Anglicans, but seldom Methodists – although the Westminster Confession that defined Calvinistic orthodoxy gave no quarter to premillennialism. Largely through the influence of Dwight L. Moody, they also took over the devotional pietism and narrow moralism of the holiness tradition, despite its Arminian theology and special appeal to Methodists. Holiness sects in turn clung to a very conservative view of biblical inspiration, even though there was no obvious historical reason why they should have done so. Tension between Pentecostalists, the chief twentieth-century heirs of earlier holiness movements, and more classically biblicist and premillennial denominations indicates that the streams have never completely coalesced. Yet Howland, a premillennialist and an Anglican, ended his career as an active supporter of the Toronto congregation of the Christian and Missionary Alliance, a congregation that had been founded by John Salmon on holiness lines with special emphasis on divine healing.[21]

Various factors helped to bring these disparate elements together. Simple conservatism was certainly operative in an era when traditional Christianity seemed to be everywhere under threat. Lay resentment of clerical leadership played its part, and in the case of Anglicans so did evangelical resistance to high church encroachments. Burwash singled out YMCA secretaries as particularly susceptible to the ideas of the Plymouth Brethren, while C.P. Mulvany described Darbyism as 'low church Protestantism carried to its logical conclusion.'[22] The desire for a new message to replace a tired evangelical orthodoxy may have led some to premillennialism or holiness as it did others to the hope of social regeneration, and both tendencies were furthered by a sense that many church activities were frivolous or mechanical. The most consistent factor, however, was resistance to any watering down of the supernatural element of Christianity. Behaviour should set Christians apart from the world, not conform them to its standards. Missions should depend on faith in God's provision, not on financial appeals. Hope for the future should be rooted in God's promises, not in human programs. Even for healing, zealots believed, one should look directly to God rather than to medicine.

The Bible was the most conspicuous symbol of disagreement, but it was not the only and probably not the chief source. There had been talk of a 'great apostasy' of the church long before the infallibility of the Bible became a contentious issue; D.J. Macdonnell, whose doubts about eternal punishment involved him in one of the most spectacular heresy trials of the period, was said by his biographer to have been little affected by biblical criticism.[23] Differing responses to biblical criticism reflected an incompatibility of outlook that extended to many other subjects. Liberals were prepared to accept the findings of biblical critics because they confirmed their own postmillennial view of history as pointing to the gradual fulfilment of God's purpose. Conservatives who resisted them were, in so doing, declining a load of philosophical and ideological baggage that usually accompanied them. Why the Bible should have become such an important symbol is entirely understandable. Protestants had always carried a special torch for it, and to those of a supernaturalist cast of mind it was of the utmost importance that it should be attributed directly to God rather than to human minds, however wise and pious.

A cleavage in evangelical ranks that was already discernible by the end of the nineteenth century would within a few years give rise to what we know as the fundamentalist-modernist controversy. It had not done so yet. Conservatives, though ready to take alarm at anything they perceived as an attack on the Bible, seem not to have been aware of the extent to which critical views had penetrated the churches. Liberals, intent on clearing new pathways to truth, were willing to let others seek theirs. Both were still more concerned to meet the assaults of sceptics than to denounce each other. Evangelicals of the left and the right shared many enthusiasms and worked together, for the most part amicably, in promoting them. Missions represented to the former a means to the regeneration of the world, to the latter a challenge to warn its inhabitants to flee from the wrath to come, and similar unequal yokings made possible co-operation in moral crusades and social action. Neither did differences yet inhibit personal friendships. The liberal D.J. Macdonnell was on excellent terms with his premillennial neighbour H.M. Parsons, and Mrs Macdonnell was active in promoting the 'Bible readings' that were a favourite means of conveying premillennial interpretation. Despite such sharp exchanges as that between Carman and Workman, many Ontarians had not yet made up their minds on a number of potentially divisive issues or would change them in one direction or another when lines were more sharply drawn.[24]

At the other end of the theological spectrum from incipient fundamentalists were a number of independent thinkers for whom the churches were too conservative. Those actively engaged in propagating fringe movements were relatively few, but their existence was indicative of a widespread mood. Some of them, such as W.D. LeSueur and the labour leader T. Phillips Thompson, went so far as to promote a secular religion of humanity, but few were prepared to deny the existence of God or to denigrate the human Jesus. Goldwin Smith, who shared many of their doubts, also shared a common Victorian nervousness about the results for society if those doubts should become general. In a number of cases, not least in Thompson's, a Voltairean indignation against the social performance of the churches was an even greater factor than intellectual questioning of their dogmas.[25]

Even among the doubting and disillusioned there were few who could leave religion alone; or perhaps it would be closer to the truth to say that doubt and disillusionment often made religious questing more intense. Mary Edwards Merrill, dissatisfied with what she heard both at church and in atheistical lectures, had a mystical experience that left her convinced that she possessed occult powers. Profession of a belief in spiritualism led to the expulsion from the Methodist ministry in 1899 of B.F. Austin, formerly the respected principal of Alma College. The place of spiritualism as the centre of esoteric interest, however, had now been taken by theosophy. This was an elaborate speculative system formulated by Madame Blavatsky, who began with an interest in occult phenomena and later drew ideas from Hinduism and Buddhism. According to her *Secret Doctrine,* a universe in which each being is essentially identical with God is evolving toward perfection through an ascending series of races and even worlds. Formally introduced to the province in 1891 by Albert E. Smythe, theosophy attracted a small but select and committed following. Among early members were Phillips Thompson (despite his secular humanism), the novelist Algernon Blackwood, and a remarkable group of women that included Dr Emily Stowe.[26] Blending an introspective mysticism with belief in inexorable progress toward a perfection of unity, theosophy was able both to satisfy the desire for personal religious experience and to inspire efforts in support of social justice and international understanding. In the twentieth century it would have an immense and not yet fully explored influence on Canadian arts and letters.

Probably no other Ontarian writer on topics related to religion has had such a wide readership as Richard Maurice Bucke, whose *Cosmic Consciousness* appears in few theological libraries but has been reprinted continually since its publication in 1901. The son of an immigrant Anglican clergyman with a well-stocked library, he spent during his youth an adventurous but harrowing winter of prospecting in the west that resulted in the loss of a foot. Settling down to a medical career, he became and remained until his death in 1902 the superintendent of the London Asylum for the Insane. In *Cosmic Consciousness* he argued that the human race, having emerged from the animal stage, is evolving toward a still higher consciousness of which individuals of the order of Jesus and the Buddha were precursors. A psychic experience in 1872 of being 'wrapped as it were in a flame-coloured cloud' convinced him that he had glimpsed this higher reality, and a reading of Walt Whitman's *Leaves of Grass* led him to regard the author as the outstanding exemplar of cosmic consciousness thus far. Bucke saw nothing supernatural in this evolutionary process; he regarded himself as a sober student of genetics and reflected many ideas then current among scientists. His writings contained significant echoes of theosophy, however, and his conclusion 'that the universe is God and that God is the universe' situated him well within the heterodox religiosity of the period.[27]

These searchers after a new heaven and a new earth resembled the more conventional social gospellers of the era in many of their assumptions and aspirations. Both conceived of history as a cosmic process rather than as a series of disparate events, and both looked for its culmination in the creation of a new society rather than the determination of individual destinies. In other respects they resembled evangelicals of the right more closely than either would have liked to admit. Both were anxious for proof rather than mere certitude, whether they sought it in an infallible book or in voices from beyond. Both were compulsive system-builders who drew up elaborate charts of universal history to illustrate biblical dispensations or theosophical stages leading to fulfilment. There seemed, indeed, to be a pervasive sense of dissatisfaction with traditional formulations that ensured a hearing for almost any new nostrum. The social gospel, dispensationalism, and theosophy all gained followings in a period that could also take seriously the identification of the British people with the lost tribes of Israel – a major topic in sermons at Bond Street Congregational Church that may have helped elect Joseph Wild Canada's most popular preacher.

At the end of the nineteenth century, despite the emergence of new religious movements on the right and left flanks of evangelical orthodoxy, the legitimacy of religious pluralism had won little acceptance in Ontario. Evangelical Protestantism was still the norm, its widening cracks largely unnoticed by the public. The status of the Church of England was such that its members could with impunity deviate somewhat from evangelical standards of belief and behaviour, but a slight whiff of ritualism was enough to call Protestants to the barricades. Individual bishops and priests might be highly respected, but Roman Catholics were still beyond an Irish pale. Modest reinforcement of the well-acculturated Jewish community by immigrants from eastern Europe was an anomaly that led to the establishment of Anglican and Presbyterian missions and pointed to future fears of a foreign onslaught.

Some old quarrels were showing signs of moderating. The provincial Conservative party quietly dropped its 'no popery' stance, thus paving the way to a long tenure in office, and Anglicans were attempting to patch up their differences. Before we conclude that Ontarians were losing their capacity for fanaticism, however, we should remember that ethnic tension within the Roman Catholic Church had still to reach its climax and that the church union controversy was yet to come. Most hopeful, perhaps, were signs of a dawning conviction that religious differences should be addressed by rational argument rather than by harassment and riot. At the time of the jubilee disturbances the *Globe* upheld the right of any religious body to assemble for peaceful purposes,[28] and thereafter its advice was usually taken.

14 *The Anatomy of Ontario Religion*

How one identifies the dominant patterns of Ontario religion will depend on the time-line one chooses. If the period since European settlement alone is considered, centre stage will inevitably be occupied by the religious systems of the West and especially by a limited spectrum of Christian beliefs. If one takes into account the entire span of human settlement in the area now embraced in the province, the hegemony of these systems will seem an incident of a day in comparison with the unchallenged sway of native traditions that endured over millennia. In this volume, which is concerned mainly with the nineteenth century, these traditions inevitably figure as prologue, and are destined to play a diminishing role as the plot unfolds. Even in the process by which the bulk of the native inhabitants of the province came to accept Christianity the most dramatic events occurred early in the century, with the result that there is little of comparative interest to record about its later stages. Justice to the native peoples, however, demands acknowledgment not only of the long reign of the spirits of the land but of the traumatic effects of their displacement by Christian missionaries who in their zeal were frequently insensitive to the cultural wounds they were inflicting. By the late twentieth century, too, it has become evident that despite their eclipse the spirits have not been totally dislodged. The minority at the Grand River adhering to the message of Handsome Lake have remained steadfast and have gained new adherents in recent years. Elsewhere, despite the acceptance of Christian belief, and despite the missionaries' disapproval, traditional practices and attitudes persisted to take on new life in an era of raised native consciousness.

The portion of Ontario's religious history that lies between the advent of European churches and the end of the nineteenth century subdivides naturally, if not so clearly, into two main periods. Until about the time of Confederation, energies and arguments were concentrated on the shaping of a pattern. During the last few decades of the nineteenth century new opportunities and challenges led to adaptations of it. No precise chronological boundary can be drawn between the two phases of religious development, for 1867 was not a particularly significant date in the religious history of the province. Church-building may have reached a peak in the 1850s, and was resumed in the late 1860s after a period of economic depression; the rethinking of religious traditions, in one form or another, had always been going on. Clearly, however, the process of formation that characterized the early decades of the century had given way well before its end to one of reformulation.

A successful effort to persuade the inhabitants of Upper Canada to commit themselves to the profession of religious – in practice, Christian – faith and to involvement in the activities of a religious organization provided the essential dynamic of the formative period. In 1842 census enumerators recorded 16.7 per cent of the population as having no religious preference or as professing no religious creed, and contemporary testimonies agree that the proportion of uncommitted Upper Canadians had been greater in earlier years. By 1871 only 1.2 per cent were so recorded.[1] The gradual maturing of the province, which stimulated in its inhabitants a desire for the amenities of civilized living and made available greater resources for securing them, was a major factor in bringing about this change. After the War of 1812 it was not uncommon for settlers to band together to seek a minister, often on the initiative of a few prominent citizens who recalled past associations or wanted to raise the tone of their communities. Most influential, however, was the missionary awakening that stirred English-speaking countries around the turn of the nineteenth century, and led to the militant evangelism of saddle-bag preachers, the involvement in proliferating missionary societies, and the rising level of piety among successive waves of immigrants. The contagious zeal, as well as the attitude of dependence thus fostered, would have continuing effects on the religion of Ontario.

From the outset the building of churches was closely associated with the social and ideological formation of communities; as a result, religion took on a strongly institutional cast. Anglicans and Methodists, vying for pre-eminence in the province, each contributed, for somewhat different reasons, to this stress on the visibility of the church. Whatever else they might associate with religion, Ontarians always understood it to imply attendance at church as well as at Sunday school, prayer meeting, or sodality. To be sure, this institutional bias should not be exaggerated. Ontarians inherited a rich supply of quasi-religious folklore from various sources, and many derived their religious orientations from intimate personal experiences. The Ojibwa Methodist missionary Shahwundais was helped to Christian belief by a vision in the woods of 'two Beings standing in the air' of whom the nearer one advised him to address his prayer to the more distant. Robert Baldwin overcame his youthful scepticism by sublimating in devotional practice his love for his dead wife Eliza. These experiences were nourished by contacts with religious organizations, however, and led to closer association with them. Whatever evidence of personal spirituality a thorough search of private journals may reveal, we do not hear of religious movements without institutional links before the later years of the century. The phrase 'To meeting as usual' with which Ely Playter punctuated his diary after conversion could be used to describe the behaviour of almost any Upper Canadian who had 'got religion.'[2]

Promoted as it was by various denominations and jurisdictions within denominations, the development of religious institutions gave rise to intense competition. In this respect Upper Canada resembled other parts of the American frontier, but with the difference that the contending forces represented not merely different theologies and polities but incompatible visions of provincial society. Often obscured by the rhetoric of political controversy, the basic question was whether one's position in society should depend on a vested interest or on the ability to outdo rivals in open competition. This, rather than the admitted intransigence of John Strachan, was why the struggle over the clergy reserves generated so much heat and called forth such a prolonged and apparently hopeless rearguard action. Conflict that would have been inevitable in any case was further complicated by the coincidence of the formative stage of the province with an era in which mercantilism was giving way everywhere to unbridled free enterprise. As each side claimed spiritual legitimation for its point of view, religion was inevitably involved. New solutions had to be worked out in a society that had not yet achieved much cohesion, a process that took time and required the clearing up of a good deal of mutual incomprehension.

Inherited mythologies that have created heroes or villains on either side should not blind us to the fact that the resolution of the controversy left the contending churches looking remarkably alike, in social function if not in theology.[3] In the process there had been movement from both sides toward the centre. There would be no established church, but neither would the churches be private organizations catering merely to the spiritual needs of their individual members. Despite the existence of an unreconstructed minority of outright voluntarists, the major churches would parcel out among themselves the functions of an unofficial moral and educational establishment. In effect, nineteenth-century Ontario society would be the sum of its religious constituencies, although the whole would sometimes feel obliged to defend itself against the parts. Religion in this setting served to legitimate the industrial and commercial activities that absorbed most of the province's energies by encouraging hard work, sobriety, thrift, and enterprise. It also promoted virtues, such as probity, restraint, and responsibility for the public good, that did not come naturally to many entrepreneurs of the period, and pointed to a dimension of reality beside which the rewards of business were mere dross.

Statistics of denominational preference both reflect and help to explain these features of the province's early religious development (see table below). The effectiveness of aggressive evangelism was dramatically illustrated by the rapid growth of denominations that practised it. Methodists, no more than a few committed families in the 1780s, constituted 17 per cent of the population in 1842 and 28.5 per cent in 1871. The Baptists, who had a later start, never rivalled the Methodists in numbers but showed equally impressive growth from 3.4 per cent in 1842 to 5.3 per cent in 1871. Churches that relied mainly on the ancestral loyalties of their members, though less successful in attracting recruits among the previously uncommitted, nevertheless accounted for a large and stable proportion of the population. Presbyterians, Anglicans, and Roman Catholics, the chief denominations that might be so categorized, accounted for 55.4 per cent of the population in 1842 and 59.3 per cent in 1871. These characterizations of the various denominations are necessarily rough approximations, and there never was a precise correlation between denominational types and attitudes to social and political questions. Nevertheless, the balance of forces indicated by these figures may help to explain why problems of relating religion to the social fabric admitted no quick or easy solution. It is also instructive, in view of its importance in determining their ultimate resolution, to recall that the formation of the Free Church represented in effect a shift from an inherited to a chosen allegiance.

	1842	1848	1851	1861	1871	1881	1891	1901
Church of England	22.1	22.9	23.4	22.3	20.4	19.0	18.3	16.9
Baptist	3.4	3.9	4.8	4.4	5.3	5.5	5.0	5.3
Methodist	17.0	19.0	22.4	25.1	28.5	30.7	30.9	30.5
Presbyterian	19.9	20.4	21.4	21.7	22.0	21.7	21.4	21.9
Roman Catholic	13.4	16.4	17.6	18.5	16.9	16.7	16.9	17.9
Others	7.5	5.5	5.9	6.2	5.7	5.6	6.4	7.0
No preference or no creed	16.7	11.9	4.5	1.8	1.2	0.8	1.1	0.5

A tendency to consensus was indicated by the inability of new religious movements to gain the adhesion of a significant proportion of the provincial population. Four denominations – Methodists, Presbyterians, Anglicans, and Roman Catholics – accounted for almost 87 per cent of those expressing a religious preference in 1842 and for almost 88 per cent in 1871. Divisions among Methodists and Presbyterians made the actual diversity greater than these figures suggest, but the number of acceptable options was still strictly limited. Even the Baptists were unable to make it into the major league, and most of the 'others' represented such familiar groups as Lutherans, Mennonites, and Quakers. That the province was predominantly Protestant there could be no doubt; if, after the manner of the time, we reckon Anglicans in this category, we find that 65.7 per cent so declared themselves in 1842 and 80.2 per cent in 1871. Among those who stated a preference in 1871, the only dissenters from orthodox Christianity were a few Universalists and Unitarians, the Longhouse people, and 518 Jews. The diversities that stood in the way of a practical consensus were real and stubborn, but they were confined within a fairly narrow range.

To follow denominational distribution to the end of the century is to receive an impression of remarkable stability. The Methodists maintained their spectacular proportionate advance until the 1870s and then levelled off. The Church of England, bedevilled by internal dissension and still carrying a large load of non-attenders, continued to lose ground. Jews, 0.2 per cent of the population in 1901, were modest harbingers of the religious pluralism of a later era. The totally uncommitted, already a negligible proportion in 1871, were down to 0.5 per cent of the population in 1901. Otherwise, minor fluctuations were more evident than significant trends, and no new movements were able to achieve more than the establishment of bridgeheads for possible future expansion. With such a small pool of unattached Ontarians on which to operate, evangelism increasingly became a means of rousing church members to greater concern for personal holiness while it directed its attention to an ever younger constituency.

To all appearances, religion had never had a more secure place in Ontario society. Full adult membership was increasing more rapidly than simple adherence in the churches that included this category in their statistics, while in the Church of England eucharistic services were being held more frequently and attended by more communicants.[4] Ontarians already habituated to activities sponsored by the churches and other religious organizations were now offered them in greater number and variety. These organizations were raising larger amounts of money and spending it more systematically. Having virtually secured the nominal allegiance of the province they were now seeking to enhance its quality and to extend their influence beyond provincial boundaries. If their resources still seemed inadequate, the enlargement of their commitments was a sufficient explanation.

Despite this appearance of orderly building on earlier foundations, there were indications that the future would not be amenable to approaches that had worked in the past. Even when the clergy were at the summit of their public repute, society was developing institutions that gradually removed such crucial activities as education from their jurisdiction. Newly emerging trade unions did not look to them for leadership, as earlier mechanics' institutes had frequently done. And while religious organizations were remarkably successful in pre-empting the growing amount of leisure time, commercial promoters were able to offer an increasing range of attractive options. Perhaps the most portentous signal of change was the virtual disappearance from church records of cases of discipline for moral offences. Even when they were urging the state to legislate morality, the churches were being eased out of the policing function that traditionally had been allocated to them.

Those who spoke for religion, on their side, were having difficulty in blessing the social order as their predecessors had done. Some said so in no uncertain terms, even if their recipes for change often displayed less certainty. Others who had no thought of subjecting the current fabric of society to serious questioning betrayed in their words and actions a growing unease with it. In 1844 John Roaf had pictured the millennium as already coming into view. He expected Antichrist to appear, but meanwhile he saw the forces of evil everywhere in retreat. Half a century later his successors, whether they expected a gradual or cataclysmic culmination of history, used images to describe it that emphasized differences from rather than similarities to the existing situation. A shift in point of view was also noticeable in a growing tendency to attribute, often reluctantly, the imperfections of society to anomalies that could not be corrected simply by converting individuals. Tracing the prevalence of alcoholism to a powerfully entrenched liquor industry suggested a critical look at industry in general, and the logic that prescribed prohibition pointed beyond it to the possibility of government involvement in a fundamental reordering of society. This was still the conclusion of a minority, but niggling doubts about the existing order were widespread.

This growing lack of congruence between church and society was exacerbated by the intellectual ferment of the period. As yet the Roman Catholic Church and other minority communities were insulated from it by their overriding concern to preserve their distinctive identities, but Protestants of the mainstream could not ignore it. The emergence of new questions created an unprecedented interest in the opinions of prominent preachers, but a well-informed public was not likely to concede to varying opinions the authority it had attributed to the pronouncements of the clergy in the days of fixed theological systems. Even more unsettling, in the long run, was the disillusionment of many of the clergy themselves with pat answers and routinized approaches that seemed inadequate to the demands of the times. Among those who took religion seriously, two contrasting approaches to intellectual issues were emerging. One alternative, which increasingly appealed to clergy who had to cope not only with outside challenges but with the questions raised by their own study, was to seek ways of reconciling new knowledge and new theories with essential elements of ancestral faith. The other alternative was to assert controverted elements of the faith with renewed vigour in defiance of the dominant intellectual trends of the period.

Although it is natural to categorize these approaches as 'liberal' or 'conservative,' in reality the pressure of modernity was compelling all parties to reformulate their positions. Indeed, this process had begun well before the later years of the nineteenth century. European movements that began to affect the province in its middle years – ultramontanism Anglo-Catholicism, and the theocratic evangelicalism of the Free Church – were all responses to the claim of the modern bureaucratic state to hegemony over all areas of life. Their varied platforms were based on authentic elements within the traditions of their churches, yet drew on them with a selectivity of emphasis that made them in many respects novel. The same can be said of positions that came to the fore within evangelical Protestantism in later years. All of them had deep roots in the evangelical heritage, and all were in some respects new inventions. Liberals who professed an optimistic social gospel were heirs of the postmillennialism that had dominated North American Protestantism since its adoption by Jonathan Edwards in the eighteenth century, but not of the biblicism that had undergirded it. Those who continued this biblicism in all its rigour were able to defend it only by adopting a new theory of its inspiration. Although premillennialism had been professed over the centuries by many reputable divines, the vision of the end times current in the later years of the nineteenth century was no older than John Nelson Darby. Holiness movements, for all their appeal to Methodist nostalgia, were branching out into a search for unaccustomed spiritual gifts such as divine healing. Most of those who opted for conservative answers would have denied that these were in any way new answers, but innovation was ingrained in the temper of the time and could not easily be escaped by those most resistant to change.

The religious situation of the late nineteenth century, in some respects the culmination of what had come before, was in others the matrix of movements that would reach maturity only in the twentieth century. The critical approach to Scripture became standard fare in almost all theological colleges (including Knox) before the First World War, and gradually percolated to the mass of the clergy and an indeterminate number of their parishioners. The search for new religious formulations that often, though not necessarily, accompanied it congealed by the 1920s into a rather bland liberalism that was shaken by a neo-orthodox reaction in the 1930s and 1940s but continues, in one way or another, to inform the minds of a great many Ontarians. The social gospel reached an initial crest in 1914, only to become a victim of post-war disillusionment in the 1920s. The term 'social gospel' could mean many things, from an almost exclusive interest in moral reformation to the formulation of radical programs of social and economic reconstruction.[5] Concern for the achievement of social justice, which came to the fore during the depression years of the 1930s, was at first most conspicuous in the United Church; it has since, in the form of political theologies, theologies of liberation, or merely heightened social awareness, spread to practically every denomination. Over the years there has been a distinct shift of emphasis from the formation of moral individuals to the liberation of oppressed collectivities, but one can trace in motives and strategies a clear line of continuity from the 'benevolences' of the early nineteenth century to the most recent movements of protest.

The negotiations that resulted in the formation of the United Church of Canada began in response to a proposal made by an expatriate Scot at a church assembly in Winnipeg, and the union was most strenuously opposed in Ontario. The Ontario-centred dream of a Canada Christian from sea to sea helped to inspire it, however, and supporters regarded it as essentially a further step beyond a series of intradenominational unions in which Ontario initiative had played a leading part. Once the United Church was in existence, the priorities it set for itself reflected the postmillennial hopes of Ontario Protestants of the nineteenth century. The wider ecumenism that has made possible working coalitions that embrace not only most Protestant denominations but the once aloof Roman Catholic Church is more difficult to trace to roots in nineteenth-century Ontario, and one does not readily think of many besides Principal Grant of Queen's who would have welcomed the prospect. Any attempt to understand the processes that led to it must, indeed, be carried far beyond provincial or national boundaries. It may not be altogether fanciful, however, to see in the unusually positive response of Canadians to this ecclesiastical thaw a belated recognition that former extremes of bigotry had become too much for reasonable people to stomach.

The dramatic growth of conservative Protestant denominations has been largely a twentieth-century phenomenon; the appearance in force of 'born-again' and charismatic Christians in major churches, including the Roman Catholic, has occurred, for the most part, in the second half of the century. Research is increasingly bringing to light, however, the existence in the late nineteenth century of factors helping to predispose many Ontarians to the appeal of such movements. Jehovah's Witnesses and Seventh-Day Adventists already had congregations in the province, although as yet they were few and inconspicuous. The initial popularity of the Salvation Army indicated the existence of an unsatisfied hunger; the alarm it aroused among church leaders suggested that they were not so sure of the solidity of their support as the growth of their operations implied. Pentecostalists would appear only in the twentieth century, but John Salmon was already making a specialty of Christian healing. Meanwhile, the Toronto Willard Tract Depository, with a board composed largely of prominent laymen, was making available a constant stream of premillennial literature. As yet there had been no explosive response to liberal theology, but the fuse was smouldering.

Can we also trace back to the last century the origins of the secularizing tendency that has led twentieth-century Ontarians in increasing numbers to abandon religious practices that were once almost universal? With hindsight we find it natural to interpret any signs of confusion or doubt as evidence of decline, and undoubtedly the façade of ecclesiastical triumphalism concealed some cracks in the plaster and even weaknesses in the construction. That there was any overall falling off in religious commitment, however, is a conclusion for which it is difficult to produce solid evidence. It seems more to the point to note that industrialization and urbanization, which had already had a weakening effect on religious structures in countries with more mature economies, were significantly present in Ontario as well. The shift from organic to mass societies, replacing coherent communities with combinations of atomistic individuals, was probably, in the long run, more corrosive of religious commitment than any of the specific questions with which the churches had to wrestle in the late nineteenth century. More satisfactory answers might have been given to these questions, but there is no great reason to think that many more people would be going to church today if they had. Social developments over which the churches had little control, rather than their response to them, were the most significant precursors of twentieth-century secularization.

To note such continuities is not to deny that history contains elements of surprise and unpredictability. Many developments of the twentieth century could scarcely have been foreseen by the most far-sighted observers of the religious situation as it was in 1900, for nothing in previous experience suggested them. To have informed an Ontarian of the late nineteenth century that before another century had run its course Islam and religions from farther east would have a significant place in the provincial spectrum, that Louis Riel would become a popular hero, that local theologians would take their cues from Latin America as readily as from Europe, that apologies would be offered to the native peoples for the missionaries' paternalism, or that churches would devote more attention to the rights of homosexuals than to the wrongs of alcohol would merely have been to invite incredulity.

Readers are likely to ask whether, among the characteristic features of nineteenth-century religion, there were any that can be identified as distinctively Ontarian. They need not expect too much. In its main outlines the story of Ontario religion in the nineteenth century was a miniature version of the general religious history of the era. Assumptions about religion prevalent in the province were those familiar in other English-speaking areas: belief in a providential order that came to look more and more like human progress or biological evolution, a close linkage between religious belief and personal morality, a frequent confusion between faith and sentiment, an expectation that religious conviction should issue in participation in a variety of voluntary activities, and, not least, the importance of being earnest. Religious impulses affecting the province were also almost invariably imported. The evangelical united front, mid-century movements that reasserted the primacy of spiritual over temporal authority, devotional practices from Ireland, French Canada, and American holiness circles all had local repercussions. In this respect Ontario showed less initiative than the maritime provinces. Whereas Henry Alline stirred great excitement there with a highly original message, the Methodists who had had equivalent success in Upper Canada disclaimed any intention of introducing doctrinal novelty.

Similarly, the religious problems faced by Ontarians were essentially those of Western Christendom. The proper relations of church and state, of faith and science, and of capital and labour were all live issues elsewhere before they were discussed in Ontario, and local debates were conducted mainly with borrowed arguments. Even the difficulties of extending religious institutions to the unreached, which attracted so much attention in the early decades of the province's history, were well understood by religious workers in the slums of Glasgow or by black preachers in the southern United States. This derivative quality need occasion no surprise. Throughout the nineteenth century imported clergy were both numerous and prominent, and British and American books, tracts, and periodicals circulated freely. Only after mid-century did a heterogeneous immigrant population coalesce into a coherent populace. If we seek to identify distinctive elements in Ontario religious history, therefore, we must content ourselves with variations in emphasis and differences in outcome.

The basic ingredients of a cake are flour, sugar, and shortening, with a dash of soda or baking-powder to make it rise, but its texture and flavour will vary enormously according to the proportions used. Similarly, the religious character of a region can vary with the ecclesiastical mix. In continental Europe it has been normal for state churches to provide for the religious needs of the bulk of the population, leaving the dissatisfied to find spiritual homes in conventicles that cultivate a more strenuous piety. Ernst Troeltsch formulated the dichotomy of church and sect to draw sharp contrasts between the two. In the United States, a wide range of ecclesiastical bodies have long enjoyed equal constitutional rights, and public opinion has accepted an unlimited plurality of churches as normal and natural. Unconvincing attempts have been made to apply Troeltsch's classification to the American situation, but Sidney Mead's concept of 'denominations' sharing the ground and selectively affirming national values fits it much better.[6] The tradition of the British Isles, though it varies somewhat from country to country, has fallen somewhere between the continental and the American. Established churches in England and Scotland, and less effectively in Ireland until disestablishment in 1869, have been at least the intended embodiments of nationally recognized spiritual values. In marked contrast with the continental situation, however, dissenting bodies have in the aggregate rivalled national churches in numbers and sometimes exceeded them in vitality.

Nineteenth-century Ontario organized its religious life in ways that suggest obvious parallels with both the United States and Europe. Especially after 1854, resemblances to the American situation were most obvious. The province had no established church, and the only ecclesiastical body that had seriously aspired to this status was neither the largest nor the fastest-growing. The major churches displayed the typical attitudes of the denomination, never more clearly than in their efforts for conservative reform near the end of the century. As in the United States, too, the dominant force was an evangelical Protestantism whose segments worked readily in tandem while insisting on their own peculiarities of belief and practice. In some other respects, however, Ontario reproduced or inclined toward Old World patterns. After the initial turnover of the pioneer period, religious affiliation represented for most Ontarians something inherited rather than something acquired. In comparison with the United States, it leaned toward the traditional end of the denominational spectrum. In the United States Baptists were numerous and Episcopalians an élite minority; in Ontario the Church of England was large and Baptists relatively few. Ontario religious practice, which struck European visitors as informal and sometimes even casual, seemed to Americans restrained and 'churchy.' Resistance to the multiplication of church bodies has also been more suggestive of Europe than of the United States, and hospitality to proposals of church union pointed to a bad conscience about the divisions that already existed.

Religious preference was related to ethnicity in ways that favoured the same balance of forces. From our present perspective the population of nineteenth-century Ontario was remarkably homogeneous, but what may seem to us to have been marginal differences mattered greatly then. Both the Dutch Reformed and the AHMS withdrew from the province for reasons that had a good deal to do with ethnicity, and immigrants from different parts of the British Isles did not always co-operate readily in local congregations.[7] Sometimes, to be sure, appropriations of ethnic tradition rested on a fair amount of historical fiction. That the architecture of many Anglican churches recalled the English countryside was probably not unrelated to their claim to represent the establishment at home; similarly, Presbyterian cultivation of Scottish associations may have reflected, consciously or unconsciously, a counter-claim resting on the establishment of the Kirk north of the Tweed. These appeals to nostalgia downplayed a very considerable Irish element in both churches, although within living memory Little Trinity Church in Toronto witnessed to continuing recognition of it by advertising itself as representing the United Church of England and Ireland. Such associations, whether altogether authentic or not, nourished a sense of rootedness in the past that contributed to the impression of stability often noted by American visitors.

The influential Wesleyan Methodists were in some respects a conspicuous exception to this cultivation of links with tradition. The spiritual offspring of pioneer American itinerants who had introduced Methodism to the province, they broke their ties with the Methodist Episcopal Church so thoroughly in 1828 that in later years American influences affected them only through the process of osmosis that was common to practically all Ontario institutions. Despite their subsequent union with the British Wesleyans, which succeeded only on the second attempt, they never absorbed the ethos of English Methodism either. They became perforce a church very much on its own, no longer American but largely impervious to British influence. Their situation had both drawbacks and advantages. Isolated to some extent from international developments, they displayed at times a rootlessness and a propensity for ad hoc solutions, a charge that is still often levelled against the United Church. At the same time they were driven to seek solutions to local problems without the handicap of precedents that had been set in very different circumstances. Understandably, Methodism was the first denomination to develop a self-conscious Canadianism that was inevitably, in view of the preponderance of Ontarians in Methodist ranks, a projection in the main of ideas conceived in the province.

Although some churches might emphasize European connections, and others look more to the United States, most denominations were mixed in their orientation. Baptists usually followed American precedents, but many of their leaders were of Scottish origin. Strachan, the last-ditch defender of British traditions, owed many of his ideas to John Henry Hobart, his contemporary as Episcopal bishop of New York.[8] John Joseph Lynch, a native of Ireland, came to Toronto from Buffalo. The Free Church, for all its talk of the Scottish covenants, was reminiscent in its crusading activism of an American Protestant denomination. The Wesleyans, who cultivated their own ethnic myth of descent from the United Empire Loyalists, embraced a large proportion of immigrants from Ireland and England. Differences in ethnic background among the denominations, useful as they might be as badges of identity, were never great enough to prevent a large amount of cross-fertilization and consensus.

In some respects the religious moulding of Ontario may not have been greatly different from that of Ohio or Lancashire, but its significance was enhanced when Ontario became the largest, wealthiest, and most strategically located province of a newly emerging nation. The responsibilities thus implied probably did not weigh heavily on the consciences of church members in Petrolia or Smiths Falls, but they could not be ignored by policy-makers and program planners in Toronto. The influence of Confederation on Ontario religion was somewhat ambiguous. On the one hand, uncertainty with respect to Canada's religious future and especially that of the developing west intensified competition among the churches and encouraged a combative spirit on both sides of the Protestant–Roman Catholic divide. On the other hand, the challenge of meeting the spiritual needs of a scattered and diverse population cast into question the prevailing denominational pattern and was a significant, if not always conscious, spur to the advocacy of church union. Not by chance did the preamble to the Basis of Union of the United Church of Canada commit it 'to foster the spirit of unity in the hope that this sentiment of unity may in due time, so far as Canada is concerned, take shape in a Church which may fittingly be described as national.' The framers did not have in mind an establishment on Old World lines, but they were certainly projecting something other than the American denominational system. Not by chance, either, did this vision meet its greatest resistance in Ontario.

This combination of ecclesiastical, demographic, and historical factors gave rise to a religious tradition that was not quite duplicated elsewhere. One is tempted to apply an analogy from economic organization. Religion might be described in continental Europe as a state monopoly with marginal provision for individual initiative, in the United States as a field for unbridled free enterprise, and in Britain as a class structure with some fluidity at the edges; in this context we might think of Ontario as preferring a typically Canadian mixed economy. One might also identify elements of the limited sovereignties for which Harold Laski argued. Religious institutions neither controlled nor were controlled by the apparatus of the state, but neither were they relegated altogether to the private realm. After 1854 they were all private corporations in law, but in matters of morality and education their public standing received practical recognition.

To note the existence of this balance of forces is not to suggest that Ontarians of the nineteenth century were incapable of ecstasy or immune to the attractions of novelty. Pioneer Methodism was noted for its 'Canadian fire.' Mormonism and Millerism made many converts in Upper Canada, and Caughey and the Palmers had unusual success. In relation to its population the province may have contributed more than its share to the early leadership of North American premillenarianism, and the meetings that were largely instrumental in shaping the fundamentalist mind were held for many years at Niagara-on-the-Lake. In the long run, however, the centripedal forces had a way of overtaking the centrifugal. Ontarians might be as responsive as others to the allure of the new and different, but before long they could be found safely back in familiar folds. This drift to the centre has been identified by a Baptist writer as a reason for his denomination's difficulty in gaining acceptance for its conception of the church as a 'gathered community.'[9]

In many respects the religious tradition that took shape in Ontario in the nineteenth century can be distinguished most readily from European and American models in terms of what it was not. It was far from representing, at least in its later stages, a mere transplanting of European institutions and values into new soil. Unlike that of New England, it was not the product of a search for the New Jerusalem; nor could Charles G. Finney's characterization of his father's westward migration as a form of apostasy have been applied with any plausibility to the bulk of settlers in Upper Canada. Whatever it was that made the local context different, missionaries of all churches discovered that they had to take account of it. This discovery lay behind the insistence of religious leaders from earliest times that the raising up of an indigenous ministry was essential to effective penetration. It was also rather dramatically illustrated in what might seem an unlikely quarter. In 1840 the African Methodist Episcopal Church organized an Upper Canada Conference, thereafter supplying it with ministers, and sending bishops occasionally to oversee its work. Sixteen years later, despite intense opposition from American delegates and bitter charges of ingratitude toward the parent church, the ministers who had been sent to the province dissolved this conference and replaced it with the independent British Methodist Episcopal Church. Their arguments virtually reproduced those that had been put forward by white Canadian Methodists in similar circumstances in 1828, noting especially 'the great disadvantages under which we labour by not having a discipline in conformity with the laws of the province in which we live.'[10]

The most conspicuous role of religion in nineteenth-century Ontario was to provide neither a completely formed tradition nor a blueprint for a new order but a set of discrete landmarks to define and delimit. As the previous quotation indicates, many of these were related to the political institutions of the province. In Ontario there was to be order without tyranny, liberty without licence, and responsible government without mob rule; many conflicts in church as well as in state resulted from the apprehension that one or more of these principles were being violated. Other landmarks claimed space and time for the spiritual in a society where the material was never in danger of neglect: a moral code, an assortment of well-supervised denominational colleges, an ingrained habit of going 'to meeting as usual,' a profusion of spires pointing heavenward. Among such landmarks, two, though not peculiar to nineteenth-century Ontario, were especially important in enabling its people to give symbolic expression to their religious attitudes.

Ontarians found many occasions on which to engage in ceremonial walks, whether in the form of parades, processions, pilgrimages, or even the 'promenades' that stood in for dances in Methodist institutions. Regiments paraded to church, maintaining a custom established when soldiers were a conspicuous presence in Upper Canada. When David Willson occasionally entered York to preach, his followers formed a cavalcade of farm wagons to escort him. The funerals of the prominent were incomplete without long and carefully planned cortèges, and local businesses often closed to allow general participation.[11] Funerals also furnished prime opportunities for the display of the regalia of the Freemasons and other fraternal orders. The processional, to which Gothic architecture was admirably suited, became an increasingly popular adjunct to the service of worship. Even secular parades and processions often had about them a distinct air of civil religion. Participation in or merely attendance at a parade of Orangemen or Hibernians enabled Ontarians to advertise their adherence to a particular religious tradition, much as Grey Cup parades today become outlets for the expression of Canadian regional loyalties; the fights that sometimes accompanied the parades provided further opportunities for demonstrating the depth of one's convictions. At such musters of strength the close association that existed in Ontario between religious and ethnic identity was often evident. The careful allocation of roles in parades and processions in relation to office or position in society also suggested the persistence of Simcoe's vision of a neatly ordered society long after its apparent rejection.

Whereas parades represented the horizontal dimension of religion, Sunday reminded Ontarians of a vertical relation to God. The *Christian Guardian* boasted that Sunday in Ontario was 'the best kept Sabbath in the world.' Whether or not the assertion was justified, the fact that it was made indicates the symbolic importance attached to Sunday. Strict sabbatarianism did not conflict with the province's preoccupation with burgeoning industry and commerce, for the injunction 'six days shalt thou labour' was held to be as binding as the command to 'remember the Sabbath day to keep it holy.' It also placed limits on materialism by defining a sacred enclosure on which business was not to encroach. One might be tempted to infer that God was allowed only one day to Mammon's six, but the assumption underlying this division of the week was that God is best served by a life spent mainly in secular pursuits. Detractors, then as now, deplored 'a Sabbatarianism which would have excluded the Master Himself with a wire fence from the cornfields on the Sabbath day.' To supporters such as W.S. Blackstock, an Ontario Sunday was 'the "pearl of days," as free from puritanic and Judaic rigour, on the one hand, as it is from anti-Christian laxity on the other.'[12]

Parades and Sundays stood for contrasting but interlocking aspects of Ontario religion. The parade or procession provided a means of publicly symbolizing different faiths and loyalties, different stations in church and society, and different roles as active participants or applauding onlookers. Sunday maintained a rhythm of labour and rest that echoed the rhythm of divine activity and provided an occasion for common recognition of dependence on an order beyond. The parade located religion in time and space; Sunday pointed it to eternity. The parade risked an over-emphasis on entrenched values that threatened to hold religion captive to vested interests. Sunday was associated with a taut moralism that too often identified religious commitment with the observance of legalistic taboos. Together they reflected the ambivalence of a society in which faith in God and loyalty to one's own were readily confused, but in which a healthy tension between sacred and secular values was also possible.

That many of the landmarks so carefully established in the nineteenth century have fallen into serious disrepair in the twentieth is scarcely open to question, although it is only necessary to reopen the separate-school issue or propose a relaxation of restrictions on Sunday business to discover that the convictions responsible for their erection are by no means dead. The hopes that inspired many Ontarians to anticipate the speedy advent of the Kingdom of God are not patently closer to fruition. Cracks in the structure of belief that began to open before the turn of the twentieth century have widened in the interim. Restraints that were expected to hasten the emergence of a new and higher type of humanity are now derided as evidence of the province's cultural backwardness. Church-going is not what it was when the *Globe* conducted its surveys, and the new religiosity touted in the 1960s has not yet shown signs of providing a substitute. Many

Ontarians still seek to be faithful to religiously inspired visions of the cosmos, although the religious systems that inspire them are of a variety that would have startled their nineteenth-century predecessors. The last word, however, belongs to those who surveyed nineteenth-century religion at close range. When religious journals greeted the advent of the twentieth century, they inevitably used the occasion to publish appraisals of the past and prognostications for the future. Most were distinctly positive in tone. Nathanael Burwash, reviewing a recent survey of nineteenth-century theology, asserted that after three generations of 'running the gauntlet of ... pantheism, materialism, and historical criticism' the world had come to 'a truer, stronger, and more universal faith in Christianity.' James H. Coyne, after summarizing progress in various secular fields, concluded by 'affirming that the mental, moral and religious outlook [had] never been so bright, so clear, so full of hope for the future, as in the closing years of the century.' The *Westminster,* looking back on a century 'of marvellous progress in every direction,' noted reports from far and near of 'quickened desire and awakened hope' and concluded that the church had 'scarcely touched the fringe of her possibilities.' The *Catholic Register,* for once agreeing with its Protestant rivals, was thankful that religion had been 'full of faith and activity in this wonderful century' and felt confident that the one then beginning would 'present to history a record of noble zeal and high intellectual culture.' Only the *Canadian Churchman* viewed the incoming century with alarm, predicting with at least partial prescience that without a radical change in customs and laws 'the race we are now proud of' would give way to 'another, with more faith in God and His promises.'[13] While most other forecasts avoided extremes of cocksureness and despair, the prevailing mood at the turn of the century was one of thankfulness for the past and optimism for the future.

Notes

ABBREVIATIONS

AA	Archives of the General Synod of the Anglican Church of Canada
AAK	Archives of the Archdiocese of Kingston
AAT	Archives of the Archdiocese of Toronto
AHMS	American Home Missionary Society
AO	Archives of Ontario
CCHA	Canadian Catholic Historical Association
CHA	Canadian Historical Association
CHR	*Canadian Historical Review*
CSCH	Canadian Society of Church History
CSPH	Canadian Society of Presbyterian History
DCB	*Dictionary of Canadian Biography*
DOA	Diocese of Ontario Archives
JCCHS	*Journal of the Canadian Church Historical Society*
KSV	King James Version
OH	*Ontario History* (before 1949 annual volumes of *Ontario Historical Society Papers and Records*)
PAC	Public Archives of Canada
QUA	Queen's University Archives
SPG	Society for the Propagation of the Gospel
SR	*Studies in Religion/Sciences Religieuses*
UCA	United Church Archives
USPG	United Society for the Propagation of the Gospel

CHAPTER I *Spirits of the Land*

1 A number of circumpolar parallels are pointed out in Åke Hultkrantz, 'The Problem of Christian Influence on Northern Algonkian Eschatology,' *SR* 9:2 (1980),

164, and in Weston La Barre, *The Ghost Dance: Origins of Religion* (New York: Dell 1970), 171ff.
2 *Globe and Mail*, 1 Oct. 1981, 19; R.E. Taylor and Clement W. Meighan, *Chronologies in New World Archaeology* (New York: Academic 1978), chart inside front cover
3 Jesse D. Jennings, *Prehistory of North America* (New York: McGraw-Hill 1968), 201–3. Evidence of the selective acceptance in Ontario of a new religion, possibly though not necessarily Hopewellian, is adduced in Michael W. Spence and J. Russell Harper, *The Cameron's Point Site* (Toronto: Royal Ontario Museum 1968), 56.
4 'All life was one in kind, and all things, potentially at least, possessed life': Diamond Jenness, *The Indians of Canada*, 7th ed. (Toronto: University of Toronto Press 1977), 168.
5 There is an illuminating discussion of the vision quest in Ruth M. Underhill, *Red Man's Religion* (Chicago: University of Chicago Press 1965), chapter 10.
6 Åke Hultkrantz, 'Myth in North American Religion,' in Earle H. Waugh and K. Dad Prithipaul, eds., *Native Religious Traditions* (Waterloo, Ont.: Wilfrid Laurier University Press 1977), 77–97; Paul Radin, *The Trickster: A Study in American Indian Mythology* (New York: Schocken 1956)
7 J.W.E. Newberry, 'Native Wholeness,' paper presented at the International Congress of Learned Societies in Religion, Los Angeles, September 1972. The expression 'sacred hoop' was apparently first used by the Sioux prophet Black Elk.
8 James A. Clifton, *A Place of Refuge for All Time: Migration of the American Potawatomi into Upper Canada, 1830 to 1850* (Ottawa: National Museums of Canada 1976), passim
9 Diamond Jenness, *The Ojibwa Indians of Parry Island* (Ottawa: King's Printer 1935), 60; Robert E. Ratzenthaler, 'Southwestern Chippewa,' in *Handbook of North American Indians*, vol. 15, Bruce G. Trigger, ed., *Northeast* (Washington: Smithsonian Institution), 757; W.J. Hoffman, 'The Midewiwin or "Grand Medicine Society" of the Ojibway,' *7th Annual Report of the Bureau of American Ethnology* (Washington: Government Printing Office 1891), 156ff
10 John M. Cooper, 'The Northern Algonquian Supreme Being,' *Primitive Man*, 6:3–4 (July–Oct. 1933), 75–6; Christopher Večsey, *Traditional Ojibwa Religion and Its Historical Changes* (Philadelphia: The American Philosophical Society 1983), 79–80, 62; John S. Long, '"Shaganash": Early Protestant Missionaries and the Adoption of Christianity by the Western James Bay Cree' (EDD thesis, University of Toronto 1986), 173–6; Werner Müller, 'North America,' in Walter Krickeberg et al., *Pre-Columbian American Religions* (New York: Holt, Rinehart and Winston 1969), 172–3
11 George Irving Quimby, *Indian Life in the Upper Great Lakes, 11,000 B.C. to A.D. 1800* (Chicago: University of Chicago Press 1960), 131; Hultkrantz, 'Christian Influence,' 171; Elisabeth Tooker, ed., *Native North American Spirituality of the Eastern Woodlands* (New York: Paulist 1979), 104–24

12 Ruth Landes, *Ojibwa Religion and the Midewiwin* (Madison: University of Wisconsin Press 1968), 11–14
13 Reuben Gold Thwaites, ed., *The Jesuit Relations and Allied Documents* (Cleveland: Burrows Brothers 1896–1901), 10:169–73, 33:191–5
14 While some scholars regard the emergence of a calendrical cycle as a relatively late development, Bruce G. Trigger notes elements of such a cycle among the Hurons: *The Children of Aataentsic* (Montreal: McGill-Queen's University Press 1976), 105.
15 Bruce G. Trigger, *The Huron: Farmers of the North* (New York: Holt, Rinehart and Winston 1969), 50–3
16 Werner Müller in Krickeberg et al., *Pre-Columbian American Religions*, 180–91
17 See Horatio Hale, ed., *The Iroquois Book of Rites* (Philadelphia: D.G. Brinton 1883).
18 Chrestien Le Clercq, *First Establishment of the Faith in New France*, trans. John Gilmary Shea (New York: John G. Shea 1881), 1:93; Gabriel Sagard, *The Long Voyage to the Country of the Hurons*, ed. George M. Wrong, trans. H.H. Langton (Toronto: The Champlain Society 1939), passim
19 An extended firsthand account of the Huron mission occupies parts of volumes 7–34 and volume 38 of Thwaites, *Jesuit Relations and Allied Documents*. The chronology is most easily followed in Trigger, *Children of Aataentsic*.
20 Thwaites, *Jesuit Relations and Allied Documents*, 34:227; 21:187ff; 31:115–19; 23:223; 33:261; 34:87–93; 34:27–33
21 Ibid., 42:135; 43:291; Keith J. Crowe, *A History of the Original Peoples of Northern Canada* (Montreal: McGill-Queen's University Press 1974), 67; Trigger, *Children of Aataentsic*, 98, 750, 828
22 James S. Pritchard, 'For the Glory of God: The Quinte Mission, 1660–1680,' *OH* 65:3 (Sept. 1973), 33–48
23 William N. Fenton and Elisabeth Tooker, 'Mohawk,' in *Handbook of North American Indians* 15:474; Edward Payson Johnson, 'The Work among the North American Indians during the Eighteenth Century,' *Papers of the American Society of Church History*, 2d series, 6:5; John Wolfe Lydekker, *The Faithful Mohawks* (Cambridge: University Press 1938), 53–5
24 Elma E. Gray, *Wilderness Christians* (Toronto: Macmillan 1956), passim; 'A Short History of the Chapel of the Delawares,' typescript in the possession of Ohsweken United Church
25 The most detailed description of the lodge is Hoffman, 'The Midewiwin or "Grand Medicine Society" of the Ojibway.'
26 Harold Hickerson, 'Notes on the Post-Contact Origin of the Midewiwin,' *Ethnohistory* 9 (1962), 404–23; Selwyn Dewdney, *The Sacred Scrolls of the Southern Ojibway* (Toronto: University of Toronto Press 1975), 167, 174. For a contrasting view see W. Vernon Kinietz, *The Indians of the Western Great Lakes, 1615–1760* (Ann Arbor: University of Michigan Press 1965), 215, 329.

27 Landes, *Ojibwa Religion and the Midewiwin*, 178; Clifton, *Refuge for All Time*, 97; Jenness, *Ojibwa Indians of Parry Island*, 61
28 Anthony F.C. Wallace,' Origins of the Longhouse Religion,' in *Handbook of North American Indians* 15:447. Wallace has analysed the movement in greater detail in *The Death and Rebirth of the Seneca* (New York: Vintage 1969).
29 'Mohawk Seminar,' in Waugh and Prithipaul, *Native Religious Traditions*, 31–2
30 Donald B. Smith, *Sacred Feathers: The Reverend Peter Jones (Kahkewaquonaby) and the Mississauga Indians* (Toronto: University of Toronto Press 1987), 19

CHAPTER 2 *Uprooted Traditions*

1 Wallace Brown, *The King's Friends: The Composition and Motives of the American Loyalist Claimants* (Providence: Brown University Press 1965), passim; William H. Nelson, *The American Tory* (London: Oxford University Press 1961), passim
2 The most comprehensive analysis of the backgrounds of Upper Canadian Loyalists is Bruce Wilson, *As She Began: An Illustrated Introduction to Loyalist Ontario* (Toronto: Dundurn Press 1981), especially chapter 1. Another rich source of statistical information is Brown, *The King's Friends*. Various interpretations are brought together in L.F.S. Upton, ed., *The United Empire Loyalists: Men and Myths* (Toronto: Copp, Clark 1967).
3 On Loyalist settlement, in addition to Wilson's *As She Began*, one may still read with profit W. Stewart Wallace, *The United Empire Loyalists: A Chronicle of the Great Migration* (Toronto: Glasgow, Brook & Company 1914). Many of the relevant documents are collected in E.A. Cruikshank, ed., *The Settlement of the United Empire Loyalists in the Upper St. Lawrence and Bay of Quinte in 1784: A Documentary Record* (Toronto: Ontario Historical Society 1934).
4 Richard A. Preston, ed., *Kingston before the War of 1812: A Collection of Documents* (Toronto: University of Toronto Press 1959), xlii–xliii
5 W. R. Riddell, ed., 'La Rochefoucauld-Liancourt's Travels in Canada, 1795,' in Alexander Fraser, ed., *13th Report of the Bureau of Archives for the Province of Ontario, 1916* (Toronto: King's Printer 1917), 75; Robert Gourlay, *Statistical Account of Upper Canada* (Toronto: McClelland and Stewart 1974), 93; J.C. Ogden, *A Letter from a Gentleman to His Friend, in England, descriptive of the different settlements in the province of Upper Canada* (Philadelphia: printed by W.W. Woodward 1795), 7
6 Estimates of the population in 1812 are little better than guesses, but the 'nearly seventy-seven thousand souls' calculated in Joseph Bouchette, *The British Dominions in North America* (London: Longman 1831), 108, on the basis of 1811 assessment rolls, is as close to credibility as any. Donald H. Akenson, who cites this figure in *The Irish in Ontario: A Study in Rural History* (Kingston and Montreal: McGill-Queen's University Press 1984), 112n, regards it as probably more accurate than other considerably higher figures.

7 Michael Smith, *A Geographical View of the Province of Upper Canada and Promiscuous Remarks upon the Government* (Hartford 1813), 62

8 Donald B. Smith, 'The Mississauga, Peter Jones and the White Man: The Algonkians' Adjustment to the Europeans on the North Shore of Lake Ontario to 1860' (PH D thesis, University of Toronto 1975), 125–7

9 E.A. Cruikshank, *The Story of Butler's Rangers and the Settlement of Niagara* (Niagara Falls, Ont.: Lundy's Lane Historical Society 1893), 15

10 Henri Têtu, ed., *Journal des visites pastorales de 1815 et 1816 par Monseigneur Joseph-Octave Plessis, Evêque de Québec* (Quebec: Imprimerie Franciscaine Missionnaire 1903), 15, 52; A.A. Johnston, *A History of the Catholic Church in Eastern Nova Scotia* I (Antigonish: St Francis Xavier University Press 1960), 312, 214, 232; Marianne McLean 'Peopling Glengarry County: The Scottish Origins of a Canadian Community,' *CHA Historical Papers, 1982*, 161–2

11 According to Frank H. Epp, *Mennonites in Canada, 1786–1920* (Toronto: Macmillan 1974), 56–7, these were 'fringe Mennonites' who belonged to no churches. L.J. Burkholder, *A Brief History of the Mennonites in Ontario* (Toronto: Livingston 1935), 30, regarded them as 'real Mennonites.'

12 Burkholder, *Brief History*, 22–5

13 Known since 1933 as 'The Brethren in Christ (Tunkers) in Canada'

14 E. Morris Sider, 'The Early Years of the Tunkers in Upper Canada,' *OH* 51:2 (spring 1959), 121–9. A naïve but highly descriptive account is George Cober, *A Historical Sketch of the Brethren in Christ Church, Known as Tunkers in Canada* (Gormley, Ont. 1953).

15 Arthur G. Dorland, *The Quakers in Canada: A History*, 2d ed. (Toronto: Ryerson 1968), 53–8; Hugh Barbour, *The Quakers in Puritan England* (New Haven: Yale University Press 1964), especially chapters 2 and 8

16 Robert Wayne Pointer, 'Seedbed of American Pluralism: The Impact of Religious Diversity, 1750–1800' (PH D thesis, Johns Hopkins University 1982), 222; William Canniff, *The Settlement of Upper Canada* (Toronto: Dudley and Burns 1869; facsimile reprint, Belleville, Ont.: Mika 1971), 316

17 James Croil, *Dundas; or, a Sketch of Canadian History, and more particularly of the County of Dundas, one of the earliest settled Counties in Upper Canada* (Montreal: B. Dawson & Son 1861), 128; Patricia Hart, *Pioneering in North York: A History of the Borough* (Toronto: General 1968), 193, 201, 213

18 *Institutes of the Christian Religion*, 1559 Latin edition, 3:21–4; 2:8

19 Alexander Macdonell to Bishop J.O. Plessis, 7 Feb. 1806, quoted in Brother Alfred [Dooner], *Catholic Pioneers in Upper Canada* (Toronto: Macmillan 1947), 181; Donald N. MacMillan, *The Kirk in Glengarry* (n.p. 1984), 8, passim

20 To SPG, 4 Oct. 1791, DOA, group II, folio 6

21 Nathanael Burwash, 'U.E. Loyalists, Founders of Our Institutions,' *United Empire Loyalist Annual Transactions, 1904–1911*, in Upton, *United Empire Loyalists*, 148; J.K. McMorine, 'Early History of the Anglican Church in Kingston,' *OH* 8

(1907), 92; Stuart to Bishop Charles Inglis, 6 July 1788, DOA II:2; Stuart to SPG,
12 Oct. 1792, *SPG Journals* 26:77, micro in AA; Raymond Albright, *A History of the
Protestant Episcopal Church* (New York: Macmillan 1964), 71; Sir William Johnson
to SPG, 1772, USPG Archives A-164, calendar series 'B,' 1702–99, micro in AA;
SPG Journals 24:122

22 'Minutes of Several Conversations between the Rev. Mr. Wesley and others; from the
year 1744 to the year 1789,' *The Works of the Rev. John Wesley, A.M.* (London:
Wesleyan Conference Office 1872), 8:299

23 Eula C. Lapp, *To Their Heirs Forever* (Picton: Picton Gazette Publishing Co. 1970),
passim; Frederick A. Norwood, *The Story of American Methodism: A History of
the United Methodists and Their Relations* (Nashville: Abingdon 1974), 74; Donald
G. Mathews, 'The Great Awakening as an Organizing Process, 1780–1830,' in John
M. Mulder and John F. Wilson, eds., *Religion in American History: Interpretive
Essays* (Englewood, NJ: Prentice-Hall 1973), 209–11

24 Luther Waddington King, 'An Historical Study of Ministerial Authority in American
Methodism, 1760–1940' (PH D thesis, Columbia University 1981), 4, 55. Wesley
ordained Francis Asbury on his own authority. The other superintendent, Thomas
Coke, was already an ordained priest.

25 Nathan Bangs, *The Life of Freeborn Garrettson*, 213 (originally published at New
York in 1829; the copy available to me lacks a title page, but contains an owner's
signature dated 1844). On Thomas Ingersoll, father of Laura Secord, at one time a
Universalist, Abel Stevens, *Life and Times of Nathan Bangs, D.D.* (New York:
Carlton and Porter 1863), 84–5

26 Matthew 18:20 (KJV); Leonard J. Trinterud, *The Forming of an American Tradition: A
Re-examination of Colonial Presbyterianism* (Philadelphia: Westminster 1949),
27–34

27 Asahel Morse, quoted in Stuart Ivison and Fred Rosser, *The Baptists in Upper and
Lower Canada before 1820* (Toronto: University of Toronto Press 1956), 52;
Stevens, *Bangs*, 361; 'Luther' (William Smart), in *Kingston Gazette*, 13 July 1816;
Stuart to Inglis, 6 July 1788, DOA II:2; Stuart, 'Answer to Queries proposed by the
Right Rev. the Bishop of Nova Scotia,' received 12 Feb. 1791, DOA II:2

28 Quotation from Dongan in E.T. Corwin, *A History of the Reformed Church, Dutch, in
the United States* (New York: Christian Literature Society 1895), 87–8; Pointer,
'Seedbed of American Pluralism,' 217ff; Robert T. Handy, *A History of the Churches
in the United States and Canada* (New York: Oxford University Press 1977), 145

29 Cruikshank, *Settlement of the United Empire Loyalists*, 133; *Christian Recorder* 1:1
(Mar. 1819), 4

30 Lennox and Addington Historical Society, 'Memoirs of Colonel John Clark,' quoted
in Preston, *Kingston before the War of 1812*, xcv; F.C. Hamil, *The Valley of the
Lower Thames, 1690 to 1850* (Toronto: University of Toronto Press 1951), 68; Egerton
Ryerson, *The Loyalists of America and Their Times: From 1620 to 1816*, 2d ed.
(Toronto: William Briggs 1880), 2:245; John Carroll, *Case and His Cotemporaries*

(Toronto: Samuel Rose 1867–77), 1:6–7; Edith G. Firth, ed., *The Town of York,*
1793–1815: A Collection of Documents of Early Toronto (Toronto: The Champlain
Society 1962), lxxi
31 Carroll, *Case,* 1:93; George F. Playter, *The History of Methodism in Canada* (Toronto: Anson Green 1862), 52; Whitney R. Cross, *The Burned-Over District: The*
Social and Intellectual History of Enthusiastic Religion in Western New York, 1800–
1850 (New York: Harper 1965), 7–8

CHAPTER 3 *Foundations*

1 Johnson to SPG, 1774, USPG Archives A-164, calendar series 'B,' 1702–99
2 Brother Alfred, *Catholic Pioneers in Upper Canada,* 183–4
3 Epp, *Mennonites in Canada,* 115–27
4 John R. Weinlick, *The Moravian Church in Canada* (Winston-Salem, NC: Provincial
Women's Board of the Southeast Province 1966), 24; Arthur G. Dorland, *The*
Quakers in Canada, 79; Leslie R. Gray, ed., 'Phoebe Roberts' Diary of a Quaker
Missionary Journey to Upper Canada,' *OH* 42 (1950), 7–46
5 E.A. Cruikshank, 'The Activity of Abel Stevens as a Pioneer,' *OH* 31 (1936), 56–90
6 Abdel Ross Wentz, *The Lutheran Church in American History,* 2d ed. (Philadelphia:
United Lutheran Publishing House 1933), 107; *The Story of the United Church at*
Morven, 1856–1966, UCA Morven file, 12–14
7 Croil, *Dundas,* 258; John S. Moir, 'Robert McDowall and the Dutch Reformed
Mission to Canada, 1790–1819,' *de Halve Moen* 53:2 (summer 1978), 4–14; Roy
Collver, 'History,' in 'Dedication Service and History, Old Windham United Church,
May 27, 1962,' UCA Old Windham file; Harry E. Parker, 'The Diary of Rev.
William Fraser (1834–1835) with an Introductory Essay on Early Presbyterianism in
Western Ontario,' *Transactions of the London and Middlesex Historical Society* 14
(1930), 31; UCA Jabez Collver file; MacMillan, *Kirk in Glengarry,* 203; on early
Presbyterianism generally, see William Gregg, *History of the Presbyterian Church*
in the Dominion of Canada from the Earliest Times to 1834 (Toronto: Presbyterian
Printing and Publishing Co. 1885); for a more analytical study, see John S. Moir,
Enduring Witness (Toronto: Presbyterian Publications 1974), 46–54, 65-7.
8 *London Missionary Society General Meeting Reports,* 1799, 1802, 1803, 1805, 1811,
1812; Moir, 'McDowall,' 15
9 Diary of Timothy Rogers, 1812, AO, Quaker Archives, 1819–1964 (Conservatives)
micro 3850; David Willson, *The Impressions of the Mind, to which are added*
some remarks on church and state and the acting Principles of Life (Toronto 1835),
passim; Dorland, *Quakers in Canada,* chapter 7; Patrick Shirreff, *A Tour through*
North America; together with a comprehensive view of the Canadas and United
States, as adapted for agricultural emigration (Edinburgh: Oliver and Boyd 1835),
112, 115; Isaac Fidler, *Observations on Professions, Literature, Manners, and Emi-*
gration, in the United States and Canada, made during a residence there in 1832

(New York: J. and J. Harper 1833), 188; D. Wilkie, *Sketches of a Summer Trip to New York and the Canadas* (Edinburgh: J. Anderson, Jun., and A. Hill 1837), 205

10 *SPG Report*, 1785, 52; J.L.H. Henderson, *John Strachan, 1778–1867* (Toronto: University of Toronto Press 1969), 7–10; Frederick H. Armstrong, 'The Oligarchy of the Western District of Upper Canada, 1788–1841,' *CHA Historical Papers, 1977*, 99; George P. de T. Glazebrook, *The Church of England in Upper Canada, 1785–1867* (Toronto 1982), 12, 14; John C. Ogden, *A Tour through Upper and Lower Canada, Containing a present state of religion, learning, commerce, agriculture, colonization, customs and manners, among the English, French and Indian Settlements*, 2d ed. (Wilmington 1800) 55–6

11 Stuart to Inglis, 17 Mar. 1792, DOA II:4; Stuart to Jacob Mountain, 18 Apr. 1797, DOA II:6; Langhorn to SPG, 6 Oct. 1812, USPG Archives A-207, 'Correspondence of J. Langhorn,' box 4A/38, folio 439, micro in AA; Stuart to son James, 3 July 1802, quoted in A.H. Young, 'The Rev'd Richard Pollard, 1752–1824,' *OH* 25 (1929), 457; Marion MacRae in continuing consultation with Anthony Adamson, *Hallowed Walls: Church Architecture of Upper Canada* (Toronto: Clarke, Irwin 1975), 37

12 Têtu, *Journal des visites pastorales ... par Monseigneur Joseph-Octave Plessis* 432–3; Cornelius O'Brien, *Memoir of the Rt. Rev. Edmund Burke, Bishop of Zion, First Vicar Apostolic of Nova Scotia* (Ottawa: Thoburn and Co. 1894), 1–2; Michael Power, *A History of the Roman Catholic Church in the Niagara Peninsula, 1615–1815* (St Catharines, Ont.: Roman Catholic Diocese 1983), chapters 12, 13

13 AAK, Letters Macdonell 1826, 584, quoted in H.J. Somers, *The Life and Times of the Hon. and Rt. Rev. Alexander Macdonell, D.D., First Bishop of Upper Canada, 1762–1840* (Washington: Catholic University of America 1931), 41

14 Robert G. Torbet, *A History of the Baptists* (Philadelphia: Judson 1959), 264; Ivison and Rosser, *The Baptists in Upper and Lower Canada before 1820*, chapter 3; Lemuel Covell, 'Visit of Rev. Lemuel Covell to Western New York and Canada in the Fall of 1803,' in Frank H. Severance, ed., *Publications of the Buffalo Historical Society*, 6 (1903), 208

15 Freeborn Garrettson, *The Experience and Travels of Mr. Freeborn Garrettson* (Philadelphia: Joseph Cruikshank 1794), 225; Bangs, *Garrettson*, 191, 219; J. William Lamb, 'William Losee: Ontario's Pioneer Methodist Missionary,' *UCA Bulletin* 21 (1969–70), 28–47. The story of Methodist advance is traced in detail in the five volumes of John Carroll, *Case and His Cotemporaries*. Carroll was apparently able to draw on records of the Genesee Conference, which from 1810 to 1824 was responsible for work in Upper Canada; these records have since disappeared.

16 *Kingston Gazette*, 3 Mar. 1812, 14; George Peck, *Early Methodism within the Bounds of the Old Genesee Conference from 1788 to 1828* (New York: Carlton & Porter 1860), 511

17 Carroll, *Case*, 2:82

18 T.R. Millman, *Jacob Mountain, First Lord Bishop of Quebec: A Study in Church and State 1793–1825* (Toronto: University of Toronto Press 1947), 283

19 Notitia parochiales, 5 Oct. 1787 to 5 Apr. 1788, 'Correspondence of Langhorn';
   Gregg, *History of the Presbyterian Church*, 175–6
20 Carroll, *Case*, 1:327; J. William Lamb, 'McCarty (McCarthy), Charles Justin
   (James),' *DCB* 4:494–5
21 Hubert to M. Brassier, vicar-general and superior of the Seminary of Montreal, 18
   July 1795, in Preston, *Kingston before the War of 1812*, 303
22 Glazebrook, *The Church of England in Upper Canada*, 51. Macdonell suggested (to
   Bishop of Solda, 4 Nov. 1819, AAK A12C6) that possible profit was the motive
   behind Protestant contributions toward the erection of a Roman Catholic chapel at
   Brockville.

CHAPTER 4 *Varieties of Pioneer Religion*

1 C.F. Pascoe, *Two Hundred Years of the S.P.G.: An Historical Account of the Society
   for the Propagation of the Gospel in Foreign Parts, 1701–1900* (London: SPG
   1901), 1:155; Strachan to Lord Teignmouth, 9 Nov. 1812, in George W. Spragge,
   ed., *The John Strachan Letter Book, 1812–1834* (Toronto: Ontario Historical
   Society 1946), 25; William Case, journal, 1808–9, typewritten copy in UCA; Isabel
   Skelton, *A Man Austere: William Bell, Parson and Pioneer* (Toronto: Ryerson
   Press 1947), 118
2 Ely Playter diary, Feb 1801–Dec. 1853, AO; Henry Scadding, *Toronto of Old*, ed.
   F.H. Armstrong (Toronto: Oxford University Press 1966), 286
3 Langhorn to the Rev. Dr Morice, 5 Oct. 1804, 6 Apr. 1805, USPG Archives A-207,
   'Correspondence of J. Langhorn,' box 4A/38, folio 439. These letters establish the
   date, which has been in doubt. For a Methodist point of view, see Playter, *Methodism
   in Canada*, 63–4.
4 *The Autobiography of Alvin Torry, First Missionary to the Six Nations and the Northwestern Tribes of British North America*, ed. William Hosmer (Auburn, NY:
   William J. Moses 1861), 40–4
5 Walter E. Houghton, *The Victorian Frame of Mind, 1830–1870* (New Haven: Yale
   University Press 1957), 218–19
6 Mulder and Wilson, *Religion in American History*, 202
7 Holly S. Seaman, 'Sketch of the Rev. William Smart, Presbyterian Minister of Elizabethtown,' *OH* 5 (1904), 179; Canniff, *Settlement of Upper Canada*, 262; Ernest
   Hawkins, *Annals of the Diocese of Toronto* (London: SPCK 1848), 18; Stuart to
   Inglis, 11 Mar. 1792, DOA II: 4
8 *A Collection of Papers printed by order of the Society for the Propagation of the
   Gospel in Foreign Parts* (London: printed by T. Harrison and S. Brooke 1788), 10,
   12, 14
9 Mountain, 1820, Archives de la Province de Québec, H.C. Stuart papers 291, quoted
   in Preston, *Kingston before the War of 1812*, xc; McMorine, 'Early History of the
   Anglican Church in Kingston,' 96–7; Spragge, *Strachan Letter Book*, 119–20, 20,

56; H.C. Stuart, *The Church of England in Canada, 1759–1793, from the Conquest to the Establishment of the See of Quebec* (Montreal 1893), 113

10 Harriet Priddis, collector, 'The Proudfoot Papers,' *Transactions of the London and Middlesex Historical Society* 8 (1917), 36–45

11 'Extracts from the Journal of the Rev. David Irish, in his late tour into Upper Canada,' *The Massachusetts Baptist Magazine* 9:1 (Feb. 1807), 260; Records, Beamsville Baptist Church, typewritten copy in Archives of McMaster Divinity College, 11 June, 1 Aug. 1808

12 Carroll, *Case* 1:178; A.E. Kewley, 'The Beginning of the Camp Meeting Movement in Upper Canada,' *Canadian Journal of Theology*, 10:3 (July 1964), 195; A.E. Kewley, 'Mass Evangelism in Upper Canada before 1830' (TH D thesis, Victoria University 1960), passim

13 Wesley's 'General Rules,' reprinted at the front of most editions of the Methodist *Discipline* throughout the world; Mrs Stanley C. Tolan, 'Christian Warner: A Methodist Pioneer,' *OH* 37 (1945), 76

14 Lemuel Covell, 'Visit ... to Western New York and Canada,' in Frank H. Severance, *Publications of the Buffalo Historical Society*, 6:209; Case, journal; Carroll, *Case*, 1:94; Abel Stevens, *Life and Times of Nathan Bangs*, 76

15 Carroll, *Case*, 1:48; Irish, 'Journal,' 260

16 Stevens, *Bangs*, 152–3

17 Ibid., 96, 101, 140; for the application of the providential theme, see symposium, *Centennial of Canadian Methodism* (Toronto: William Briggs 1891): by George Douglas to the original Wesleyan mission (title to chapter 1), by Albert Carman to North America (238), and by Alexander Sutherland to Canada (254).

18 Armine W. Mountain, *A Memoir of George Jehoshaphat Mountain, D.D., D.C.L., Late Bishop of Quebec* (London: Sampson Low, Son and Marston 1866), 139

19 Torry, *Autobiography*, 59; Stevens, *Bangs*, 39; A.H. Young, 'The Rev. Robert Addison and St. Mark's Church, Niagara,' *OH* 19 (1922), 177, 179, 181–2; Stuart to Inglis, 22 Oct. 1792, 25 June 1793, DOA II:4. Apparently, Addison's bishop had been eager to be rid of him for some time when he recommended him for colonial service: John Burtnick and Wesley B. Turner, *Religion and Churches in the Niagara Peninsula: Proceedings, Fourth Annual Peninsula Conference, Brock University, April 1982* (St Catharines, Ont.: 1982), 29.

20 *Story of the United Church at Morven*, 11; Epp, *Mennonites in Canada*, 115, 118, 124, 127; Case, journal

21 John Howison, *Sketches of Upper Canada, Domestic, Local, and Characteristic: to which are added, practical details for the information of immigrants of every class; and some recollections of the United States of America* (Edinburgh: Oliver and Boyd 1821), 135

22 J. William Lamb, 'McCarty (James),' 495; Carroll, *Case*, 1:113; S. Houston, 'Early History of Presbyterianism in Kingston,' *Queen's Quarterly*, 2:2 (Oct. 1894), 95

23 Gourlay, *Statistical Account of Upper Canada*, 119; S.D. Clark, *Church and Sect in Canada* (Toronto: University of Toronto Press 1948), chapter 3

24 *SPG Collection of Papers*, 42ff; Robert E. Chiles, *Theological Transition in American Methodism, 1790–1935* (New York: Abington 1965), chapter 2; Edmund Burke, *A Treatise on the First Principles of Christianity, in which all difficulties stated by ancient and modern sceptics are dispassionately discussed* (Halifax: John Howe and Son 1808), passim

25 Peter Russell to Serjeant Shepherd, 9 Jan. 1800, in Firth, *The Town of York, 1793–1815*, 231

26 J. Donald Wilson, 'The Teacher in Early Ontario,' in F.H. Armstrong, H.A. Stevenson, and J.D. Wilson, eds., *Aspects of Nineteenth-Century Ontario: Essays Presented to James J. Talman* (Toronto: University of Toronto Press 1974), 219; George W. Spragge, 'John Strachan's Contribution to Education, 1800–1825,' in J.K. Johnson, ed., *Historical Essays on Upper Canada* (Toronto: McClelland and Stewart 1975), 74–85; Carroll, *Case*, 1:153

27 W. Perkins Bull, *From Strachan to Owen: How the Church of England Was Planted and Tended in British North America* (Toronto: George J. McLeod 1937), 71; Burke to Plessis, 13 Sept. 1798, in O'Brien, *Memoir of the Rt. Rev. Edmund Burke*, 40; Smith, *A Geographical View of the Province of Upper Canada*, 67

CHAPTER 5 *Atlantic Triangle*

1 *The Report of the Loyal and Patriotic Society of Upper Canada* (Montreal 1817), quoted in C.P. Stacey, 'The War of 1812 in Canadian History,' *OH* 50:3 (summer 1958), 155

2 Akenson, *The Irish in Ontario*, 20–3; Michael B. Katz, *The People of Hamilton, Canada West: Family and Class in a Mid-Nineteenth Century City* (Cambridge: Harvard University Press 1975), 23

3 Cruikshank, 'Abel Stevens as a Pioneer,' 90; Fred Landon, ed., 'The Proudfoot Papers,' *Transactions of the London and Middlesex Historical Society* 11 (1922), 47

4 Freda Ramsay, 'The Churches and Emigration,' *CSPH Papers*, 1976, 24

5 James J. Talman, 'Some Notes on the Clergy of the Church of England Prior to 1840,' *Royal Society of Canada Transactions*, 3d series, 32 (1938), sect. 2: 57; Gregg, *History of the Presbyterian Church in Canada*, 493

6 D. Welsh to William Morris, 30 Mar. 1830, QUA, William Morris Papers, box 1; *Records of the Lives of Ellen Free Pickton and Featherstone Lake Osler* (Toronto 1915), 25; Thomas Beveridge, 'An Account of the First Mission of the Associate Synod to Canada West,' transcribed and annotated by Andrew W. Taylor, *OH* 50:2 (spring 1958), 103 (compare Report of St Andrew's Church, Niagara, n.d. but perhaps 1831, QUA, Presbyterian Church Papers, box 1); John C. Banks, 'The Reverend James Magrath: Family Man and Anglican Cleric,' *OH* 55:3 (Sept. 1963),

231–42; George Pashley, 'Journal of a Voyage to Upper Canada to Cobourg, 1833,' typewritten copy in PAC, MG24.J12.

7 T.R. Millman, *The Life of the Right Reverend, the Honourable Charles James Stewart, D.D., Oxon., Second Anglican Bishop of Quebec* (London, Ont.: Huron College 1953), 37, 53, 142; W.J.D. Waddilove, ed., *The Stewart Missions* (London: J. Hatchard 1838), xiv; W.J.D. Waddilove, ed., *Report and Correspondence of the Late Bishop of Quebec's Upper Canadian Travelling Mission Fund, 1844* (Hexham: printed by Edward Pruddah 1844), 2; *SPG Report*, 1832, 9; E.A. McDougall, 'Early Settlement in Lanark County and the Glasgow Colonial Society,' *CSPH Papers*, 1976, 43; Parker, 'The Diary of Rev. William Fraser,' 58; C. Glenn Lucas, 'Presbyterianism in Carleton County to 1867' (MA thesis, Carleton University 1973), 98; minutes of directors, Glasgow Colonial Society, 4 June 1830, UCA, Glasgow Colonial Society collection, box 5, no. 3

8 Moir, 'McDowall,' 15; Beveridge, 'First Mission of the Associate Synod,' 110; AHMS *Report*: 4th (1830), 12; 11th (1837), 56; 1st (1827), 55–6, UCA, micro D2.1 16; Goldwin S. French, *Parsons and Politics* (Toronto: Ryerson Press 1962), 85. In 1836 the AHMS, recognizing the affiliation with itself of the Montreal-based Canada Education and Home Missionary Society, announced that 'its name would not henceforth limit the field of its appropriations' (*10th Annual Report*, 79), but in the following year severe financial losses combined with the rebellions to render this change of policy virtually stillborn.

9 Reuben Butchart, *The Disciples of Christ in Canada since 1830* (Toronto: Canadian Headquarters' Publications, Church of Christ [Disciples] 1949), passim; P.A. Henry, *Memoir of the Rev. Thomas Henry: Christian Minister, York Pioneer, and Soldier of 1812* (Toronto 1880), 178, 185–8; information on the Christian Connection supplied by Prof. Allan Gleason; Louise Foulds, *Universalists in Ontario* (Olinda, Ont. Unitarian Universalist Church 1980), passim; Richard E. Bennett, 'A Study of the Church of Jesus Christ of Latter-Day Saints in Upper Canada, 1830–1850' (MA thesis, Brigham Young University 1975), 26–47; Carroll, *Case*, 4:23; *Kingston Chronicle and Gazette*, 14 July 1838

10 Carroll, *Case*, 3:294, 485; Millman, *Stewart*, 194; P.E. Shaw, *The Catholic Apostolic Church, Sometimes Called Irvingite: A Historical Study* (New York: King's Crown Press 1946), chapters 12, 13; D. Johnson, 'The Church of the Good Shepherd,' *Waterloo Historical Society* 31 (1943), 39–40

11 William Bettridge, *A Brief History of the Church in Upper Canada* (London: W.E. Painter 1838), 138; Carroll, *Case*, 2:141; 3:294, 486; 4:345, 451; Thomas Webster, *History of the Methodist Episcopal Church in Canada* (Hamilton: Canada Christian Advocate Office 1870), 384

12 *Records of ... Osler* 153; Waddilove, *Stewart Missions*, 45; Harriet Priddis, 'Proudfoot Papers,' *Transactions of the London and Middlesex Historical Society* 6 (1915), 37; Marilla Marks, ed., *Memoir of the Life of David Marks, Minister of the Gospel* (Dover, NH: Free Will Baptist Printing Establishment 1846), passim

13 D.W. Clark, *Life and Times of Rev. Elijah Hedding, D.D.* (New York: Carlton and Phillips 1856), 315; compare Peck, *Early Methodism*, 501, 504.

14 Zander Dunn, 'The Great Divorce and What Happened to the Children,' *CSPH Papers*, 1977, 58–96

15 The fullest account of these Methodist troubles is French, *Parsons and Politics*, 67–79, 134–95. They are described from the perspective of Egerton Ryerson in C.B. Sissons, *Egerton Ryerson: His Life and Letters* I (Toronto: Clarke, Irwin 1937).

16 To Robert Alder, annual report on missions for 1834, photocopy in UCA, the Wesleyan Methodist Church (Great Britain), Missions in America, the British Dominions in North America, Correspondence, 113:3

17 Dale A. Johnson, 'The Methodist Quest for an Educated Ministry,' *Church History* 51:3 (Sept. 1982), 304

18 To James Richardson, 30 Apr. 1833, in Sissons, *Ryerson*, 1:178. George Ryerson (to Egerton, Bristol, England, 6 Aug. 1831, UCA, Egerton Ryerson Papers, box 1, file 8) wrote, 'The whole morning service of the Church is now read in most of the Wesleyan Chapels & with as much formality as in the Church.' The two statements may well both have been correct.

19 Quoted in Gregg, *History of the Presbyterian Church*, 441; for a detailed account of these negotiations, see Moir, *Enduring Witness*, chapter 5.

20 Edward Marsh to Absalom Peters, 19 Sept. 1835; Samuel Sessions to Peters, 4 Oct. 1834; Joseph Marr to Peters, 6 Apr. 1836; S.W. Armstrong to Peters, 5 Apr. 1828; Marsh to Peters, 19 Sept. 1835; all in UCA, AHMS correspondence, 1822–38, micro D2.3 39

21 Gregg, *History of the Presbyterian Church*, 493; Priddis, 'Proudfoot Papers,' *Transactions of the London and Middlesex Historical Society*, 6 (1915), 67

22 W.F. Curry to Milton Badger, 27 Sept. 1837, AHMS correspondence; John Kenyon, 'The Development of Congregationalism in Early Nineteenth-Century Ontario,' *CSCH Papers*, 1978, 11–25

23 This paragraph is largely based on the research of Donald A. Goertz, a doctoral student at the Toronto School of Theology.

24 C.R. Cronmiller, *A History of the Lutheran Church in Canada* (Toronto: Evangelical Lutheran Synod of Canada 1961), 109; A.G. Dorland, *The Quakers in Canada*, chapters 8, 9, 255–63; Epp, *Mennonites in Canada*, 135–7

25 Letters of Bishop Macdonell, AO, section E, 9:1321–31, quoted in Somers, *Life and Times of ... Alexander Macdonell*, 128

26 J.E. Rea, *Bishop Alexander Macdonell and the Politics of Upper Canada* (Toronto: Ontario Historical Society 1974), 61; Helen I. Cowan, *British Immigration to British North America, 1783–1837* (Toronto: University of Toronto Library 1928), 97–101

27 Millman, *Stewart*, 54, 58; Bull, *From Strachan to Owen*, 72, 93, 115, 127, 138–9; Waddilove, *Report and Correspondence ... 1844*, 224; Richard Ruggle, 'The Canadianization of the Church of England,' *CSCH Papers*, 1981, 81

28 (W.S. Darling), *Sketches of Canadian Life, Lay and Ecclesiastical, Illustrative of*

Canada and the Canadian Church by a presbyter of the Diocese of Toronto (London: David Bogue 1849), 230–2; Waddilove, *Report and Correspondence ... 1844*, 33

29 *Colonial Advocate*, 29 July, 2 Sept. 1824; 9 Mar. 1826; 30 Aug. 1827

30 Of the Anglican clergy who served Upper Canada prior to 1840, 31 have been identified as being from Ireland, compared with 32 from England, 15 native to the province, and a scattering from various other places (Talman, 'Some Notes on the Clergy,' 63). Lucas, 'Presbyterianism in Carleton County,' 11, 117, 154–5, 376. As early as 1830, 13 of 62 Methodist itinerants were from Ireland, compared with 27 from Upper Canada, 12 from the United States, and 3 from England (*Christian Guardian*, 1 Jan. 1831). According to Donald H. Akenson (*The Irish in Ontario*, 349), Anglicans constituted the largest single category of Protestant Irish to migrate to Canada.

31 A.H. Young, 'The Church of England in Upper Canada (1791–1841),' *Queen's Quarterly* 37:1 (winter 1930), 158; Millman, *Stewart*, 90; Talman, 'Some Notes on the Clergy,' 62; Power, *The Roman Catholic Church in the Niagara Peninsula*, 135; Somers, *Macdonell*, 90, 162; Skelton, *A Man Austere*, 201. That the sponsors of the Hillier seminary counted on American backing is indicated by a letter of 13 Oct. 1831 from its agent, Eliakim Corry, asking the AHMS to supply a professor (AHMS correspondence), and by a letter to the editor of the *Kingston Chronicle* (8 Oct. 1831), denouncing the project as a deliberate step toward political union with the United States.

32 Robert Wallace, 'Reminiscences of Student Life in Canada Fifty Years Ago and the Origin of Two Presbyterian Colleges,' *Knox College Monthly* (Aug. 1892), 193–4

CHAPTER 6 *Religion on the Hustings*

1 Gourlay, *Statistical Account of Upper Canada*, 116

2 Articles 36 and 37

3 James J. Talman, 'The Position of the Church of England in Upper Canada, 1791–1840,' in Johnson, *Historical Essays on Upper Canada*, 58–73; Young, 'The Church of England in Upper Canada,' 145–66; Alan Wilson, *The Clergy Reserves in Canada*, CHA Historical Booklet 23 (Ottawa: Canadian Historical Association 1967), 4. Although a strict reading of the Constitutional Act would suggest that the clergy reserves should consist of one-eighth of the total land granted, the act was interpreted as conferring one-seventh.

4 Armstrong, 'Oligarchy of the Western District,' 89. Armstrong credits this point to Fred Landon ('The Common Man in the Era of the Rebellion in Upper Canada,' in Armstrong et al., *Aspects of Nineteenth-Century Ontario*, 154–70, originally published in *CHA Annual Report, 1937*).

5 For British and American parallels, see E.R. Norman, *The Conscience of the State in North America* (Cambridge: University Press 1968), passim. Since the primary

focus of this chapter is on the implications of political involvement for the religion of Ontarians, I include here only as much of the narrative of the controversy as seems essential to understanding. Readers who wish a more detailed account are referred to Alan Wilson, *The Clergy Reserves of Canada: A Canadian Mortmain* (Toronto: University of Toronto Press 1968). Useful discussions with reference to particular denominations are: for the Presbyterians, Moir, *Enduring Witness*, chapters 4, 5; for the Methodists, French, *Parsons and Politics*, chapters 5–7; for the Church of England, Millman, *Life of ... Charles James Stewart*, chapters 6, 11, 12, 14.

6 Quoted in Gerald M. Craig, *Upper Canada: The Formative Years, 1784–1841* (Toronto: McClelland and Stewart 1963), 56

7 Donald H. Akenson (*The Irish in Ontario*, 160) argues that the existence of the reserves facilitated settlement in Leeds and Lansdowne townships. This may well have been the case once satisfactory provision had been made for leasing them, but the lack of such provision in earlier years was certainly instrumental in creating a sense of grievance. Among Gourlay's respondents (*Statistical Account*, 293) 24 complained of absentee ownership, 19 of the Crown and clergy reserves, and 14 of a lack of people, especially those with capital and a spirit of enterprise.

8 R. Burns, 'God's Chosen People: The Origins of Toronto Society, 1793–1818,' *CHA Historical Papers, 1973*, 213

9 Egerton Ryerson, *Claims of the Churchmen and Dissenters of Upper Canada Brought to the Test, in a controversy between several members of the Church of England and a Methodist Preacher* (Kingston: printed at the Herald Office 1828), 13, 25–51

10 James J. Talman ('The Position of the Church of England,' 72) and T.R. Millman (*Stewart*, 110) suggest that the Canadian Methodists received a government grant before their union with the Wesleyans. This grant was made to Ryan's small Canadian Wesleyan Methodist Church. See French, *Parsons and Politics*, 165, n26.

11 *Christian Guardian*, 30 Oct. 1833; Journal of Conference, 1830, manuscript in UCA

12 At first, the salaries of the missionaries were cut severely. In 1834 it was arranged that they should receive 85 per cent of their previous salaries for life, but that future missionaries should be entirely the responsibility of the SPG (Millman, *Stewart*, 118). For a lucid and fair account of the rectories question, see ibid., 139–41. G.M. Craig, ed., *Lord Durham's Report: An Abridgement of the Report on the Affairs of British North America by Lord Durham* (Toronto: McClelland and Stewart 1963), 95

13 Landon, 'The Common Man,' 167–8; John Roaf to T. Baker, 26 Dec. 1837, AO, James R. Roaf Papers; *Kingston Chronicle and Gazette*, 27 and 30 Dec. 1837; 1 July 1838; *Kingston British Whig*, 11 May, 8 June 1838; Pascoe, *Two Hundred Years of the S.P.G.*, 1:161

14 Wesleyan Methodist Church in Canada, *Minutes of Conference* 4 (1837), 164–6; Bettridge, *Brief History*, 76, 80

15 *Christian Guardian,* 23 Feb. 1842

16 John S. Moir, 'The Upper Canadian Roots of Church Disestablishment,' *OH* 60:4 (Dec. 1968), 252

17 Bettridge, *Brief History*, 139
18 Hawkins, *Annals of the Diocese of Toronto*, 101–2; *Kingston Gazette*, 21 Apr. 1812; *SPG Report*, 1839, 84–5; Bettridge, *Brief History*, 36; *Christian Recorder* 1:1 (Mar. 1819), 12
19 Anyone who compares Chalmers's arguments in these 'Lectures on the Establishment and Extension of National Churches' (in Chalmers, *Works* [Glasgow n.d.]) with those of Strachan's letter of 1830 to the Rt Hon. Thomas Frankland Lewis (in J.L.H. Henderson, ed., *John Strachan: Documents and Opinions* [Toronto: McClelland and Stewart 1969]) will be struck not only by the close resemblance of the ideas but by near-identities of phraseology. Compare, for example, 'Nature does not go forth in quest of Christianity, but Christianity must go forth in quest of nature' ('Lectures on the Establishment,' 17:27), with 'Nature does not go forth in search of Christianity, but Christianity goes forth to search at the door of nature' (*Documents and Opinions*, 110). Since we are told that Chalmers regularly sent Strachan copies of his works on publication (A.N. Bethune, *Memoir of the Right Reverend John Strachan, D.D., LL.D., First Bishop of Toronto* [Toronto: Henry Rowsell 1870], 328), he may have used these words on a previous occasion. It is at least conceivable, however, that he borrowed them from Strachan. Chalmers, *Works*, 17:322–3.
20 Craig, *Upper Canada*, 108; Strachan to Sir George Arthur, 2 May 1838, in Charles R. Sanderson, ed., *The Arthur Papers* (Toronto: Toronto Public Libraries and University of Toronto Press 1943), 104; Waddilove, *Report and Correspondence ... 1844*, 176
21 W.R. Ward, 'Church and Society in the First Half of the Nineteenth Century,' in Rupert Davies, A. Raymond George, and Gordon Rupp, eds., *A History of the Methodist Church in Great Britain* 2 (London: Epworth 1978), 13–17; E.A. Cruikshank, ed., *The Correspondence of Lieutenant Governor John Graves Simcoe, with allied documents relating to his administration of the government of Upper Canada* 1 (Toronto: Ontario Historical Society 1923), 31–5, 251–2; John Strachan, *An Appeal to the Friends of Religion and Literature on behalf of the University of Upper Canada* (London: printed by R. Gilbert 1827), 21
22 To Absalom Peters, 19 June 1835, UCA, AHMS correspondence
23 Mark 12:17 (KJV); Parker, 'The Diary of Rev. William Fraser,' 115; Playter, *Methodism in Canada*, 226; Thomas H. Wilson, 'An Historical Study of the Relationship of the Anglican Church of Canada to Kingston Penitentiary, 1835–1913' (PH D thesis, University of Ottawa 1978), 13
24 J.C. Grant to J. Rose, 'Reasons and Considerations in favour of the Claims of the Church of Scotland in Canada,' May 1825, PAC, MG24, G36; Macdonell to Thomas Weld, Dec. 1828, AO, Macdonell Letters, series E, vol. 3, 351–2; Memorial of Synod, 28 Mar. 1835, QUA, Presbyterian Church Papers, box 1; Francis G. Morrisey, OMI, 'The Juridical Status of the Catholic Church in Canada (1534–1840)' (D.Can.L. thesis, Saint Paul University, Ottawa, 1972), 210–11; 'The Petition of David Wilson [sic] to the Honorable the House of Assembly of Upper Canada,' photocopy in PAC,

MG24, J36; John Bayne to William Morris, 2 Apr. 1839; A.H. Gale to Morris, 19
Apr. 1839; in leaf 2 QUA, William Morris Papers, Correspondence, 1823–41, collection 2139, box 1
25 J. Partington to Absalom Peters, 7 July 1836, AHMS correspondence; M.A. Garland,
'Proudfoot Papers,' *OH* 31 (1935), 98, 105; A.H. Newman, 'Sketch of the Baptists of Ontario and Quebec to 1851,' *Baptist Year Book (Centennial Number) for Ontario, Quebec, Manitoba and the North West Territory, and British Columbia, 1900*, 87. From 1833 to 1838 Wesleyan membership dropped from 16,039 to 15,190: George A. Cornish, *Cyclopaedia of Methodism in Canada* 1 (Toronto: Methodist Book and Publishing House 1881), 32. The Methodist Episcopals went from zero to 4,180: S.G. Stone, 'Historical Sketch of the Methodist Episcopal Church in Canada,' in *Centennial of Canadian Methodism*, 192.
26 Leeds to SPG, 5 Feb. 1828, *SPG Journals*, 38:67–8; Waddilove, *Report and Correspondence ... 1844*, 215; Bethune, *Strachan*, 249
27 Ryerson, *Claims of Churchmen and Dissenters*, 35; Edwy to Egerton Ryerson, 26 Nov. 1833, quoted in Sissons, *Ryerson*, 1:217

CHAPTER 7 *New Measures*

1 *Report of the Upper Canada Clergy Society* 3 (1840), 24; Anson Green, *The Life and Times of the Rev. Anson Green, D.D.* (Toronto: Methodist Book Room 1877), 111, 209
2 *Past and Present; or a description of persons and events connected with Canadian Methodism for the last forty years* (Toronto: Alfred Dredge 1860), 39
3 Marion MacRae, *Hallowed Walls*, passim; Harold D. Kalman, *The Conservation of Ontario Churches* (Toronto: Ontario Ministry of Culture and Recreation 1977), 107–10
4 *Colonial Advocate*, 16 June 1825; L.E. Smith, 'Nineteenth-Century Canadian Preaching in the Methodist, Presbyterian and Congregational Churches' (TH D thesis, Victoria University 1953), 45–7; *Records of ... Osler*, 138; Green, *Life and Times*, 70; Edward Gordon to Macdonell, 11 Mar. 1850, quoted in Edward Kelly, ed., *The Story of St. Paul's Parish, Toronto* (Toronto 1923), 57
5 M.A. Garland, 'Proudfoot Papers,' *OH* 32 (1937), 97; G.P. de T. Glazebrook, *Life in Ontario: A Social History* (Toronto: University of Toronto Press 1968), 62; William Lamb, 'Canadian Methodism's first tunebook, *Sacred Harmony*, 1838' in John Beckwith, ed., *Sing Out the Glad News: Hymn Tunes in Canada* (Toronto: Institute for Canadian Music 1987), 91–118; Margaret A. Filshie, 'Sacred Harmonies: The Congregational Voice in Canadian Protestant Worship, 1750–1850,' *Canadian Themes* 7 (1985), 294–5; John Howison, *Sketches of Upper Canada*, 135; Frederick H. Rennie, 'Spiritual Worship with a Carnal Instrument: The Organ as Aid or Obstacle to the Purity of Worship in Canadian Presbyterianism, 1850–1875' (TH D thesis, Knox College 1969), 72–3; Hilary Spooner, 'Sharon Temple and

the Children of Peace,' *OH* 50:4 (Dec. 1958), 222; Scadding, *Toronto of Old*, 140

6 *Scobie and Balfour's Canadian Almanac* (Toronto 1850), 52, quoted in Allan Greer, 'The Sunday Schools of Upper Canada,' *OH* 67:3 (Sept. 1975), 172–3; *Christian Recorder* 1:10 (Dec. 1819), 368; *Christian Guardian*, 23 Apr. 1831

7 *Kingston Gazette*, 2, 9, and 16 Dec. 1817; Margaret Angus, 'Health, Emigration and Welfare in Kingston, 1800–1840,' in Donald Swainson, ed., *Oliver Mowat's Ontario* (Toronto: Macmillan 1972), 120–35; *Colonial Advocate*, 11 Dec. 1828; *Christian Guardian*, 30 Jan. 1833

8 Useful studies of the international evangelicalism of the period are Richard Carwardine, *Trans-Atlantic Revivalism: Popular Evangelicalism in Britain and America, 1790–1865* (Westport, Conn.: Greenwood 1978), and Charles I. Foster, *An Errand of Mercy: The Evangelical United Front, 1790–1837* (Chapel Hill, NC: University of North Carolina Press 1960).

9 Webster, *The Methodist Episcopal Church in Canada*, 156; Playter, *Methodism in Canada*, 243; Jane Agar Hopper, *Old-Time Primitive Methodism in Canada* (Toronto: William Briggs 1904), 30; Carroll, *Case*, 4:12; Leviticus 6:13 (KJV), quoted by George Petrie, 27 Aug. 1844, in Waddilove, *Report and Correspondence ... 1844*, 193

10 Robert J.A. Samms, 'Revivalism in Central Canadian Wesleyan Methodism, 1824–1860' (PH D thesis, McGill University 1984), 70; F.A. Cox and J. Hoby, *The Baptists in America: a narrative of the deputation from the Baptist Union in England to the United States and Canada* (New York: Leavitt, Lord and Co. 1836), 190; Richard Kay to Absalom Peters, 20 Apr. 1837, AHMS correspondence, UCA; Green, *Life and Times*, 148

11 Judith Fingard, '"Grapes in the Wilderness": The Bible Society in British North America in the Early 19th Century,' *Histoire sociale/Social History* 9 (Apr. 1972), 6–7; Upper Canada Bible Society, minutes of committee, 12 Dec. 1831, PAC, MG17, FI; William Case, *Jubilee Sermon delivered at the request of and before the Wesleyan Canada Conference, assembled at London, C.W., June 6th, 1855* (Toronto: G.R. Sanderson 1855), 14

12 'George Ryerson to Sir Peregrine Maitland, 9 June 1826,' introduction by C.B. Sissons, *OH* 44:1 (Jan. 1952), 27; *Christian Guardian*, 24 Apr. 1830; Greer, 'Sunday Schools,' 173

13 *Christian Recorder* 1:5 (July 1819), 185; O'Grady to Macdonell, 29 Oct. 1829, cited in Kelly, *Story of St. Paul's*, 55; Epp, *Mennonites in Canada*, 126; Fidler, *Observations on Professions, Literature, Manners, and Emigration*, 190–1; Wesleyan Methodist Church in Canada, *Minutes of Conference* 44 (1867), 34–5

14 Millman, *Life of ... Charles James Stewart*, 41; *Christian Guardian*, 11 July 1838; Lucius G. Matlack, *The History of American Slavery and Methodism from 1780 to 1849; and History of the Wesleyan Methodist Connection of America* (New York

1849), 180–2; *London Anti-Slavery Reporter*, reprinted in *New York Watchman and Wesleyan Observer* 5:14 (31 Oct. 1840), 174

15 James J. Talman, 'Pioneer Drinking Habits and the Rise of the Temperance Agitation in Upper Canada Prior to 1840,' in Armstrong et al., *Aspects of Nineteenth-Century Ontario*, 184; W.R. Ward, *Religion and Society in England, 1790–1850* (London: B.T. Batsford 1972), 289; James M. Clemens, 'Taste Not, Touch Not, Handle Not: A Study of the Social Assumptions of the Temperance Literature and Temperance Supporters in Canada West between 1839 and 1859,' *OH* 64:3 (Sept. 1972), 145; F.L. Barron, 'The American Origins of the Temperance Movement in Ontario, 1828–1850,' *Canadian Review of American Studies* 11:2 (fall 1980), 136–8; W.F. Curry to Absalom Peters, 4 Aug. 1837, AHMS correspondence; Green, *Life and Times*, 154

16 Webster, *History*, 238; Abner Nash to James Dougall, 29 July 1831, AO, James Dougall Papers; Cox and Hoby, *Baptists in America*, 224–5; Cross, *The Burned-Over District*, 216–17

17 Gray, *Wilderness Christians*, 184–5; Case, journal, 1808–9; Donald B. Smith, *Sacred Feathers*, chapters 5 and 6

18 I have told the story of Christian missions among the Indians of Upper Canada in greater detail in *Moon of Wintertime* (Toronto: University of Toronto Press 1984), chapter 4.

19 Carroll, *Case*, 3:130; Daniel G. Hill, *The Freedom-Seekers: Blacks in Early Canada* (Agincourt, Ont.: The Book Society of Canada 1980), chapter 8; Robin W. Winks, *The Blacks in Canada: A History* (Montreal: McGill-Queen's University Press 1971), 148

20 *Christian Guardian*, 24 Apr. 1830; Catherine L. Albanese, *America: Religions and Religion* (Belmont, Cal.: Wadsworth 1981), 267; Carroll, *Case*, 3:169; Liz Muir, 'Petticoats in the Pulpit: Three Early Canadian Methodist Women,' *CSCH Papers*, 1984, 26–49; Dorland, *The Quakers in Canada*, 131; Foulds, *Universalists in Ontario*, 3

21 W.P.J. Millar, 'The Remarkable Rev. Thaddeus Osgood: A Study of the Evangelical Spirit in the Canadas,' *Histoire sociale/Social History* 19 (May 1977), 59–76; Nathan H. Mair, 'An Account of the Deeds of the Reverend Thaddeus Osgood, Beggar,' *UCA Bulletin* 30 (1983–4), 31–43; DOA II:2; Methodist Missionary Society, Minutes, 8 Oct. 1830, UCA, micro D6.4 57; *The Panoplist*, Jan. 1809, 304–5; Aug. 1811, 139–40

22 *Christian Advocate*, 1 Sept. 1832; Foster, *Errand of Mercy*, 138–9; Clemens 'Taste Not,' 146; Winthrop S. Hudson, 'A Time of Religious Ferment,' in Edwin S. Gaustad, ed., *The Rise of Adventism; Religion and Society in Mid-Nineteenth-Century America* (New York: Harper & Row 1974), 4; Foster, *Errand of Mercy*, 179

23 Green, *Life and Times*, 107; *Christian Recorder* 1:8 (Oct. 1819), 284; Clemens, 'Taste Not,' 146; Richard E. Ruggle, 'Itinerant Clergy in Upper Canada,' *JCCHS* 27:2 (Oct. 1985), 64

24 Fingard, '"Grapes in the Wilderness,"' 14; W.P. MacDonald in *The Catholic*, Dec. 1830, quoted in Stewart D. Gill, 'The Sword in the Bishop's Hand: Father William Peter MacDonald, a Scottish Defender of the Catholic Faith in Upper Canada,' *CCHA Study Sessions* 50 (1983), 447

25 *Christian Guardian*, 30 Nov. 1836

26 *Witness of Truth* 4:8 (1849), 175; Willson, *Impressions of the Mind*, 16

27 *A Letter to the Congregation of St. James' Church, York, U. Canada, occasioned by the Hon. John Elmsley's Publication of the Bp. of Strasbourg's Observations on the 6th Chapter of St. John's Gospel* (York: Stanton 1834)

28 George to Egerton Ryerson, 6 Apr. 1832, UCA, Egerton Ryerson Papers; Carroll, *Case*, 4:243-4, 259, 321, 335, 356

29 Gerald M. Craig, ed., *Early Travellers in the Canadas, 1791–1867* (Toronto: Macmillan 1955), xxxi, 213; Andrew Reed and James Matheson, *A Narrative of the Visit to the American Churches, by the Deputation from the Congregational Union of England and Wales*, 2d ed. (London: Jackson and Watford 1836), 2:246, 267; Waddilove, *Report and Correspondence ... 1844*, 90; (Darling), *Sketches of Canadian Life*, 163; *Records of ... Osler*, 141; Skelton, *A Man Austere*, 175

30 Green, *Life and Times*, 31-2; Torry, *Autobiography*, 169; *Records of ... Osler*, 36; Wilkie, *Sketches*, 163

CHAPTER 8 *Echoes of Europe*

1 Desmond Bowen, *Paul Cardinal Cullen and the Shaping of Modern Irish Catholicism* (Waterloo, Ont.: Wilfrid Laurier University Press 1983), passim; Emmet Larkin, 'The Devotional Revolution in Ireland, 1850–75,' *American Historical Review* 77:3 (June 1972), 636

2 Michael Power, circular to clergy, 31 Dec. 1846, AAT, LBOI.166; J.J. Lynch, letter on occasion of *ad limina* visit, 1879, LBOI.275; Murray W. Nicolson, 'The Catholic Church and the Irish in Victorian Toronto' (PH D thesis, University of Guelph 1980), 108; Gerald J. Stortz, 'John Joseph Lynch, Archbishop of Toronto: A Biographical Study of Religious, Political and Social Commitment' (PH D thesis, University of Guelph 1980), 12; Power, circular, 1846; 'l'esprit de l'independance et d'insubordination,' Power to Joseph Signay, 13 Jan. 1847, LBO2.295; Charbonnel to Charles Juhel, 27 Dec. 1858, LBO2.019; Franklin A. Walker, *Catholic Education and Politics in Upper Canada* (Toronto: Dent 1955), 53; Power to Jean-Philipp Roothan, general of the Society of Jesus, 2 Nov. 1842; Roothan to Power, n.d., but received at the beginning of June 1843; last two in AAT

3 Quoted in J.G. Hanley, 'Marian Devotion in the Diocese of Kingston: The Early Days,' *CCHA Report* 21 (1954), 20. The significance of parish missions in the United States is discussed in Jay P. Dolan, *Catholic Revivalism: The American Experience, 1830–1900* (Notre Dame, Ind.: University of Notre Dame Press 1978).

4 Christopher F. Headon, 'The Influence of the Oxford Movement upon the Church of

England in Eastern and Central Canada' (PH D thesis, McGill University 1974), 61ff; D.F. Cook, 'A Survey of Hymnody in the Church of England in Eastern Canada to 1909,' *JCCHS* 7:3 (Sept. 1965), 41–2; S.W. Horrall, 'The Clergy and the Election of Bishop Cronyn,' *OH* 58:4 (Dec. 1966), 218; J.L.H. Henderson, *John Strachan, 1778–1867* (Toronto: University of Toronto Press 1969), 59; Oliver R. Osmond, 'The Churchmanship of John Strachan,' *JCCHS* 16:3 (Sept. 1974), 46–59; John Kenyon, 'The Influence of the Oxford Movement upon the Church of England in Upper Canada,' *OH* 51 (1959), 79–94

5 Alan W.G. Stephenson, *The First Lambeth Conference, 1867* (London: SPCK 1967), 150

6 Christopher F. Headon, 'Developments in Canadian Anglican Worship in Eastern and Central Canada, 1840–1868,' *JCCHS* 17:2 (June 1975), 30, 34; Oliver R. Osmond, 'Anglican Parish Church Worship in the Diocese of Toronto from the Consecration of John Strachan to the Outbreak of the Second World War, 1839–1939' class essay for the Toronto School of Theology

7 R. McGill to W. Morris, 27 Jan. 1845, QUA, William Morris Papers; R.F. Burns, *Life and Times of the Rev. R. Burns, D.D., Toronto* (Toronto: James Campbell and Co. 1871), 194–6, 211; C. Glenn Lucas, 'Presbyterianism in Carleton County to 1867,' 150–2

8 A.P. Stanley, *The Life and Correspondence of Thomas Arnold* (London: Ward, Lock & Co. 1844), 2:187; Harold J. Laski, *Studies in the Problem of Sovereignty* (New Haven: Yale University Press 1917), 263–4

9 65,203 in 1842, 258,151 in 1861

10 This is the thesis of Nicolson, 'The Catholic Church and the Irish,' and of Brian P. Clarke, '"To Bribe the Porters of Heaven": Poverty, Salvation, and the Saint Vincent de Paul Society in Victorian Toronto, 1850–1890,' *CSCH Papers*, 1983, 97–115.

11 The relevance of Anglo-Catholicism to the colonial situation is discussed in Elliott Rose, 'The Castle Builders: High Anglican Hopes of the Frontier in the Mid-Nineteenth Century,' *CSCH Papers*, 1975, 42–63.

12 QUA, Presbyterian Church Papers, box 4, file 35; Hugh Scobie to Morris, 2 Nov. 1843, William Morris Papers; Ian Rennie, 'The Free Church and the Relations of Church and State in Canada, 1844–1854' (MA thesis, University of Toronto 1954), 49–59

13 Cecil J. Houston and William J. Smyth, *The Sash Canada Wore: The Social Geography of the Orange Order in Canada* (Toronto: University of Toronto Press 1980), 4; Power, pastoral address for Lent, 2 Feb. 1846, LBO1.146; Moir, *Enduring Witness*, 155

14 Alan L. Hayes, 'The Struggle for the Rights of the Laity in the Diocese of Toronto, 1850–1879,' *JCCHS* 26:1 (Apr. 1984), 5-17; Benjamin Cronyn, *Bishop of Huron's Objections to the theological teaching of Trinity College as now set forth in the letters of Provost Whitaker, published with the authority of the Corporation of Trinity College* (London 1862)

15 Robert Choquette, *L'Eglise catholique dans l'Ontario français du dix-neuvième siècle* (Ottawa: Editions de l'Université d'Ottawa 1984), 175–6

16 But 'Little Willy' Jones wore a white cotton gown on the Ancaster circuit (Carroll, *Case*, 2:225), and in 1829 the noted, if eccentric, evangelist Lorenzo Dow was observed at a camp meeting in 'a long white surplice over all, without pockets or buttons' (Carroll, *Past and Present*, 140). L.E. Elliott-Binns, *Religion in the Victorian Era*, 2d ed. (London: Lutterworth 1946), 110–11

17 *The Wesleyan* (Toronto), 26 Jan. 1842; Green, *Life and Times*, 298

18 *Christian Guardian*, 21 May 1845, 122; 21 Jan. 1846, 54; 6 May 1846, 114; 21 May 1845, 121; 'To the official and other members of the Wesleyan Methodist Church in Canada assembled at the Quarterly Meetings,' circular of conference, 19 Nov. 1846, UCA, Methodist Union Papers, Methodist Reunion 1847–8, Missionary Operations; Minutes of the Methodist Missionary Society, 14 Sept. 1846, UCA micro D6.4 57

19 *Gospel Tribune* 2:1 (May 1855), 16, on Presbyterian union; 1:2 (June 1854), 47, on open communion; 1:3 (July 1854), 78–9, on the YMCA; 3:12 (Apr. 1857), 326, on co-education; Richard West, *Christian Union in Canada: Its Desirableness, Possibility, and Extent* (Toronto: W.C. Chewett and Co. 1865), 9–10; John 17:21 (KJV)

20 Green, *Life and Times*, 395; for statements pro and con on the relative importance of philosophical idealism and historical criticism in Canada, A.B. McKillop, *A Disciplined Intelligence: Critical Inquiry and Canadian Thought in the Victorian Era* (Montreal: McGill-Queen's University Press 1979), 206, and Michael Gauvreau, 'The Taming of History: Reflections on the Canadian Methodist Encounter with Biblical Criticism, 1830-1900,' *CHR* 65:3 (Sept. 1984), 336

21 *Ecclesiastical and Missionary Record*, Dec. 1848, 18; D.C. Masters, 'Patterns of Thought in Anglican Colleges in the Nineteenth Century,' *JCCHS* 6:4 (Dec. 1969), 65

22 *The Banner*, 6 Oct. 1843, 30; Sydney E. Ahlstrom, 'The Scottish Philosophy and American Theology,' *Church History* 24 (1955), 257–72; Nathanael Burwash, *The History of Victoria College* (Toronto: Victoria College Press 1927), 76; Bethune, *Memoir of the Right Reverend John Strachan*, 192; McKillop, *A Disciplined Intelligence*, 33; Masters, 'Patterns of Thought,' 63

23 Carl Berger, *Science, God, and Nature in Victorian Canada* (Toronto: University of Toronto Press 1985), 3–27, 56–60; McKillop, *A Disciplined Intelligence*, 102–3

24 Daniel Wilson, quoted in Clifford Holland, 'First Canadian Critics of Darwin,' *Queen's Quarterly* 88:1 (spring 1981), 103; Nathanael Burwash, *Manual of Christian Theology on the Inductive Method* (London: Horace Marshall and Son 1900), 1:v-vi; Marguerite Van Die, 'Nathanael Burwash: A Study in Revivalist Canadian Culture, 1839–1918' (PH D thesis, University of Western Ontario 1987), 115, 222; S.S. Nelles, cited freely in C.B. Sissons, *A History of Victoria University* (Toronto: University of Toronto Press 1952), 95; Nathanael Burwash, manuscript autobiography, chapter 10, UCA, Burwash Papers, file 619

CHAPTER 9 *Affairs of State*

1 Morris to Lord Sydenham, 2 Oct. 1840, QUA, William Morris Papers
2 F.H. Armstrong, 'The York Riots of March 23, 1832,' *OH* 55:2 (June 1963), 67
3 Robert McGill to Robert Burns, 10 Oct. 1837, reprinted in *UCA Bulletin* 21
   (1969–70), 19; E.C. Kyte, 'Journal of the Honourable William Morris's Mission
   to England in the Year 1837,' *OH* 30 (1934), 239; *Proceedings of the General
   Assembly of the Free Church of Scotland*, May 1843, quoted in Hugh Watt,
   Thomas Chalmers and the Disruption (Edinburgh: Thomas Nelson and Sons 1943),
   306
4 Burns, *Life and Times of the Rev. R. Burns*, 385; William Gregg, *Short History of the
   Presbyterian Church in the Dominion of Canada from the Earliest to the Present
   Times* (Toronto 1892), 130–1; Richard W. Vaudry, 'Peter Brown, the Toronto *Banner* and the Evangelical Mind in Victorian Canada,' *OH* 77:1 (Mar. 1985), 7–8
5 Walter Pitman, *The Baptists and Public Affairs in the Province of Canada, 1840–1867*
   (New York: Arno 1980), 36; *Canadian Independent* 12:4 (Oct. 1865), 133; Presbyterian Church of Canada in Connection with the Church of Scotland, *Minutes of
   Synod, 1843* (Toronto: Scobie & Balfour 1849), 118
6 Green, *Life and Times*, 385
7 Cornish, *Cyclopaedia of Methodism in Canada* 1:32; Carroll, *Case*, 4:434, 437, 484
8 Egerton Ryerson, *The Story of My Life*, ed. J. George Hodgins (Toronto: William
   Briggs 1883), 23. He made this point on the occasion of the restoration of the
   imperial grant in 1847.
9 For a detailed examination of the course of this controversy, see Wilson, *Clergy
   Reserves: A Canadian Mortmain* and, for the various issues discussed in this
   chapter, John S. Moir, *Church and State in Canada West, 1841–1867* (Toronto:
   University of Toronto Press 1959).
10 *Journals of the Legislative Assembly*, 1849, app. JJJJ
11 *Christian Observer*, Apr. 1851, quoted in Pitman, *Baptists and Public Affairs*, 86
12 C.B. Sissons, *Egerton Ryerson: His Life and Letters* 2 (Toronto: Clarke Irwin 1947), 33
13 Laurence K. Shook, *Catholic Post-Secondary Education in English-Speaking Canada:
   A History* (Toronto: University of Toronto Press 1971), 135
14 Wilson, *Clergy Reserves*, 216; Gregg, *Short History*, 115; Moir, 'The Upper Canadian Roots of Church Disestablishment,' 257; Green, *Life and Times*, 355
15 J. George Hodgins, ed., *Documentary History of Education in Upper Canada* (Toronto: Warwick Bros and Rutter 1894–1910), 10:129
16 Spragge, *Strachan Letter Book*, x
17 Kelly, *St. Paul's Parish*, 77
18 David Onn, 'Egerton Ryerson's Philosophy of Education: Something Borrowed or
   Something New?' *OH* 61:2 (June 1969), 77–86; Egerton Ryerson, *First Lessons
   in Christian Morals for Canadian Families and Schools* (Toronto: Copp, Clark 1871),
   10, 16, 46, 70–80, 60ff

19 Sissons, *Ryerson*, 2:116n
20 Walker, *Catholic Education and Politics in Upper Canada*, 13; Charbonnel to Ryerson, 24 Mar. 1852, AAT, LB02.317
21 To the Warden of the London District Council, Miscellaneous Proudfoot Papers, University of Western Ontario, quoted in Stewart D. Gill, 'The Canadianization of the Scottish Church: The Reverend William Proudfoot and the Canadian Frontier, 1832–1851,' 12, *CSCH Papers*, 1982; Debates of Legislative Council, 1841, quoted in Hodgins, *Documentary History*, 4:32
22 *Church*, 28 July 1845; *Church Chronicle*, 3:3 (June 1865), 37; *Seven Letters on the Non-Religious School System of Canada and the United States* (Toronto: Henry Rowsell 1853), quoted in Alison L. Prentice and Susan E. Houston, eds., *Family, School and Society in Nineteenth-Century Canada* (Toronto: Oxford University Press 1975), 133
23 In 1846 the Congregation for the Propagation of the Faith declared non-sectarian religion a danger to youth: Watson Kirkconnell, 'Education,' in George W. Brown, ed., *Canada* (Berkeley: University of California Press 1954) 437.
24 Charbonnel Lenten pastoral, 1857, quoted in Nicolson, 'The Catholic Church and the Irish,' 376; Katz, *The People of Hamilton*, 39
25 22 Feb. 1867
26 Prentice and Houston, *Family, School and Society*, 21; Walker, *Catholic Education and Politics*, 313
27 H.C. McKeown, *The Life and Labours of the Most Rev. John Joseph Lynch, D.D., First Archbishop of Toronto* (Toronto: J.A. Sadlier 1886), 308; R.A. Billington, *The Protestant Crusade, 1800–1860* (New York: Macmillan 1938), 156; Nicolson, 'The Catholic Church and the Irish,' 398–401
28 J.A. Raftis, 'Changing Characteristics of the Catholic Church,' in John Webster Grant, ed., *The Churches and the Canadian Experience* (Toronto: Ryerson Press 1963), 89; Nicolson, 'The Catholic Church and the Irish,' 415–16
29 Egerton Ryerson, quoted in J.L.H. Henderson, 'The Abominable Incubus: The Church as by Law Established,' *JCCHS* 11:3 (Sept. 1969), 65
30 *Church Chronicle*, 1 Dec. 1867; William Westfall, 'Order and Experience: Patterns of Religious Metaphor in Early Nineteenth-Century Upper Canada,' *Journal of Canadian Studies* (spring 1985), 5–24

CHAPTER 10 *Mission Accomplished*

1 The Anglican figures were extracted by Robert Black from church society reports and synod journals; those for the Wesleyans are taken from Cornish, *Cyclopaedia of Canadian Methodism*, 1:813; on Anglican midweek services, Osmond, 'Anglican Parish Church Worship in the Diocese of Toronto,' passim; Presbyterian Church of Canada, *Minutes of Synod*, 1860, 49
2 Murray G. Ross, *The Y.M.C.A. in Canada: The Chronicle of a Century* (Toronto: Ryerson Press 1937), 15–16, 19

3 William E. de Villiers-Westfall, 'The Sacred and the Secular: Studies in the Cultural
   History of Protestant Ontario in the Victorian Period' (PH D thesis, University of
   Toronto 1976), 5–6, and passim
4 'Report of the Education Committee,' Canadian Wesleyan Methodist New Connexion
   Church, *Minutes of Conference*, 1865, 20; William H. Elgee, *The Social Teachings of the Canadian Churches: Protestant: The Early Period, before 1850* (Toronto:
   Ryerson Press 1964), 183; R.N. Grant, *Life of Rev. William Cochrane, D.D.*
   (Toronto: William Briggs 1899), 169
5 Marion V. Royce, 'Methodism and the Education of Women in Nineteenth Century
   Ontario,' *Atlantis* 3:2 (1978), 130–43; PAC, MG24, D16, Buchanan Papers, vol.
   116, 75548
6 Wallace, 'Reminiscences,' 199; Richard W. Vaudry, 'The Free Church in Canada,
   1844–1861' (PH D thesis, McGill University 1984), 237–8; R.P. Bowles in *On the
   Old Ontario Strand*, addresses at the centenary of Victoria University and the Burwash Memorial Lectures of the centennial year (Toronto: Victoria University
   1936), 158; Cornish, *Cyclopaedia of Canadian Methodism* 1:32; Albert Burnside,
   'The Canadian Wesleyan Methodist New Connexion Church, 1841–1874,' typescript in UCA, 165; J. Edwin Orr, *The Fervent Prayer* (Chicago: Moody 1974), 2–3;
   G. Smellie, *Memoir of the Rev. John Bayne, D.D., of Galt* (Toronto: James
   Campbell and Sons 1871), 47; J.A. Johnston, 'Factors in the Formation of the Presbyterian Church in Canada' (PH D thesis, McGill University 1955), 68; J.A. Raftis,
   'Changing Characteristics of the Catholic Church,' in J.W. Grant, *The Churches and
   the Canadian Experience*, 86
7 F.W. Collaton, 'The Story of Algoma, 1830–1939,' *JCCHS* 2:2 (Apr. 1954), 21;
   'Third Annual Report of Mission to Lumbermen,' 1871, QUA, Presbyterian Church
   Papers, file 190; Alexis de Barbézieux, OFM Cap., *Histoire de la province ecclésias-
   tique d'Ottawa et de la Colonisation dans la vallée de l'Ottawa* (Ottawa: La Cie
   d'Imprimerie d'Ottawa 1897), 1:233; Sally W. Weaver, 'Six Nations of the Grand
   River, Ontario,' in *Handbook of North American Indians*, 15:530
8 Howard Law, '"Self-Reliance Is the True Road to Independence": Ideology and the
   Ex-Slaves in Buxton and Chatham,' *OH* 77:2 (June 1985), 107–22; James K.
   Lewis, 'Religious Nature of the Early Negro Migration to Canada and the Amherstburg Baptist Association,' *OH* 58:2 (June 1966), 117–32; Daniel Payne, *History
   of the African Methodist Episcopal Church* (Nashville: AME Sunday School Union
   Publishing House 1891), 128, 361–92
9 G.O. Stewart circularized the clergy of the projected diocese of Ontario for contribu-
   tions to a delegation requesting an appointment from England (*Church*, 16 Mar.
   1854). Robert McGill noted a similar feeling in the Niagara area that all professors at
   Queen's should be Scottish (to William Morris, 10 July 1840, QUA, William
   Morris Papers, box 1). Smith, 'Nineteenth Century Preaching,' 67; Spencer Ervin,
   The Political and Ecclesiastical History of the Anglican Church of Canada (Ambler,
   Pa.: Trinity 1967), 54; John S. Moir, 'The Canadianization of the Protestant

Churches,' *CHA Historical Papers, 1966*, 67

10 *Canadian Independent* 12:3 (Sept. 1865), 104; Ervin, *Political and Ecclesiastical History*, 84; various items under 'Correspondence 1870,' QUA, Presbyterian Church Papers, file 170

11 Ruggle, 'The Canadianization of the Church of England,' 84–5

12 *Presbyterian Record*, Oct. 1884, 256. The Sunday school of Knox Church, Toronto, made a contribution to foreign missions in 1849 (PAC, Buchanan Papers 75634), but in 1870 the Foreign Missionary Committee of the Kirk lamented that 'only one or two' congregations made annual contributions (QUA, Presbyterian Church Papers, file 170).

13 *Canadian Baptist*, 7 May 1863; Connolly to E.J. Horan, 3, 19 Oct., 9 Nov. 1866, AAK, DI2C42; J.W. Grant, 'Canadian Confederation and the Protestant Churches,' *Church History* 38:3 (Sept. 1969), 327–37; F.J. Wilson, 'Roman Catholics and the Confederation Movement' (MA thesis, Queen's University 1936, 64–5); Macdonald to Horan, 5, 23 Sept. 1865, AAK, DI5C36

14 *Christian Guardian*, 1 Jan. 1879

15 Rennie, 'The Free Church,' chapter 7; Burkhard Kiesekamp, 'Response to Disruption: Presbyterianism in Eastern Ontario, 1844,' *CSCH Papers*, 1967, 30–51

16 Katz, *The People of Hamilton*, 26

17 Alexis de Barbézieux, *Histoire*, I:iv, 244; Robert Choquette, *L'Ontario français historique* (Montreal: Editions Etudes-Vivantes 1980), 90; Alexis de Barbézieux, 'Une paroisse canadienne,' in Gaetan Vallières, ed., *L'Ontario français par les documents* (Montreal: Editions Etudes-Vivantes 1980), 117–19; J.A. Lenhard, 'German Catholics in Ontario,' *CCHA Report* 4 (1936–7), 41–5; James A. Wahl, 'Father Louis Funcken's Contribution to German Catholicism in Waterloo County, Ontario,' *CCHA Study Sessions* 50 (1983), 513–31. In 1871 Ontarians of French origin numbered 75,383, Roman Catholics 274,162.

18 *Gospel Tribune* I:2 (June 1854), 47. The most convenient summaries of early Baptist struggles to organize are still the articles of A.H. Newman and F. Tracy in *Baptist Year Book*, 1900, 73–112.

19 Cronmiller, *The Lutheran Church in Canada*, 109–19, 249–50; J. Henry Getz, ed., *A Century in Canada, 1864–1964* (Kitchener: Evangelical United Brethren Church 1964), 5–11

20 Carroll, *Case* 4:396; *Christian Guardian*, 15 Mar., 10 Apr. 1844; Waddilove, *Report and Correspondence ... 1844*, 271–2; Clark, *Church and Sect in Canada*, 308–13; Carl Ballstadt, Michael Peterman, and Elizabeth Hopkins, '"A Glorious Madness": Susanna Moodie and the Spiritualist Movement,' *Journal of Canadian Studies* 17:4 (winter 1982–3), 88–100; *Christian Guardian*, 16 and 23 Jan. 1867; *Canadian Independent* 12:4 (Oct. 1865), 131–2; Ernest R. Sandeen, *The Roots of American Fundamentalism: British and American Millenarianism, 1800–1930* (Chicago: University of Chicago Press 1970), 71

21 Stephen A. Speisman, *The Jews of Toronto: A History to 1937* (Toronto: McClelland

and Stewart 1979), chapters 1, 2; Louis A. Kurman, 'The Hamilton Jewish Community,' *Wentworth Bygones* 8 (1969), 8. The census of 1871 listed 1,088 Unitarians and 1,722 Universalists. The latter had peaked in 1851 with 2,684 adherents.

22 F. Keith Dalton, 'The Reverend William Arthur Johnson: Clergyman, Artist, Teacher, 1818–1880,' *JCCHS* 8:1 (Mar. 1966), 10; *Christian Guardian*, 14 Dec. 1864; W.D. McIntosh, *One Hundred Years in the Zorra Church* (Toronto: United Church Publishing House 1930), 79, 83; QUA, Presbyterian Church Papers, file 193; W.H. Pearson, *Recollections and Records of Toronto of Old, with References to Brantford, Kingston and Other Canadian Towns* (Toronto: William Briggs 1914), 268, 300; John Macdonald, 'Recollections of British Wesleyanism in Toronto from 1842 to the Union with the Canadian Methodists in 1848, and of St Andrew's Church (Presbyterian) from 1840 to the Disruption,' *Canadian Methodist Magazine* 29 (Feb. 1889), 329; James Nisbet, 'Diary of a Tour of Canada West, April–September, 1848, on behalf of the Canada Sabbath School Union, including a record of expenses and a draft report to the Union,' PAC, MG24, J25

23 *Canada Presbyterian Church Pulpit*, 1st series (Toronto 1871), 16–21; A. Osborne, M. Punshon, *Sketch of His Life with Sermons* (London 1871), 57, quoted in Smith, 'Nineteenth-Century Canadian Preaching,' 97

24 Peter George Bush, 'James Caughey, Phoebe and Walter Palmer and the Methodist Revival Experience in Canada West' (MA thesis, Queen's University 1985), 12, 83, 126; James Caughey, *Earnest Christianity Illustrated* (London: Charles H. Brown 1855), 404; *Christian Guardian*, 9 July 1856, and, for a positive assessment of the state of religion, especially revivals and camp meetings, 4 July 1866; Hopper, *Old-Time Primitive Methodism*, 124

25 Memorials of congregation and government employees to Synod, 1844, QUA, Presbyterian Church Papers, file 39; *Christian Guardian*, 2 Jan. 1867; Nathan H. Mair, *John Dougall (1816–1886) and His 'Montreal Witness'* (Montreal: Archives Committee of the Montreal and Ottawa Conference of the United Church of Canada 1985), 5; 'Circular by ministers and delegates of Congregational churches assembled in Montreal 15 July 1848,' Presbyterian Church Papers, file 35; Ruth E. Spence, *Prohibition in Canada* (Toronto: Dominion Alliance 1919), 92; Kelly, *St. Paul's Parish*, 108

26 Rennie, 'Spiritual Worship,' 61, 63, 85, 111, 133

27 S.S. Nelles, 'Introduction,' in Green, *Life and Times*, viii; Richard Carwardine, *Trans-Atlantic Revivalism*, 24; Neil Semple, '"The Nurture and Admonition of the Lord": Nineteenth-Century Canadian Methodist Response to "Childhood,"' *Histoire sociale/Social History* 27 (May 1981), 168, 172; Burwash, *History of Victoria College* 464–6; Samms, 'Revivalism,' 245

28 Charles Edwin Jones, *Perfectionist Persuasion: The Holiness Movement and American Methodism, 1867–1936* (Metuchen, NJ: Scarecrow 1974), 83; Melvin Easterday Dieter, *The Holiness Revival of the Nineteenth Century* (Metuchen, NJ: Scarecrow 1980), 27–8, 32

29 Fred Landon, 'The Anti-Slavery Society of Canada,' *OH* 48 (1956), 125–32
30 John Roaf, *Lectures on the Millennium* (Toronto 1844), 99, 160, 35. William E. de Villiers-Westfall points out in a more detailed analysis of these lectures ('The Sacred and the Secular,' 210–18) that Roaf was not an optimist in secular matters. Strictly speaking, Miller himself appears not to have been a premillennialist: Leonard I. Sweet, 'Millennialism in America: Recent Trends,' *Theological Studies* 40:3 (Sept. 1979), 522–3.
31 Minutes of the Beamsville Baptist Church, Baptist Archives, McMaster Divinity College; Egerton Ryerson, *Scriptural Rights of the Members of Christ's Visible Church* (Toronto: Brewer, McPhail 1854), especially at 14; Sissons, *Ryerson*, 2:288–99; on similar concerns in the United States after 1850, Robert E. Chiles, *Theological Transition in American Methodism, 1790–1935*, 56
32 Sissons, *Ryerson*, 2:252; S.S. Nelles, quoted by L. Smith in *On the Old Ontario Strand*, 130; Winthrop S. Hudson, 'The Interrelationships of Baptists in Canada and the United States,' *Foundations* 23:1 (Jan.-Mar. 1980), 28; Muir, 'Petticoats in the Pulpit,' 41

CHAPTER 11 *The Activist Temper*

1 *Canadian Church Magazine and Mission News* 15 (Sept. 1887), 360; Alexis de Barbézieux in Vallières, *L'Ontario français par les documents*, 117–19; W.H. Withrow, *Life in a Parsonage* (London: T. Woolner 1885), 44
2 Harry Manning, 'The Changing Mind-Set of Canadian Methodism, 1894–1925,' *Canadian Methodist Historical Society Papers* 1 (1978), 10; Roger W. Lynn and Elliott Wright, *The Big Little School: Sunday Child of American Protestantism* (New York: Harper and Row 1971), chapter 4; John Webster Grant, *George Pidgeon: A Biography* (Toronto: Ryerson Press 1962), 34–5
3 *Irish Canadian*, 2 Feb. 1883, 3; *Catholic Register*, 11 Jan., 8, 15 Feb. 1894
4 Wendy Mitchinson, 'Canadian Women and Church Missionary Societies in the Nineteenth Century: A Step Towards Independence,' *Atlantis* 2:2 (spring 1977), 57–75
5 J.S. McGivern, SJ, ed., *The Saint Vincent de Paul Society (Toronto) 1850–1975* (Toronto: Society of Saint Vincent de Paul 1975), passim; Speisman, *The Jews of Toronto*, 56–7
6 Stephen A. Speisman, 'Munificent Parsons and Municipal Parsimony: Voluntary vs Poor Relief in Nineteenth Century Toronto,' *OH* 65:1 (Mar. 1973), 41; B.E. Bull, 'City Mission Work,' *Canadian Methodist Magazine and Review* 37 (June 1893), 598–9, 583; J.F. McCurdy, ed., *Life and Work of D.J. Macdonnell* (Toronto: William Briggs 1897), 288–303
7 Ross, *The Y.M.C.A. in Canada*, passim
8 Wendy Mitchinson, 'The YWCA and Reform in the Nineteenth Century,' *Histoire sociale/Social History* 24 (Nov. 1979), 376; Mary Quayle Innis, *Unfold the Years: A History of the Young Women's Christian Association in Canada* (Toronto: McClelland and Stewart 1949), 15

9 Veronica Strong-Boag, in Susan Mann Trofimenkoff and Alison Prentice, eds., *The Neglected Majority: Essays in Canadian Women's History* (Toronto: McClelland and Stewart 1973), 89–90; T.R. Morrison, '"Their Proper Sphere": Feminism, the Family and Child-Centered Social Reform in Ontario, 1895–1900,' *OH* 68:1 (Mar. 1976), 154–9

10 John Fletcher Hurst, *The History of Methodism* 7 (New York: Eaton and Mains 1902), 84; Wesleyan Methodist Church of Canada, *Minutes of Conference* 43 (1866), 93; Walter E. Ellis, 'Gilboa to Ichabod: Social and Religious Factors in the Fundamentalist-Modernist Schism among Canadian Baptists, 1895–1934,' *CSCH Papers*, 1975, 16–17

11 *Toronto Daily Mail*, 9 Apr.–28 May 1891. This contest is analysed in greater detail by Margaret Prang in a forthcoming article.

12 *Knox College Monthly*, July 1892, 104; C.S. Clark, *Toronto the Good: A Social Study: The Queen City of Canada as It Is* (Montreal: The Toronto Publishing Co. 1898), 155; C. Pelham Mulvany, *Toronto Past and Present until 1882* (Toronto: W.E. Caiger 1884), 169; *Westminster*, Sept. 1896, 181–2; A.B. Hyde, *The Story of Methodism throughout the World* (Springfield, Mass.: Willey 1889), 799

13 *Acts and Proceedings of the General Assembly of the Presbyterian Church in Canada*, 21st (1895), 70; 35th (1909), 78; Lynn and Wright, *The Big Little School*, 82–3; Dorland, *Quakers in Canada*, 264; Butchart, *Disciples of Christ in Canada*, 196, 245; Foulds, *Universalists in Ontario*, 111

14 Nicolson, 'The Catholic Church and the Irish,' 108; Stephenson, *The First Lambeth Conference*, 200; Albright, *History of the Protestant Episcopal Church*, 246; *Canadian Church Magazine and Mission News* 1 (July 1886), 1, 36

15 According to the census of 1901 the population of Ontario was 2,182,947, the seating capacity of its churches 2,203,869. The fullest account of Presbyterian union is Johnston, 'Formation of the Presbyterian Church in Canada'; of Methodist union, J. Warren Caldwell, 'The Unification of Methodism in Canada, 1865–1884,' *UCA Bulletin* 19 (1967), 3–61.

16 *Christian Guardian*, 20 Feb. 1867, 20; Albert Carman, 'The Methodist Church,' in *Centennial of Canadian Methodism*, 249

17 W. Ormiston to Moderator of Synod of Church of Scotland, 18 Apr. 1870, QUA, Presbyterian Church Papers, box 15, file 170; Caldwell, 'Unification of Canadian Methodism,' 28; *Proceedings of the Provincial Synod of Canada*, 1886, 84; for the formation at London of the Canadian Church Union to promote national unification, *Canadian Church Magazine and Mission News* 10 (Apr. 1887), 243

18 *Evangelical Churchman*, 18 May 1876, 4; Margaret Prang, 'The Evolution of a Victorian Liberal,' in Ontario Historical Society, *Profile of a Province: Studies in the History of Ontario* (Toronto: OHS 1967), 130–1; Reginald Stackhouse, 'Sam Blake: A Man for Then and Now,' *Insight* (bulletin of Wycliffe College), 1978, 2–3

19 Green, *Life and Times*, 441

20 *Annual Report of the Woman's Foreign Misionary Society of the Presbyterian Church in Canada (Western Section)* 2 (1878), 11. Cecilia Jeffrey, secretary of the WFMS, made several tours of inspection of the Presbyterian Indian missions in the west (*Acts and Proceedings of the General Assembly of the Presbyterian Church in Canada* 16 (1898), 180). According to the *Westminster* (June 1896, 62–3), a provision that the Methodist WMS should be under the direction of the missionary society had become a dead letter.

21 John D. Thomas, 'Servants of the Church: Canadian Methodist Deaconess Work, 1890–1926,' *CHR* 65:3 (Sept. 1984), 381

22 Sabbath School Association of Ontario, Minutes, 1887–1903, UCA; Ronald George Sawatsky, '"Looking for that Blessed Hope": The Roots of Fundamentalism in Canada, 1878–1920' (PH D thesis, University of Toronto 1985), 227–9; W.C. Langdon, 'The Early Story of the Confederation of the Y.M.C.A.S,' in *Y.M.C.A. Year Book*, 1888, 57, quoted in Ross, *The Y.M.C.A. in Canada*, 34

23 *Westminster*, June 1896, 43. Compare Filshie, 'Sacred Harmonies,' 305.

24 *Canadian Methodist Magazine* 21 (Jan. 1885), 75–8; clipping noted as excerpted from *Montreal Star*, under dateline 21 Feb. 1888, in UCA, John E. Hunter, Personal Papers, scrapbook of evangelistic meetings held jointly with Rev. Hugh Thomas Crossley; Pearson, *Recollections and Records of Toronto of Old*, 244-5

25 R.G. Murison, 'The Early Worship of the Church,' *Knox College Monthly*, Dec. 1895, 309; Veronica Strong-Boag, ed., *A Woman with a Purpose: The Diaries of Elizabeth Smith* (Toronto: University of Toronto Press 1980), 53; Arie Korteveig, 'Dr J.R. Jaques and Albert University, 1875–1885,' *Canadian Methodist Historical Society Papers* 4 (1984), 9, citing *Canada Christian Advocate*, 5 Mar. 1879

26 Rennie, 'Spiritual Worship,' 208; John Thompson, 'The Home: Women's Work in the Church,' *Knox College Monthly*, Sept. 1892, 232; E.R. Fitch, *The Baptists in Canada: A History of their Progress and Achievements* (Toronto: Standard 1911), 171; Neil Semple, 'The Impact of Urbanization on the Methodist Church in Central Canada, 1854–1884' (PH D thesis, University of Toronto 1979), 188ff. In 1900, the Toronto Conference defeated a motion to forbid invitations from circuits (*Globe*, 16 June 1900). J.C. Wilson, a minister who served mostly on rural circuits, noted in his journal only one instance when he was sent to a circuit that had not invited him, and on that occasion conference officials felt it necessary to visit the circuit to explain their reasons. This journal is in the possession of the Reverend David W. Morris of Waterloo, Ontario, who kindly made it available to me.

27 *Irish Canadian* 20:5 (2 Feb. 1882), 3; *Catholic Register* 2:4 (25 Jan. 1894), 4; for a complaint about the musical quality of services, *Catholic Register* 8:50 (13 Dec. 1900), 4; Choquette, *L'Eglise catholique dans l'Ontario français*, 216–19; Lynch to A.D. Cavanagh, 30 June 1887, AAT, LB05.171; William Perkins Bull, *From Macdonell to McGuigan* (Toronto: The Perkins Bull Foundation 1939), 340–3

28 Semple, '"Nurture and Admonition of the Lord,"' 159–62; Manning, 'Changing Mind-Set of Canadian Methodism,' 5; Ross, *The Y.M.C.A. in Canada*, 168–9

CHAPTER 12   *The Beckoning Vision*

1 William Westfall, 'The Dominion of the Lord: An Introduction to the Cultural History of Protestant Ontario in the Victorian Period,' *Queen's Quarterly* 83:1 (spring 1976), 60

2 *Home and Foreign Record of the Canada Presbyterian Church 1:1* (Nov. 1861), 2–3; 1:2 (Dec. 1861), 29–30

3 Ross, *The Y.M.C.A. in Canada*, 49; Alvyn J. Austin, *Saving China: Canadian Missionaries in the Middle Kingdom, 1888–1959* (Toronto: University of Toronto Press 1986), 67–9, 76; *Missionary Outlook*, Oct. 1900, 222; Apr. 1901, 92; Stephen Neill, *A History of Christian Missions* (Harmondsworth: Penguin 1964), 459. The SIM later merged with the Andes Evangelical Mission to form the Society of International Missionaries.

4 C.H. Mockridge, *The Bishops of the Church of England in Canada and Newfoundland* (Toronto: F.N.W. Brown 1896), 372; *Canadian Church Magazine and Mission News* 18 (Dec. 1887), 437; James Allen, *Missions in New Ontario* (Toronto: Department of Missionary Literature of the Methodist Church 1906), 1–6; C.W. Gordon, *The Life of James Robertson* (Toronto: Westminster 1909), passim

5 *Ocean to Ocean* (Toronto: J. Campbell 1873), 345

6 *Toronto Daily Mail*, 23 Mar. 1883; *Canada Presbyterian*, 4 Apr. 1883, 221; *Discipline of the Methodist Church*, 1886, para. 35

7 Peter B. Waite, 'Sir Oliver Mowat's Canada: Reflections on an Un-Victorian Society,' in Swainson, *Oliver Mowat's Ontario*, 12–32

8 *Globe*, 9 May 1883; Christopher Armstrong and H.V. Nelles, *The Revenge of the Methodist Bicycle Company: Sunday Streetcars and Municipal Reform in Toronto, 1888–1897* (Toronto: Peter Martin Associates 1977). The index contains sixteen references to Caven. That the Lord's Day Act failed to satisfy many of the desires of evangelicals is pointed out in Paul Laverdure, 'Sunday Secularism? The Lord's Day Debates of 1906,' *CSCH Papers*, 1986, 85–107.

9 *Canada Presbyterian*, 14 Feb. 1883, 104; W.L. Grant and Frederick Hamilton, *Principal Grant* (Toronto: Morang and Co. 1904), 381–92; McCurdy, *Life and Work of D.J. Macdonnell*, 213, 215. The fullest account of the prohibition movement is Spence, *Prohibition in Canada*.

10 W.H. Withrow, 'Legal Prohibition of the Liquor Traffic: The Duty of the Hour,' *Canadian Methodist Magazine* 6 (July 1877), 69; Edward Barrass, 'Our City Churches,' *Canadian Methodist Magazine and Review* 38 (Sept. 1893), 259; Toronto Conference, Methodist Church, *Minutes*, 1895, 88

11 Richard Allen, 'The Background of the Social Gospel in Canada,' in Richard Allen, ed., *The Social Gospel in Canada*, National Museums of Canada History Division Paper no. 9 (Ottawa: National Museums of Canada 1975), 15–16; *Mail and Empire*, 14 May 1897; Methodist General Conference, *Minutes* 4 (1894), 300

12 Ramsay Cook, *The Regenerators: Social Criticism in Late Victorian English Canada*

(Toronto: University of Toronto Press 1985), 105–22; S.S. Craig, 'The Church and the Money System,' *Knox College Monthly*, Jan. 1896, 371–81; *Canada Presbyterian*, 10 Jan. 1885, 25; A.S. Ross in *Knox College Monthly*, Jan. 1896, 387; John S. Moir in Jerald K. Zeman, ed., *Baptists in Canada: Search for Identity amidst Diversity* (Burlington, Ont.: Welch 1980), 150–1; *Knox College Monthly*, May 1892, 8–9

13 These groups are discussed in detail in Gene Howard Homel, '"Fading Beams of the Nineteenth Century": Radicalism and Early Socialism in Canada's 1890s,' *Labour/Le Travailleur* 5 (spring 1980), 7–32.

14 'The Woman Question,' *Canadian Methodist Magazine* 17 (June 1883), 559

15 John Thompson, 'The Home: Women's Work in the Church,' 238; *Canada Presbyterian*, 31 Oct. 1879, 1; *Westminster*, June 1896, 25; Aug. 1896, 101; David Macleod, 'A Live Vaccine: The YMCA and Male Adolescence in the United States and Canada, 1870–1920,' *Histoire sociale/Social History* 21 (May 1978), 9; Carol Lee Bacchi, *Liberation Deferred? The Ideas of the English Canadian Suffragists, 1877–1918* (Toronto: University of Toronto Press 1983), 66; William H. Magney, 'The Methodist Church and the National Gospel, 1884–1914,' *UCA Bulletin* 20 (1968), 61

16 D.C. Masters, *The Rise of Toronto, 1850–1890* (Toronto: University of Toronto Press 1947), 139–40; Macdonald, 'British Wesleyanism in Toronto,' 233–4

17 Grant, *George Pidgeon*, 31

18 *Montreal Daily Witness*, Evangelical Alliance extra, Oct. 1874, 40–5; T.R. Millman, 'The Conference on Christian Unity, Toronto, 1889,' *Canadian Journal of Theology* 3:3 (July 1967), 165–74

19 S.G. Phillips, *The Need of the World* (Toronto: William Briggs 1882), 95–7; *Canada Presbyterian*, 18 Jan. 1888, 56; Richard Ruggle, 'Herbert Symonds and Christian Unity,' *JCCHS* 18:2, 3 (June–Sept. 1976), 53–83; Alfred Gandier, 'Church Union,' *The Theologue* 10:4 (Mar. 1899), 114

20 Clark, *Church and Sect in Canada*, chapter 8; Semple, 'Impact of Urbanization on the Methodist Church,' especially chapters 5, 6; Bacchi, *Liberation Deferred?* 59; Cook, *The Regenerators*, 4

21 Neil Semple, 'The Impact of Urbanization on the Methodist Church of Canada, 1854–1884,' *CSCH Papers*, 1976, 52–3; Bush, 'The Methodist Revival Experience,' 138; Phyllis D. Airhart, 'The Eclipse of Revivalist Spirituality: The Transformation of Canadian Methodist Piety, 1884–1925' (PH D thesis, University of Chicago 1985), chapter 5. That professional evangelists never made good their promises to deliver increased membership is argued in William G. McLaughlin Jr, *Modern Revivalism: Charles Grandison Finney to Billy Graham* (New York: Ronald 1959), passim.

22 Sissons, *Ryerson*, 2:638; Clark, *Toronto the Good*, 98–9; Ralph C. Horner, *Ralph C. Horner, Evangelist: Reminiscences from his own pen, also reports of five typical sermons* (Brockville: Standard Church Book Room n.d.), 34

23 *Globe*, 7 Feb. 1872; 5 May 1896; Reed and Matheson, *A Narrative of the Visit to the*

American Churches 2:246; Henry Scadding and J.George Hodgins, *Jubilee of the Diocese of Toronto 1839–1889* (Toronto: Diocese of Toronto 1890), 79, 76. I have taken this analysis of the 1896 *Globe* figures from Peter F.M. Hanlon, 'Moral Order and the Influence of Social Christianity in an Industrial City, 1890–1899: A Social Profile of the Protestant Lay Leaders of Three Hamilton Churches, Centenary Methodist, Central Presbyterian and Christ Church Cathedral' (TH M thesis, McMaster University 1984), 6n.

24 Clark, *Toronto the Good*, 7; Pearson, *Toronto of Old*, 234

25 Cook, *The Regenerators*, 6; Gauvreau, 'The Taming of History,' 334–5

26 Gaston Carrière, OMI, *Le voyageur du Bon Dieu: Le Père Jean-Marie Nedelec, omi (1834–1896)* (Ottawa: Rayonnement 1961), passim; Stortz, 'John Joseph Lynch,' 210–15; J.R. Teefy, ed, *Jubilee Volume, 1842–1892, The Archdiocese of Toronto and Archbishop Walsh* (Toronto: George T. Dixon 1892), xvii; Lynch to P.J. McCabe, 31 Dec. 1887, AAT, LB05.258; Choquette, *L'Eglise catholique dans l'Ontario français*, 217–18; *Irish Canadian* 20:2 (12 Jan. 1882)

27 Lynch to Archbishop Gibbons, 23 Mar. 1887, AAT, Letterbook 2

28 Stortz, 'Lynch,' 90, 79, 116; Armstrong and Nelles, *Revenge of the Methodist Bicycle Company*, 117; *Catholic Weekly Review* 5:44 (12 Dec. 1891); *Catholic Register*, 13 Dec. 1900, 4

29 Murray W. Nicolson, '"Six Days Shalt Thou Labour": The Catholic Church and the Irish Worker in Victorian Toronto,' paper presented to CHA Vancouver 1983, 22–32; Jeanne R. Beck, 'Henry Somerville and Catholic Social Thought' (PH D thesis, McMaster University 1977), passim

30 Despite the title of the article, this is the general conclusion of M.G. Decarie in 'Paved with Good Intentions: The Prohibitionists' Road to Racism in Ontario,' *OH* 66:1 (Mar. 1984), 18.

31 Marcus W. Hansen, *The Immigrant in American History* (Cambridge, Mass.: Harvard University Press 1940), 111; Nicolson, 'The Catholic Church and the Irish,' 31, 173, 230, 444–6; *Catholic Register* 3:8 (21 Feb. 1895); 1:2 (12 Jan. 1893)

32 *Catholic Register*, 4 Jan. 1894; T.W. Anglin, 'The Life and Times of the Most Rev. John Joseph Lynch,' in Teefy, *Jubilee Volume*, 186; AAK, FI7ED28; Nicolson, '"Six Days Shalt Thou Labour,"' 18; John S. Moir, 'The Problems of a Double Minority: Some Reflections on the Development of the English-Speaking Catholic Church in Canada in the Nineteenth Century,' *Histoire sociale/Social History* 7 (Apr. 1971), 53–67; Clarke, '"To Bribe the Porters of Heaven,"' 111

33 *Rouge et Noir* 7:1 (Feb. 1886) 4–5; 7:6 (Dec. 1886) 11; 7:1 (Feb. 1886) 17; 7:2 (Mar. 1886) 5; 7:3 (June 1886), 3–4; Edward Pulker, *We Stand on Their Shoulders: The Growth of Social Concern in Canadian Anglicanism* (Toronto: Anglican Book Centre 1986), 25; *A Brief History of the Sisterhood of Saint John the Divine, Toronto and Willowdale, Ontario, 1884–1970* (no publishing details; copy in Trinity College Library, Toronto), 7

CHAPTER 13 *Strains in the Fabric*

1 Leroy Edwin Froom, *The Prophetic Faith of Our Fathers: The Historical Development of Prophetic Interpretation* 3 (Washington: Review and Herald 1949), 228, 251; *Catholic Register* 1:2 (12 Jan. 1893); Gerald J. Stortz, 'Archbishop John Joseph Lynch and the Anglicans of Toronto, 1860–1888,' *JCCHS* 27:1 (Apr. 1985), 7, 9; Mark McGowan, '"We Endure What We Cannot Cure": John Joseph Lynch and Roman Catholic-Protestant Relations in Toronto, 1864–1875; Frustrated Attempts at Peaceful Coexistence,' *CSCH Papers*, 1984, 89–111; for a catalogue of anti-Catholic arguments, J.R. Miller 'Anti-Catholic Thought in Victorian Canada,' *CHR* 66:4 (Dec. 1985), 474–94
2 Mark A. Galvin, 'The Jubilee Riots in Toronto, 1875,' *CCHA Report* 26 (1959), 93–107; J.R. Miller, *Equal Rights: The Jesuits' Estates Act Controversy* (Montreal: McGill-Queen's University Press 1979), 96–111; James T. Watt, 'Anti-Catholicism in Ontario Politics: The Role of the Protestant Protective Association in the 1894 Election,' *OH* 59:1 (Mar. 1967), 57–67
3 Franklin A., Walker, *Catholic Education and Politics in Ontario* (Toronto: Nelson 1964), 111
4 Hereward Senior, 'Orangeism in Ontario Politics, 1872–1896,' in Swainson, *Oliver Mowat's Ontario*, 149; A. Burnside, 'The Bible Christians in Canada, 1832–1884' (TH D thesis, Victoria University 1969), 317; Albert Carman, 'The Church's Working Doctrines,' *Canadian Methodist Magazine* 28 (July 1888), 52; Alfred Gandier, 'Church Union,' 112; 'They never did, and they never will, act fairly by us': *Catholic Register* 2:3 (18 Jan. 1894); *Christian Guardian*, 13 Apr. 1870, 58
5 B.F. Austin, 'Protestant Girls in Roman Convent Schools,' *Canadian Methodist Magazine* 27 (Feb. 1888), 181; Choquette, *L'Ontario français historique*, 134; *A Brief View of the State of the Catholic Church in Upper Canada, showing the evil results of an undue predominance of the French foreign element in the administration of ecclesiastical affairs, and of the advisableness of petitioning the Sovereign Pontiff for a more just proportion of bishops and priests from the old country, by an association of Irish gentlemen, to which is added the notices and letters of 'Legion,' 'An Irishman,' and 'An Irishman, Father of a Family'* (Toronto 1858), 5, 45
6 Choquette, *L'Eglise catholique dans l'Ontario français*, passim
7 J.V. Cleary to the Bishops of Hamilton and Peterborough, 14 Mar. 1889, AAK, FIIC14
8 J.O'Mahony to Cleary, 15 Feb. 1887, AAK, FIIC9; Lynch to Cleary, 24 Dec. 1884, FIIC13; circular, 18 Feb. 1888, AAT, LB04.194; to L. Hand, 9 Mar. 1888, LB04.304; to D. Morris, 10 Mar. 1888, LB04.307; *Catholic Register* 2:8 (22 Feb. 1894); *Irish Canadian* 20:2 (12 Jan. 1882); 20:3 (19 Jan 1882); 20:5 (2 Feb 1882)
9 The low church Evangelical Association should not be confused with the German-language church of the same name. Headon, 'The Influence of the Oxford Movement,' 193; Bull, *From Strachan to Owen*, 375; Scadding and Hodgins, *Jubilee Volume*, 38; Bruce S. Elliott, 'Ritualism and the Beginnings of the Reformed

Episcopal Movement in Ottawa,' *JCCHS* 27:1 (Apr. 1985), 18–41; *Catholic Register* 1:6 (9 Feb. 1893)

10 Alan L. Hayes, 'The Struggle for the Rights of the Laity in the Diocese of Toronto,' 5–17; D.C. Masters, 'The Anglican Evangelicals in Toronto, 1870–1900,' *JCCHS* 20:3–4 (1978), 51–65; Mockridge, *Bishops of the Church of England*, 252

11 *Dominion Churchman*, 6 Jan. 1876, 2: *Canadian Churchman* 26:45 (29 Nov. 1900), 725

12 R.G. Moyles, *The Blood and Fire in Canada: A History of the Salvation Army in the Dominion, 1882–1976* (Toronto: Peter Martin Associates 1977), chapters 1–6; with emphasis on the urban aspects of the revival of the period, Clark, *Church and Sect in Canada*, chapter 8

13 Horner, *Ralph C. Horner*, xii-xv, 82, xix, 55, 127; Brian R. Ross, 'Ralph Cecil Horner: A Methodist Sectarian Deposed, 1887–1895,' *UCA Bulletin* 26 (1977)/*JCCHS* 19:1–2 (Mar.-June 1977), 94–103; Ronald Sawatsky, 'Unholy Contentions about Holiness: The Canadian Holiness Association of the Methodist Church,' *CSCH Papers*, 1982, 20; Semple, 'Impact of Urbanization on the Methodist Church' (PH D thesis), 320; Burkholder, *Mennonites in Ontario*, 193

14 In 1891, 'other' comprised 1.7 per cent of the population. This figure included the Mennonites, who were reckoned at 0.6 per cent in 1901. Salvation Army adherents in 1891 accounted for 0.4 per cent of the population of the province. They were most numerous in Ontario South (1.52 per cent) and Norfolk South (1.48 per cent), as compared with 0.85 per cent in Kingston, 0.67 per cent in London, 0.47 per cent in Toronto, 0.44 per cent in Hamilton, and 0.11 per cent in Ottawa.

15 George C. Workman, *Messianic Prophecy Vindicated* (Toronto: William Briggs 1899), 43; Goldwin Smith, *Guesses at the Riddle of Existence* (New York: Macmillan 1897), vi; George C. Workman, *The Old Testament Vindicated as Christianity's Foundation Stone* (Toronto: William Briggs 1897), 9. The Workman case is described in detail in George A. Boyle, 'Higher Criticism and the Struggle for Academic Freedom in Canadian Methodism' (TH D thesis, Victoria University 1965), part 2. A more recent analytical study is Tom Sinclair-Faulkner, 'Theory Divided from Practice: The Introduction of the Higher Criticism into Canadian Protestant Seminaries,' *SR* 10:3 (1981), 321–43.

16 James H. Coyne, 'A Century of Achievement,' *Canadian Methodist Magazine and Review* 53 (Feb. 1901), 123; John S. Moir, *A History of Biblical Studies in Canada: A Sense of Proportion* (Chico, Cal.: Scholars Press 1982), 9

17 Warfield and Hodge, quoted in Sandeen, *Roots of American Fundamentalism*, 123, 127–8; Moir, *Enduring Witness* 176

18 Ernest R. Sandeen, *The Origins of Fundamentalism: Toward an Historical Interpretation* (Philadelphia: Fortress 1968), 3; Robert Obradovic, 'The Development of Adventist Higher Education in Canada, 1916–1980' (PH D thesis, University of Toronto 1984), 27–8; M. James Penton, *Jehovah's Witnesses in Canada: Champions of Freedom of Speech and Worship* (Toronto: Macmillan 1974), 35–6

19 Sawatsky, '"Looking for That Blessed Hope,"' passim
20 John A. Irving, 'The Development of Philosophy in Central Canada from 1850 to 1900,' *CHR* 31:3 (Sept. 1950), 259-64, 268-76; McKillop, *A Disciplined Intelligence*, chapter 6; Nathanael Burwash, manuscript autobiography, 18, UCA, Burwash Papers, box 28, file 619
21 Sawatsky, '"Looking for That Blessed Hope,"' 4-5; George M. Marsden, *Fundamentalism and American Culture: The Shaping of Twentieth Century Evangelicalism, 1870-1925* (New York: Oxford University Press 1980), 78; Lindsay Reynolds, *Footprints: The Beginning of the Christian and Missionary Alliance in Canada* (Toronto: Christian and Missionary Alliance in Canada 1982), 115
22 Burwash, *History of Victoria College*, 465-7; C.P. Mulvany, *Toronto Past and Present,* 188
23 Froom, *The Prophetic Faith of Our Fathers*, 3:615; Reynolds, *Footprints*, xi; J.F. McCurdy, *Life and Work of D.J. Macdonnell*, 282
24 Ronald Sawatsky, 'Henry Martyn Parsons of Knox Church, Toronto (1818-1913),' *CSPH Papers*, 1982, 116; McCurdy, *Macdonnell*, 351; Airhart, 'Revivalist Spirituality,' 189-91
25 Cook, *The Regenerators*, chapters 3, 4
26 Cyril Greenland, 'Mary Edwards Merrill, 1858-1880, "The Psychic,"' *OH* 62:2 (June 1976), 81-92; Cook, *The Regenerators*, 69-78; Michèle Lacombe, 'Theosophy and the Canadian Idealist Tradition: A Preliminary Exploration,' *Journal of Canadian Studies/Revue d'études canadiennes* 17:2 (summer 1982), 100-18
27 For the printing history of *Cosmic Consciousness*, M.A. Jameson, ed., *Richard Maurice Bucke: A Catalogue Based upon the Collections of the University of Western Ontario Libraries* (London, Ont.: University of Western Ontario 1978), 40-1; R.M. Bucke, *Cosmic Consciousness* (Philadelphia 1901), 7-8, 14; R.M. Bucke, 'Mental Evolution in Man,' *British Medical Journal* 2 (11 Sept. 1897), 645; Leslie Armour and Elizabeth Trott, *The Faces of Reason: An Essay on Philosophy and Culture in English Canada, 1850-1950* (Waterloo, Ont.: Wilfrid Laurier University Press 1981), 365-77; S.E.D. Shortt, *Victorian Lunacy: Richard M. Bucke and the Practice of Late Nineteenth-Century Psychiatry* (Cambridge: University Press 1986), 109-11
28 Speisman, *The Jews of Toronto*, 190-7; *Canadian Church Magazine and Mission News* 103 (Jan. 1895), 169-70; Galvin, 'Jubilee Riots,' 96, 103

CHAPTER 14 *The Anatomy of Ontario Religion*

1 Inconveniently for the historian, the first credible religious census of the province was taken only in 1842. In 1839 returns to the clerk of peace of each district included information on denominational preference. Gathered during the controversy over the clergy reserves, they were so generally discounted that they are passed over here in favour of information gathered three years later. Even the available statistics suffer from subjectivity on the part of enumerators, serious inconsistencies in classification, and continuing confusion about the nature of divisions within denominational families.

It should also be remembered that such figures, which represent merely individual expressions of preference, can give no indication of the quality of denominational affiliation; some of those who listed themselves as adherents of a particular body may never have darkened a church door.

2 *Missionary Notices of the Methodist Church of Canada* 3:6 (Mar. 1876), 98; Michael S. Cross and Robert L. Fraser, '"The Waste That Lies Before Me": The Public and Private Worlds of Robert Baldwin,' *CHA Historical Papers, 1983*, 169; AO, Ely Playter diary, Feb. 1801–Dec. 1853

3 De Villiers-Westfall, 'The Sacred and the Secular,' 60, 80–1

4 Osmond, 'Anglican Parish Church Worship,' 8–11, 17–19

5 The liberalism of the 1920s may be sampled most conveniently in the columns of the *Canadian Journal of Religious Thought*. Adherents of the social gospel are classified as conservative, progressive, or radical in Richard Allen, *The Social Passion: Religion and Social Reform in Canada, 1914–28* (Toronto: University of Toronto Press 1971), 17.

6 Ernst Troeltsch, *The Social Teaching of the Christian Churches* (London: George Allen and Unwin 1931), I:331ff; Sidney E. Mead, *The Lively Experiment: The Shaping of Christianity in America* (New York: Harper and Row 1963), chapter 7

7 Fred Landon, ed., 'Proudfoot Papers,' *OH* 27 (1931), 445; *Records of ... Osler*, 140. That in the United States differences of ethnic background have been sublimated into those of denominational affiliation is the thesis of Will Herberg, *Protestant, Catholic, Jew: An Essay in American Religious Sociology* (Garden City, NY: Doubleday 1955), 272–3. The American development is portrayed, in terms more reminiscent of the description of Ontario here, as one in which the churches helped to create or shape ethnicity in Timothy L. Smith, 'Religion and Ethnicity in America,' *American Historical Review* 83:5 (Dec. 1978), 1155–85.

8 Joseph D. Ban, 'The Scottish Contribution to Baptist Life in Canada,' unpublished address; Mark C. McDermott, 'The Theology of Bishop John Strachan: A Study in Anglican Identity' (PH D thesis, St Michael's College 1983), 76–81

9 S. Ivison, 'Is There a Canadian Baptist Tradition?' in Grant, *The Churches and the Canadian Experience*, 66–7

10 David L. Weddle, 'The Law and the Revival: A "New Divinity" for the Settlements,' *Church History* 47:2 (June 1978), 206; Payne, *History of the African Methodist Episcopal Church*, 322

11 Scadding, *Toronto of Old*, 61; Smellie, *Memoir of the Rev. John Bayne*, 35; Grant, *Life of Rev. William Cochrane*, 163–4, 195; Bethune, *Memoir of the Right Reverend John Strachan*, 359–60

12 *Christian Guardian*, 1 Jan. 1868; Mulvany, *Toronto Past and Present*, 102; W.E. Blackstock, 'The Sabbath Question,' *Canadian Methodist Magazine* 18 (Aug. 1883), 173

13 Nathanael Burwash, 'Nineteenth-Century Theology: Its Tendencies and Probable Outcome,' *Canadian Methodist Magazine and Review* 53 (Feb. 1901), 166; Coyne, 'A Century of Achievement,' 120; *Westminster* 9:24 (15 Dec. 1900), 739; *Catholic Register* 8:52 (27 Dec. 1900), 4; *Canadian Churchman* 27:1 (3 Jan. 1901), 5

PICTURE CREDITS

Index